The Old Army

0 11557 02897 3

Harris & Ewing

General Parker

The Old Army

Memories, 1872–1918

JAMES PARKER

BRIGADIER GENERAL UNITED STATES ARMY, RETIRED,

MAJOR GENERAL NATIONAL ARMY, M.H., D.S.M.

With a new introduction by Sandy Barnard

STACKPOLE
BOOKS

Published by
STACKPOLE BOOKS
5067 Ritter Road
Mechanicsburg, PA 17055
www.stackpolebooks.com

Cover design by Tracy Patterson

Cover photo courtesy of the United States Military History Institute, Carlisle, Pennsylvania

Printed in the United States of America

10 9 8 7 6 5 4 3 2 1

FIRST EDITION

Library of Congress Cataloging-in-Publication Data

Parker, James, 1854–1934.
The old army : memories, 1872–1918 / by James Parker ; with a new introduction by Sandy Barnard.— 1st ed.
p. cm. — (Frontier Classics)
Originally published: Philadelphia : Dorrance & Co., c1929. With new intro.
ISBN 0-8117-2897-8
1. Parker, James, 1854–1934. 2. Generals—United States—Biography.
3. United States.
Army—Biography. 4. United States—History, Military—19th century.
5. United States—History, Military—20th century. 6. Indians of North America—Wars—1866–1895.
I. Title. II. Series

E181.P241 2003
355'0092—dc21
[B]

2003042455

INTRODUCTION

by Sandy Barnard

Some years ago, I began researching the life of frontier journalist Mark H. Kellogg, thinking that perhaps the little known reporter for the *Bismarck (Dakota Territory) Tribune* was a possible candidate for a biography. Uncertain whether to proceed, I contacted Dr. William Taft, my journalism history professor at the University of Missouri School of Journalism. He issued a "thumbs up" to my proposal, telling me that "We have had plenty written about the Bennetts, the Pulitzers and the Greeleys. What we need are more stories about the little people of journalism." Kellogg certainly fit that latter description, and eventually I published my biography, *I Go With Custer: The Life and Death of Reporter Mark Kellogg*.

In reading the memoirs by Brig. Gen. James Parker, *The Old Army: Memories 1872–1918*, I sensed that Dr. Taft's statement about the potential of journalist Kellogg's life story might apply to the ex-soldier's. As was true of Kellogg, Parker was not a household name. Of course, as a military figure, he offered more historical significance than Kellogg. During his 42-year military career, he advanced from second lieutenant to major general and received the Medal of Honor for his courage in combat in 1899 in the Philippines. He participated in many events that influenced the society of his day and that still touch us today.

A description that author Heath Twichell, Jr., wrote about Gen. H. T. Allen in the preface to his 1974 book, *Henry T. Allen: The Biography of an Army Officer 1859–1930*, also assists in assessing Parker's own standing. Allen served as commander of the American occupation forces in the Rhineland from 1919 to 1923.

"[Allen's] life began before the Indian frontier had disappeared and the last blank spaces on the maps of American territory were filled in. Before he died the United States had transformed itself, under the imperatives of its manifest destiny but with many a reluctant backward glance, into a first-rank world power with great international responsibilities. During this process of national transformation, Allen took part in nearly every major step involving the participation of the U.S. Army. Although few of the roles he played were individually of outstanding historical importance, collectively they entitle him, in my opinion, to consideration as a significant figure in American history."

Twichell continued, again in a way that fits Parker's own role and influence in the army of that period:

"Interwoven with the colorful strands of Allen's life is a paradoxical theme: the growing tendency of the army to become involved in affairs not purely military all the while there has been an increasing amount of professionalization within the organization in an attempt to define, emphasize, and preserve its internal standards and unique ethic. Allen's career is a perfect example of this paradox."

The two books are different, of course. Twichell's is a biography, while Parker's own is a memoir. Yet, as Twichell indicates, both cover much of the same terrain. Immediately after his graduation from the U.S. Military Academy, standing No. 31 in the class of June 1876, Parker was assigned to the 4th U.S. Cavalry. He clearly enjoyed the life of a line officer, especially his role as a company officer leading men, whether they faced Utes in Utah, Apaches in the Southwest, Spaniards in Cuba, or insurrectionists in the Philippines. As his obituary in the *New York Times* stated in 1934, "General Parker liked fighting. He got plenty of it against the Indians, and his hard-riding, hard-hitting ways, his horsemanship won him the sobriquet of 'Galloping Jim.'"

Undoubtedly, his greatest disappointment in 42 years as an officer came in the 12 months before age forced him into retirement in 1918. His country was about to fight its largest war since the Civil War, against a major European power, and Parker, despite his age of 63, was as zealous about participating as he had been in 1876. Yet his country said it no longer had a place for him at the head of its troops in combat. While he had honed the 32nd Infantry Division to a level of combat readiness that ranked it among the elite units the U.S. Army would dispatch to the European Theater, another general replaced him to take it overseas. In his last months before retirement, Parker was reassigned to a figurehead position as commander of another division in training, the 85th.

This final sequence of events personally devastated the general. In a letter of June 11, 1917, to the Adjutant General's Office, Parker asked to be retained on duty beyond the next February, the date of his retirement for age: "I believe it can be demonstrated that I am, as to vigor of mind and body, a man of middle age, as are many men over sixty-four now commanding on the battlefields of this war. I believe also that my experience in handling and training troops, and my experience in war, will be of value to the government in the present emergency."

In his memoirs, he related how he tried vainly to be continued in service: "What I wanted was to command troops in France, in what grade little mattered. I felt that I still had a right to serve my country."

It was not to be. "The day arrived," he wrote. "I received from the War Department the customary, cold-blooded order severing me forever from the service and from those whom I loved and who looked up to me."

Fortunately, his memoirs and the historical record document his fine service. They show that during his career Parker was not only a courageous and accomplished leader, but also an astute observer and a fine writer. In his memoirs, he could be blunt and opinionated, yet his book, originally published in 1929, remains an essential reference source for the late Indian Wars—those that are often overlooked in that period after Custer's Last Stand of 1876—as well as for the Spanish American War, the Philippines Insurrection, and the period that marked the professionalization of the Regular Army at the turn of the century.

The eminent Western collector and scholar Everett D. Graff described Parker's book as a "very interesting account of frontier Indian warfare and life at the forts in the Southwest and West during the 1870's and 80's. He gives a fine account of the Geronimo campaign, and his appreciation of General [Ranald] Mackenzie as an Indian fighter is excellent."

Parker's book opens simply enough, noting that he was born on February 20, 1854, in Newark, New Jersey, the second son of noted lawyer Cortlandt Parker, a former president of the American Bar Association, and his wife, Elizabeth Wolcott Stites Parker. James, who had been named for his paternal grandfather, had five brothers—Richard Wayne, Cortlandt, Charles, Chauncey, and Robert, all of whom had their own distinguished careers—and three sisters—Katherine, Frances, and Elizabeth. Richard Wayne served several terms as a congressman and frequently sought to advance his brother's career.

In 1864, James Parker began his schooling at Englewood Academy, Perth Amboy, New Jersey. His grandfather, James, then 88, lived in Perth Amboy, and his father's summer home, known as the old "Castle," was also there. The house, only a stone's throw from Raritan Bay, had been built in 1720. Its basement served the Parker boys well as a boathouse, while an old garden across the street doubled as a playground. Nearby stables contained horses and ponies, assuring that by age 10, he was already a competent horseman.

Parker, an intelligent individual, was well-educated, attending the Newark Academy; the well-regarded Phillips Academy of Andover, Massachusetts; and the United States Military Academy at West Point, New York. In addition, in 1878, he earned a master's of arts degree from

Rutgers College of New Brunswick, New Jersey. Thus, it is not surprising that his book offers a well-written and articulate summary of both the events of his military life and his opinions. In fact, the first two-thirds of the book focus more on the chronology of his career with only an occasional editorial comment slipping into his text. The last third is highly opinionated, perhaps reflecting his increasing frustration with an ever-growing Army bureaucracy that had failed to advance him past company grade for nearly a quarter century. While he rose rapidly in the next 13 years from captain to brigadier general, even his promotion to the latter rank was touch and go. Despite possessing many influential friends, especially within the Army itself, he seems to have lacked the political contacts who could have assured his promotion at a faster pace.

In late September of 1876, just three months after Custer's fall at Little Bighorn, Parker, who at six feet four inches was tall for a cavalryman, rode the final 165 miles along rough trails in a "ramshackle old affair" of a stagecoach to join his regiment at Fort Sill, Oklahoma. In colorful language, he describes the scenes along his way:

"The country was generally level, with park-like alternations of post-oak groves and open prairies. . . . [On] the morning of the third day we crossed a broad, deep creek bordered by picturesque cottonwoods and emerged on an elevated plateau. In the distance loomed mountains of bare granite; in the foreground what seemed like a small, well-built town, the national flag on a lofty flagpole waving above the buildings."

In rapid order, he describes the fort itself, the "American Desert," and the officers and men of the army on the Plains. He found in the ranks many men who were Civil War veterans, some on the Confederate side. Drink often was a problem for men, but on the whole, "for active service in the field they were a splendid class of men."

His early years in the army provided a multitude of experiences for the young officer:

> There is a widespread idea that the military profession is an easy one to learn, and that its difficulties are soon overcome, after which it becomes a comparative life of leisure. It has been my experience, however, that the intricacies of a thorough knowledge of command are looked upon lightly only by those who have never encountered them; that the life of a young officer for many years is merely an apprenticeship.
>
> I indeed found up to the time I was retired as an officer, after forty-two years' service as such, that every day I

> was learning some new thing about commanding troops, this especially after I had attained high rank.

The 4th U.S. Cavalry Regiment he found had gained "a high reputation" under its commander, Col. Ranald S. Mackenzie, legendary for his successes on the battlefields of the Civil War as well as on the Plains. Most young officers stood in awe of Mackenzie, and Parker was no exception.

"Mackenzie had an unusually magnetic influence on his officers, his personality impressing itself upon them. . . . [T]he Mackenzie spirit reigned long after his death," Parker noted, even as late as the Spanish-American War among such men as Gens. H. W. Lawton and S. B. M. Young.

Life as an officer could be demanding and often required men to live far from their wives and families. In November 1879, he married Charlotte M. Condit, whom he had known from childhood days in Newark. Her family had been concerned about her living in the wilds of the west with Parker, but consented to their marriage. In his bachelor days, or when military circumstances required living apart from Charlotte, he found that the officers developed among themselves a spirit of individuality and originality. He uses a modern phrase to describe the bonds among them: "We were a band of brothers often deeply devoted to one another."

Much of his first decade as an officer involved frequent contacts with Indians, both in garrison as well as on campaign. At times, his memoirs reflect great admiration for the Indian, but at the core he thought like most men of his times: The Indian's culture could be admired, but, as Parker saw it, the Indian, as a person, still ranked below the white man.

"In everything but war the Indian was in the Stone Age. Like our ancestors, he had no special spur to invention, which after all is the basis of our modern civilization.

"The American Indian was a warrior, pure and simple. While he had intervals of peace, he lived for war. It is as a warrior he is admired. . . . And if killing is war, the American Indian was one of the greatest warriors that ever existed."

Despite his admiration for their ability as warriors, Parker pointed out, "I never became an Indian lover. I never was in sympathy with much that has been written about the 'poor Indian.' It was inevitable that the whites should demand that the land should be divided between the whites and the Indians."

In one of his more frank opinions, he debunked the government's traditional decision to view the tribes as separate nations: "In my opinion most of the trouble we have had with Indians has been due to yielding to the demands of the Indians to be recognized as separate nations and to a policy of conciliation instead of law."

The highlights of his career during his first decade and a half included service on the Mexican border from 1878 to 1879; the Ute Campaign in Colorado between 1879 and 1881; and the Geronimo Apache Campaign of 1885–86. He was promoted to first lieutenant in 1879 and to captain in 1888, but it would take another 13 years, 1901, before he would be promoted to major in the Regular Army. Fortunately, he rose rapidly after that. Just two years later in 1903, he was promoted to lieutenant colonel in the 13th U.S. Cavalry, and in 1907, he was appointed colonel in the 11th U.S. Cavalry.

He actually had enjoyed higher rank in the late 1890s during the Spanish-American War and the Philippines Insurrection. He was initially appointed as major and then lieutenant colonel for the 12th New York Volunteers during the war and later lieutenant colonel for the 45th U.S. Volunteers during the Philippines Insurrection between 1899 and 1901.

Throughout his career, Parker was known for two strong characteristics: In garrison, he was a marvelous organizer, and on the battlefield he was a courageous leader. For example, in mid-August 1899, near San Mateo in the Philippines, he led one of three reconnaissance columns that came under fire. As Brig. Gen. S. B. M. Young described it in his after-action report, "Captain Parker immediately formed his lines of skirmishers and gallantly led his command against the entrenchments and after forty minutes of sharp fighting drove the enemy back. In the attack, which I personally witnessed, the men had to advance for a full mile under a heavy fire, through mud and water up to their knees with only the slight protection afforded by the small dikes in the rice fields, and I cannot too highly commend the gallantry of Captain Parker and all the offices and men of his command."

The action took place about 7:00 A.M., August 12, 1899. Just two days later, on August 14, Young praised Parker again in a letter the general wrote to his subordinate's wife: "'Captain Jim' covered himself and his command all over with glory—besides smashing the enemy and scattering the fragments to the Mountains. . . . [And I] am very glad, for certainly no officer could have executed it any better, and I do not know of any one in my command who could have done it so well. . . . He is simply superb on the battlefield."

Later that year, this time at the town of Vigan, Parker again led a mixed column of troops that came under an attack just before 4:00 A.M. by some one thousand insurrectionists who caught the Americans off guard. Parker responded by personally leading small groups of his men to various points to post them to withstand heavy enemy fire. At one point, when the fire from a hospital slackened, he ordered a charge by six men, whom he personally led. "On nearing the stone fence, a tremendous fire belched forth and three of the six men with me were killed, the remainder resuming their former position."

Shortly, he led another charge "under a hot fire" against insurgents who had taken refuge in the town's cathedral. His counterattack succeeded, and by 8:00 A.M., his force of fewer than 250 men had repulsed the enemy. Some 40 dead insurgents were found, although Parker believed their casualties were higher. Another 30 were taken prisoner. Parker wrote to Young, "It speaks well for the forbearance of our men that so many prisoners were taken, owing to the desperate character of the fighting, there was a strong inclination to give no quarter."

For his actions during that four-hour fight, Parker would receive the Medal of Honor in 1902. In January 1900, one of his captains, Charles Van Way, recommended his colonel for the medal, writing, "All this time this daring officer was first one place, then another, ever exerting every energy toward increasing our fire, and apparently unmindful of his own danger. His daring example had much to do with the steadiness and determination of the men."

It wasn't the first time that his quick response to an enemy attack had saved his unit. In May 1885, he was second in command of a 4th Cavalry detachment chasing the band of Apaches under Geronimo. Just after noon on May 22, the troops camped by a narrow, shallow creek on the floor of Devil's Canyon, New Mexico, despite Parker's immediate misgivings about the site. When his captain headed off to bathe in a nearby stream, his concerns rose. Shortly, Apache warriors began firing down on his men. He immediately responded by leading an uphill charge, explaining in his memoirs, "It is, I believe, when ambushed, always the safest course to attack. The enemy's belief in his secure position fades, he loses morale, he is in turn surprised."

Fortunately, Indian scouts under Lt. Charles B. Gatewood had been detailed along the summit of the canyon to act as videttes for the camp. Their presence close to the hostiles' nearby camp prompted the firing. Lt. Leighton Finley, 10th U.S. Cavalry, noted in his own report to Parker that the latter did not hesitate to lead 17 men to the top of the canyon wall, firing all the time. "You took us by rushes, taking advantage of the cover of various ledges of rocks to protect us. The hill was particularly steep and I cannot believe that it was less than five hundred feet high."

The troops' surprise response had the intended effect envisioned by Parker, as the Indians fled from the crest of the canyon, leaving some 17 fires still burning. Finley added, "If you will permit me to say so, I would like to state that, in my own humble opinion, you saved the command from probable grave disaster. . . . It was a case of being almost 'all surrounded' in a very bad box. In my judgment, if you had not done what you did do, or if you had hesitated a moment, it is not pleasant to contemplate what might have happened."

In April 1898, Parker, perhaps feeling disappointed by his long tenure as a company grade officer, petitioned the Adjutant General's Office to be awarded the Medal of Honor for his Devil's Creek action, but his request was rejected. Brig. Gen. George Crook had made no reference to his performance or filed a recommendation, forcing the AGO to assume Parker did not merit the nation's highest military honor on that occasion. Much later, in 1928, he was awarded the Silver Star for gallantry in action during what was called the "shirt-tail fight" at Devil's Creek.

In 1886, Parker was appointed by Gen. Nelson A. Miles to command another detachment that crossed the Mexican border searching for Geronimo. While cooperating with other troops under Capt. W. H. Lawton, later a general, they assisted in the capture of the Indian leader, bringing the Apache war to an end. When Lawton himself was promoted, Parker received his own boost to captain. Soon after the war broke out in 1898, Parker sought the colonelcy of a New Jersey volunteer regiment from the state's governor, Foster A. Voorhees. Lawton, who as a major general would be killed in action in the Philippines the next year, wrote on June 1, 1898, to the governor that Parker was "a courageous, zealous officer of excellent judgment, high character, and a thorough soldier. There is not another person either in or out of the Military Service, whom I can recommend more strongly for such an appointment."

Yet despite such support, Parker was overlooked for high command. He had to settle for an initial assignment as a mustering officer for all the volunteer regiments in New York. In May 1898, he was appointed as major in the 12th New York, and in October, he was appointed its lieutenant colonel, commanding the important post of Cardenas in Cuba. The latter assignment proved important in demonstrating his superb administrative capabilities. He would spend another 20 years on active duty, and frequently his assignments would involve administration.

Earlier, he had prepared for such work, first with an assignment to Fort Myer, Virginia, with his company of the 4th U.S. Cavalry. Later, the company was transferred to the Presidio in San Francisco. By 1894, he was ready for another kind of assignment, one that overlapped his command skills with his administrative ability. He was appointed as senior cavalry instructor at West Point and commanded the academy's own cavalry detachment for his four years there. His considerable success can be seen in his efficiency report for June 1897. Col. O. H. Ernst wrote, "[He is] well fitted for his present detail or for duty with National Guard or as an attaché, or for Adj. Gen.'s Dept. Has good literary talent."

The colonel concluded: "He has raised the standards of the Cavalry Detachment at this place from that of a body of laborers and grooms to that of an excellent troop of cavalry."

In 1899, after returning from Cuba, Parker rejoined his troop as a captain in the 4th U.S. Cavalry, which was transferred to the Philippines that summer. While Parker was in the Philippines, his father had predicted, "If James is not killed, he will distinguish himself."

That Parker would do. By August, he was involved in the campaign against San Mateo. About that time, he had been appointed lieutenant colonel of the 45th U.S. Volunteers, but remained on special duty on the staff of General Young for several months. That November, while accompanying troops under Major Swigert of the 3rd Cavalry, they encountered resistance from troops led by General Aguinaldo near Manoag. Seeing the enemy about to fire, Parker ordered a charge. In an affidavit later, Parker's orderly, Pvt. Eugene F. Hannum, told how the lieutenant colonel, Pvt. Joseph Lugenbrouk and he rode at a gallop, pistols drawn, toward the enemy.

"The insurgents broke into a panic into three parties," Hannum stated. The three men, now two hundred yards ahead of their comrades, chased one of the groups, firing their weapons at them, for about half a mile.

Parker's own statement is more vivid than the private's. Apparently, Swigert was hesitant about charging, so Parker, on Young's staff, effectively seized command: "As Major Swigert showed no signs of giving any command and considering instant action all important, I called out, 'Draw pistols and charge,' and in order to get the column under way quickly, gave the example by taking up the gallop.

"In a moment I found myself among the insurgents, some of whom stood their ground firing wildly, while others plunged into the bushes on either side of the road, a few fired wildly at us. It took but a minute or two to discharge all the six cartridges in my revolver."

Parker was lucky to survive, although apparently the circumstances aided him and his two enlisted comrades on their mad dash through one thousand enemy troops. According to a 1907 newspaper account of Parker's life, his "miraculous escape from death" occurred because the road curved, the day was dark, and the enemy, surprised by Parker's boldness, fired wildly at the three men. For his action, Young received a brevet of lieutenant colonel.

Beginning in January 1900, Parker took part in a series of engagements with the 45th Regiment. Also, as administrator in the districts of

Lagonoy and Iriga, he successfully restored order and reestablished local government, schools and police. All in all, in the Philippines Parker commanded six important expeditions and participated in 20 engagements. He was recommended for brevet commissions three times, before returning to the United States in May 1901 with the permanent rank of major in the 4th Cavalry.

On his return from the Philippines, his brothers Cort and Bob greeted him and his wife. Back in the Newark home of their father, "the three brothers approached a sideboard at the east end of the dining room where a Colonial ancestress looked down from an oval frame. A bottle of bourbon was produced and glasses were filled and emptied. 'Jim,' asked one of the hosts, 'did you kill any of the insurrectos?' The tanned colonel grinned, 'No,' he replied, 'I don't think so. Anyhow, I hope not.'"

Assigned as an assistant under Maj. Gen. H. C. Corbin in the Adjutant General's Office in Washington, D.C., he worked on revising the cavalry drill regulations and served as president of a board which prepared new firing regulations. His duties were broad and gave him plenty of opportunity to state his opinions: "As I have never been backward in presenting my views I did not hesitate to submit memorandums on matters, which, in my opinion, could be improved."

In January 1903, he changed emphasis when he became director of the AGO's Division of Militia Affairs, displaying remarkable skill in working with the National Guard. He enjoyed close contact with Secretary of War Elihu Root, whom he described as "the greatest man and patriot" of that time. Prior to this, the militia had not been, in Parker's view, "properly organized," and so he set about to improve the situation. That meant implementing the so-called "Dick Bill," passed by the 1902–3 Congress, which formally organized guard and militia units into one uniform force.

Surprisingly at one point in this period, Parker claimed that he would not let friends in the militia push his name for promotion to brigadier general. He feared that "I might be separated permanently from the line and from command of troops." He further claimed that he had supported the promotion of John J. Pershing to general because the latter had proved himself so competent in Philippines, "even though in so doing I asked that he be promoted over my head—an action for which Pershing did not fail to thank me." At times in his memoirs, Parker comes across as atypically lacking in personal ambition, apparently believing that in the end appropriate honors would come his way. His record shows that his approach ultimately proved best for himself.

In any case, he worked hard at building up the capabilities of the new militia to the point where he viewed it as "a nucleus of patriotic citizens animated by the soldierly spirit, who make considerable sacrifices of time and money in its behalf. It is a school for officers and soldiers who, graduating from its ranks, add to the defensive power of the country. And among those who witness its undoubtedly fine parades and close order drills it serves to keep the military spirit alive."

Despite his success in handling the Army's bureaucracy, during this period Parker appears to have undergone some change in attitude. Up to the mid-point of the first decade in the 20th century, his memoirs had provided a straight forward narrative of his experiences. Now, a forceful bluntness becomes more evident in his text. For example, he relates how he befriended Theodore Roosevelt and even exchanged letters with him, but that Roosevelt, as president, tended to promote younger men to general, especially those whom he had known in Cuba during the Spanish-American War. That meant bypassing more senior officers with longer careers.

"Roosevelt, while he was yet a young man," Parker wrote, "was the great exponent of the theory that in war youth counts far more than experiences. It is a creed held by many in our service. But it is a false creed."

He further argues that many of history's great commanders were older men with considerably more experience during their careers. "In war the rashness of ignorance has no value," he commented. "And to imagine that in a few short years an officer may fully learn to command is folly; in my forty-two years of service there was scarcely a day I did not learn some new thing, and it seemed to me that it was towards the end of my career that my eyes were opened most. The art of war is an intricate study."

Despite the harder edge apparent in his memoirs' last 100 pages, he still found humor in aspects of his career. For example, after his promotion to lieutenant colonel in April 1903, he noted with amusement how often he had reached that rank: once in the 12th Infantry, a second time in the 42nd Infantry, and again in the 45th Infantry. "I now became lieutenant colonel 'military secretary.' Later I was lieutenant colonel adjutant general. And later lieutenant colonel 13th Cavalry."

In January 1904, he transferred to St. Louis as adjutant general of the new Northern Division, and in the spring of the next year, he was ordered to Fort Riley, Kansas, returning to command, this time of a full cavalry regiment, while serving as director of the cavalry school. He had served there in 1881, but found the place much changed in the passage of 24 years.

In October 1906, the Army returned to Cuba on pacification duty. Parker, initially assigned as provost marshal of Havana, spent much of his time as president of a general court-martial. On April 18, 1907, he gained his third promotion in six years when appointed colonel of the 11th Cavalry Regiment stationed at Pinar del Rio, Cuba, 125 miles west of Havana.

In March 1909, his regiment marched in the inauguration parade for President William H. Taft and then moved to Fort Oglethorpe, Georgia, where it would remain for three more years under his command. "I was able . . . to make the 11th Regiment incontestably the crack regiment of the cavalry arm of the service." He believed he was fortunate in having the entire regiment under his control, unlike most regiments that were scattered at various stations. He trained and retrained his men in virtually every aspect of military life, leaving his people with little leisure time.

"It is a well-known fact that the more time to idle the soldier has the more likely he is to grumble," he stated. "If you want to make him contented, give him plenty to do, always providing that he can see the work you provide is good for training, for the command or for the post."

His superiors and friends recognized his talent as a regimental leader. For example, Maj. Gen. Jesse M. Lee, writing to support Parker's promotion to brigadier general in December 1911, stated enthusiastically:

> Colonel Parker possesses the rare quality of knowing how to handle and instruct officers and men—promoting their military efficiency to the highest degree. He imbues them with his own spirit of devotion to every possible phase of military duty, as fully evidenced by the splendid reputation of his regiment—the 11th Cavalry—one of the best instructed and most efficient regiment [sic] I have ever known since my entry into service in 1861.
>
> Suffice it to say that Colonel Parker is an ideal commander of the Mackenzie and Lawton type. His great capacity, untiring energy, conspicuous efficiency and inspiring example, mark him as one of the very best officers in our army. . . . As a cavalry leader he has few equals and no superiors in the Army.

At the same time, Maj. Gen. Daniel Sickles noted: "He is an accomplished officer, a thorough master of his profession, of which his regiment is a conspicuous example." He added that during his visit to Fort Oglethorpe, he was impressed with "the excellent discipline of his regiment and the precision of its maneuvers, and the excellent tone and appearance of his men."

Despite such enthusiastic reviews, Parker lingered as a colonel for several more years, until finally attaining his general's star on March 3, 1913. As he tells it in his memoirs, even then it was a close call, as the U.S. Senate divided over which men to promote. If his promotion had not been finalized by March 4, he had feared the incoming President Woodrow Wilson would have favored other men, notably his classmate, Col. Hugh L. Scott.

The new general was ordered to Fort Sam Houston, San Antonio, Texas, to command the 1st Cavalry Brigade. He would spend four years in Texas, where at the outset, he commanded what he considered "the biggest brigade of cavalry in the world." His three regiments—the 2nd, 3rd and 14th Cavalry—numbered three thousand men. Much of his time in Texas involved being prepared to march after Pancho Villa, whom he termed a "powerful bandit."

In 1916, after Villa's raids across the border, the U.S. government ordered Pershing to pursue Villa into Mexico, but without much success. Now, at age 62, Parker found himself manning a desk, as he had been ordered to Brownsville in early May 1916 to take command of the district headquarters there. He organized a local defense force, built around two Texas National Guard regiments; the next month, after a Mexican raid, he ordered a squadron of cavalry to pursue the enemy across the border. Later that summer, after a presidential order concentrated some 100,000 National Guard troops on the Rio Grande, Parker found himself commanding the equivalent of two divisions or one army corps from his Brownsville headquarters.

Despite the large number of troops along the border, President Wilson for political reasons forbade any further crossing or other acts of aggression toward Mexico. Parker criticized the president in his memoirs for not allowing the Mexican question to be decided and for not keeping fully intact the National Guard regiments that had been trained to a high degree of readiness for the European war that he expected the United States to be drawn into soon.

Parker's blunt opinions soon led to what may have been the most controversial episode in his life, one that resulted in an official reprimand from his ex-classmate, Maj. Gen. Hugh L. Scott, now the chief of staff in Washington, D.C. Interestingly, it is one that goes unreported in his memoirs. It began undoubtedly innocent enough, when on September 10, 1916, Parker, as commander of the Brownsville District, inspected the 4th and 5th Nebraska regiments at Camp Llano Grande. Unfortunately, Parker may not have realized that a newspaper reporter was lurking about, recording his words.

"How fine it would be if you men could only be kept down here until you are thoroughly trained and as well prepared as any regular organization to go into battle," stated the general, mounted on a black horse. He paused and rubbed his chin. According to the reporter's account, datelined

September 10, "Something was coming, the militiamen sensed it and were thrilled with expectancy."

Parker supposedly continued: "Yes, and how much better it would be if we could go across the Rio Grande and whip hell out of those 'greasers.' That is what I am hoping for and praying for."

Of course, Brigadier General Parker later would tell his superiors that he had been misquoted, but the reporter, Buehler Metcalfe of the *Omaha (Neb.) World-Herald*, had overheard even stronger comments. Meeting the previous day with the officers at Camp Llano Grande, the reporter wrote, "he told the officers that he believed it was only a question of time when the American troops would be sent across the border and that if the militiamen are sent home now, they will return in a very short time. He said he expected the troops to remain on the border from three to six months longer."

The Wilson administration and the Army quickly responded. A September 22 directive required Parker to explain his remarks. In his statement, dated September 29, 1916, he acknowledged making "some remarks in confidence to the officers and soldiers of the command."

He added: "The tenor of my remarks was to compliment these soldiers on their fine work and showing during some trying times, and with the idea of encouraging them in keeping up their spirit and morale, and to combat the tendency on the part of many soldiers to demand a return to their homes. To accomplish this I tried to impress them with the fact that they were supporting the diplomacy of the administration by being ready if necessary to cross the Rio Grande, well fitted for successful action."

He next blamed the reporter for misquoting his privately intended comments: "Such remarks as I made were not intended for the public, but for men in training to act and fight as soldiers. They were expressed in soldiers' language but not exactly as reported. The color and character of the newspaper article herewith, taken with the absence of context and surroundings, gave wrong impression of my words and intention."

The Army refused to accept his blame-the-press explanation. On October 10, 1916, Major General Scott issued an unemotional statement that carried the force of a directive: "The Secretary of War directs that Brigadier General James Parker be informed . . . that the Secretary of War expects officers of the Army, especially of those of the grade of general officer, to so guard their actions and words that the Department will not be embarrassed by having newspaper reports of such words and actions brought to its attention by outside parties."

How important to his career was this setback for Parker? At first glance, it seems it barely affected him. The country's involvement in World

War I was only about six months away, and it would enable Parker to gain his second star. At the same time the flap occurred only seventeen months from his sixty-fourth birthday, when he faced forced retirement for age. Try as he might, he was unable to obtain an overseas combat command or forestall the date of his retirement. One could surmise that the army leadership had determined that Parker's best days were behind him and it had little reason to retain him on active duty.

In his memoirs, he states that shortly after this time he came near to being ordered to Russia as military attaché. The secretary of war, however, decided he could not be spared from his duties along the Rio Grande. Or, perhaps he lacked the sophisticated polish necessary for such a diplomatic role.

At this time we have no way of knowing how much his Texas comments undermined him in the eyes of his superiors. Just a few months later, even before war was declared by the United States, Parker himself sought to ensure that he would not be left on the sidelines by penning a one-sentence note to the Adjutant General: "In case of a foreign war, I request my name be considered for service with an early expeditionary force."

As noted earlier, that would not prove to be the case. Instead, he remained as a training commander in this country. In June 1917, when Gen. John J. Pershing yielded command of the Southern Department, Parker succeeded him, overseeing troops in Texas, Oklahoma, New Mexico, Arizona, and Southern California. Soon, he was ordered to establish from among troops in his department what became the First Division. In his memoirs, he claimed that he had been designated as its commander, but that President Wilson preferred another man, who was a political friend. Parker commanded the Southern Department for three months, organizing new encampments for training and being promoted to major general, National Army, effective August 5, 1917. On August 26, he was appointed to organize the 32nd Division at Waco, Texas. Made up of four regiments and two brigades, it numbered some twelve thousand National Guard troops from Wisconsin and Michigan, about a third of whom he had previously trained. In his obituary in the *New York Times* in 1935, he was described as "keeping half an eye on the Rio Grande and one and a half on the men he was training for service in France" for several months in 1917.

The division, as was generally true, lacked any cavalry regiments, a point which Parker, as an old cavalryman, criticized. While he was unable to gain a combat command, his friends who did recalled his abilities, and at least two of them missed him and his aggressiveness on the field of battle. In speaking of the American breakthrough at the battle of Soissons on July 18, 1918, Maj. Gen. Robert Bullard, an old friend, wrote in his own memoirs, "I longed for one single American cavalry division, led by an American cavalryman that I knew." That cavalryman was James Parker.

Likewise, Gen. Hunter Liggett, who commanded the 1st Army in France, wrote to Parker in 1921, recalling how he told his staff that "If I had Jim Parker here and now, and a division of American cavalry, not one of the enemy's organizations and none of his material would ever get across the Meuse River. And it was so. We did think of you over there, you see."

Undoubtedly, both men spoke from their hearts. But the cavalry's practical role in war was drastically altered by the European fighting. Galloping Jim wrote General Pershing in the spring of 1918, asking, "If you break through the enemies' line you will need cavalry and lots of it. Have you no use for an old cavalry drillmaster to train the horsemen you need?"

Sadly, he noted, "I received no answer."

Parker, who had led cavalry against Indians in the Southwest and on the Plains and against insurrectionists in the Philippines, would have found a different reality on the battlefields of Europe. Times had changed, and the means of warfare had also.

While he would not lead troops in Europe, in the fall of 1917 he was sent as an observer to France. Leaving in late September, he spent two months overseas and made it to the front lines, where he came under fire on several occasions while visiting British, French, and American troops. He returned home on November 26, 1917.

On his return, he and a number of other senior officers were ordered to undergo physical examination in Washington, D.C. In his memoirs, he notes the tests effectively ended the careers of a number of men, but not his, noting proudly he achieved a score of "almost one hundred per cent."

Having passed his exam, he returned to the 32nd Division at Waco. A few days later, on December 7, 1917, he learned that the division would go to France, but his joy was tempered by a telegram the next day. He was relieved of command and ordered to Camp Custer, Battle Creek, Michigan, to assume command of the 85th Division. His retirement was just two months off.

"One may judge of my feelings on receiving this message," Parker wrote. "I had hoped that in view of my record I would be retained in charge of the 32nd Division and would command it in France. However, I obeyed the order loyally, hoping against hope."

He added, "It was hard to say good-bye to my friends at Waco. I hurried off, grief in my heart."

In a different context, James Parker might have been labeled a good company man, for he was a loyal, efficient and dedicated officer. Across a career of forty-two years, no matter what task his nation and the army asked of him, he responded with enthusiasm and a high degree of competency. Despite his short term with the 85th, he performed well in preparing that division for combat. Parker had begun his career facing the Indian tribes of the West on the back of a horse. Now he had American Indians under his command, preparing to engage in a war that certainly marked a change in how men fought each other. The horse's day was done.

He spoke with admiration for the Indians. "To see those great fellows, armed with a bayonet, go at the dummies arranged for bayonet exercise was really a wonderful sight, for they certainly were in earnest."

At his retirement he received the Distinguished Service Medal, whose citation he noted "shows that my efforts to prepare my troops for this great exigency were not forgotten."

He would live another 16 years, much of that time at Greenvale Farms, Portsmouth, Rhode Island. His memoirs, which well documented his career, were published in 1929. His wife, Charlotte, died September 17, 1933, at their Greenvale home. The general himself died of pneumonia, after an illness of six weeks, on June 2, 1934, in New York City. They were survived by their four children: sons Cortlandt and James, Jr., and daughters, Mrs. Guy Murchie, Jr., and Mrs. Ronald T. Lyman. In his obituary in the *Army and Navy Journal*, a friend was quoted as saying, "A great light has gone out for the army, and a gallant gentleman has left the ranks."

CONTENTS

CHAPTER		PAGE
I	My First Post	13
II	The Buffalo Hunt	55
III	Horse Thieves and Outlaws	67
IV	Service on the Rio Grande	85
V	The Ute Campaign	116
VI	In the Navajo Country	138
VII	The Geronimo Outbreak	149
VIII	The Geronimo Campaign	168
IX	Fort Myer and San Francisco	191
X	The Spanish-American War	201
XI	The Philippine Insurrection	222
XII	Vigan	274
XIII	The Capture and Defense of Lagonoy	321
XIV	Service as Adjutant General	368
XV	The World War	431

ILLUSTRATIONS

General Parker .... *Frontispiece*

FACING PAGE

Officers of the 4th United States Cavalry 32
Comanche and Kioway Chiefs............. 64
Apache Chiefs 96
Major General Ranald Slidell Mackenzie. 128
Horace Jones, Indian Interpreter......... 160
Major General Henry W. Lawton 192
Fort Riley 224
Fort Bowie 224
Fort Wingate 224
Fort Sill 224
Major General Leonard Wood 256
Major General George Crook 288
First Lieutenant Charles B. Gatewood.... 288
Apaches at Home......................... 320
Apache Scouts Stripped for Action........ 320
En Route to Bowie After Geronimo's Surrender 320
Geronimo and Natchez, Prisoners at Fort Bowie 320
Major General S. B. M. Young............. 352
Officers of 12th New York Volunteers, Cuba 384

FACING PAGE

COLONEL R. W. LEONARD.................. 384
GENERAL PERSHING AND GENERAL PARKER..... 416
CAPTAIN JAMES PARKER, 4TH CAVALRY....... 416
CAPTAIN JAMES PARKER, WEST POINT 416

INTRODUCTION

This is the life of a restless, daring soldier in active service on both sides of this varied earth, a life unusual, apart perhaps from the common life of men and representing conditions that are past, but for all that none the less interesting; a life full of personal and human incidents.

Here are the "Memories of the Old Army," but they are scenes, thoughts and happenings of interesting times, men and regions known in the author's life. They are very full memories. All the better. The historian of the West in its making and of America in the Philippines here will get the view of eyes that were not strained for sensation, but saw things as they were. As the author lived them consecutively, so he gives you consecutively the acts, scenes, thoughts and incidents of his life. With him you make an excursion over the wild plains of the Southwest tracked only by Indian and buffalo; or after Geronimo you go with him into the Sierras of Arizona and Mexico, the Sierras looming , frowning, rugged to awfulness and sublimity; or in pursuit of Aguinaldo, amid the strange, unknown, tropical scenes and peoples of the Philippines. Seeing with the eyes of a newcomer, he makes all his story new to the reader.

These memories are an inexhaustible store of occurrences and conditions that will be of interest and value to him who would understand the times and the places in which General Parker lived.

Major General Robert Lee Bullard

THE OLD ARMY

MEMORIES

I

MY FIRST ARMY POST

I WAS born in Newark, New Jersey, February 20, 1854. My father was Cortlandt Parker, a noted jurist; my mother was an exceptionally gifted woman, Elizabeth Wolcott Stites, of Morristown, New Jersey. I had five brothers, all of whom had distinguished careers. I was educated at Newark Academy; Phillips Academy, Andover, Massachusetts; Rutgers College, New Brunswick, New Jersey; and at West Point. In 1876 I was graduated from West Point, thirty-first in a class of fifty cadets, and was appointed Second Lieutenant of the Fourth United States Cavalry.

Complying with orders received from the War Department, I started in the latter part of September to join my regiment at Fort Sill, Indian Territory. Stopping for some days at St. Louis, I found there a number of my classmates who were also en route to join their regiments, and I had a joyous time in their company.

Resuming my journey, at Caddo, Indian Territory (now Oklahoma), I left the railroad and took the "stage" for a trip of two days and two nights to Fort Sill. This stage, a ramshackle old affair drawn by two horses, made the trip of one hundred sixty-five miles at an average speed of four miles an hour. The road was exceedingly rough and at times boggy—long detours from the original road often had to be made in places where the settlers, farming on the government sections allotted to them, had run their fences across the former highway. These settlers were sometimes semi-civilized Oklahoma Indians, Chickasaws or Choctaws, and at other times whites who had married Indian women and had been inducted as members of the tribe and had thus obtained the right to take up this very rich Indian land. The country was generally level, with park-like alternations of post-oak groves and open prairie. At times we stopped at stage stations, log huts, to obtain our meals and change our horses. The stage, holding but four persons, was crowded with packages and mail and was exceedingly uncomfortable—I obtained but little sleep during the two nights on the road. I was greatly relieved when on the morning of the third day we crossed a broad, deep creek bordered by picturesque cottonwoods, and emerged on an elevated plateau. In the distance loomed mountains of bare granite; in the foreground what seemed like a small, well-built town, the national flag on a lofty flagpole waving above the buildings.

Fort Sill, like nearly all frontier posts at that period, was not a fortified place, but rather what might properly be called a cantonment. In most posts the buildings were arranged in the form of a square, enclosing a parade ground, the officers' residences on two sides, the men's barracks on a third, the hospital on the fourth. In other posts one side was left open, a preferable method, since it allowed for the extension of the post. The stables, storehouses and guardhouses were usually in the rear of the men's quarters, and the sutler's store just outside the post. Drills and parades were conducted on the parade ground.

I was received with every kindness by the captain of my company (we called troops of cavalry "companies" in those days, and squadrons of four troops we called "battalions") and by the Commander of the Post, General John P. Hatch, Lieutenant Colonel of the 4th Cavalry. The post was very crowded then with troops; in addition to four companies of cavalry of the ordinary garrison, there were a number of batteries of heavy artillery. The artillery had been sent from seacoast forts to Fort Sill, soon after the "Custer Massacre" of June, 1876, to take the place of six companies of the 4th Cavalry which had gone to the North under Mackenzie to fight the Sioux and Cheyennes.

Fort Sill was one of a line of forts, running approximately North and South, established along the edge of the "American Desert," an area extending generally from about the line of the 100th meridian west of Greenwich, to the Sierras of California and Oregon. I say "American Desert" because in my opinion that expression was correctly used at that time. It is an arid country. There are oases of considerable extent, and much has been done to improve the country by irrigation, digging wells and ingenious methods of dry soil farming, but the fact remains that in this section, comprising over one-third the area of the United States, the average population even now is shown by the Census of 1920 to be less than four persons per square mile. In 1876, in this vast arid section of over one million square miles, filled with game and buffalo, freely roamed the Indians, who nevertheless fiercely resented the advance of the white settlers towards its borders. These settlers, engaged in the peaceful occupation of farming, demanded to be protected—hence this line of posts. Later, when these Indians had become more peaceful and were given reservations, some of these posts, like Fort Sill, were maintained for the purpose also of looking after the rights of the Indians.

In 1876 the officers of the army of higher rank than second lieutenant were all veterans of the Civil War. In the ranks, too, were many war veterans. These soldiers were as a rule men who had gone back to civil life after the war was ended but who were too restless to become good business men. Such in my company were Wettstein, formerly Lieutenant Colonel 103 N. Y. Volunteers, sometime a non-commissioned officer, at other times a private, often in the guardhouse for "revelling." Another was Kimball. Captain in the Confederate service, a good bugler, reliable ordinarily. Another was Harley, 1st Sergeant of Company K, formerly in the war a Major of Volunteers, six feet four inches tall, handsome, well proportioned, erect. Harley had a dignity which at first altogether abashed Second Lieutenant Parker, appearing in officer's uniform for the first time. For, ignorant as I was of military matters, I had to give orders to this splendid veteran!

Drink was often the impelling reason in those days for enlistment in the Army. Pay day was irregular—sometimes once in two months, sometimes, on account of absence in the field, once in four or six months. The soldier's pay, though only $13 a month, and at times reduced by fines, might amount on pay day to a considerable sum. Pay day often was a debauch, an orgy of drunkenness. I had seen over ten per cent of the enlisted men of a Command in the guardhouse for intoxication, and there was much desertion as well on pay day.

But for active service in the field they were a splendid class of men. Inured to hardships, acquainted with the many methods the experienced soldier learns for maintaining his health, vigor and comfort when on the march, anxious for adventure, for peril, they were looked upon with admiration and respect by their officers.

It was true at that time, and it still is true, that each company in the American Army is in a certain way a *Club,* from which officers are excluded. The men, while they do not ever dream of questioning the orders of their officers, are as a body independent. They do not want a fatherly supervisor, they resent being patronized and cuddled by their superiors. They demand their rights, but no more than their rights. They resent having any one of their number too familiar with his officers. They persecute and call "dog robber" any soldier who acts as an officer's servant.

Naturally, with such a feeling as this reigning it is difficult to obtain good non-commissioned officers. The best men do not want to serve as such. This makes a situation altogether different from that, for instance, in the German or English armies. In those armies a non-commissioned officer is a young satrap, with power to punish. In our army such a thing would be impossible.

In those days there was no army test of literacy, citizenship or nationality in our army. It was composed in the ranks largely of Americans, with many Irishmen, and some Germans. Of the foreigners, I preferred the Irish—they were more intelligent and resourceful as a rule. However, if a German was fit to be a non-commissioned officer he usually made a good one—he was feared by the men, did not curry favor, but was rigid in carrying out orders. I had a sergeant, Richard Weege, who served me for many years and who finally retired and went back to Germany. He used to write me a letter, on my birthday every year, couched in very broken English. In Germany his retired pay made him quite a personage among the local men of means and he was in the habit there of vaunting the prowess of the American Army, which he proclaimed was the best in the world. But when the World War came the Germans had no use for this patriotic "American" —he was obliged to return to the United States, and when we entered the war he took service again in our army!

In the regiment there was a line of cleavage between the older officers, veterans of the Civil War, and the younger set who had seen no war service, but who prided themselves on their energy and youth, and rather mocked at the oldsters. My captain, Edward M. Heyl, had a rat-tailed black horse, well bred and powerful, he called Nigger, and whom he was in the habit at times of driving in a two-wheeled, one-seated cart. On one occasion, driving past one of the houses and seeing seated there two of the most bumptious of the younger lieutenants, Heyl pulled up and cordially invited them to take a drive. Accepting with some hesitation, they took their places on each side of the Captain, who whipped up and drove off down the road leading to the ford over Cache Creek. The lieutenants wondered, knowing that the creek was up and the ford swimming deep —however, they said nothing, nor did the Captain. Thus in silence they arrived at the ford. Heyl gave the horse a cut and shouting, "Whoop, Nigger," the powerful animal plunged in and swam to the other side. The lieutenants, standing up, held on like grim death, the water up to their necks, and they emerged dripping. As they drove about on the other side of the creek ordinary topics were discussed but of the ford they said nothing. On their return, they again came to the ford—the Captain again shouted, "Whoop, Nigger!" They again came safely through, and were duly deposited dripping at their quarters. This occurrence pleased the lieutenants, who held Heyl in greater estimation.

There is a widespread idea that the military profession is an easy one to learn, and that its difficulties are soon overcome, after which it becomes a comparative life of leisure. It has been my experience, however, that the intricacies of a thorough knowledge of command are looked upon lightly only by those who have never encountered them; that the life of a young officer for many years is merely an apprenticeship. I indeed found, up to the time I was retired as an officer, after forty-two years' service as such, that every day I was learning some new thing about commanding troops, this especially after I had attained high rank.

I was fortunate in the regiment to which I was assigned on leaving West Point. At graduation the cadets in order of rank choose a regiment, but it is literally a leap in the dark. If they ask for advice from their officers they cannot depend on it, for each officer cracks up his own regiment and branch. Perhaps the only unprejudiced officers at West Point are the doctors, for they usually have served with all, and can better than any prescribe infantry, cavalry, or artillery to the bewildered cadet.

The 4th Cavalry had a remarkable record. It was one of the new regiments organized in 1855 when Jefferson Davis was Secretary of War, and to it were then promoted many brilliant young officers, most of whom attained high rank later. During its first ten years of existence there served in it the following officers who afterward became generals:

COLONELS

E. V. Sumner — John Sedgwick
*Robert E. Lee** — L. P. Graham

LIEUTENANT COLONELS

Joseph E. Johnson — W. H. Emory
W. J. Hardee — T. J. Wood

MAJORS

D. B. Sackett — S. D. Sturgis
George Stoneman

CAPTAINS

George J. Anderson — George B. McClellan
Robert S. Garnett — E. M. McCook
James Oakes

*Note—Confederate Generals in *Italics*.

FIRST LIEUTENANTS

W. N. R. Beale	*George H. Stewart*
Jas. McIntosh	*Robert Ransom*
Eugene A. Carr	*Alfred Iverson*

Frank Wheaton

SECOND LIEUTENANTS

Davis S. Stanley	*J. E. B. Stewart*
Elmer Otis	Jas. B. McIntyre
Eugene W. Crittenden	Francis L. Vinton
George D. Bayard	*L. L. Lomax*
Wirt Davis	Eli Long

These included three commanders-in-chief: McClellan, Lee, and Johnston, and numerous corps and division commanders.

The record of the 4th Cavalry in the War of the Rebellion was unique. It was a prominent factor in the campaigns which kept Missouri in the Union in the early part of the war. Later it served in Kentucky, Tennessee and Georgia. As a part of the celebrated "Minty's Brigade," in 1863 and 1864, it marched over 5800 miles, and was in action against the enemy 76 times. In 1865 it took part in Wilson's Cavalry raid of over 800 miles, which had an important share in terminating the rebellion. In action it had an uninterrupted series of successes. For many of them it relied upon the sharpened saber and the charge. Since the war it had been engaged almost continuously in campaigning against the Indians in the Southwest. Under General Mackenzie it gained a high reputation.

In those days in a cavalry post on the frontier there were few military exercises. In the first place, due to the penury of government appropriations, a large part of the men were engaged in work as mechanics or laborers: cutting timber, repairing and constructing buildings, making roads, logging, in the winter cutting and storing ice, etc. Numerous detachments were absent in the field, escorting trains, pursuing deserters and horse thieves, and scouting. After each prolonged scout the horses, which had gone most of the time without grain and were run down, were unfit for mounted drills. The recruits when they arrived were often put to work at once on special duty as laborers, teamsters or mechanics, and learned to ride only when on a campaign. After fifteen or twenty days of marching the raw recruit had become a horseman! Consequently, equitation was not of a high order. There were no target ranges and very little rifle practice. There was no system of target practice then in the army. This seems incomprehensible, but it was unfortunately a fact. During the War of the Rebellion entire regiments went into battle without previous rifle practice, many men firing their guns for the first time. Thus at Gettysburg, after the battle was over, 25,000 muskets were picked up, useless, having two or more loads in the barrel. And history shows that foreign armies were also deficient in musketry preparation. The unexpected results of some wars might be traced to lack of this preparation on one side or the other. It seemed to be assumed by military men that *volume* of fire was all that was necessary and that *accuracy* of fire was needful only to a few sharpshooters. We know differently now. The rifle is a scientifically constructed instrument and its use requires long, careful teaching. Much of the success our troops in Europe gained in the World War may be traced to their careful preliminary training in rifle practice. But so little was known of the capabilities of our cavalry carbine in 1876 that the disastrous "Custer Massacre" was generally accounted for by the theory that the Indian was armed with a superior weapon. It was only later that we found out how fine a weapon was our Springfield carbine.

The officer of today on duty with troops works hard at long drills; much study is required. Not so in 1876. When not in the field he had many hours of idleness. There was much guard duty to be done, but drill hours were few, and study of the art of war was not the fashion. Today there is an officers' school in each post, and promotion is conferred only after a long and difficult examination—these things were then absent. Most of the older officers scoffed at study, did not believe in books; they claimed that such things were for the ignorant, that they had graduated in the school of war, that book learning was as nothing compared to experience of war. The younger officers were impressed by this dictum; besides, on graduating from the treadmill of West Point, they hated the sight of a book. Only a few read or studied.

Naturally, cards, billiards and liquor attracted many of these; the last even more because of the intermittent hardships of campaigning. Further, Fort Sill was the most malarious post in the army —many of the men were weakened by chills and fever. It was a common occurrence on meeting the civilian farmer in the Indian Territory and saying, "Good-morning, Mr. Smith, how are you today?" to have him answer, "Oh, pretty well;

I'm chillin' today!" It used to be said that 3-grain quinine pills passed current for 5 cents. By order of the doctors we took a pill each morning for breakfast. We were told that some years before during the day a ration of whiskey was customarily issued; the company would be lined up each morning at reveille and a gill of whiskey with 3 grains of quinine administered to each man.

The 4th Cavalry was a "bachelor" regiment. I found at Fort Sill only three ladies in the post: the wives of a captain, of a doctor, and the elder sister of another doctor. We had dances occasionally, but most of the officers present at the "hop" played cards. The ladies took turns dancing with the youngsters. There was a big bowl of "fish house punch" and much merriment. When a lanciers or a quadrille was announced, one of the officers danced as a lady.

Our principal recreation at Fort Sill was hunting. Buffalo could only be found forty miles to the westward, but there were plenty of deer, turkey and smaller game near the post. Quail abounded. It was noted that quail stuck close to civilization and were not found beyond the settlements. There was no "closed season" then for game. But the thing I enjoyed most was hunting with greyhounds.

In the prairie west of Fort Sill were to be found numerous jack rabbits, a species three or four times as large as a cottontail rabbit, larger than a Belgian hare and extraordinarily fleet. So fleet is the jack rabbit that on a surface which is smooth and devoid of grass he can run away from the greyhound, provided he goes straight. Particularly is this the case if he is running up an incline. Here the superior weight of the dog is a handicap.

But if the jack rabbit dodges about, the straight-running pack of hounds gains distance on him. Also, if he gets into long grass he cannot run as fast as the greyhound, since, on account of his inferior height, the grass impedes him more. Among the jack rabbits which infested this region, there were several that Jones said he had "trained," they were so clever in picking their ground, and had been so often run without success.

But the jack rabbits were not always "trained" and usually the hunt ended in two or three having been run down and killed. I remember on one occasion on my horse, Bayard, I had outstripped all my fellow-riders. I was alone, all the dogs but one had given up the chase; this one, a beautiful little hound named Jenny, was following the hare at a pace which, on account of fatigue, had become not much faster than a slow trot; my horse seemed almost used up. Finally the pace became a walk, then the jack rabbit, overcome by fatigue, fell in its tracks; the hound, also overcome, lay down with his muzzle on the hare, too tired to bite.

With greyhounds also we hunted the prairie wolf or coyote. Usually these animals were to be found near the prairie dog towns, watching for a chance to pounce upon an unwary marmot. Keeping the dogs closed in, or at heel, in perfect silence we approached behind the cover of the nearest hill. Carefully reconnoitering, the ghostly form of the wolf, which was almost exactly the color of the prairie, would be seen stealing away. With a shout we rushed at him at full speed. The hounds, with their noses in the air looking vainly this way and that, dashed to the front. Watching us as we pointed to the game, the leaders soon caught sight of it and the whole hunt, with yells of encouragement to the hounds, swept on.

The prairie wolf is a match in speed for jack rabbit, hound or horse, and the chase is ordinarily a long one. But he has a foolish habit of dodging instead of running straight forward; the hounds know this and run far apart so as to take up the chase by turns. The wolf, exhausted at last, halts, turns and faces the pack, his dangerous teeth glittering in the light, snapping fiercely at the hounds, who form a circle around him. Afraid to tackle him in front, some run in and tear at him from behind; the wolf turns on them like a streak of lightning and blood is seen running from their ears and jowls. Again he is attacked from behind, again he turns and tears his enemies. Their teeth are no match for his, as they well know; they approach him with much trepidation; the fight is now to be a long one; the wolf will succumb in the end, but not without much danger to the hounds. So a horseman dismounts, runs in and shoots the wolf, who falls, the hounds in a yelling mass biting him fiercely.

On one occasion in chasing a wolf I found myself far in front of the remaining horsemen, who had fallen behind out of sight. It was a hot day. The wolf was making for a creek, over the bank of which he disappeared, the hounds following. When I arrived at the bank and looked over I was astonished at the spectacle which met my eyes. The hounds and the wolf were swimming around the pool lapping up the water—the wolf in the center seemed to be paying no attention to the hounds, or they to him; all, including the wolf, were engrossed in the pleasure of cooling off after the hot and fatiguing run. But presently the wolf saw me, left the water and disappeared over the opposite bank unpursued; all my efforts, shouts and cries would not distract the hounds from their pleasant occupation. The wolf accordingly escaped.

This same pack we took with us to Fort Clark and afterward to Fort Riley. There an amusing thing occurred. At Riley, in a settled country, wolves were scarce. Capturing a litter of young wolves, they were kept in a cage near the hounds' kennel. In course of time the wolves grew to maturity and we arranged a wolf hunt.

Followed by the huntsmen and the pack, a wolf in a box was carried in a wagon to the center of a big prairie, and then turned loose. The hounds made for him, snapping and barking, but just at that moment a hound on the outskirts of the pack flushed a jack rabbit. Away went the pack after the rabbit. The wolf, with his tail between his legs, seemed undecided what to do, when to our great astonishment he rushed off after the pack, reached it, and joined merrily in the chase! We followed. After a long chase, in which the pack became scattered, the jack rabbit was caught, but the wolf was nowhere to be seen. Late that night he returned to his cage and was found there next morning!

Besides the greyhounds, we had at Fort Sill General Mackenzie's pack of foxhounds, kept for running wild cats and bears. The General kept them in the yard adjoining his quarters, where they were attended to by Private Strobel, the General's orderly, a Russian by birth. Strobel was of the short, solid, Mongolian type; extremely taciturn, and devoted to the General and his interests. He was an amusing fellow. At Pueblo,

Colorado, in 1881, in the Ute campaign, I watched him aiding the men, leading the General's pack mules aboard a cattle car for transportation to the front. One of the mules pulled back, objected to being pushed and lashed out with both heels, knocking Strobel down. Strobel jumped up, and with fire in his eye rushed at the mule, kicking him with a tremendous kick. The mule retaliated; Strobel went down once more, recovered himself, and kicked again; the kicking, much to my astonishment, was finally decided in favor of Strobel, and the mule entered the car.

This pack of hounds was trained not to follow deer, coon, rabbits or anything except wild cat and bear, the dogs being severely punished when they followed other animals. I once saw one amusing instance of this on the banks of the Red River. After a long chase through rough and bushy country we heard a terrible commotion ahead, a torrent of squeals and grunts. Reaching the pack we found that we had been chasing, not wild cats, but semi-wild pigs! The rage of Strobel and the General was frightful! In the end the hounds suffered almost as much as the pigs!

But a real "cat hunt" was thrilling. Wild cats abounded in the timbered valleys of the creeks, which near Fort Sill ran through the prairie country, and were usually bushy and bordered by precipitous slopes. Through these valleys the creeks, sometimes swift and deep, meandered. With the pack, some fifteen or twenty in all, preceding us, we would slowly ride along the bottom, the hounds apparently unconcerned, in perfect silence, Strobel occasionally dashing off with whip in hand to drive back a wandering puppy. Suddenly there would be a halt, the hounds, with nose to ground, circling about examining this and that patch of grass and brush with increasing interest. Some of the younger hounds would perhaps give a yelp or two but to them no attention was paid; the critical examination of the seniors would proceed in silence. Presently a long-drawn howl would be heard on the outskirts of the pack; one of the older and more reliable dogs had found the trail; his discovery was immediately echoed by another hound, and away the pack went in full pursuit and cry. What a joyous refrain; what a triumphal song! Through woods, over fallen logs, smashing through brush, jumping down and up precipitous banks, followed the huntsmen, encouraging the pack with horn and cry, our horses trembling with excitement and ploughing over obstacles at break-neck speed. The cliffs echo back the song of the hounds and the cries of the riders. The cat is wily, a check comes; to hide his trail he jumps into the stream and follows it, traveling in the water for a considerable distance. The hounds are silent, but presently the trail is found again and away the pack sweeps in full cry. Whenever a fallen tree is encountered the cat runs along the trunk, up into the branches, again descending to the ground and thus resumes his flight. This always causes a temporary check. Presently, as the chase proceeds, we catch a glimpse of the cat itself far in front, a brown figure, stealing along, casting an occasional glance behind at the baying dogs. They on the other hand do not see the cat; their attention is concentrated entirely upon the spoor. The trail grows hot, the scent of the cat is strong and fresh, and the hounds rush forward more quickly; they distance us, they disappear from sight; a wild and fierce mingling of cries is heard, and then —silence!

We emerge from the brush, we ride rapidly to the place where the cries of the hounds were last heard. A curious scene presents itself. In a circle, around a lofty tree, on their haunches, their noses pointing toward the sky, sit the pack, gazing intently toward the upper recesses of the tree. In its topmost branches sits the cat, gazing down at the hounds, grimacing. Occasionally a low hiss is heard as the cat faces his enemies.

When the cat was treed it became the duty of the youngest officer present to dislodge him, so that the hounds might get at him. As I was always the youngest and often the only officer with Mackenzie on the hunts (the average lieutenant stood too much in awe of the General really to enjoy his society), I had that experience often. In this way I found that wild cats are rather tame and cowardly creatures when confronted with man. The cat usually retreated as I approached. Running out on a side branch he would stay there glaring and grimacing and showing his teeth until poked with the short stick which I carried, when he would run out to the end of the branch, leap from there to the ground and after a fierce fight, be dispatched by the pack. Only once did a cat seem to threaten me: on that occasion he came directly towards me, and when almost within reach of my hand he turned under the branch, passed under me to the main trunk and thence to the ground.

I imagine that the alliterative saying, "he could whip his weight in wild cats," was originated with some person not well acquainted with the animal, which in my opinion is not nearly as fierce when cornered as is the domestic cat. The fighting qualities of the mountain lion or cougar are also much exaggerated. On one occasion, his troop being on an Indian scout, Lieutenant Wentz Miller of our regiment saw a flock of wild turkeys to one side of the road and, dismounting, shot one. The turkey fell in long grass, and Miller, stooping to pick it up, found the head of the turkey in the possession of a mountain lion. Both held on for a moment, then the animal let go and slunk away. This occurred in sight of a whole troop.

Bears were not plentiful around Fort Sill, and they had usually to be sought at a distance and in the mountains, entailing an expedition of a day or more. The chase, a long and arduous one, was generally terminated by the bear taking refuge in a cave or rock crevice, where he very often badly mauled the unlucky hound who came within his reach. The horsemen, when they came up, usually dispatched the bear.

Fort Sill at that time, like most other posts, had no officers' club. Neither had it the present Government-controlled "canteen" or post exchange. The functions of these two institutions were then supplied by the "post trader's store." Many of these post traders or settlers, who were appointed by the Government at Washington, were good fellows, and a welcome addition to the society of the post. Some of them were married and had charming families. The post trader maintained a bar room for enlisted men, a general merchandise store for men and officers, and a large lounging room, with billiard table, etc., for the officers. He was obliged to turn over a certain proportion of his profits to the Post Fund maintained for contingencies.

The post trader was one of the fixtures at the post. Garrisons might move and the personnel of the post change to the last man, but the post trader remained. His was the store, too, which supplied the civilians of the surrounding country. He also often acted as a kind of banker for officers, cashing their pay accounts, sometimes for long periods in advance, a thing then not prohibited by regulations. In many ways he could be of service. In 1878, when Congress allowed the army to go a whole year without pay, the post traders on the frontier cashed our pay accounts regularly, lending us the amounts without exacting interest. I, in common with other officers in those days, received many kindnesses from post traders, to whom I wish to render this tribute, in spite of the fact that as a class they were later much reviled and depreciated.

Mackenzie used to call Comanche the Court language of the plains. I believe the Indians have some five or six hundred different languages and dialects. But a smattering of Comanche was common to all the Indians of the Southwest. This was first because Comanche was easy; second, because the Comanches, in their raids, traveled everywhere. One old Comanche chief told us he had been where he had "seen little hairy men with long tails, in trees," which seems to prove he had been as far south as Central America.

However, the universal language among Indians was the sign language. This they had developed to such a point that it was not uncommon for Indians, usually of different tribes, to spend long hours together in perfect silence, conversing

Maj. E. B. Beaumont

Maj. Wirt Davis

Capt. H. W. Lawton

Capt. A. E. Wood

Capt. T. J. Wint

Capt. W. M. Thompson

Capt. E. M. Heyl

1st Lt. Jos. H. Dorst

1st Lt. Alex. Rodgers

OFFICERS OF THE 4TH UNITED STATES CAVALRY

by signs. Lieutenant Lawton (afterward General), whom the Indians, like ourselves, respected and admired greatly, was an adept at this language. We all learned a few expressions. Numbers were expressed by the fingers (and thus, of course, originated the decimal system), twenty-four-hour periods by *"sleeps,"* or putting one hand like a pillow to the ear, animals by some distinguishing trait or mark, as a deer by indicating with the fingers antlers, a cow curved horns, etc. It is a curious fact that many of these signs are identical with the gesticulations of the natives of southern Italy. It is, in fact, not an artificial but a natural sign language.

At Fort Sill the Indians we guarded on the extensive reservation were the Comanches and the Kioways. They numbered several thousands. Of the Kioways the entire tribe had been pacified. Of the Comanches all were present except a few of the Cohardie Comanches, still hostile. Their camp was said to be somewhere out on the Staked Plains or Llano Estacado. The Cohardie Comanches, the scourge of Texas and the Southwest, were in 1874 attacked by Mackenzie with the 4th Cavalry, at their camp in the Paladuro Cañon of the Staked Plains. Twelve hundred Indian ponies were captured and shot to prevent their recapture. Most of the Indians then surrendered.

The Kioways and Comanches apparently differed little in dress, appearance, or customs. Both tribes were "plains Indians" and thorough horsemen. They disdained to go on foot. They had many herds of horses, or rather ponies. Their camps were located in different places on the reservations. They lived in large tepees or wigwams, conical, with pole frames over which buffalo hides were stretched. They received from the Government an allowance of clothing, rations, etc. These supplies were issued to them by the Indian agent, who was an Interior Department official and not under the control of the War Department. The beef was issued on the hoof, and slaughtered by the Indians. The Indians eked out the food thus supplied by gathering and storing berries, wild plums, roots, etc. In summer they were permitted to go under escort of soldiers to the buffalo country, some forty to a hundred miles west of Fort Sill, where they killed great numbers of buffalo, drying the meat. The skins they sold to the Indian trader, who paid from five to ten dollars apiece for them, according to quality.

The Kioways and Comanches, while similar in appearance, were not so in language or customs. Their languages were entirely different, their customs largely so.

In fact, customs among the different tribes of Indians vary so much that one should receive with great caution the statement, so common in books, "the American Indian does so and so." There are even four or five hundred tribes, all with different customs as to marriage, funeral rites, burials, housing, food, drink and what not. For instance, the Comanches considered turkeys bad medicine and would not eat them, the Apaches shrank from the sight of fish. The Sioux loved whiskey, the Comanches would not touch it.

There is one thing all Indians are fond of—tobacco, and it was difficult for the younger officers to keep their houses from being invaded by bucks and squaws who gave you by sign and word the impression that they would not object to receiving sugar, tobacco or some other commodity, for the Indian does not consider it beneath his dignity to beg. Very curious and inquisitive, they were, too, about our personal belongings, including photographs. On one occasion a young buck, after looking at my mother's picture and then at me said interrogatively, "You?" And then pointing to the picture made the Indian sign of birth, thus asking me if I were her son. Our conversation consisted largely of signs and a few Indian and American words which we in turn possessed. That reminds me that the Comanche word for food was *chuckaway.* As they often prowled around the men's kitchens, the soldiers picked this up, and the cook's call to meals thus became *"Chuckaway! Chuckway!"* This became shortened into *chuck,* from which, without doubt, came the modern tramps' argot *chuck,* for eatables in general.

We often wonder at the Indian stoicism. As a matter of fact, it was a matter of pride with him to conceal his perpetual astonishment at the white man's devices. To him a wheelbarrow was as wonderful almost as a steamboat or a locomotive—he could have constructed neither. But he greatly appreciated our inventions, when he could use them—especially those pertaining to war. It was often noticed that the Indian on the warpath was equipped with the most modern firearms. Thus many of the Indians who fought in the Custer "Massacre," in which Custer and his men were wiped out, were armed with magazine guns while the troops had only single loaders. It was charged at the time that some vile traders made a practice of selling arms to the Indians; that they could by no means obtain them otherwise. But, in fact, many of the arms were sold to the

Indians by the settlers, the very persons who feared the Indians most. The Indian would see in a settler's home the rifle that he coveted. He would offer a pony for the gun. "No!" said the settler. Two ponies. "No!" Three, four, five ponies. It was too much for the farmer. He was offered ten times the value of the gun; he gave it up. But he did not tell his neighbor.

To the Indian the rifle meant life or death. The same was the case with cartridges. In 1885 we found that the Apaches who had gone on the warpath had been paying our soldiers a dollar apiece for cartridges. And he reserves his cartridges for close range. He must shoot at point blank distance; he does not understand the graduation of the rear sight leaf, or how to use it. Thus when he kills a deer he crawls up close, within a few yards, before he shoots. If he can, he will do the same with a man. He can conceal himself marvelously. On the warpath he strips and covers his body with mud; a few feet off he is as indistinguishable on the ground as a young quail, spreading itself flat on the soil at the alarm call of its mother.

Speaking about cartridges, we were rather surprised at Fort Sill by the avidity with which the Indians sought and collected the empty cartridge shells left on the target ground. For our cartridge shells had a solid base, and we thought they could not be reloaded. But we were mistaken. The Indians would drive a nail of a certain length into the base of the shell. Around the nail they would pack powder, and on the point of the nail a percussion cap. On top of all, fitting in the shell, they placed a bullet. In firing, the point of the firing pin struck the head of the nail, the point of the nail hit the cap in the base of the bullet and fired the cap and the powder. This was an example of a mind quickened to inventiveness by the demands of war. But in everything but war the Indian was in the Stone Age. Like our ancestors, he had no special spur to invention, which after all is the basis of our modern civilization.

The American Indian was a warrior, pure and simple. While he had intervals of peace, he lived for war. It is as a warrior he is admired. War brings out many heroic traits and it makes a man of pride. We admire a proud man. And if killing is war, the American Indian was one of the greatest warriors that ever existed. I have marched through northern Mexico, and I make bold to say that in the lifetime of the oldest Indians now in the Chiricahua tribe, that tribe has killed ten thousand Mexicans—men, women and children. The same thing could have been said of the Comanches. In northern Mexico you can find whole towns abandoned in the wilderness, once wiped out by Apaches.

War does not tend to increase of population, which is the main reason why the Indians have decreased in numbers. And the wars between Indian tribes have been by far more bloody than those with the whites. In war the Indians give no quarter. Whole tribes have thus been wiped out. Other tribes have been driven into the desert to starve. The losses which the Indians have incurred in fighting the whites are not to be compared with their losses in inter-tribal hostilities.

The Indian is a natural warrior. He loves war. Thus the whites never had any difficulty in enlisting Indian soldiers or scouts to fight other Indians. These Indians were regularly enlisted like soldiers, carried on the muster rolls as privates and non-commissioned officers, wore our uniform, and were proud of the flag. They were as ready to fight their own relatives as to fight foreign tribes. In 1885 part of the Chiricahua Apaches broke from the reservation and went on the warpath, and we enlisted many of the remainder to pursue the hostiles. Their war dances at night around an immense fire, their naked bodies shining in the blaze as they danced and sang their savage chant, firing their rifles into the air, was one of the most thrilling sights I ever saw.

Speaking of the stoicism of Indians, we were occasionally visited by some of the chiefs who had visited Washington, seen the great father, had been shown the large cities, etc., with the object of impressing upon them the tremendous power and numbers of the whites, and the futility of opposing them. It was naturally expected by the authorities that their experiences and impressions would be communicated to the tribes. Not so; the chiefs, while amazed and greatly impressed by what they saw, knew that if they told these experiences they would be regarded as pacifists, and correspondingly lose power and influence among the others. It would be said in the tribe that they had been hoodooed; their minds had been affected; that they were crazy. It was the business of the war chiefs to preach the doctrine that the scattered whites one saw on the frontier were the only foe to be overcome, and could by a strong effort be exterminated; that the rations and supplies issued to the Indians at the agencies were in the nature of a tribute, which the whites found necessary to make, in order to postpone war.

But these same chiefs were often garrulous enough regarding their experiences in the East when they found themselves alone with the whites. They showed that they were particularly impressed by the enormous lodges (hotels) they lived in; by the elevators, by the great canoes (ships), by the enormous extent of country and the multitudes of people, by the Capitol at Washington. They were glad of an opportunity of boasting of these experiences when it could be done without danger to their prestige. Interpreter Jones, who had several times accompanied them on these trips, and who, by the way, was at times almost as astonished himself as any Indian by some of the things he saw, had many amusing tales to tell of these journeys.

While in camp near Mount Sheridan in 1877 a frequent visitor from a neighboring camp of Comanche Indians was a young chief named Quinah. Quinah was one of the handsomest Indians I ever saw, over six feet tall, lithe, straight as an arrow, finely cut features, light-colored complexion, an ideal savage! His dress was exceedingly ornate; his manner proud and haughty. He was one of the leaders of the young men and preached war.

On one occasion he happened in on us while we were eating midday dinner, and we invited him to join us at the table, an invitation which he readily accepted, showing during the meal a tremendous appetite. Whether he regarded this unusual hospitality as a sign of weakness I don't know, but some days afterward, as I was busily engaged at my correspondence, he entered my tent, and without preliminary called out, "Tabac!" "What?" said I. "Tabac!" he shouted, looking at me haughtily. "Get out of here!" I yelled, advancing on him. He turned tail and left.

My experience with Indians has been that they are likely to regard hospitality as a proof of weakness. They never invited us into their tepees; in fact, a visit to their camps was usually met by scowling looks, the squaws being particularly venomous towards the army ladies whom they evidently regarded as weak, pampered creatures.

This same Quinah, later known as Quinah Parker, became afterward the head chief of the Comanches, and a very rich man. The story is quite a romance. Some time in the fifties the Comanches, while on a raid in Texas, encountered Judge Parker and his wife driving through the country. They killed the Judge, and dragging Mrs. Parker, who was a handsome woman, off into captivity, she became the wife of one of the chiefs. By this alliance she had a son, Quinah, who must have been born along about 1855. Judge Parker was a rich man, possessed of lands and herds, this property at his death descending to his wife, and at her death to her child. Years after I saw Quinah, he laid claim to the estate and won it. Quinah died some years ago.

It was not unusual in the early days to find whites among the Indians. In the Comanche tribe was a boy named Schmidt who had been captured by the Indians at one of the German settlements north of San Antonio. When the Indians were brought into Fort Sill Reservation, the authorities sent this boy back to his parents. Some months later he reappeared with the tribe, having run away from home. The fascination of Indian life was too much for him.

In truth, there was much to attract about the life of the plains Indian. There was a wild dare-devil recklessness especially alluring to a certain class of men. The summer was one long camping picnic, full of adventure, moving from place to place. The men hunted and amused themselves, and the women did all the work of camp. The women were slaves, the men knights. Naturally, there was something about the Indian character which attracted. I have even known some officers, detached for Indian scout duty, and thus obliged to spend long periods alone with Indians, to become for a time almost Indian-like in habit and thought, such was the influence of their environment. Gatewood was an example.

But I never became an Indian lover. I never was in sympathy with much that has been written as to the wrongs of the "poor Indian." It was inevitable that the whites should demand that the land should be divided between the whites and the Indians. The Indians were first given enormous tracts of territory on which to roam and hunt. Holding to a sentimental feeling for the Indians, we continued to treat with each tribe as a "nation." In the treaty we would agree to respect the boundaries of their reservation, while on their part the Indian tribe would engage to refrain from acts of war "as long as water runs and grass grows." But the tribe was not a nation, and the chief was not able to prevent his young men from harassing the settlements. Thus most of the treaties were first broken by depredations and murders committed by the Indians. It was a mistake to treat them as nations; we erred through a desire to be just. The Canadians never did it; they had very little trouble. As for ourselves we should have forced the Indian to settle, take up land and cultivate it, as we did finally in 1890. In my opinion most of the trouble we have had with Indians has been due to yielding to the demands of the Indians to be recognized as separate nations and to a policy of conciliation instead of law.

If the author of *A Century of Dishonor* had seen as I saw in 1885 in peaceful, quiet farming settlements a reign of horror, caused by a raid of murderous devils who went on the warpath for no reason, except that they wanted a murder debauch, as a white man goes on a drunken debauch; if she had seen women and children huddled together in houses, shaking with terror, afraid even to go to sleep lest they should suffer the same fate as their husbands, fathers and brothers, she never would have written that book.

Speaking of the curious customs of Indians, I was once hunting in the woods near Mount Sheridan when I heard a weird musical sound. At first I paid no attention to it, thinking it was the wind. But it grew louder and, presently, as I emerged in an opening in the forest a curious sight met my eyes. Seated on the ground was an Indian squaw stripped to the waist. In her hand she held a shell, with the sharp edge of which, with rapid motions, she was lacerating her breasts, at the same time crooning a doleful Indian lament. Blood ran down her body. Near by was her husband busily engaged in hanging shirts and other articles of clothing on the bushes.

Inquiring what this all meant, he informed us by signs and words that his wife was mourning on the anniversary of her former husband's death. He evidently was much impressed with the ceremony and took part in it with pride.

It is amusing to me in these latter days to see Indians pictured, even when engaged in the most ordinary occupations, as being dressed in beaded and fringed buckskin garments with feathered headdresses. As a matter of fact these were regalia costumes, and were never assumed except on grand occasions. In twelve months I never saw the Comanches rigged out this way, except on one occasion when they had a kind of mounted parade. Usually their dress consisted of a shirt, a gee-string, moccasins and a blanket. They were, however, lavish in the use of paint, which they applied to their faces. Indians did not wear hats but were very fond of umbrellas, generally of the particularly loud style, such as are used by us as advertisements. On some occasions, as a distribution of supplies, you would see hundreds of Indians riding along the road, in solemn silence, carrying these gaudy umbrellas.

An account of Fort Sill in 1876 would be incomplete without a description of the officers who garrisoned it. Life in those days was rough; the absence of woman at our frontier posts, and the state of celibacy in which our officers lived did not contribute to the refinements of our life. But it developed individuality and *originality*. Besides, there is no question, but that in the absence of female influence there is scope for more intimate relations between men. We were a band of brothers, often deeply devoted to one another. As our Colonel and Regimental Commander we had Ranald Slidell Mackenzie, a great cavalry leader of the Civil War.

Under him the regiment was constantly employed in the pursuit of hostile Indians, having many skirmishes. In 1873 the Rio Grande frontier was being harassed by Kickapoo and Lipan Indians, who, when pursued, escaped into Mexico. Mackenzie took the responsibility of crossing into Mexico, and by a forced march surprised the Indian camps near Remolino at dawn, utterly defeating them. The next morning he was back on American territory. This violation of foreign territory, though it led to much diplomatic correspondence, was approved by our Government, putting an end, as it did, to these murderous Indian raids insufferable to a self-respecting nation.

In 1874 the regiment under Mackenzie defeated the main body of the Comanches on the Staked Plains, capturing nearly 2000 horses. Knowing from previous experience the impossibility of protecting this vast herd from a stampede by Indians, who would thus regain their hostile influence, he was compelled to order the herd destroyed. The bones of these poor animals still mark the site of "Mackenzie's Battleground," but the power for evil of this tribe was broken and they soon came in and surrendered. From that time on, by his wise control, Mackenzie, at Fort Sill, I. T., completely changed the aspect of the Indian question in that part of the country.

In 1876 there was an Indian outbreak in Wyoming. Six companies of the regiment accompanied Mackenzie there, where he captured and deposed Red Cloud. Later commanding the Powder River expedition, in the dead of winter he surprised the Cheyenne Indians in the Big Horn Mountains, captured their camp and left them fugitives, without shelter or food. Their surrender soon followed, with lasting peace. Returning to Fort Sill, thence to Fort Clark, Texas, in May, 1878, he again led an important expedition across the Rio Grande into Mexico, against the Lipans and Kickapoos, who were raiding our settlements. This expedition brought the Mexican Government to terms. Mexico, by it, was compelled to send a considerable body of troops to the Rio Grande, which punished the Indians and restored order. In 1879 the Utes in Colorado killed their agent and defeated a column of troops sent against them; again Mackenzie and his regiment was called for, and in 1881, as Colonel Dorst says, "In one sublime moment he averted war" and forced the Uncompahgre Ute Indians to submit. They were removed to a new reservation in Utah. Immediately afterward the Apaches in Arizona went on the warpath and Mackenzie and his regiment were sent there in pursuit. In 1881 and 1882 he commanded his regiment during the Indian troubles in New Mexico.

Mackenzie had an unusually magnetic influence on his officers, his personality impressing itself upon them. This influence was lasting with all those who served under him or with him. I remember in 1899, during the Philippine Insurrection, General Lawton said to me, "Whenever I am in a tight place, whenever I am uncertain what to do, I say to myself, 'What would Mackenzie do?'" And several times during that campaign General Young, who was serving under Lawton, said to me, "Mackenzie wants me to do this; I mean Lawton." Thus the Mackenzie spirit reigned long after his death.

Of those who served this remarkable officer the closest of all, the one in whom Mackenzie most confided was Lawton, afterward Brigadier General. Lawton, who came from civil life, enlisting as sergeant in the Indiana Volunteers, in April, 1861, emerged, in 1865, a Lieutenant Colonel, was one of those great soldiers produced by the war, a better school than West Point, since it graduated in the higher ranks fighters, not merely students. Lawton was a confirmed woman hater: a conviction, shared to a great extent by Mackenzie, was that a married officer was never so fit for the active service of the frontier as was a bachelor. In this connection I remember an amusing incident in 1878 at Fort Clark, Texas. We were having lunch at the General's house, when in the course of the conversation Lawton announced that he did not think women ought to be allowed at frontier posts. Hearing a peculiar sound, we discovered that one of our fellow-guests, a remarkably pretty woman who had just joined the regiment as a bride, was sobbing. Lawton was astonished, flabbergasted, and sought to make amends. "Why, Mrs. T.," said he with reddened face and stammering voice, "as for really meaning what I said, I would like to see the army entirely composed of women."

"You horrid man!" said Mrs. T., mopping up her tears and leaving the room in much indignation. Lawton was repentant, but Mrs. T. always afterward alluded to him as "that horrid Lawton."

In 1886 Lawton, then a captain, became well known in connection with the capture of Geronimo, the Apache chief, a campaign in which I co-operated with him. In 1898, in the campaign of Santiago, Lawton, then a major general, took

El Caney, an outwork of Santiago, after an obstinate and bloody fight. Later, in the Philippines, he greatly distinguished himself, being the "fighting general" of our forces. In July, 1900, serving under him I took the town of San Mateo, near Manila, after a bloody fight. General Otis ordered it evacuated, considering it a point in our line too advanced. Five months later, in retaking San Mateo, Lawton was killed.

Mackenzie repaid the devotion of his younger officers by assiduously working for their promotion. In those days we had "regimental" promotion—that is, up to the grade of captain, officers were promoted in their regiments, and not transferred to other regiments, as is now the case when officers obtain a grade. Officers thus remained many years in the same regiment, a fact which cemented regimental feeling and regimental pride. In war or in arduous active service (which as in war resulted in many casualties among the officers) it was considered only fair that the regimental officers should profit. In the strenuous work of Mackenzie's regiment an unusual number of officers became incapacitated for duty. The retired list in those days was very limited, and in many cases worn-out officers remained long years absent from their regiments, but still on the rolls, blocking promotion. This, Mackenzie successfully fought at Washington. His disabled officers were promptly retired, a number resigned, and thus the 4th Cavalry was envied for its quick promotion. Some officers obtained a captaincy after only twelve years of service, a rate of promotion then regarded as extraordinary.

In return, we were indignant that Mackenzie did not receive the reward of his services. But there were many older officers at that time who had held high command during the Rebellion and rendered brilliant services. For these Mackenzie had to wait. At one time Miles was Mackenzie's rival for the coveted star. In camp one night Mackenzie abstractedly was gazing into the heavens when an officer remarked laughingly, "I'm afraid, General, there's Miles between you and that star!" The General turned away, snapping his fingers nervously.

One of Mackenzie's most distinguishing traits was his brilliant success in the management of Indians. Turbulent, dangerous when his suspicions were aroused, the Indian was childlike and easily led by one he trusted. At the same time weakness would not do with the Indian; benevolence had to be mixed with determination and force of character. The Indian was a man and a warrior, and recognized and appreciated warrior traits. Many military commanders made the mistake of parleying with him; that was fatal, for the Indian, like the schoolboy, was never at a loss for words. Nothing pleased him more than prolonged conferences. In these the Indian shone by the grand manner in which, with his blanket wrapped around him, his head erect, he rolled forth the eloquence of his primitive language, full of imagery. These conferences were likely to gain nothing useful.

The Indians had faith in Mackenzie; they knew by his acts that he was continually endeavoring to better their condition, to make "the white man's road" of peaceful effort more acceptable. They knew he was watching the Indian agent, that he was striving with the Government at Washington to obtain them more food, clothing, comforts; that he was even having his soldiers build them houses, and spending money out of his own pocket to provide them with cows and sheep. But they feared him as well as loved him, for they had learned through many a struggle that he was a great war chief.

A single incident will illustrate his way with Indians. In the summer of 1877 a number of Cohardie Comanches, a tribe then hostile and on the warpath, had stolen in to the Comanche camp near Sill. Mackenzie heard of this, and sent word to the Comanches that they must deliver over these hostiles, to be put in the guardhouse. Of these facts I was ignorant, as I sat at my desk as acting adjutant. A hubbub attracted my attention to the adjoining office of the General—the office was full of Indian chiefs holding, through Jones, the interpreter, a conference with Mackenzie. Mackenzie sat at his desk apparently saying nothing, while Jones interpreted the remarks of the Indians. One after another of the chiefs strode forward and, with flashing eyes and haughty mien, delivered his oration, which was received with many "ughs" of approval by the others. Presently Mackenzie called me, and I entered the room. "Come close," said he, and in a low tone directed me, "have all the troops saddle up, leaving the horses in their stalls, the men to be armed and equipped with 100 rounds of ammunition. Do this quickly but quietly, in such a manner that the preparations will not be seen by the Indians." Going out I found the troop commanders and gave them these instructions, and in the course of a half-hour returned and reported to Mackenzie that all was ready.

The discussion was still going on, the Indians

showing some excitement, Mackenzie sitting by in silence. As soon as I had made my report Mackenzie rose and took his hat.

"Jones!" said he, "tell these Indians I have listened to their talk long enough. Tell them," he said slowly, "that if they do not bring those renegade Cohardie Comanches to the guardhouse in twenty minutes"—here he made a pause and spoke deliberately—"I will go out to their camps and kill them all. Repeat that, Jones, just as I have said it. I—will—go—out—to—their—camps—and—*kill*—them—all!" This he said without the least appearance of excitement, in a quiet, deliberate voice. He then left the room.

The effect on the Indians was instantaneous—they seemed thunderstruck. They rushed for their horses, galloped madly from the post, and in a very few minutes a party reappeared bringing the renegades. A less decisive action might have ended in war.

In 1881 I was present when Mackenzie, by his boldness, initiative, and knowledge of the Indian character, averted a bloody Indian war. The Ute Indians, a powerful Indian tribe, which up to that time had suffered no defeats at the hands of the whites, inhabited the western part of Colorado. There were three reservations, one for the White River Utes in the North, one for the Southern Utes near Fort Lewis, in the South, and one for the Uncompahgre Utes, the most numerous tribe of all, on the Uncompahgre River in the extreme western part of Colorado. The White River Utes in 1879 had revolted and killed their agent, Meeker; an expedition sent under Major Thornberg to restore order met with disaster; Major Thornberg and many of his command being killed. As a consequence the State of Colorado demanded the removal of all these Indians to Utah; and a Commission was sent from Washington to the Uncompahgre River to arrange for their transfer.

The Indians fiercely resented the demands of the Commission, and the whole of the summer of 1880 was absorbed in protracted negotiations; the troops, cavalry and infantry, under Mackenzie, standing idly by. These parleyings were conducted by the Interior Department; Mackenzie, under the War Department, having no part in them. They were finally apparently crowned with success. The Indians, in exchange for a certain sum of money, agreed to move to Utah the following summer.

The next summer (1881) with a smaller command we again marched out to the Uncompahgre River. It was apparent at once that there was a hitch in the proceedings; the Indians had thought little of their promise to move; they claimed they had misunderstood the terms of the treaty and they refused to budge. The Commission appeared and began to parley; the Indians were collecting ammunition, were armed to the teeth, and were exceedingly surly and hostile in demeanor.

The negotiations dragged on all summer without success. Finally in September the Commission found that their efforts were useless, and notified the Government to that effect. The matter was turned over to the War Department to settle, and Mackenzie was ordered to take such steps as were in his opinion necessary and proper.

All was excitement on the Uncompahgre; the Indians, some two thousand in number, were evidently preparing for a fight, and had intrenched themselves on the summit of a lofty mountain, where they evidently proposed to defend their wives and children while the main force raided the settlements. These, consisting of mining outfits, were numerous and isolated and would fall an easy prey. The civilians about the Indian agency, including the agent, Bundy, regarded war as certain. Upon the receipt of the telegram from Washington, the force of troops present, about ten companies of infantry and cavalry, some 300 or 400 men, was ordered to stand equipped with 200 rounds of ammunition per man and three days' cooked rations. This done, Mackenzie sent word to the chiefs to come in for a conference.

It took place the following morning. Mackenzie informed the chiefs that the matter had been turned over to him for settlement; they had promised to move to Utah, and he wished to know whether or not they were going. Somewhat daunted by his cool, determined manner, the leading chief commenced an oration in which he denounced the whites for wanting to deprive the Indians of their land, and was proceeding to more violent expressions when Mackenzie, with his hat in his hand, stood up.

"It is not necessary for me to stay here any longer," he said. "You can settle this matter by discussion among yourselves. All I want to know is whether you will go or not. If you will not go of your own accord, I will make you go. When you have sufficiently discussed this matter and have arrived at a conclusion, send for me. Remember, you are to go, at once."

The Indians were full of consternation. They expected a long parley, lasting weeks. In the meantime they would have time to finish their preparations, which were not nearly complete, should the war become necessary. And they had thought the white man was afraid.

After a debate lasting several hours they sent for Mackenzie. They proposed a compromise. They said they had concluded they must go, but first they wished to go back to their camp and talk with their old men. "No," said Mackenzie. "If you have not moved by nine o'clock tomorrow morning, I will be at your camp and *make* you move."

The next morning, shortly after sunrise, we saw a thrilling and pitiful sight. The whole Ute nation on horseback and on foot was streaming by. As they passed our camps their gait broke into a run. Sheep were abandoned, blankets and personal possessions strewn along the road, women and children were loudly wailing. Poor things! they were leaving the land which had been theirs for centuries, their home, their country, for an unknown destination hundreds of miles away.

Mackenzie, too, felt a pity for them. But it was inevitable that they should move, and better then, than after a fruitless and bloody struggle. They should think, too, that the land was lost beyond recovery. And so as we marched behind the Indians, pushing them out, he sent word to all the surrounding whites, who hurried after us, taking up the land and at once commencing the erection of their houses. As we pushed the Indians onward, we permitted the whites to follow, and in three days the rich lands of the Uncompahgre were all occupied, towns were being laid out and lots being sold at high prices. With its rich soil and wonderful opportunities for irrigation, the Uncompahgre Valley—before a desert—

soon became the garden spot of Colorado, covered with fruitful fields and orchards.

Mackenzie was promoted to the grade of brigadier general in 1882 and retired from the army for disability in 1884. He died in 1889 at the age of forty-nine after a brief but brilliant career. His memory will always be cherished by those who knew him. As Colonel Dorst says in Cullum's biographical register of West Point graduates: "Braver than a lion, yet sensitive and gentle as a woman, uncompromising, determined and just, yet kind, generous and deeply sympathetic with humanity in any walk of life; imperious, impetuous and dashing, yet modest, diffident and simple . . . the example of such a man can never be lost in death."

He was a *soldier*.

II

THE BUFFALO HUNT

While I have qualified as sharpshooter, I am not a good game shot. In fact, though I have had considerable success in hunting it has been due to good luck. But one hunting expedition which deserves to be recorded took place before our western country was stripped of game.

In 1877, Captain Albert H. Markham of the English Navy, a noted Polar explorer, later a distinguished admiral, was touring the country. At Chicago, meeting General Sheridan, he expressed his desire to take part in a buffalo hunt. General Sheridan sent him to General Mackenzie at Fort Sill, and in November, 1877, we took him out to the buffalo country. Our party consisted of First Lieutenant Thompson ("Hurricane Bill"), commanding; Captain Markham, Lieutenant Sandy Rodgers, myself, sixteen soldiers, six Indians and my mulatto servant. The Indians went along to take care of the hides and dry the beef of the slain buffalo. We had with us two wagons with teams, nine spare horses, and four greyhounds.

Markham was a dapper little Englishman of pleasant manners. In contrast with our rough get-up he was always carefully and neatly clothed in sporting equipment, while his array of rifles and shotguns filled us with admiration.

We marched westward over flat country toward the Staked Plains, camping the first night at

West Cache Creek. The next day, while on the march, an amusing thing occurred. Markham, riding at the head of the column with Thompson, had expressed a great desire to kill a prairie hen. Suddenly Thompson exclaimed: "There is one!" "Where? Where?" said Markham, greatly excited and loading his shotgun. "There!" shouted Thompson, and with equal excitement grabbed Markham's gun from his hands and before he could utter a protest shot the prairie chicken dead. He then returned the gun. We who knew Thompson's eccentricities had difficulty in concealing our laughter at the flabbergasted expression on the face of our guest.

But Markham later had plenty of opportunities to kill prairie chickens, as well as other small game. Reaching Otter Creek, we found the country full of ducks and geese. It had been a wet season and the buffalo wallows were full of water, making hundreds of little ponds. These ponds, usually bordered by a growth of high grass, covered the country in all directions and were exceedingly easy to approach without alarming the game. On one occasion the simultaneous discharge of two guns killed twenty ducks. We also saw curlew and occasionally wild swans.

We spent several days in this sportsman's paradise. Taking up our line of march again, we crossed the north fork into the buffalo country. Almost immediately we encountered buffalo.

I had never killed buffalo, and my first chase was an exciting one. Sighting a herd at a distance, the officers left the column and approached by a circuitous route, keeping some high ground between us and the herd. Arrived at the ridge, we crossed at a gallop and charged down on the herd peacefully grazing in the hollow beyond. As we approached, one by one they raised their heads and, sighting us, began slowly to turn and get under way. A few moments more they were rumbling along at full gallop, throwing mud and stones behind them in their awkward scramble to get away. When we reached them they were going at a run almost as fast as a horse. Singling out a fat animal, Markham and the others each rushed it at full speed. My choice fell on a young bull who gave my horse, Bayard, a lively chase. I had learned that the proper way to kill a buffalo is to ride up alongside and then with the revolver shoot him about the center of the body, just in rear of the foreshoulder, the ball thus reaching the vitals. But whenever I attempted this the buffalo dodged. In my excitement this did not prevent me from shooting; in all I fired sixteen shots, emptying my revolver again and again. The unfortunate beast was pierced fore and aft and diagonally, until from loss of blood he fell, but this did not occur until I had ridden several miles, and my steed was badly winded from the long run. Some horses are afraid of the shaggy-headed buffalo and shy when brought near; this happened to Markham, and to his great disappointment he made no kill.

I learned later how to overtake and when to hit the buffalo, and usually dropped him at the first shot. If the bullet goes through the lungs, the animal staggers for a few paces and then sinks back on his haunches after taking a sitting position; the blood gushes from his nose until finally he falls over and expires.

The tidbit to the Indian was the liver. This, when the animal was butchered, he ate raw, the blood streaming down his front, presenting a gory and ludicrous spectacle.

After a buffalo was killed it would be stripped of its hide, butchered, and loaded on a wagon. When it reached camp, the choice portions would be distributed to the officers' mess and the soldiers' cook fire; the remainder, with the hide, would be turned over to the Indians. They tanned these hides and later sold them to the post trader. Some of the meat was cut into strips which were hung on bushes to dry, thus constituting "jerked beef," a favorite food with Indians and plainsmen. But much of the meat they ate, feasting by day and night. All night long they sang and ate.

The next day we crossed the Salt Fork of Red River and after a long march camped on Turkey Creek, a branch of Red River. And here a curious thing occurred. All that hot afternoon, while on the march, we had seen at a distance small bands of turkeys, feeding upon the grasshoppers on the plain. After getting into camp Thompson and Markham started out again to hunt deer and buffalo; but my friend Sandy Rodgers and myself, lazy, like most newly graduated cadets, remained in camp. As the evening sun declined and we were lying in our tent, smoking and enjoying our ease, we heard some soldiers shouting, "Head off these mules, they are going out towards that herd of buffalo!" It must be explained that mules are very inquisitive, and will readily join a moving herd of animals. Rodgers and I turned out to look at the herd of buffalo, which seemed to extend for a mile. Going back into my tent I got a telescope and discovered that they were not buffaloes but turkeys!

Running along the ridge they showed up against the sky, which had the effect of magnifying their proportions.

They were running toward the creek just above us. Seizing our guns, a carbine and a muzzle-loading shotgun, we ran up the bank to intercept them. I think we and the turkeys arrived about the same time. At any rate, there was a tremendous fluttering, flying and squawking combined with shooting for a minute or two. When this ceased we went around to pick up the dead and did not find one! We had been too excited to shoot straight!

As we disconsolately returned to camp we met Markham and Thompson who, when they heard our story, jeered us greatly.

It turned out we were camping at an immense turkey roost. The valley contained a grove of large cottonwood trees, and was bordered by high cliffs on top of which was the plain where the turkeys roamed during the day. At night they returned to the cliffs from which they flew off into the trees.

The turkeys seemed to be bewildered by our presence at their roost, but instead of fleeing our presence they were always near at hand, strolling around, uttering their plaintive calls; and there never was a time when our cook, who had his fire at the base of the cliff near the creek, did not have turkeys within rifle range. Sometimes indeed they wandered among our tents!

I had no difficulty in revenging myself on the turkeys for my bad fortune on the first day we camped there. Armed with my old muzzle-loading shotgun, I would encounter a small flock of turkeys at a distance, driving them before me.

Presently they would enter a thicket of bushes, and crowd together there, while I would slowly approach. Arrived at a suitable range, I would fire at the cluster of turkey heads, killing two or three, which I bore back to the camp in triumph. Roast turkey was a regular item on our bill-of-fare as well as on that of the soldiers.

The Indians, however, would not eat turkey; they considered it "bad medicine." Neither would they shoot turkeys, but they had no objection to catching them alive for us. To accomplish this the Indian would ride about the plain until he encountered a flock of turkeys. By cautious and slow maneuvers he would separate one of the turkeys from the flock, driving it before him. He was careful at first to ride slowly, so that the turkey could travel at a slow trot. For if he increased his pace too much, the turkey would take to his wings. They can fly extraordinarily fast and far, soaring after they reach a certain height. If the turkey flew, he escaped.

But moving at a slow trot, presently the turkey would become so tired that he could not fly! When that moment arrived the Indian would put spurs to his horse, and the unfortunate bird, chased at full speed, his open beak showing his fatigue, vainly dodging his pursuer, would finally, like an ostrich, plunge his head into a hole in the ground and allow himself to be taken a prisoner.

I remember one day we set out in a party to visit a new hunting ground. We took our four greyhounds with us, hoping to scare up a deer. On the way we saw off to the left a lone bull buffalo, an old fellow, forced from his herd by younger bulls. Such bulls were often very savage. The greyhounds pursued him, barking at his heels, while he trotted away fiercely lunging from side to side at the dogs.

I put spurs to my horse and followed. When he caught sight of me he stopped, turned around and charged me. By that time I had perfect confidence in my horse, Bayard, who showed himself not the least afraid of buffalo. I therefore halted, took good aim and, as the old bull neared me, fired, striking him in the forehead. At the same moment I jumped my horse to the front, dodging the rush of the bull. The bullet did not faze him, but, the dogs attacking him just then, he turned his attention to them and ran off, the dogs barking at his heels. I followed and when he saw me he turned and again charged me. Once more I planted a bullet in his forehead and jumped aside. Three times this happened; then tiring of this sport I rode up beside him, planted a bullet in his lungs and he fell.

The hunting party proceeding on its way was then at a considerable distance, and the dogs left me to overtake them. Tying my horse to the old bull's horns, I proceeded to remove the tongue, a choice bit. This is done by cutting a long slit under the chin, pulling the tongue through this hole and cutting it off.

I was thus engaged when I heard a noise and looking up saw a considerable herd of buffalo passing me at a fast gallop. They had probably been alarmed by the hunting party. Mounting my horse I pursued, riding into the flank of the herd. Instead of firing from a distance I determined this time to put the muzzle of the revolver against the body of the animal before I fired. The buffalo were then going at a tremendous pace. Picking out a fat cow I rode up close to her and shoved my pistol against her side; but at the same moment and before I could pull the trigger, the cow lashed out with her heels, hitting my horse a tremendous lick, causing him to jump to one side. Simultaneously the gun went off in the air. The cow dashed between two other animals and escaped. Just then there passed a buffalo cow and her large calf. I pursued the cow and with a well-directed shot brought her to a stand. She, however, made fight and I then discovered the cartridges in my revolver were exhausted. Dismounting and running in, I dealt her a tremendous blow between the eyes with the sharp point of the hilt of the revolver. This was too much for her and she reeled over. I still have the .45-calibre revolver with which I hit her, a big piece knocked out of the handle. After an exhilarating day, we returned in great spirits to sit down to a bounteous game supper. Often we had four kinds of game: duck, turkey, antelope or deer, buffalo. The game was roasted as only a soldier cook using the Dutch oven could do it. The Dutch oven, an iron pot with legs, stood in a bed of coals; the cover, with projecting rim, held more coals, and all the juices and flavors of the dish were conserved. It was usual to start a feast of this kind with a mallard duck apiece!

After supper we sat around a roaring fire, talking over the adventures of the day. Presently Markham would say: "Well, I must write up my little log!" and return to his tent, soon followed by Thompson. As we sat by the crackling fire gazing into its glowing depths we listened to the Indians feasting in their camp near by, singing their guttural chant, "Hi-ya-ya, hi-ya-ya, hi-ya, hi-ya, hi-ya-ya." Imitating the Indians we cut off great cubes of buffalo flesh and threw them into the fire, withdrawing them later, using a pointed stick. These when cut open were a delicious morsel.

On a night following one of these feasts I had a dream. I dreamed the whole world, the whole universe, had joined in one vast song. Louder it swelled and louder until I awoke to what seemed a cataract of melody. Before I had fully recovered my senses and fully realized what it was, the hyena-like bark of the coyote, coming from a thousand throats, interrupted it. It was merely the night serenade of the wolves, attracted by the smell of flesh, a remarkable sound when heard for the first time. They used to tell a story of an officer of our regiment, Jack Martin, on his way from Caddo to Fort Sill to join, having with him a party of recruits. In the middle of the night he was aroused by the unearthly noise. "Sergeant, what's that?" he called. "Coyotes, sir!" "What?" "Coyotes, sir!" "Turn out, men! Turn out!" Martin yelled, "the Kioways are upon us!"

When about ten days of the trip had elapsed our rations and forage began to run out, and the day of our expected return to the post was approaching. Naturally, we did not want to cut short this ideal experience. Thompson, always full of resources, was equal to the occasion. He knew that if he sent the wagons to Fort Sill for supplies, he would probably be ordered to return. So instead he determined to obtain his supplies from Fort Elliott, about a hundred miles northwest of the camp. It was a greater distance than to Sill, but that did not bother Thompson.

Accordingly, with two wagons and a detachment of men, Sandy Rodgers and I set out for

Fort Elliott. We started north, to cut the wagon road between Sill and Elliott, marching through an unknown country without a guide.

We soon found ourselves in difficulties. Much of the region we were to pass over consisted of "bad lands," a desolate region of bare washed-out ravines. In this connection Thompson, who always rode with Markham, and who frequently amused himself by using the most astounding Americanisms with which Markham was greatly impressed, once pointed to the north as he said, with his peculiar drawl, "Captain, did you ever see such a ravinous country as that?" "What? What?" said the Captain. "A ravinous country," said Thompson. "You see, it is full of ravines!" The Captain, jotting down this new Yankee word in his "little log," was delighted.

This year, 1877, was one of the great years of the buffalo's destruction. It is calculated that in '76 and '77 over a million buffalo were butchered for their hides. This was accomplished by buffalo hunters, a class of men who made a regular business of it, traveling in bands of two or three, accompanied by a wagon. They were armed with an accurate, breech-loading, sharpshooter's weapon, sometimes equipped with a telescopic sight and having a long range. Spotting a herd of buffalo, the hunters, approaching under cover, would take a position 500 or 1000 yards away. At this distance the noise of the discharge was not sufficient to alarm the buffalo. Their first shots would be sighting shots; then, having determined their range exactly by the dust kicked up by the bullet, they would begin to shoot to kill. A buffalo would be hit and fall; the others interrupted in their grazing would raise

Lone Wolf

Quinah

Salose

Big Tree

White Horse

COMANCHE AND KIOWAY CHIEFS

their heads, stupidly gaze at the struggling animal and then, as if reassured, go on with their occupation. In this way an entire herd would be exterminated.

I think, also, many buffalo died from the "Texas fever" caught from cattle. Often cattle, strayed from the great herds being driven north from Texas, would be seen running with the buffalo.

Whatever the cause, the great herds of buffalo suddenly ceased to exist about 1879. For years afterward a profitable business was carried on by men who collected their bones and shipped them east to be ground for fertilizer.

One day, while on this trip to Fort Elliott, I saw a herd near and gave chase. Presently it was joined by several other herds and in a few minutes I had stretched out before me a rushing, thundering mass of thousands of these shaggy-headed beasts. My horse was not in good condition and I finally gave up the chase. But it seemed ludicrous that this great horde should be fleeing from a single man when, by resisting, they could overthrow and crush him in a moment.

Fort Elliott, Texas, was situated near the present town of Mobeetic. Having struck the main road from Fort Sill, we arrived at Elliott without further incident, and I was to discover, by our reception, how welcome to the people of an isolated frontier post was the coming of visitors. Belonging to the same regiment we had many interests in common and our visit, though short, was most delightful. Our new-found friends vied with one another in entertaining us at breakfasts, luncheons and dinners, and at night a "hop" was given in our honor at which we danced till late.

Our wagons loaded with rations and forage, we took leave of the hospitable people of Fort Elliott. On the fourth day we reached our camp on Turkey Creek. There the days of sport passed only too rapidly and we finally, to our great regret, had to pack up and commence the return march to Fort Sill, where we arrived after a march of four days, bringing plenty of game for our friends. Altogether we killed on the trip over 50 buffalo, a number of bear, deer and antelope, over 150 turkeys and 300 wild fowl.

III

HORSE THIEVES AND OUTLAWS

In the spring of 1877, being stationed at Fort Sill as a Second Lieutenant of the 4th Cavalry, I received orders from General John P. Hatch, commanding that post, to pursue some horse thieves who, the night before, had run off a band of horses from the Indian herds.

At that time the Comanche and Kiowa Indians, then on the Fort Sill Reservation, were possessed of numerous herds of horses, which were often the prey of horse thieves, as a rule coming from Texas. The stolen horses, after having been driven across the Red River, were then offered for sale publicly in the Texas towns. The ordinary horse thief who stole from whites generally received short shift; but Indian ponies were considered by the Texans fair game, whether taken from friendly or hostile Indians.

On this expedition I was furnished with a detachment of mounted men, six men and a corporal; also with a guide—a colored man.

This negro, whose name was Smith, informed me that the band of horses was undoubtedly being driven toward Old Fort Arbuckle, an abandoned army post about seventy-five miles east of Fort Sill; and that the horse thieves, he had reason to believe, were three desperadoes: Bill Mahardy, Limber Jim and John Anderson.

Smith had passed these men on the Arbuckle road coming towards Sill, and believed that they were there for no good purpose. He gave them a wide berth when he saw them on the road, each party circling around the other at the distance of a long rifle shot, but he was sufficiently near to recognize them.

The pursuit started late in the afternoon, and we picked up the trail of the herd of horses a few miles from Sill. Over the level, treeless country the detachment moved at a steady trot, occasionally walking to rest the horses, at times dismounting and leading. Just before dark, at some distance, we saw a party of five cowboys riding a little to one side of the road. I galloped up to them to ask if they had seen the fugitives. They received my inquiries with cocked rifles, over which they answered my questions in short and unsympathetic negatives! Seeing that I could get no information from them, and tiring of looking into the muzzles of their guns, I rejoined my detachment and continued the pursuit. Nightfall came, but it had rained, and the trail was clearly visible in the light of the moon.

By this time I had become sufficiently acquainted with my negro guide, Smith, to discover that he was a good deal of a desperado himself, and that it was a case of set a thief to catch a thief. He evidently had some grudge against the men I was pursuing. I had discovered, too, that my corporal, whose name was Anderson, was a frontiersman himself, and an expert trailer. He had lived with Indians, spoke the Comanche language, was well acquainted with the principal outlaws, and was an exceptional man. Taciturn and respectful, his advice, when asked, was straight and to the point. He was a wonderful plainsman. His name was evidently assumed, and

I have often wondered what his history was and how he came to enlist.

Some time after midnight we reached the broken and partly wooded country around Old Fort Arbuckle, and the trail led us to the log cabin of "Babe" Mahardy. Silently dismounting and stationing the men around the cabin, we burst open the door and rushed in, grabbing "Babe" just as he was getting out of bed with a loaded pistol in his hand.

Securing Babe on a led horse, his feet tied under the horse's belly with hobbles, we proceeded to the neighboring home of John Anderson, outlaw. It was empty, but we secreted ourselves in and about the cabin until daylight; when Anderson appeared we nabbed him.

The sparse settlements around Old Fort Arbuckle (abandoned in 1861) were inhabited by negro-Indian half-breeds, runaway slaves, and deserters from negro regiments. It was evident that they were more or less in sympathy with the horse thieves, but they seemed friendly, and as we had thus far recaptured only about ten of the horses, we decided to enlist their help in recovering some more. So, after we had ineffectually ridden many miles in search of the concealed and scattered animals, I offered a prize of one horse for every six turned in to me by these non-committal and nondescript settlers.

This was making rather free with the Indians' horses—as I was informed on my return by General Hatch—but I had no way of obtaining funds to use as rewards, and I assumed that my Indian friends would approve of this method, as it was evident the horses would not be recovered otherwise. By this stroke of diplomacy, beside the preceding more direct methods, I got about twenty-five horses.

After five days of hard riding, in which I had traveled two hundred and fifty miles, and after numerous adventures, we returned to Fort Sill, where to the surprise and amusement of the other officers, I drove my herd of horses with the prisoners in triumph across the parade ground to the post commander's house. I was informed by my laughing friends that, while I was inside the house reporting to General Hatch, my captured horses eased their fatigue by leaning up against the fence!

So ended my first independent scout. Limber Jim with a dozen more horses was captured later while on a scout by Corporal Anderson, who chased him into a log cabin from which he drove out the family and withstood a siege; with many oaths he alternately fired through the chinks and fried bacon on the stove until at last he was forced to give up.

The prisoners, soon after, were taken by the Deputy U. S. Marshal from the guardhouse where they were confined, to Fort Smith, Arkansas, the seat of the U. S. District Court for the Western District of Arkansas, which included the Indian Territory. Some weeks later I was summoned by this court as a witness. And with four mules, an ambulance ("Dougherty Wagon"), and a driver I started for Fort Smith, three hundred and thirty miles away.

My route lay due east across the beautiful country now included in the State of Oklahoma. In contrast with the arid, treeless plains west of Fort Sill most of it was park-like, with a succession of groves and prairies, in which deer and turkeys roamed freely. We passed few settlements, although we saw many half-civilized Indians—Cherokees, Choctaws, Chickasaws, Seminoles and Creeks—who lived in rude dwellings at a short distance off the road, on farms that were small but apparently sufficient for their needs. Their light-colored skin gave them the appearance of ordinary white farmers, though many of them boasted pure Indian blood. It is my opinion, fortified by what I have seen in Mexico, that the Indian who lives in a house tends to lose his coppery hue.

The roads were good, many of them having been constructed by the Government before the war and leased to parties who maintained toll gates and repaired the routes. We traveled from thirty to forty miles a day through this paradise, camping each night by a convenient stream.

My driver, Jones, slept under the ambulance, while I slept inside on the seats, which let down to form a comfortable bed. Every evening on arriving in camp, Jones staked out and attended to the mules while I got my mess chest from the tail of the wagon, got out the utensils, built a fire, fried eggs and bacon and perhaps a piece of venison, and made coffee. This done, I called Jones and we ate our frugal meal together. Then while Jones cleaned up the dishes, I took my gun and wandered off in search of game.

This ideal life was interrupted at Caddo, a hundred and sixty-five miles from Sill, where our road crossed the railroad and where we encountered a telegraph office. There I received orders from General Mackenzie to go by rail south to Denison, Texas, with a view to recovering some horses which had been stolen from Indians and sold to parties in Denison.

I found Denison, just south of the Red River, a typical railroad-frontier town, very "wild and woolly!" It consisted of three parallel streets at right angles to the railroad. The southern one was the street of the prostitutes, the middle one contained the banks, stores and liquor saloons, and the northern one the respectable residences. Near the railroad was a fairly good hotel.

The town, though it had many decent people—some northerners—was the resort of desperadoes, and was accustomed to being shot up by cowboys. It was also a market for stolen Indian ponies.

While I was there the notorious Jesse James, train robber and terror of the Southwest, spent some days in town. No one dared arrest him; he was spoken of rather with pride, as a distinguished visitor. I was even invited to meet him. I considered trying to arrest him, but thought better of it when I remembered that I had no authority under the law, troops no longer being allowed to be used as a *posse comitatus*.

Having secured a lawyer to take legal steps to recover the horses, and having met a number of the best people in town, I wandered out the second morning of my stay and found an auction sale of horses going on. As they looked very like Indian ponies, I stopped to examine their brands; a mounted cowboy, intentionally, ran his horse violently against me.

I backed off and cautioned him not to do that again, whereupon he again tried to run me down. I hauled off and hit him under the chin, knocking him off his horse. He jumped up and came for me; I threw him down and sat upon him. While we were in this position two other men ran up and attempted to strike me; I am pleased to say that I got each of them in the eye. About this time a whole crowd rushed in, shouting, "Kill the —— of a ——! He's a stranger!"

They were too close to use their weapons, but they piled in on me and presently I was buried in a fighting, kicking mass of humanity. At this juncture some of my friends, seeing the fracas, and shouting that I was an army officer, dragged me out of the turmoil, and took me across the street to a clothing store. There I brushed off the dust and dirt, straightened my hat, and discovered that I did not have even a scratch!

To celebrate this remarkable piece of good luck we adjourned to a bar room to take a drink. While I was engaged in this grateful occupation, a police officer came up and said he would like me to make complaint against the cowboy who had assaulted me, and who was then in the lock-up.

"Let him go," I said. "I gave him a good black eye, and that's enough."

The policeman disappeared. Presently he returned.

"I'm sorry," he said, "but the Mayor has ordered me to put you under arrest—you'll have to come to the Mayor's office."

Upon reaching the Mayor—a little stumpy fellow about five feet high—I asked him why I had been arrested.

"For fighting in the streets," says he.

"But I was fighting in self-defense. I was attacked by that cowboy when I was behaving in an entirely peaceful manner."

"That doesn't matter," he said, with a great

show of dignity, "we have an ordinance here against fighting in the street. I would advise you to plead guilty; I will make the fine merely nominal."

"All right; guilty!"

"Fine, one dollar; costs, seven dollars and a half!" said the Mayor.

I paid eight dollars and a half and departed, using strong language about justice in Denison City.

A few minutes later I had to pay sixteen dollars to get Jones out of jail. It seems that he had abandoned his mules and come down to Denison to get drunk. In this he had thoroughly succeeded, and I began to think that I was becoming a considerable source of revenue to Denison.

Nevertheless, I had a good time in Denison. I drilled the local militia company; went to various entertainments where I met the reigning belles; and was celebrated by the local newspapers, even being alluded to as "The Terror of the Plains."

But my business did not progress—"the law's delays" are many and tedious when public opinion favors procrastination.

One day Chief Mowaway, Comanche, arrived accompanied by an interpreter. As witness for the prosecution he was required to make an affidavit. When the formula for the oath was administered to him, with arm extended, he pointed to the skies, and with a grave uplifted countenance, spoke a sentence solemnly in Comanche. It was impressive.

"What did he say?" asked the notary.

"He said," answered the interpreter, "'The Great Spirit knows that I am telling the truth'."

But time was flying, I was summoned by the

Court at Fort Smith and I had to go back to Caddo and resume my journey. I never saw Denison again. But in 1917, forty years later, being at Fort Sam Houston, and commander of the Southern Department, I found in my office a solemn delegation of the Mayor and Board of Trade of Denison, Texas. I was selecting sites for six World War training camps, for forty thousand men each, and naturally Denison wanted one. In declining their request (for other reasons entirely) I did not tell them that I had once been assaulted and then arrested and fined in their belovèd city!

Continuing my journey, with driver Jones and the ambulance, I arrived in the town of Fort Smith, Arkansas. This old town, the head of navigation of the Arkansas River, was the shipping point whence, before the advent of the railroads, supplies were sent by team to the various military posts in the Indian Territory, and along the river were grass-grown quays and venerable looking warehouses.

The army post, surrounded by a stone wall, still stood, in fair condition, and was used by the District Court for its courthouse and jail. The court was presided over by Judge Parker and District Attorney Clayton, two eminent jurists. They were celebrated for the amount of work they dispatched. It was said that on one occasion, at the end of one session of three months, sixteen murderers were hanged. Truth to tell, they had no alternative, if justice was to be done, for the Indian Territory, since the Civil War, had become the resort of vast numbers of outlaws, including renegade Indians, deserters, and many types of fugitive criminals.

Fort Smith was full of memories of the old days when the fort was an important military post before the war. A number of distinguished Southern families resided there, and nearly all of them were connected by marriage with the old army. Many army officers, in the old days, married the belles of Fort Smith and the surrounding country, and it was said that one regiment of infantry lost all of its bachelors during its sojourn at the town.

Some days after arriving there I met a gentleman who said to me, "General Bonneville has asked me to tell you that he would very much like you, with your Indian witnesses and the interpreter, to lunch with him at his residence, just out of town."

"Bonneville?" I said. "What Bonneville?"

"Why, the celebrated General Bonneville."

"You don't mean *Captain* Bonneville, do you, about whom Washington Irving wrote a book?"

"I do; the same Bonneville."

"Why, I read that book when I was a young boy," I said. "I thought Bonneville was dead long ago."

"He is, on the contrary," said my friend, "very much alive, as you will see. It is only day before yesterday that he married a young wife, in spite of the fact that he is eighty-four years old."

Bonneville was one of the most picturesque and romantic characters in the history of the American Army. Graduating from West Point in 1815, he served for years in the Indian country of the Southwest. In 1825 he accompanied General Lafayette to France. In 1831 he obtained a leave of absence for two years, and headed an exploring expedition in the Rocky Mountains and the far Northwest.

On this expedition he was gone for nearly four years, and being absent without leave for nearly two years, his whereabouts unknown, he was dropped from the rolls of the army. It was claimed by some that he had been captured by Indians; others insinuated that he had been seen in Paris, having gone there in a European whaler, which he had boarded on the western coast. He was, however, finally restored to the army by President Jackson. It was said that Jackson energetically remarked that he did not care a damn where he had been, he was too good an officer to be lost to the army! His journal was taken possession of by Washington Irving, who did not fail to embellish it. Bonneville afterwards served with great credit in the Mexican War, and was retired in 1861.

On the appointed day we went out to his home, and were received by the General and his bride. Bonneville was a stocky little Frenchman, dark complexioned, with the bright eyes of a squirrel, active and lithe. I remarked that I had read about him in Irving's books, but that that was a long time ago.

"People say that I am too old to marry," said he, "but ask my wife if I am not a good husband." She blushingly assented.

He was very much interested in my Indians, and presently we sat down to lunch.

The Indians, who are great mimics, copied my movements exactly. They had never seen plates, forks, napkins or a table before. They had never before been in a house. But, with their eyes fixed upon my every action, they unfolded their napkins, laid them on their laps, took up their knives and forks and used them, exactly as I did, and with perfect dignity.

One would not have known that they had not always dined in a palace.

During the repast General and Mrs. Bonneville stood behind our chairs and waited on us, General Bonneville entertaining the Indians with stories of his experience, when, as a young lieutenant, he was stationed at Fort Smith, and scouted against hostile Pawnees, in the year 1822!

General Bonneville died eleven months after we saw him at his home. His widow, I am informed, still resides at Fort Smith.

In due time the trial of Babe Mahardy, Limber Jim, and John Anderson began. To expedite matters, previous to the trial the prisoners and witnesses were informally examined by the judge and district attorney, who acquainted themselves thoroughly with the facts of the case. As there were no intricacies and the result of the trial was a foregone conclusion, time was not wasted in procedure. After the evidence was all in the judge gave the counsel for the defense five minutes to make his plea. The judge's charge was direct and to the point. A verdict of guilty was rendered and the prisoners were sentenced to two years in the penitentiary.

On my return to Fort Sill I learned that it had been reported that at Denison I had been attacked by a mob of a thousand men, and had stood them all off! Well, that was a fair recompense for the money that I had contributed to the city treasury!

In those days the cowboy was not the admirable character depicted later by such writers as Theodore Roosevelt. As a rule he was either a desperado or the associate of desperadoes. In 1880 I knew of a case where a farmer in New Mexico had settled on land claimed by a neighboring ranch owner. He was told to get out. He did not heed the summons, and one day the ranch owner with all of his twenty cowboys went to the farm, killed the farmer, his wife and his children in cold blood and burned down the house, and for this, I believe, they were never prosecuted!

To the cowboys of Texas and the Indian Territory, military men, being men of the law, were anathema; they never lost a chance to show their contempt of them. I have seen General Mackenzie at the head of a marching regiment answered with insult by a cowboy from whom he had inquired his way. Murders were frequent among them. The "bad man," who usually murdered by shooting men in the back, was hail-fellow-well-met among them. Negro and half-breed desperadoes mingled with them. A pay day was a drunk, and to shoot up a town was their joy and recreation.

But on one occasion I got even with the cowboys. In the fall of 1880 my squadron was returning by rail from the Ute campaign in Colorado, our destination being Fort Riley, Kansas. It was our custom to travel at night, unloading the cattle cars, which contained our horses, every morning, feeding, watering and grooming the horses during the day, and in the evening loading our animals on the cars again for the night's journey. We had stopped and spent the day thus at a cattle station in western Kansas. It was on the cattle trail from Texas, and a half-mile from the station was a herd of cattle, kept rounded up by a dozen cowboys. During the day one of my soldiers, being drunk, sold his revolver to a cowboy. We had loaded up the train in the afternoon, and the men were in the passenger cars when this was discovered. I saw the boss, a black-bearded, low-browed, piratical-looking fellow near the train. I went over and told him, politely enough, that one of his men had one of my revolvers and I would be glad if he would return it. He answered, with many oaths, loud enough for my men to hear, that he didn't know anything about my damned revolver. I told him I had authority under United States laws to confiscate the revolver, as it was United States property, and that if he couldn't help me I would have to go out to the herd and get it myself. "Mister, you better not go out near my herd and bother my cattle. If you do there may be some shooting!"

This was great joy to me. Without replying I ran to the train and ordered my men to turn out, bringing their guns with them. Forming hastily we rushed to the front in skirmish line, the men having 10-yard intervals, the line thus being nearly 400 yards long. Nearing the herd the flanks swung around enveloping it and the cowboys. The trick was accomplished so quickly they were unable to get away. Being near the left flank I made sure the envelopment was complete and then returned to the center. A pleasing sight met my eyes. The twelve cowboys, boss and all, ghastly white, their hands held up to heaven, were begging for their lives, while they looked into the muzzles of my men's carbines. The black-browed boss seemed the most terrified of all.

I let him go on for a while, begging for mercy,

and then I told him I would spare their lives. "But," I said, "before I let you go I want to let you know what I think of you and all your kind." And I gave them a tongue lashing. I described in vivid terms their faults and their crimes. I gave them a fair dose of their own medicine. They had nothing to say in rebuttal.

It is needless to add that I recovered my revolver.

My experiences with outlaws have led me to believe they are not as redoubtable as the ordinary tales of the frontier would have led us to think. On one occasion at Fort Sill, being officer of the day, I was ordered to arrest a murderer named Ben Hogan. I was told he was with an outfit camped on the other side of Cache Creek and that he wore a red shirt. Arrived at Cache Creek I found it bank full and swimming deep. Forcing my horse in, I reached the opposite shore after a violent struggle, and as I emerged, dripping, a man coming down the bank shouted, "You got pretty wet, didn't you, Loot'nant?" He had on a red shirt!

"Yes," said I, "hold up your hands!"

He looked astonished, then pale, but he put up his hands promptly, though I did not have to draw my revolver. I took his pistol away from him, and turned him over to a soldier who managed the ferry. Arrived at the other side I marched him to the guardhouse. I believe he afterward escaped from a deputy marshal. His pistol which I kept in my desk disappeared mysteriously some time later.

Another thing I discovered was that criminals in the West surrendered much more readily to troops than to officers of the law, who were too often accused of killing their prisoners "while attempting to escape." On the other hand a strict construction of the law prohibited troops, when not on Indian reservations, from arresting citizens.

The outlaw's favorite arm was the revolver, preferably the army Colt revolver. Such high prices were offered and paid for these revolvers that it was practically impossible to leave them in the hands of the soldiers without loss. At the post, revolvers had a habit of disappearing so frequently that after each drill or inspection, when they were served out to the men, I had them gathered in after the drill and put in a box, which was then locked and put under my bed in my quarters. The revolver was responsible for most of the crimes of violence on the plains. The revolver is a weapon of assassination; it can be concealed and is thus doubly dangerous. In 1885 I found ranches in New Mexico where the cowboy was armed with a rifle but was not allowed to carry a revolver. This had a very marked effect in preventing crime.

I have seen many frontiersmen who were extremely expert in the use of the pistol. But I have satisfied myself that this expertness, especially on horseback, can only be acquired by an immense expenditure of ammunition. With our limited allowance of cartridges in the army we in the cavalry were never able to attain this expertness. In fact, I proved by experiment that when in motion on the horse the rifle is a more accurate weapon than the pistol. This is largely due to the shortness of the pistol barrel, its tendency to be canted, and the fact that the rifle has a shoulder rest. The sights are thus easier to catch quickly.

The cowboy as a rider, in the days that I knew him, was not what he claimed to be or what he was cracked up to be. The saddle he rode in, an adaptation of the Mexican saddle, was difficult to fall out of; so trussed up was the man, before and behind, by the high pommel and cantle, and supported on each side by immense wooden stirrups. This enormously heavy saddle was fastened to the animal under his girth and under his belly by two leather cinches, which worked like a pulley, with great force. Enormous sweat leathers protected the legs but made it impossible to get them against the horse's body, the man riding stiff-legged. A powerful, cruel curb bit was used, and the cowboy was equipped with great spurs having rowels two inches wide, with revolving spikes. These, when jabbed into the horse's side, could wound frightfully.

The horse, under these conditions, was ruled entirely by terror. As the herds of cow ponies subsisted entirely on grass they seldom were fat and the saddle, which did not always fit, so wrenched the horse's withers that it was seldom one saw a cow pony without a sore or festering back. When one pony was used up he would be turned out and another ridden. No mercy was shown.

The cowboy's notion of training a horse was crude in the extreme. The method was to break the horse's spirit. Captured by the lasso the wild horse was first starved for several days to make him weak. Then he was roped and thrown to the ground, and saddled and mounted while on the ground. Allowed to rise, fighting the bit, the saddle and the rider, the animal would be put at full speed until so exhausted that he was barely able to stand. After several such experiences he was conquered, "trained," "broken." Thereafter, quivering with terror, he obeyed his brutal rider. Both cowboys and Indians treated their ponies in this manner.

As for the cowboy himself, he was the tough, the rowdy, the anarchist of the plains. As a rule, driven from the eastern states, "he had left his country for his country's good." Usually he never went back.

In 1879 near Fort Hays, at Hays City, a cattle station, there was a cemetery of considerable size. It was said then, with considerable pride, that no man was buried there except those who had "died with their boots on." In the West there were many similar "boot cemeteries," as they were called, notably at Dodge City, Kansas; Tombstone, Arizona; Tucson, Arizona, and other places, where in the early days gamblers, horse thieves, cattle thieves, stage robbers, buffalo hunters, rustlers, bad men, and outlaws "owned the town."

It was along in the early 'eighties that the advent of decent people forced a clean-up of these pests by officers of the law. Some were shot or hanged, some imprisoned, some emigrated to Mexico; a very few reformed. Things have changed since those days. Then our bad men "went West"—now they stay with us, to recruit our train bandits, bank robbers and hold-up men.

IV

SERVICE ON THE RIO GRANDE

It is not generally known how near we came to war with Mexico in 1878. There had always been disorder in that country. As the *Encyclopedia Britannica* says, speaking of the revolution of 1810 which gained Mexico its independence, "thenceforward till the second election of Porfirio Diaz to the presidency in 1884 the history of Mexico is one of almost continuous warfare." Naturally, these troubles created disorder along the Rio Grande and affected diplomatic relations with the United States. In 1877 the government of Porfirio Diaz, having been established by force, followed by a so-called election, was not recognized by the United States. This greatly embittered the ruling party in Mexico, which was further excited by an order by our Secretary of War, to General Ord, commanding the department of Texas, authorizing our troops, when necessary, to pursue Mexican marauders across the frontier. The Mexican Minister of Foreign Affairs, Vellarta, charged that a scheme had been concocted to bring about a war. Our Minister to Mexico, John W. Foster, in his *Diplomatic Memoirs,* says in regard to this: "There is no doubt of the correctness of his statement that there had been a change of policy as to recognition after the inauguration of President Hayes and there was some foundation for the charge that a scheme had been formed to bring on a war through the Texas troubles." This scheme he explained was the project of certain politicians in high places who believed that such a war would consolidate the new administration in the United States by diverting attention from pending issues, namely, the Hayes-Tilden presidential embroglio and the disturbed condition in the southern states.

There was then, as there is now, a strong sentiment in the United States, that the turbulent history of Mexico, only one-ninth of whose inhabitants are of white blood, demonstrates that only a protectorate similar to that established over Cuba will ever ensure to its inhabitants the blessings of peace and prosperity.

Such was the political atmosphere when, on December 17, 1877, the 4th Cavalry started on its march to the Rio Grande. Its destination was Fort Clark, Texas, 125 miles west of San Antonio and near the border. The part of the regiment I accompanied, starting from Fort Sill, Indian Territory, consisted of five troops with a considerable train of wagons. General Mackenzie, who took command, joined us just before starting. He had been on a flying visit to Washington where he conferred with the authorities. One day as we were riding at the head of the column he said to me: "As sure as that sun rises and sets there will be war with Mexico within six months!"

In view of my youth and inexperience I was greatly surprised and flattered at being appointed adjutant of the expedition. But I was conscious of the fact that serving Mackenzie I had not an easy road to travel, and so it turned out.

From the first we encountered difficulties. Starting out in a pouring rainstorm we camped in the mud ten miles from Sill. It continued to rain.

Next day we found, as the teamsters said, "the bottom of the whole country had dropped out." Marching along, a leading wagon would bog. When this happened two troops would dismount. Attaching a long picket line to each side of the wagon the dismounted men would haul, the teamsters yell, the whips crack. With the mules straining in the harness, the men pulling and cheering, the wagon would slowly emerge from the morass and move on to firmer ground. Attempts by the wagons following to pull out of the road and avoid the boggy ground would often fail, and the march was checked until all of the wagons had been pulled through the mud hole.

Mackenzie, never a patient man, was furious. He had 600 miles to go, and was anxious to arrive and take command of the force to be concentrated at Fort Clark.

This continued day after day. To make a long story short, it took us thirteen days to reach the Red River, distant only forty miles! Every day at four o'clock, long before daylight, we had reveille, breakfasted, and packed up. Every day before we had gone far the wagons began to bog. Every day it rained. We were wet through, officers and men, and remained so day and night. Our blankets and bedding were wet. Mud covered everything. This journey was celebrated in after years as the "Mud March" of the 4th Cavalry.

One day I remember we marched but three-fourths of a mile and then the wagons, being hub-deep in mud, were obliged to make camp.

But Mackenzie would not give up. We made an attempt to march every day. At last we arrived at the Red River which we expected to ford easily. It was running bank full, with a very rapid current. The only means of crossing was an old scow which was poled across. Naturally, the swift stream carried the scow downstream a considerable distance each time it crossed. It then had to be laboriously poled upstream to the landing place. Each trip took a long time.

We attempted to cross the horses by swimming. The horses of all the troops, some 300 in all, were led down into the water. In advance, some men in a boat led their horses into deep water; others, good horsemen and swimmers, rode forward to lead the way; others with shouts urged on the herd from behind.

The horses went in willingly enough and seemed to understand what was wanted. Then suddenly several in the forefront with snorts of fear recoiled; in a moment the whole mass had turned and was rushing for the shore. Nothing could stop them; they knocked down several men, trampling upon and badly injuring them, and then furiously stampeded on the road back toward Sill.

Fortunately at the last camp, five miles from the river, some wagons had halted for repairs. When the frightened horses, winded by their long run, saw the mules thus peacefully grazing, they halted and allowed themselves to be caught up.

My friend, Lieutenant Thompson, was one of those knocked down. He suffered a broken rib.

We took three days in crossing the Red River. Everything had to be ferried over. New Year's Day we spent in this sloppy work, as we had spent Christmas in hauling wagons through the mud. Many exciting incidents occurred. Among others, a young officer, Lieutenant Murray, just from West Point, joined us at the Red River; in crossing he fell overboard; impeded by his long overcoat, he was nearly drowned, but was hauled up with a boathook in the nick of time. This amused the men.

Two days after marching south we reached the town of Henrietta, Texas. On our way we were met by a delegation of the principal citizens. They informed us that, some years before, their town had been attacked by Indians and had been saved by our regiment. They wished to testify to their gratitude by giving the officers a "banquet" and a "ball."

This bored Mackenzie greatly. He was not in a mood for festivities. At first he dissented, but he finally gave in. We arrived at Henrietta early in the forenoon. It was a typical frontier town, dirty streets, unpainted houses. On account of a plague of cowboys who had been in the habit of getting drunk and shooting up the town, a local prohibition law had been passed. The leading citizens, however, all carried flasks, but instead of whiskey the flasks contained alcohol, flavored with a fruit extract obtained at the drug store. There were supposed to be no saloons.

After we had pitched camp, we dug down in our chests, arrayed ourselves in clean uniforms and went to the banquet. It was a cold collation, largely canned goods. To it were invited, apparently, all of the male population of the town, so that some officers who arrived a little late were crowded out and had to wait for a second table very meagerly supplied. There were the usual high-flown speeches by the mayor and the principal citizens, responded to with difficulty by Mackenzie, who was not an orator. Much to our amusement the mayor, who sat next to General Mackenzie and who was pretty well "primed," insisted on Mackenzie taking a drink from his flask of alcohol, which he repeatedly drew from his breast and shoved at the General. At last the General, making use of some pretext, left the mayor and seated himself on the opposite side of the table.

The ball took place about eight that evening. Being fond of dancing I entered upon the festivities with great zest, but I soon discovered that my education in dancing had been neglected. Neither the waltz nor the polka, the lanciers or the quadrille was danced. No such refinements had penetrated to the wilds of Texas. We danced the hoedown, a kind of jig quadrille. Some of the officers were adepts; my attempts to master it were awkward and ludicrous in the extreme. The music was provided by two fiddles execrably played.

The ball was at full height, and my buxom partner was rapidly teaching me the step, when a terrific fusillade punctured by the whirring of bullets was heard without. We reached for our revolvers. My partner seized me. "Don't go!" she beseeched. "It's only the cowboys shooting up the town; they do that every night." I broke away and rushed for the door, accompanied by the other officers. Outside a battle was raging.

The soldiers, worn out by the hardships of the march, had sought liquor. They had found it in what the inhabitants called a "blind tiger." It was a kind of saloon in which the proprietor evaded the terms of the law by remaining concealed. At the end of the room was a revolving dumb-waiter; when money was placed in this it revolved and presently turned again, exposing to view a glass of fearful whiskey, or "rot gut." Soon many of the soldiers were fighting drunk and created such disturbance that the saloon was closed.

The soldiers attempted to tear down the building. The sheriff with some other citizens interfered. A fight ensued; weapons were drawn and presently a fusillade commenced, the soldiers using their revolvers.

Upon our appearance many of the soldiers decamped, running back to camp. But many were too drunk to obey, and some had to be knocked down with the butts of our revolvers. A few lay on the ground maddened by liquor, resisting, cursing and screaming; these we had to tie and gag before conveying them to the lock-up. In one case a bar of soap was used for gagging. When the soldier opened his mouth to yell the soap was thrust into his mouth. It was harsh, but effective. In returning to camp the soldiers had to cross a log spanning a deep ditch. Many fell by the wayside. Some slept there.

Suffice it to say there was no more dancing that night. I never again saw my fascinating partner.

The next day we stayed in camp to rest the animals. That evening the troops were assembled to muster for pay, a ceremony which in the old army took place every two months, conducted by the commanding officer, who, reading the muster roll, identified each man. Greatly to Mackenzie's irritation, some of the men were still under the influence of liquor. Some had to be severely punished. A few of the most violent had to be spread-eagled, or stretched out on the ground with ropes, until they had recovered their senses. Many, the next day, under charge of the guard, walked, leading their horses.

The following morning, when we attempted to pull out of camp, some of the wagons were found to be frozen fast in the mud and had to be dug out. From Henrietta we marched south fifty miles to Fort Richardson, near Jacksboro, Texas. On this march we had snow, rain and mud. In one camp the prairie was so deep in mud that it was thought safe to turn the horses loose, to graze, without hobbles. But in spite of the deep mud we had a stampede. The horses were unable to gallop fast, however, in this quagmire, and several trumpeters mounting in haste, blowing their trumpets, were able to lead the herd in a circle, bringing the horses back to camp in an exhausted, blown condition, plastered with black soil.

Fort Richardson was garrisoned by a portion of the 10th Cavalry under the command of its Lieutenant-Colonel, General John W. Davidson, a veteran of the Mexican and Civil Wars. The 10th Cavalry was one of the four negro regiments of the United States Army. The officers were white, the rank of sergeant-major being the highest which could be attained by a negro. Thus officered, they were excellent regiments and a credit to the service. They had very high *esprit de corps,* the men being proud of their profession and enlisting practically for life, the officers claiming that these men were superior to white soldiers in discipline, fidelity, neatness, sobriety, and equal in bravery. The young officers always repelled with indignation the suggestion that they would willingly transfer to a white regiment. In my subsequent career I often served in garrison with colored troops and I found them to have very estimable qualities. I believe that the colored race are a valuable military asset. But the regiments must be officered by whites else they are of no account.

At Fort Richardson we received much attention from the officers and ladies of the 10th Cavalry. Miss Davidson, the colonel's daughter, a beautiful brunette, being the only unmarried lady of the garrison, was the reigning belle of the post, and accompanied the general and myself on a delightful horseback ride. But our time was short and within forty-eight hours we were obliged to part with our new-found friends and resume our march.

From Fort Richardson our route took us southwestward towards Fort Griffin, Texas. On the way we had another stampede. It occurred at night. The horses that were picketed out on grass (each horse being tied by a lariat to an iron "picket pin" driven into the ground) rushed off, dragging their picket pins after them. Most of the horses were recovered the next day, many seriously wounded by the flying picket pins, but my horse, Bayard, was among those not found. In fact, I did not get him back until several months afterwards, when two of our officers, driving south through Texas, found him working in a cotton gin, many miles from the scene of the stampede.

Bayard was a noble horse. In a herd he was always the leader, the "boss," as it were, the other horses following and imitating him. Consequently he had to be watched. Nevertheless, he was greatly admired and loved by the enlisted men. In 1880, when after a long absence I returned to my troop, it was my horse that my men greeted with ardent demonstrations of affection.

In marching southwest from Jacksboro we left the rich lands of the "black belt," which runs southward through Texas, for the barren plains which border the Llano Estacado. Fort Griffin, garrisoned by a portion of the 10th Cavalry, we reached in a blinding snowstorm. It was a peculiar post, built like no other I have ever seen. The men's quarters, instead of being barracks, were wooden huts the size of a tent, and arranged to accommodate only a small squad.

Fort Griffin was in the buffalo country, and on several occasions herds of buffalo had stampeded over the parade and through the post. They told us there that Lieutenant "Bill" Davis (brother of the celebrated General Jeff C. Davis), had a short time before attempted to kill a buffalo with a saber. The saber stuck in but did not kill the buffalo—the buffalo ran away with the saber!

We stayed at Fort Griffin a day, long enough to strip that post of a large portion of its supplies. Our soldiers needed clothing and shoes, which Mackenzie, by virtue of his superior rank, took, despite the protest of the post commander.

In examining a map of the western part of the United States it is easy to determine the more populous regions by the fact that there the names of towns and villages are crowded closely, while in the sparsely settled country the paper looks blank. Thus the fact that the western part of Texas is well-nigh a desert can be determined at a glance. Our route from Fort Griffin due south, passing to the west of the settlements, thus keeping in open country and avoiding fences, was over a prairie country watered by occasional streams, which became more wooded and picturesque. The weather also was more settled as we moved south. Passing by the old abandoned forts, Camp Colorado, Camp San Saba, Fort Mason, we arrived, after a march of about 400 miles, at Fredericksburg. From Fredericksburg the road to Fort Clark, 150 miles away, diverged to the southwest. At Fredericksburg I was informed by General Mackenzie that I would accompany him by stage to San Antonio, where he was going, in order to confer with the department commander, General Ord. I feebly protested, asking the General if I would not be more useful by staying, as adjutant, with the regiment. The General snapped his fingers and replied that he wanted me to go to San Antonio "to have a good time." When I told this to my brother lieutenants they were much amazed; the General did not have the reputation of giving his officers a "good time," As it turned out my good time was of short duration.

Fredericksburg, a considerable town, was an isolated German settlement, founded about the time of the Mexican War. It was entirely German, no other language was used, even the negroes talked German. The town looked German and the hotel, built around a courtyard, was German in the extreme. We stayed at this hotel and in the morning, when I came down to breakfast, I found the General walking up and down the platform outside snapping his fingers nervously and looking at a green and gold stagecoach, "the General McKinzy," drawn up in front of the door. "Such is fame," said he, laughing, "to have your name spelled wrong."

The Irish decorated coach—"General McKinzy" —did not take us far. It was an old coach and broke down on the big hill just outside Fredericksburg. Another stage was sent for and duly landed us that evening at San Antonio. We stayed at the Menger Hotel, a very different hostelry from the hotel of that name of the present day. I remember that copying the Spanish style the toilet rooms were just outside of the kitchen, and in front of them hung joints of beef.

San Antonio de Bexar is famous as the former capital of Texas, when it was a province under Mexican rule. The history of Texas' revolt against Mexico is an astonishing one. It occurred in 1835. After a few skirmishes, in January, 1836, a Mexican army of 6000 men, under Santa Anna, President of Mexico, entered Texas by several different routes. At San Patricia, February 26, a Texas force, which had been sent to capture Matamoras at the mouth of the Rio Grande, was encountered and of its 100 Americans nearly all were killed. At San Antonio 188 Texans entrenched themselves in the Alamo; it was taken by assault March 6th and all were killed. At Goliad, on the San Antonio River, March 12, a force of 47 Texans was all killed. Near Goliad, March 27, Fannin's army of 500 Texans was encountered and, having surrendered, 357 were killed.

The only remaining force of Texans, about 500, afterward increased to 1200, under "General" Sam Houston, hearing of these disasters, retreated toward the east, destroying their homes and property. They were pursued by Santa Anna with

Chatto

Mangus

Geronimo

Dutchy

Natchez

Victoria

APACHE CHIEFS. WITNESS THE SAVAGERY OF THESE FACES

a small part of his force, and overtaken near the present city of Houston. Both armies confronted each other for several days, and then Santa Anna entrenched. On April 21 Houston moved forward to reconnoiter the Mexican position; he found the Mexicans, 1150 strong, unprepared, rushed the camp, killed and wounded 838 and captured all except 40 of those left. The next day a small party of Texans was out collecting stragglers—they saw in a swamp a man's head above the long grass; they brought him into camp, whereupon the other prisoners arose and saluted, exclaiming, *"El Presidente!"*

They had captured the President of Mexico! The rest was dead easy. In fear of his life, Santa Anna ordered his remaining forces, over 4000, to march back to Mexico, and Texas was free!

No more miraculous change of fortune can be cited in history. I spent the day after reaching San Antonio having a "good time." Late that evening, returning from a party, I was told at the door of the hotel that General Mackenzie wanted to see me. I found him in his room, closeted with Lawton, who had arrived from Fort Sill, bringing the band and soldiers' wives by rail from Caddo. Evidently Lawton, too, had been having a "good time," but in a way the General did not approve. The General was somewhat agitated.

"Mr. Parker," said he, "I want you to proceed to the camp of the band of the regiment, take command, and tomorrow start on the journey to Fort Clark."

I saluted and retired. It was the end of my "good time." Lawton grinned sardonically.

After inquiring, I found that the band and the

soldiers' wives were camped about two miles out from San Antonio, near the water tower. I tried to engage a vehicle, but the cabmen's charges were so excessive that I determined to make the trip on foot.

It was near midnight. San Antonio was surrounded by a forest of mesquite trees, which at that time reached nearly to the Menger Hotel. It was traversed by many confusing roads or tracks. After an hour's marching I discovered I was lost.

Fortunately, I arrived at a telegraph line. "Shinnying" up one of the poles, I was able to look over the tops of the mesquite trees. In the dim starlight a dark column loomed some distance away. It was the water tower. Sliding down the pole I proceeded in that direction. At the water tower a man directed me to the camp, where no one was awake. I picked out a tent, apart from the others, as probably the Commanding Officer's; in it I found Lawton's striker asleep on his bed. Ejecting the striker I took possession.

Next day I started for Clark with my charges in wagons. My "command" consisted of some fifteen bandsmen, and thirty "ladies," some not quite so ladylike as others. There were frequent violent disputes among them. I acted as peacemaker. The distance was 125 miles by stage road.

The trip was without incident. I remember the stage station at Castroville was kept by Colonel Le Normand, an officer of Napoleon's old guard. He was one of those old soldiers of Napoleon's who, under the lead of General Lallemand, made up in 1818 an expedition to Texas which they called the *Champ d'asile.* Balzac mentions it; the poet Beranger immortalized it. They started with great expectations. But money was wasted; the expedition was dispersed by Spanish troops, and the whole affair was a failure. The Colonel, who was then in 1878 over ninety years of age, was the last survivor.

Fort Clark, a post established before the Civil War, was built on a plateau at the head of Las Moras Creek, which flowed from an immense spring near the post. The country near the post was flat, covered with groves of mesquite. The climate was dry. According to a Mr. Cornell, who kept a large store in Brackettville, the small town which adjoined the post, "You can't rise corn in Kinney County without litigation." He meant irrigation, of which there was little, as Las Moras Creek ran between high banks. The post, built upon land leased by the Government, was then, and has always been since, in a dilapidated condition. It has several times been abandoned as a station for troops and occupied afterward. Along about 1880 it was expected that the Southern Pacific Railroad from San Antonio to El Paso would run through it, but the town of Brackettville failed to subscribe to the company's bonds and so the railroad made a semi-circle around it, not approaching nearer than seven miles.

Shortly after I arrived, the garrison in and about the post was increased to a battalion each of the 10th, 20th and 24th Infantry, three batteries of light artillery and thirteen troops of cavalry, from the 4th and 8th Regiments. Twenty-one of these organizations were at the post; some of the cavalry was camped out on the Pinto River, ten miles distant; other troops were at Fort Duncan, twenty-four miles distant. There was also a detachment of "Negro-Indian-Seminole-Scouts" in their village on Las Moras Creek, several miles below the post. These scouts, who originally were runaway slaves from the Seminole nation, were good trailers and fighters, and intimately acquainted with the wild country along the Rio Grande. They were commanded by Lieutenant (afterward General) Bullis. In those days the price of land in western Texas was a dollar per acre, but as Texas scrip was worth only fifteen cents on the dollar, and scrip could be exchanged for land, it cost the buyer only fifteen cents. Bullis in his scouting operations discovered and bought many choice bits of land which made him eventually a rich man. He also discovered and became the owner of several valuable mines.

The commander of Fort Duncan, a sub-post of Fort Clark, was Lieutenant-Colonel W. R. Shafter. Shafter also commanded Fort Clark whenever Mackenzie happened to be absent. Shafter afterward gained much fame, as well as considerable criticism, as major-general in command of the Santiago expedition which, in 1898, brought our war with Spain to a conclusion.

In person Shafter was not *distingué,* being short and corpulent. His language, too, at times was likely to be a little inelegant. But he was a soldier, energetic and thorough. Officially his manner was vigorous, nervous, abrupt. In this he somewhat resembled Mackenzie, whom he greatly admired. In return Mackenzie had great confidence in Shafter, as did General Ord, the Department Commander. On the other hand, he was greatly disliked by many officers. He hated a slacker. A private letter of his to General Ord, freely commenting on the failings of a number of officers in his command, had by an unlucky chance been included in some papers regarding the "state of affairs on the Rio Grande frontier," a resumé published by Congress. It was bitterly resented. From that time on Shafter was more or less in hot water. In 1879 his enemies in the Senate fought his promotion to colonel and nearly defeated it.

Despite his corpulence, Shafter was one of the most active officers in the army. On the Rio Grande frontier he had, although an infantryman, distinguished himself by much arduous cavalry work, commanding a number of cavalry raids and expeditions.

Shafter had had a curious history. A colonel, and brevet brigadier general of volunteers at the close of the Civil War, with a gallant record, he had retired to civil life in Michigan, his native state. The regular army was then being reorganized; commissions were in such demand that some of the most distinguished volunteer officers were glad to accept low rank. Shafter, residing near Kalamazoo, Michigan, engaged in cutting and hauling cord wood for a living, made application for a majority and was told by his Congressman that he had a mighty slim chance.

They say that one day, coming into town, perched upon his load of wood, he was passing the post office, when the postmaster ran out and handed him a long envelope postmarked Washington. Opening it, Shafter found he was the lieutenant-colonel of the 41st Infantry! It turned out that his Congressman had failed to obtain him a majority commission. But after the list was made up a lieutenant-colonel declined, and they gave Shafter the vacancy.

On the Santiago campaign Shafter did not go out of his way to be polite to the mob of war correspondents or newspaper reporters. This incensed a number of them, resulting in much rabid criticism. A great deal of this was highly unjust. After General Miles, of whom the Government fought shy for political reasons, Shafter was the most competent of our general officers. Leaving out details, what he accomplished at Santiago was marvelous. His force consisted of 17,000 men; the enemy, in and about Santiago, had over 32,000. Ordered to land near Santiago, he debarked on a surf-beaten shore commanded by heights in such a way that the landing could not have been protected by the fire of the fleet. He then found that the enemy in Santiago greatly outnumbered him and was in a secure position. Instead of delaying the attack and calling for reinforcements and siege guns, as many other commanders would have done, he at once assaulted the enemy's works. Failing to capture them in spite of great losses, he sent a demand for surrender. The enemy, convinced that Shafter's force was stronger than it was, sacrificed its fleet and capitulated.

It is singular that military critics have not contrasted this campaign with that of Sebastopol, in 1859. The map of the coast, of the city on its bay, might almost be taken for that of Santiago. In each case was the capture of a hostile fleet involved. Sebastopol, having at first but a small garrison, could have been taken by an immediate assault. Instead, the allies, by landing on the wrong side of the city and other bad management, gave the enemy time to fortify it. In the end they took a year to capture Sebastopol and lost 252,000 men, mostly by disease. At Santiago, with yellow fever and malaria rampant, our experience would have been similar, but for Shafter's determination to "put his fate to the touch." Shafter deserved well of his country.

In March, 1878, being assured that no military movements were then contemplated, I obtained leave of absence to visit my home at Newark, New Jersey. This leave was afterward extended to two months. Returning by sea via Galveston, we ran into a tremendous storm in which, during the night, a tram car, carried as freight on an upper deck, broke loose. The noise was frightful, but I was too sick to care whether we sank or not. At Galveston I heard that military movements were in progress and hurried on to Fort Clark, where I was fortunate enough to overtake Shafter's command on May 8, 1878, the day it started for Mexico.

Mackenzie with eleven troops of cavalry had already, some days before, crossed the Rio Grande near Del Rio, and was on his way by forced marches to the haunts of the Kickapoo Indians in the mountains some 150 miles distant from the Rio Grande. These Indians had been depredating on the American side of the river, stealing into Texas in the dark of the moon, hiding in the hills, and when the moon was full and they could travel day and night, raiding through the country. Sometimes these raids took them completely round the city of San Antonio, 150 miles in the interior. They killed men and women without mercy, peaceable farming families being found dead and mutilated, their houses rifled, their stock run off. These were often people who had never seen an Indian and who had lived the most peaceful lives. Returning to Mexico with their booty the Indians found a ready sale for it in the small Mexican towns. These raids with many other similar outrages had continued for many years, unchecked by Mexico, in spite of protestations by our authorities. The American Government had at last determined to put a stop to that, even should it involve a war with Mexico.

The plan of the expedition was as follows: following the eleven troops of cavalry under Mackenzie, the main body of the expedition under Shafter, consisting of three battalions of infantry, three batteries of artillery, and two troops of cavalry, with forty wagons, laden with thirty days' rations for the whole command, was to march to the town of Santa Rosa, 150 miles in the interior, and there establish a supply camp which the cavalry under Mackenzie were to use as a base for their succeeding operations against the Indians.

The commander of "M" Troop, to which I was temporarily assigned, was Captain William O'Connell, born in Ireland, raised in the army, a gallant fighter, tall and powerful, with a picturesque brogue. As the sequel will show, he almost brought on the war with Mexico.

Our first day's march was in the direction of the Rio Grande. The day was excessively hot and the white infantry arrived in camp fagged out. Not so the colored infantry battalion. I was astounded to see them, after reaching camp and throwing off their impediments, turn out for drill. They were commanded by a war veteran, Major Bentzoni, born in Prussia, risen from the ranks during the Civil War. In a stentorian voice, with a strong German accent, he drilled his troops for an hour, largely at double time, completing the maneuvers by a grand charge on a neighboring hill which was taken with a rush amid great cheers. The tired white soldiers looked on with distinct disapproval.

I had occasion to notice their battalion the next day when a long march was being made, the thermometer registering over 100 degrees in the shade. The white soldiers, bowed under their heavy packs, seemed half-dead with fatigue; the colored troops tramped along with a springy step, joshing each other, with loud bursts of darkey laughter. Whenever a halt took place there was a rush for the battalion wagon some distance in the rear, the soldiers running gleefully back to their places, their mouths full of hardtack.

The second day's march brought us across the Rio Grande, the river being easily forded. That night we camped on a small stream on Mexican soil. Outposts were established around the camp. Being assigned to outpost duty I was given part of the line. My orders were transmitted to me by Lieutenant Dodt, acting adjutant general. Dodt told me that if natives approached my outposts to allow them to pass, if unarmed. If armed, to arrest them and bring them into camp. If Mexican soldiers appeared, to fire on them at once.

"Why, this is war!" I exclaimed.

"Of course it is war!" said Dodt.

However, during my hour of guard no Mexicans appeared.

The next day, after passing an old stone fort, which appeared strangely out of place in that wilderness, we camped on the San Diego River, a mountain stream, icy cold. Here to our great surprise we were joined by Mackenzie with his cavalry. His expedition into the mountains had been disastrous. On account of the dryness of the season, water holes on which they had counted proved dry. Also the guides misled them. After suffering great hardships from lack of water, they were obliged to retrace their steps. Our plan of campaign was consequently modified.

That afternoon was excessively hot. There was no shade. We had no tents. The surface of the bare plain was like heated iron, almost unsupportable. To cool myself off I took a swim in the icy cold river.

That night I had a raging fever. I lost consciousness. The next day, awaking, I found myself stretched out in an ambulance. Looking out of the ambulance I saw alongside a field cannon in battery, ready for firing. My orderly was near by, holding my horse. It was about noon.

I staggered out and mounted my horse. Going to General Shafter's headquarters I was informed of the situation. It appeared we had reached Remolino, a little town at the head of the San Rodriguez River, a kind of headquarters for the Kickapoo Indians for disposing of their plunder. We had arrived about seven o'clock that morning. Instead of Indians we had found there a considerable body of troops of the Mexican Army under command of a General Winkler.

The Mexicans showed fight. A parley ensued. They were asked what their intentions were. They replied that they had received orders to "fire on any American troops crossing the Rio Grande." We asked them, then, why they did not fire. They explained that we were a little too strong for them, but that they expected reinforcements, and that when the additional troops arrived they would attack us, if we had not retired.

"When will you receive these reinforcements?" Mackenzie asked.

"At two o'clock."

"Very well, then, I will go into camp; at two o'clock I will advance."

Joining my Troop K of the 4th Cavalry and reporting to Captain Heyl, I found preparations for the movement being made. Eleven troops of cavalry in line of masses were facing the village of Remolino. The artillery and gatling guns were disposed on heights bearing upon the Mexican camp. The infantry accompanied by two troops of cavalry was on the right.

At two o'clock the infantry advanced. There was a tense moment, then the Mexicans fled. As someone expressed it, there was not one Mexican patriotic enough to fire off his gun, else the war with Mexico would have begun. Old Captain O'Donnell preceding the infantry with his troop dashed at the Mexicans with uplifted pistol; he was with difficulty restrained. The Seminole Scouts riding through the Mexican camp looted it of pots and pans.

Winkler's servant, a young negro, deserted him and joined us just as the advance began. He afterward became Lieutenant Dorst's servant. He told us that Winkler and the Mexican officers were for fighting, until they learned we had with us a battery of gatling guns. That was too much for them.

Our officers called this, jokingly, "the battle of Remolino." It resembled the battle of Fontenoy, when the French said to the English, "Gentlemen, fire first," except that there was no bloodshed! Curiously enough there was no account of the incident in the eastern papers, except in the *New York Sun,* at that time rabidly hostile to the Hayes administration. Appearing only in that paper people may have thought the story unreliable.

We were in Mexico about nine days. From Remolino we marched generally parallel to the Rio Grande, to the head of the San Rodrignez, then down that river. I suffered a great deal with fever but remained on duty with my troop. The Mexican force paralleled our march. Several times it took up a position threatening our line of march. When we deployed into line of battle the Mexicans decamped.

We had along with us a number of civilians, who came for the purpose of reclaiming cattle which had been stolen and driven across the Rio Grande. A quantity of beeves were thus recovered.

On arriving at the Rio Grande, not far from Piedras Negras, a town opposite Eagle Pass, we found the Mexican force posted on a high hill commanding the crossing. Mackenzie sent an officer to ask what their intentions were. They sent back a surly message to the effect: "Go ahead, but look out for yourself." Mackenzie was angry and it is said discussed with Shafter the advisability of seizing Piedras Negras. He sent a couple of troops of cavalry in skirmish line toward the hill, to hold the Mexicans while we crossed. The cavalry was not stopped in time and rushed at the hill. The Mexicans again decamped, leaving much camp property.

We then crossed the river. The ford was too

deep for infantry, so each cavalry horseman took up an infantryman behind. This made the crossing expeditious. I was sorry to lose a fine setter dog, which I called Tomp after my friend Thompson, which accompanied me on the expedition. He could not face the deep water of the ford, and I left him howling on the bank; I suppose the Mexicans captured him.

Arrived on Texan soil, the command dispersed to their various camps. Preparations were made for a second crossing, to take place as soon as the drouth ended. Accordingly, on July 4th we marched down to the river and began crossing the command. On this occasion I acted as Mackenzie's adjutant-general.

The river had risen and the ford was deep. Some of the pack mules, deviating from the ford, got into deep water and were drowned. A large portion of the cavalry had passed over the ford into Mexico when a courier arrived at a gallop bringing from Fort Clark a telegraphic despatch sent from Washington. The movement was ordered stopped and the troops recrossed the river.

The threat of war had had its effect. The Mexican Government, under Diaz, engaged to police the Rio Grande. Six thousand regular troops were sent to the Texas border, and short work was made of the Kickapoo Indians and other bandits. In a few months robberies, raids and disorders largely ceased. A strong government under Diaz was established and until 1910, when he was overthrown, comparative peace prevailed along the Rio Grande.

These effects did not, however, show themselves at once, and a strong garrison under Mackenzie continued to be maintained at or near Fort Clark.

In fact, it will probably always be necessary to keep a strong guard along our border. Diaz's administration, a dictatorship, as autocratic and ruthless as that of the czars of Russia, held down the people for a time but was finally, in 1910, overthrown, and the reign of terror was resumed with added force. The fact is the trouble with Mexico is deep-seated. Most of the inhabitants of Mexico are Indians, illiterate, semi-savage, held in a state of peonage by laws inherited from the Spanish conquerors. They are debased by cheap drink, *pulque* and *mescal*. They are virtually in a state of bondage by debt. Owning no property of value they have nothing to lose, and with their turbulent Indian nature take part readily in insurrections. In these uprisings, engineered by ambitious military chiefs, they know and care nothing about the ends to be gained. If defeated or captured they go over to the enemy. As soldiers they are accompanied by their wives and children and often receive better pay than during peace. Their instinct for fighting is hereditary. As for Americans, they hate and despise us; they think we are afraid of them. When, as is often the case, diplomatic relations between the two countries are strained, they talk freely of invading us and extending their territory to the Mississippi. Anarchy is normal; law and order are exceptional. In the last one hundred years there have been over one hundred insurrections and revolutions, and sixty rulers.

The decline in the condition of Mexico has been continuous since the revolution of 1910. Owing to the constant warfare, sixty per cent of the horses, mules, cattle, goats, etc., have disappeared.

Due to the agrarian laws which break up the great estates, distributing them to poor laborers, crops have largely decreased. A large portion of the Mexican population is impoverished, and the effects are seen in the generally anæmic appearance of the common people. The labor situation grows worse, as a result of constant strikes and of the acceptance by the laborers of bolshevik doctrines. Laws have been passed making it difficult or impossible for Americans or other foreigners to own property; many estates owned by them have been expropriated by the government without compensation. Other confiscatory laws were directed against the foreign oil companies; in consequence the output has been reduced by nearly one-half. As the tax on oil constitutes a large part of the government revenues, the government (1928) defaulted on the interest on its bonds.

One of the few things left in Mexico leading to peace and order was the influence of the priests; laws against the church are destroying this. Many priests are leaving the country. So is the better class of the Mexicans—those formerly rich and prosperous. Mexico is now almost stripped of those Mexicans who prior to 1910 constituted the aristocracy of the country. They are exiles. But it is not only the rich who emigrate. In 1923, we are told, 500,000 Mexicans entered California, besides immense numbers who crossed into other states. We have in this country 3,000,000 Mexicans, chiefly refugees.

That we are largely responsible for maintaining this adjoining country in a state of anarchy, for perpetrating the misery and ruin of its inhabitants, there can be no question. We will not interfere or permit others to interfere. It is as though we saw a fire raging in an adjoining house, people and property perishing, and refused to render aid. The magnificent domain of Mexico, with its boundless undeveloped riches, would be a refuge and a home for millions of impoverished Europeans, wrecked by the World War, were order restored. Moreover, their presence in Mexico alone would be sufficient to end the era of revolutions.

There have been many occasions when things have come to such a pass that our duty to intervene was plain. There have been occasions when we have suffered wrongs at Mexico's hands which with any other nation would have brought about an instant declaration of war. The reason generally given why we have not intervened is that Mexico is weak, and we wish her to work out unhindered her way to civilized government. This is hypocrisy! We know well that under present conditions Mexico is proceeding from bad to worse.

And yet at times we have indulged in *partial* intervention. In 1912 the U. S. Navy attacked Vera Cruz and after some fighting, accompanied by loss of life, captured it. The city was then occupied by a division of our troops under General Funston, which held the city, confronting a Mexican army, from April until November.

Again, in 1916, a force of U. S. troops under General Pershing, numbering 12,000, entered Mexico in pursuit of the bandit Villa. This force operated in the northern states of Mexico nearly twelve months. Incidentally the Mexican troops attacked one of our outlying detachments of cavalry, killing, wounding, and capturing over twenty men. This insult was swallowed.

There have been other occasions when we have used our troops to bring pressure on the Mexicans, but without actually invading their country. Thus, in 1911 conditions were so grave that the Taft administration sent a force of 12,000 men to the border, and in the expectation of war ordered all Americans out of Mexico. Many poor people lost their homes and all their property. This accomplished, the government changed its mind about having a war. The pacifists had gained the upper hand.

Again, in 1916 when it was found that Carranza and Obregon, incited by Germany, were considering the prospect of sending a large force across the Rio Grande to invade Texas and loot San Antonio, our government, to defend the frontier, took 100,000 men of our National Guard from their homes, families and occupations, and sent them to the Rio Grande to defend the United States against invasion!

These occurrences have not improved our relations; they have merely angered the people of Mexico and made their hatred and disdain more intense.

In this connection it is interesting to study the French Intervention of 1863-66. Then, as now, Mexico was split by a struggle between the Catholic and anti-Catholic parties. Then, as now, there was disorder, and foreigners were maltreated.

The French (30,000 men) marched from Vera Cruz to Mexico City. They did not then have the aid of railroads, and it is doubtful if a railroad would have helped much, as an army based on a railroad loses half its strength guarding it, and is deprived of much liberty of maneuver. Arrived at the cultivated plains of the interior food and forage were found in plenty.

On the way to Mexico City, except for the siege of the city of Puebla (which was unnecessary), they had no fighting. Arrived at Mexico City they were received with open arms by the people.

They announced they intended to restore order and make of Mexico an independent nation under French protection. They convoked a government, formed of the most representative citizens. This government elected a ruler, passed many good laws, and raised an army of Mexican soldiers which was largely used to do the dirty work of cleaning up the country, suppressing bandits and putting down small insurrections. It is quite likely these Mexican troops could have done the whole work of restoring law and order, leaving to the French merely the duty of garrisoning Mexico City and a few important towns. But the party of Juarez, the liberals, opposed to Maximilian, were supported and secretly aided and armed by the United States, necessitating that the French troops (which, including some few Austrian and Belgian troops, never numbering over 40,000) were used partly as "flying columns" supporting the Mexican Army. On account of rains, active operations had to be restricted to the dry season, October to May.

When, in the fall of 1865, resistance was practically at an end, the American Government interfered by sending a large force of troops to the Rio Grande. It accompanied this threat with a demand couched in significant language, that the French troops be withdrawn and sent back to

France. Compliance with this demand followed. The retirement of the French, combined with the hostility of the United States, struck terror into the hearts of the Mexican Imperialists, and weakened their resistance, resulting finally in the capture of their last stronghold, Queretaro, and the execution of Emperor Maximilian.

Since then, with the exception of President Diaz's autocratic rule, Mexico has been a prey to revolutions, insurrections and savagery. Recently, before the Pan-American conference, the United States has proclaimed that it is its right and duty to intervene in Central American states, to restore order and protect Americans. Does this apply to Mexico, as well as to San Domingo, Hayti and Nicaragua?.

Intervention here would be a work of humanity. It would rescue from a thralldom of disorder millions of people. It would bring them civilization, education, order, prosperity. As in the case of Cuba, it would in time be remembered with gratitude and appreciation. It would require but a small effort on the part of the American Republic. It is the only remedy.

V

THE UTE CAMPAIGN

In July, 1879, I was promoted First Lieutenant of the 4th Cavalry and assigned to Troop A, of that regiment. I was loath to leave my old troop, the Black Horse Troop of the 4th Cavalry. I had come to know the men and they me. I will tell later how I rejoined it.

The most fortunate day of my life was the day of my marriage, November twelfth, 1879. The young girl who on that day joined my fortunes gave me love, a home, five splendid children, ambition to excel. Coming from luxurious surroundings she made light of the perils of the Indian country, and faced the hardships of the frontier without a murmur. To her, as to me, the romance of army life made a vivid appeal. In our rough western posts, attracting all by her grace, the charm of her personality and her wit, she made devoted friends who were ever faithful to our fortunes. She was an ideal soldier's wife.

While on leave of absence at Newark, New Jersey, just before I was married, we heard the news of the Ute outbreak. The White River Utes in the northern part of the State of Colorado had revolted and killed their agent, Meeker. Troops under Thornburg were sent to the agency to suppress the outbreak. They were attacked before they reached it, were roughly handled, and took up a defensive position; their commander, Thornburg, was killed. The 5th Cavalry under

General Merritt made a forced march, relieved Thornburg's command, which was besieged by the Indians, and marching to the agency engaged in restoring order.

In the meantime General Mackenzie with the 4th Cavalry was ordered from Texas to the Uncompahgre Agency in the west central part of the State. The Uncompahgre Utes, as they were called, showed signs of revolt and had killed several miners and teamsters. With the six troops of the regiment then in Texas, Mackenzie proceeded by rail from Texas to Fort Garland, Colorado, leaving the band and Troop A, to which I had been assigned, at Fort Hays, Kansas. At Fort Garland, Mackenzie made preparations for the march across the Rocky Mountains to the Uncompahgre Reservation, to commence in the early spring.

In December, 1879, with my bride, I joined my new troop at Fort Hays, Kansas. The post, adjoining the small town of Hays City, 290 miles west of Kansas City, was established in 1873 as a supply point for expeditions against hostile Indians, who formerly overran that wild and arid country. Hays City, at one time a boom town and the rail head of the Kansas Pacific Railroad which was being built, had then an unenviable reputation as a wild and woolly western town, the headquarters for cattlemen, outlaws, gamblers, and desperadoes. In 1879, however, it was a quiet enough place—the railroad had gone on, the country had been settled by peaceable farmers, and the cattle trails coming from Texas led to stations farther west. But the farmers around Fort Hays were not prosperous; the country was then undergoing one of its periodical droughts which generally last for two or three years. Cycles of wet and dry weather are a peculiarity of the dry country which extends from the neighborhood of the 100th meridian to the Rocky Mountains. The dry weather lasts two or three years, and is followed by more or less normally wet weather for the next seven or eight. I have observed a number of these cycles. During the favorable period there is a boom; the people are informed by the farmers and the real estate men that the "climate has changed"; that railroads, telegraph lines, upheaval of the soil, cultivation, have so altered conditions that droughts are no more to be feared. In consequence there is a rush to occupy this cheap farming land. A settler with his family takes up a quarter section; the first year he constructs a sod house, a dugout to live in; he obtains credit from the local dealer for seeds and tools. At the end of the first year he has perhaps raised a good crop; he is able to put a mortgage on his land, and with the money build a small house or barn. The second year, if crops are good, he pays off the first mortgage and borrows more money for further improvements. This goes on until the year of drought arrives; at the end of the second year of dry weather his crops having failed, the crash comes; the farmer is bankrupt; mortgaged to the hilt and unable to pay his interest! He abandons everything except a wagon, a pair of horses and some tools and moves "farther west." The mortgage companies are left with some useless land and buildings on their lands and *they* go broke. The banks fail. The railroads having no freight to carry pass their dividends. These fatal periods of difficulty often coincide with financial crises in the Eastern centers of capital.

The country around Fort Hays was a flat, treeless plain. A small creek bordered by a few cottonwood trees skirted the post. The post itself, in a form of a quadrangle, was built for four troops of cavalry. The buildings of wood, all painted yellow, were so lightly constructed they rocked in the wind. The garrison in 1879 consisted of Troop A, 4th Cavalry, the regimental band, a few officers' and soldiers' wives, whose husbands were absent in the field, and a chaplain too old to be of any service. He regularly went on sick report every Sunday morning to escape from preaching! He informed me that Fort Hays would probably soon be abandoned—that they always sent him to such posts. "I expect the next post they send me to will be 'Sitky'." By which he meant Sitka, Alaska, that being the most out-of-the-way place he could think of. He was one of the type of old worn-out parsons, who, in those days, as a result of religious pressure brought on the authorities, were accommodated with a billet in the army. When too worthless to be of any use they were ignored, a condition of affairs which they did not resent too strongly. Of course, there were many exceptions. I am glad to say that today the corps of chaplains in the army is doing good work.

The chaplain, to be at his best, must possess the entire confidence of the soldiers. (It is they who need his ministrations.) But this is impossible if he is intimate with the officers. The best chaplain I ever knew, who was wonderfully efficient in bringing about contentment, thus preventing desertion and disorder, made a rule of living apart from the officers and devoting himself principally to the men. He sacrificed much, but he had our deepest respect and admiration. This was Chaplain, now Monsignor, George J. Waring.

With my young bride I arrived one December night at the railroad station, two miles from Fort Hays. It was "cold enough to freeze the tail off a brass monkey," as Lieutenant Lockett, who came to greet us, remarked. Getting into a sleigh drawn by two horses we were drawn rapidly through the deep snow, and after a short drive were received with great hospitality at the quarters of the commanding officer, Captain Leopold Parker. A few days later, our baggage having arrived, we moved into our own home.

Leopold Parker was a remarkable officer. Of medium height, dark sallow complexion, coal-black hair and beard, piercing eyes, a black pipe always between his lips, an habitual user of strong coffee, he was what one might call "intense." An officer of a "Galvanized Yankee" regiment in 1865 (a Galvanized Yankee was a converted Confederate prisoner), he joined the 4th Cavalry in 1869, where for several years he was Mackenzie's trusted adjutant, absorbing from Mackenzie that officer's extraordinary devotion to duty. He might be said to consider nothing, think of nothing, but his military duty.

There was an amusing example of this some few days after I arrived. One of the men of "A" Troop deserted. Now Parker had just been promoted; he was commanding a troop for the first time; he seemed to regard this desertion as a personal affront to himself, and moreover, he abhorred desertion as a military disorder of the worst type. To our astonishment (for Lockett and I had become somewhat calloused to the very common offense of desertion), Leopold Parker entered upon a night and day campaign against this unfortunate derelict; he became for the time being a chief of police, an expert detective; the clerks at headquarters were worn out writing letters and telegrams to towns and villages, to mayors and chiefs of police, constables, sheriffs, United States marshals, deputy marshals, railroad authorities; journeys were made, traces investigated, scouting parties sent out, nothing left undone. At last after four or five days of turmoil and excitement the man was discovered. A party of officers went after him, he was conveyed in triumph to the post, securely manacled, and placed in the darkest and securest dungeon in the guard-house. Leopold Park was grimly pleased; the crime against the honor of his command had been appeased, the criminal would be punished. But it was not long before another misguided individual attempted to escape from military discipline. Immediately the same excitement reigned at headquarters, the same campaign was waged. Finally, as before, the poor wretch was captured and locked up securely.

Lockett and I had seen many desertions; we deplored it, but we thought it was a necessary concomitant of the service; we did not think it could be entirely prevented. But to our astonishment desertion in A Troop, 4th Cavalry, stopped right there! The men were afraid to desert! "Black" Parker was too much for them.

There are few desertions in the army today, but in those days it was a terrible scourge, especially in the West. The men complained of poor pay, restricted food, hardships in the field, excessive guard duty, long hours of non-military labor on roads and buildings, entire lack of amusement and recreation, the monotony of the desert. When pay day, which occurred once in two months, came along, accompanied by the inevitable soldiers' orgy, bad whiskey would have its effect and men up to that time trusted and noted for good behavior would desert. As a consequence the West was full of former deserters. One of our former Secretaries of War was even heard to say, "Let them desert, they build up the West!" There was no proper public sentiment in the West against deserters and deserters had no difficulty in finding people who aided and concealed them.

Shortly after my arrival at Fort Hays I was appointed quartermaster and commissary of the post, attending to those duties as well as my duties as First Lieutenant of Troop A. Mrs. Parker found novelty and amusement in a great many of our military developments and exclaimed, "I had imagined you a dashing commander of men—I now find your principal duties are keeping a grocery store and a junk shop." Likening the quartermaster's storehouse to a junk shop was a happy comparison. For while it was difficult to find in it much that was really useful for household purposes, it had in the former Indian campaigns become the dumping ground of vast quantities of field and camp equipment deposited there by marching columns, never reclaimed, and allowed for years to slowly moulder and rust.

This was not the only case where my sprightly bride with her spirit of fun made me see ridiculous aspects in things which I had hitherto regarded only in a matter-of-fact way. And she, like me, was proud of doing her part to serve our country. Like a true soldier, she soon came to love the regiment, the troop, the uniform, the trumpet calls, the pomp and parade of the cavalry squadron. She developed into an expert horsewoman, and mounted on Bayard, I on another mount, we galloped over the far-reaching plains. With her, life was a poem.

But it was not to last.

In March, 1880, by the dismissal of an officer, the first lieutenancy of my old Troop K became vacant and at my request I was transferred to it. Being ordered to join Mackenzie's command at Fort Garland, on March 30th I took leave of Captain Leopold Parker and my friends at Fort Hays. The furniture in our little home was packed up and while I went West, Mrs. Parker took the train East. It happened that my train was scheduled to leave in the night, before the departure of hers; but a favoring west wind came up, held back my train and expedited hers so that I had after all the opportunity of seeing her off before I embarked for the campaign.

Denver, through which I passed for the second time, was then a stirring town filled with miners, who were beginning to open up the rich silver deposits of Colorado, and with cattle men, who were engaged in stocking the great western ranges. Money was easy with both; play ran high; and there was a general atmosphere of recklessness. Prices were exorbitant. It was no place for a poor lieutenant in the army to abide, and I hurried on. But during my stay of twelve hours I met many young Easterners, some of them society men, strangely out of place, in from the ranches for the winter, spending with a free hand the riches they believed they had in sight. Ranching at that period was a tempting proposition. With the departure of the Indians vast ranges of Government land, covering territory that seemed unfit for cultivation, were to be had for the taking. Once the territory around the few water holes and streams had been filed upon, the rest of the area, including the range, being considered worthless except for grazing, was regarded as securely held. Some of these ranges were twenty or thirty miles square. The principal expense in establishing the ranges was the cost of the cattle. And it seemed an easy mathematical demonstration that in a few years the natural increase in the cows would bring large returns.

But they reckoned without the market. In a few years after 1879, hundreds, perhaps thousands, of new ranges were producing, and throwing their stock upon the market. The price of cattle was cut in half. Added to this there came droughts in summer, zero weather in winter. The cattle died by thousands. Many of the cattle men went bankrupt.

Later on, when the country to the east became more settled, it was found that much of the country included in the limits of these ranches, which had not been filed upon, was capable of cultivation by "dry soil farming" or otherwise. Farmers came; the ranges were encroached upon; the land became too valuable for cattle raising; the cattle men's holdings became fewer in number and more restricted. Few of the great ranches are now left. And cattle raising, to succeed, must be conducted scientifically with full provision for the cattle in time of drought or blizzard.

At the time I was there, Denver was mining mad. Rich strikes had been made in the mountains and the country was overrun by prospectors. Few men who could afford it did not have grub stake prospectors out in the hills. The "grub stakers" (two men usually worked together) were furnished by their employer, at the cost of several hundred dollars, with two pack mules, tools, a tent, and enough bacon, flour, etc., for three or four months' subsistence. Thus equipped, the prospectors would sally forth in quest of fortune. When a strike was made, half of the mine went to the employer.

In case a silver vein or deposit was found, the difficulty was to find a buyer. Unless the ore showed up exceedingly rich, usually the mine could not be sold unless it had been "developed." Developing a mine meant sinking a shaft down through the vein to determine its depth, then tunneling along it to determine its length, and then cross cut it to find its width. This done, a body of ore, so many cubic yards, of such and such an average richness, had been exposed, and the purchase was no longer a gamble. But to properly develop a mine costs about $25,000. The West is covered with "prospect holes," many of them perhaps rich strikes but abandoned for lack of a purchaser. Ruined hopes!

The officers of the 4th Cavalry while in Colorado sank several thousand dollars in this game. Our grub stakers found several promising leads, but for want of a purchaser they were finally abandoned.

At Fort Garland I found my Troop K. My captain, E. M. Heyl, was then absent on a detail of several years' duration on duty in the East.

This, to my great contentment, left me in command of the troop. We learned about this time that the State of Colorado, desiring to develop its western territory and impatient at the outrages continually being committed on miners, teamsters, and settlers, had demanded of the general Government that all the Utes should be moved west into Utah, to the Vintah Reservation of 270 square miles. This move the Indians angrily opposed and a bloody fight was expected. The Utes, mountain Indians, held the reputation of being formidable fighters, having in the past had numerous engagements with the plains Indians, whom, in their mountain fastnesses, they invariably defeated. Up to 1879 when they killed Agent Meeker and waylaid the troops sent to rescue him, they had never had a war with the whites.

I remember that in spite of drills, life was not all drudgery. All my companions, the young lieutenants of the command, Wentz Miller, Jug Wood, Joe Dorst, Squire Mason, Sandy Rogers, Murray, Wilder, McDonald, Wheeler, and Richards, found time for numerous diversions. There were deer and duck in the vicinity, horse racing was a favorite sport, foot races were indulged in. We constructed a primitive gymnasium where we held numerous events. At night it was cold on the mountain plateau, but in our fireplace great piñon logs crackled, throwing out an aromatic odor. There was much singing, under the leaderships of Dr. Munn, our surgeon, and Colonel Beaumont, commanding officer of the cantonment. There was considerable card playing, while some of the officers, more studious, utilized the evenings to improve their minds by study. No women were present with our command.

On May 18, 1880, we started on our 200-mile march to the Uncompahgre agency. The command of six troops was in splendid condition, the officers and the men keen, the horses fit. As a result of Lawton's careful preparations we were magnificently fitted out—clothing, equipment, armament, ammunition, food supplies, wagon trains and pack train.

At Saguache, a town at the northern end of San Luis Valley, we entered the mountains. From here on we marched through an entanglement of mountains, range after range running north and south, buttressed laterally by splendid spurs, dominated by tremendous peaks. The ragged, narrow, precipitate peaks of European mountains seemed insignificant compared with this billowing grandeur.

Bear, deer and elk abounded and on one march we saw quantities of immense antlers lying near the road bleaching in the sun. It is a curious provision of nature that these animals should shed twenty or thirty pounds of bone each year.

We traveled over the Cochetopa Pass, thence westward along a route south of the Gunnison River and generally parallel to it. The Gunnison River most of the way travels in a tremendous canyon, the "Black Canyon," which is now one of the scenic attractions of the Denver and Rio Grande Railroad. The country boasted few inhabitants and few buildings except an occasional store or gin mill, selling, usually, liquor whose corroding potency defies description. I remember while one day in charge of the rear guard, seeing ahead of me a sergeant of the train escort leave his post of duty without permission, ride up to one of these saloons, dismount and enter, immediately emerge, mount, and having ridden perhaps a distance of a hundred feet, fall from his horse, dead drunk. That whisky surely was of the kind that "killed at forty paces."

In the mountainous regions, while there was plenty of timber, grass was scarce, and horse feed was lacking. I saw one settler who advertised hay at twenty cents a pound. He had taken possession of a small *cienaga* or mountain meadow of perhaps three acres at the side of the road; from this he gathered almost six tons, or 12,000 pounds of hay per year and the passing teams going to the mines bought every pound of it. It will easily be seen that this man was in receipt of a considerable income.

Descending Cedar Creek May 31, 1880, the road entered the valley of the Uncompahgre River, a furious torrent. Occasionally, along the riverbank there was a narrow stretch of grass and it was on one of these that we camped, grateful after our arduous two weeks' march to find a resting place.

We were near the Uncompahgre agency, now the town of Montrose. And it was not difficult to see why the Uncompahgre was so much desired by the whites. It was practically the only piece of land within hundreds of miles available for cultivation; could be easily irrigated, and had an inexhaustible supply of water.

Getting to Ouray was rather difficult. The Uncompahgre River valley narrowed into a canyon and the road from the north, to avoid the canyon, ascended by an easy grade to a plateau. Near Ouray the plateau came to a sudden end,

Major General Ranald Slidell Mackenzie, Colonel of the
4th United States Cavalry

and there was a drop of 1,000 feet down which the road descended, on a grade of forty-five degrees, seemingly almost perpendicular. On such a grade brakes were useless; it was equally useless to lock the wheels; in spite of everything the wagon would slide down upon the horses, especially in places where smooth road was encountered. The procedure, therefore, was, on arriving at the descent, to cut down a large tree, preferably a foot in diameter; this tied by a rope to the rear of the wagon, the branches dragging, held back the vehicle sufficiently to enable the descent to be made without danger. As a result the bottom of the plain was covered with hundreds of dead trees, dragged there by the teams which had preceded our ambulance.

To get back up the hill was a different matter. The wagons were "snubbed" to the top. For this two long ropes were attached to the body of the wagon. One of them was carried forward and wound around a tree bordering the road ahead of the team. With yells and shouts and cracking whips the ascent would begin, the mules, struggling desperately up the steep slope. As they ascended, the slack in the rope would be taken in, the team would come to a halt, the wagon held by the rope, the mules resting. In the meantime the other rope would be carried forward and wound around a tree and the first rope unfastened. Again the team would struggle to the front. Thus "snubbing" with alternate ropes, the wagon would finally arrive at the top of the grade.

Besides the cavalry there was a considerable force of infantry in the valley, making a body of troops several thousand strong, all under the command of General Mackenzie.

The force of troops was made necessary by the uncertain attitude of the Indians, with whom the Indian Commission was negotiating to abandon the valley and move over into Utah. This plan many of the Indians violently resented. They were a fine-looking tribe, rich in herds of horses, cattle and sheep, well provided with property, many richly clad in garments lined with the fur of the beaver and other animals, and armed to the teeth. It was easy to see they would make dangerous fighters. Their bearing towards the troops was sullen but not hostile. Of the progress of the negotiation we knew nothing and we were rarely brought into contact with the Indians. I could even say we never heard a hostile shot, if one day, returning from a hunting expedition, I had not heard a bullet whiz by me. Looking around I saw that it had been fired at a very long range by a small Indian boy high up on the slope of the mountain. The boy, in great trepidation, decamped. I did not follow him nor did I think it worth while to report the incident.

When in the field punctiliousness in dress and training is seldom maintained. This was not the case, however, with the troops commanded by Mackenzie. In our semi-permanent camps the usual routine of post life was pursued. Neatness in dress was demanded and the troops drilled many hours a day to fit them for active service. There was much competition. The "black horse troop," K, which I commanded, was noted for good horsemanship and precision in drill. To spur the men to further efforts I used to tell them, "I want you to be the best troop, in the best regiment, in the best army, in the world!" And they did not fail to respond.

But there was considerable marching and scouting. From July 2nd to July 8th we marched one hundred miles east and south through the mountains. From July 26th to August 8th we marched over one hundred miles, first westward along the Gunnison River and the Grand River, thence northeast up the Grand River mesa, thence through Leon Park and Surface Creek. We saw much game on this trip and the streams were full of trout. Several nights when we camped near the Grand River we used fire stones for fuel—the shale was so impregnated with oil that it burned readily.

On August 26th General Sheridan, commander of the Division of the Missouri, with headquarters at Chicago, visited us. It was the first time I had ever seen that famous cavalry leader. He was a great friend of Mackenzie, who had commanded a division of cavalry in Sheridan's Corps at the battle of Five Forks and in the operations around Richmond which ended in Lee's surrender at Appomattox. Sheridan was accompanied by his brother, Mike Sheridan of the Adjutant General's Department, and by the inspector and a number of staff officers. The next day there was an inspection of the cavalry command at which General Sheridan expressed himself as highly pleased. Later, with Mackenzie and two troops of cavalry as an escort, Sheridan departed for Gunnison City, hunting and fishing on the way.

By now I had been nearly six months away from my bride and this enforced absence, especially in view of the fact there had been no fighting, was becoming very irksome. I remember that in my extremity I even considered the advisability of a temporary detail of duty at West Point, which I was glad afterwards did not materialize. I was also offered a transfer into the Quartermaster's Department, but that would have taken me from my beloved regiment and troops, and given me instead of the life of a cavalry soldier, a sedentary billet. I would not consider it. Nor would I be influenced by the urgent appeal of my father, who was anxious that I should leave the army and join his law firm. I took pride in the fact that of his six sons I was the one who had from a boy made his own way in life. I also was proud of my profession, of serving my country. Life at the frontier was arduous; promotion in the army was at a standstill and I had few hopes of advancement, but there was a source of pride even in the feeling that I might be making sacrifices for my country.

To my wife I wrote daily, as did she to me. This continued during all of my active service in the army, whenever I was absent. Occasionally in times of stress when there was fighting the mails were held up. In October, 1881, I received thirty-one letters from her in a batch, and in January, 1900, there were forty-two at one time! When this happened I read the latest letter and sewed the remainder into a book, poring over them at my leisure.

It was with feelings of joy that we learned at the end of August that arrangements had been concluded with the Indians, and that the troops, no longer needed for the protection of the peace commissioners, would be withdrawn for the winter. Accordingly, on October, 1880, we left the supply camp and proceeded on our return march to Fort Garland. The road back we found much easier, as the State of Colorado during the summer had made many improvements. There, however, we were held in camp until November 4th, before we took rail to our new post, Fort Riley, Kansas. It was during the march to Fort Garland that we passed a train of six army wagons loaded heavily with silver dollars for the Uncompahgre Indians. The silver, amounting to some hundreds of thousands of dollars, was, we understood, a first payment under the treaty signed by the Indians to vacate Colorado.

As the spring of 1881 advanced we heard rumors of threatened hostilities on the part of the Utes. Having signed the treaty to evacuate and having accepted payment in reparation they now claimed that they were deceived and did not understand the treaty. Accordingly on May 9th the command entrained for Fort Garland by rail via Denver and Pueblo.

Fort Riley had been a pleasant post, the quarters were comfortable and life was easy. Since my marriage in 1879 many young officers had followed suit; the 4th Cavalry was no longer a "bachelor regiment." The young women who had joined the regiment were without exception charming companions and a credit to it, and post life was full of gayety. Dances, picnics, horseback parties, rabbit hunts took up our spare time, and brought happiness into our life.

It was therefore not without deep regret that we exchanged farewells while the band played "The Girl I Left Behind Me." Poor girls, their lot was harder than ours, for we were buoyed up by the stern joy and hope of battle!

The post with its ladies was left in charge of a small detachment of men, mostly unfit for active service, commanded by Lieutenant Patch, post commander and quartermaster, a fine officer who had been crippled by the loss of a leg. We knew with him they would be safe and well cared for.

When we arrived at Fort Garland we did not stop to refit but at once started for the Uncompahgre which we reached June 3 without incident. The cavalry command consisted of companies A, B, I, K and L of the 4th Cavalry. At the supply camp on the Uncompahgre was also a force of six companies of the 23rd Infantry, which had remained all winter. They had constructed themselves barracks and quarters of upright pickets with mud roofs; their families had joined them and it was wonderful how comfortable and contented they were in those rough habitations.

The Indians were sulky and semi-hostile; many of them had removed to a mountain which they had fortified; they were well armed; citizens and others prophesied they could not be moved without a fight. The force of troops present was plainly not in numbers equal to the emergency—however, the War Department preferred not to greatly increase the force, for fear of precipitating matters. On July 1st the Peace Commissioners arrived and commenced a long parley.

Our stay on the Uncompahgre River came to an end September 5, 1881. I have already described, in my accounts of General Mackenzie, how on the 30th of August the crisis arrived, how the Indians refused to treat any longer and resolved to fight, and how Mackenzie by his undaunted bearing and quick action, boldly demanding instant compliance, so terrorized the Indians that they yielded.

Following the retreating horde, herding them along, my troop marched August 31st seven miles down the river. Next day I marched to the mouth of the Uncompahgre River, moving the following day to the north side of the Gunnison River, where I was joined by Captain Lawton's troop.

Lawton's troop and mine camped on the north side of the river while A. E. Wood's troop and Abiel Smith's troop followed in the rear of the Indians. Our task at the mouth of the Uncompahgre River was to hold back the civilians. They followed us closely, taking up and "locating" the Indian land thrown open for settlement. For obvious reasons it was not desirable to let these civilians come in contact with the Indians; thus we were holding a crowd of these people on the south side of the Gunnison until the Indians had passed Kahnah Creek, thirteen miles distant.

At eleven that evening a courier rode into camp with a telegraphic dispatch received at headquarters, to the effect that the Apaches in Arizona had gone on the warpath and after a bloody fight with the troops at Cibicu Creek were now attacking the post of Fort Apache. I immediately started with my troop for Fort Apache, 1000 miles distant, via the nearest railway point, Gunnison City.

At Gunnison City our horses and men boarded trains for Pueblo and Albuquerque. From Albuquerque we went by the new Atlantic & Pacific Railroad (now the Atchison, Topeka & Santa Fe) 224 miles to Billings, Arizona, the head of the railroad. There we disembarked and took up our march for Fort Apache, Arizona, 138 miles distant, which we reached by forced marches in six days, on September 26, 1881.

We found that the Indian excitement, made much of by the newspapers, had largely quieted down. After the Cibicu affair in which the Indians, while conferring, had treacherously fired on the troops, killing and wounding a number of officers and men of the 6th Cavalry (the affair was then called the "Cibicu Massacre"), the post of Fort Apache had been attacked, but not seriously. The hostile Apaches had then dispersed into small bands.

The White Mountain Apache Indian Reservation in which we found ourselves was a savage-looking country—as savage as its denizens, the Apaches, a fierce race, who delighted in war and to whom intervals of peace were merely resting periods in the normal life of warfare. There were two tribes of Apaches, on the White Mountain Apache Indian Reservation—the White Mountain Indians and the Chiricahua Indians. The former in preceding years had suffered heavily in their wars with the whites and settling down as agency Indians near Fort Apache had been somewhat tamed by a long period of peace and prosperity. The Chiricahua Apache Indians, on the contrary, had never abated their fierceness.

We arrived too late at Fort Apache to take part in any of the fighting. Instead, we proceeded by forced marches to the San Carlos Agency, some hundred miles southwest of Fort Apache, to restrain the Chiricahua Apaches under Geronimo in their camp near there. But on our arrival we found the bird had flown. Geronimo and his tribe hearing of our approach had fled to

Mexico where they remained, killing and plundering the natives for three years.

In November, 1880, the regiment received orders to proceed to New Mexico where we were distributed at various posts, my troop being stationed at Fort Wingate.

VI

IN THE NAVAJO COUNTRY

It was in the month of November, 1881, that we arrived at Fort Wingate, New Mexico. The post was old, in rather a tumble-down condition, and overcrowded, being occupied by eight companies of the 13th Infantry and our two troops, A and K, of the 4th Cavalry, the whole under Colonel Bradley, a noted general officer during the Civil War. The Navajos (pronounced Navahos), a powerful tribe, inhabited the country to the north of the post; a branch of the Apache family, they had been a moderately peaceful tribe since 1848 when a force of U. S. troops under Kit Carson had inflicted a crushing defeat upon them. Since then they had acquired thousands of sheep, and, being property owners, were not inclined to go on the warpath. It is curious that the Government, which furnished them with these sheep, did not pursue the same policy with the other Apache tribes, which could easily have been brought in like manner to appreciate the advantages of quietude and order. These sheep made the Navajos practically self-supporting.

As the Navajo or Apache language is akin to that spoken by tribes in the Northwest, it is probable that they came from that direction. In fact, there is good reason to believe that some of our plains Indians came from a stock reaching America via Behring Straits. I knew an old guide, packer and miner, Chris Gilson, who told me that in 1890 or thereabouts he was employed by the Government to live with a tribe in Alaska and observe their habits. During the winter that he was with them, many of them crossed the ice to Asia in order to hunt deer!

The country was full of the remains of ancient houses. Along the Puerco River were a number of small hillocks, each hillock crowned by the stone foundation of a small house, the ground around being strewn with fragments of broken pottery. An old irrigation ditch could be followed along the top of the bluff which bordered the river. These were evidences of the earliest civilization when the natives lived in detached houses and irrigated their fields with river water.

The cliff dwellings, in my opinion, show where these primal cultivators of the soil fled when the savage Apaches arrived. They took to the rocks. Around Fort Wingate these cliff dwellings are numerous, and are evidently of much later date than the isolated houses. It would seem evident that the original natives on the arrival of the Apaches banded together for defense, constructing, so to speak, small castles backed up against the cliffs, where they could defend themselves more easily, and yet could look out for their tilled fields.

Later, it seems evident, they abandoned these cliff dwellings for the "pueblos." These are large edifices sheltering a whole village, the only entrance into the houses being by holes in their roofs. Having arrived at the roof, the ladder is drawn up and the people in their houses are secure.

In some pueblos, as at Pueblo Hopi and Acoma, the town, for further safety, is placed on top of a high rock, a single path leading to the top.

Fort Wingate was an overcrowded post, some of the lieutenants, for lack of quarters, being obliged to live in tents. In the 13th Infantry there had been great stagnation of promotion, so much so that I was the junior first-lieutenant in the post. Consequently I had some difficulty in obtaining quarters for my family. Even when we had settled down in a moderately desirable home we were in constant fear of its being taken from us. On one occasion a new officer having arrived, we thought it prudent to entertain him and his wife. Our would-be beguilement did not protect us, however, for after a few weeks our guests calmly informed us that they had taken a fancy to our house and would we please move elsewhere! So we packed up, bag and baggage, and I moved my little family to a less desirable set of quarters which happened to be vacant.

It was not long after this that I went out on a scout of several weeks' duration. Returning, I rode to my quarters and found it was *occupied by another family.* After considerable difficulty, I finally discovered where my family lived; and at the same time I discovered that I had offended a certain officer (who shall be nameless) and that this was his way of getting even with me!

All this gives a faint idea of one of the drawbacks of service. Congress in its wisdom enacted a law that quarters should be provided at posts as follows: for a second lieutenant, one room and a kitchen; for a first lieutenant, two rooms and kitchen, with an adidtional room for each grade. Of course, the lieutenant with a family would be out of luck if post commanders and bachelors did not help him out. So also in the more important posts the houses were built with "attic" rooms, which by a convention did not count as "rooms" but nevertheless served as such.

On May 10, 1882, we had an exciting but ludicrous experience. It was about midnight and I was sleeping soundly when suddenly Mrs. Parker shook me by the shoulder and cried, "Jim, there's an Indian in the room!"

I started up, half-asleep, my wits still wool gathering. Over the foot of the bed the light of the night lamp showed an Indian standing. I gave one jump, seized him by the throat and began to maul him about choking him. If I had had a weapon I would have killed him. He made little resistance but muttered feebly, "Agua! Agua!" (Water).

Suddenly my wife cried, "Jim, that's the smallpox Indian!" Then I remembered that a Navajo apparently suffering with smallpox had been driven away from the post that afternoon.

I dragged him to the door and shouted for the corporal of the guard, who took him in custody. Then I went for the doctor who made an examination of the man. Sure enough, it was the smallpox Indian. Returning home I was fumigated. That is, my nightclothes were cremated, while I stood in an atmosphere of burning sulphur until I cried for help.

Fortunately, no harm resulted, although while I was grappling with the Indian his face was in contact with mine. But our anxiety lasted during two weeks. I left the post the very next day after this occurrence for a scout of fifteen days, during which time I had no means of communication with my wife, and we were mutually in ignorance of each other's fate.

It was during this year we were visited by

General John Pope, and afterwards by General John A. Logan. They were very different personalities. Pope, a product of the regular army and of that self-sufficient body, the corps of engineers, composed supposedly of the intellectual élite of West Point (not always of its best fighters), was then the commander of the department of the Missouri, which included New Mexico within its boundaries. Not very tall but handsome, of fine presence, a man who had commanded great armies, to a subaltern he was a person to be approached with awe, which his manner of receiving subordinates did not lessen. All the same, as one looked at him, he could not help remembering Pope's bombastic order of 1862, dated, "Headquarters in the saddle," and Lee's rejoinder, "Pope has his headquarters where his hindquarters ought to be!"

What makes a general? Courage and common sense, I think, most of all. Granted, the advantages of military training, experience, reading; but in war the general of a division, a corps or an army of today must possess in a larger degree those two requisites, else he is a failure. He must not be like McClellan: an engineer with a factor of safety of 7 to 1.

I did not see much of Pope, who remained only a day or so. But I became very well acquainted with General Logan, who was a man of an altogether different type. Tall and angular, with high cheek bones, deep-set, piercing black eyes, coal-black hair and a great black mustache, Black Jack, as his soldiers called him, had a contour of face very like a Sioux Indian chief. They even said he had Indian blood in his veins.

Logan was a contemporary of Lincoln and, like

Lincoln, he was, before the war, one of the cleverest politicians and lawyers of Illinois. Politics helped to gain him his rank of General Officer, but he afterwards earned that rank by eminent service in battle and campaign. He was a fighter.

At the time that he visited Fort Wingate, he was a United States Senator, perhaps the most powerful and influential man in that body. He was accompanied by Mrs. Logan, then and always a masterful woman.

Logan's conversation was extraordinarily interesting. He was a product of those days when political passion ruled the country, and when the West was fast coming into its own as an arbiter in the Nation's destiny. But one of the most remarkable incidents that I remember about him was how on one occasion being at the trader's store, he took up a pack of cards and proceeded to deal at will to his three opponents and himself, in an imaginary game of poker, hands in which his own hand was always the superior! It was evident that in his early days he had learned the game from its most noted champions!

In May, 1883, I received orders from the War Department to make a topographical reconnoissance or exploration of the north and west portions of New Mexico. By June 18 we were about 90 miles from Wingate. On June 20 I reached Cañon Largo, an immense canyon running toward the northwest. Descending Cañon Largo I reached the San Juan River, a turbulent stream coming from the snow-clad mountains of Colorado. Crossing the Colorado line and marching up the La Plata River, I reached Fort Lewis, Colorado, June 24th.

Resting a few days at Lewis I resumed my march, passing near the southwest corner of Colorado where one can stand in four States—New Mexico, Arizona, Nevada and Colorado uniting at that point. On July 3rd I arrived at old Fort Defiance. The small cantonment, the houses built of adobe bricks, was surrounded by a stone wall for defense. A capital error, however, had been committed by putting the post near the base of a high mesa, from the top of which, it is said, the Indians in olden days often shot arrows into the post!

Old Professor Hank Kendrick, our most beloved instructor at West Point, whose subjects were chemistry and mineralogy, often used to give point to his remarks by citing his experiences at Fort Defiance in the year 1859. Kendrick was a noted wit and one of his toasts is still celebrated in New Mexico. Speaking at a dinner at Albuquerque, given to the officers of his expedition by one of the Armijos, the most distinguished family in New Mexico, old Hank said, "I propose a toast. Here's to the Army and Navy, the Armyjoes and the Navyjoes!"

On July 5, 1883, I arrived at Gallup, pretty well used up by the long desert march. I was pleased to receive later, on the subject of my map, a commendatory letter from the War Department.

In September, 1883, I took my family East where we spent a delightful four months at my home in Newark, New Jersey, and elsewhere. We returned in January. On June 2, 1884, at 1:30 a. m., I was summoned to the quarters of the Post Commander, Colonel Crofton, who informed me that in returning from Coolidge, New Mexico, a quarter of a mile away, two soldiers of the garrison had been ambushed by Indians, one, Blake, being killed, the other, von Moth, being slightly wounded. He desired me to go at once and "investigate."

I took but a few minutes to mount my troop and get on the road. The wounded soldier who accompanied us, informed me that they had been attacked by Marianna, a chief with whom they had had a quarrel and who had a camp not far from Coolidge.

I determined to surround the camp and capture Marianna. It was still dark, but nearing the camp I dismounted the troop, and with the assistance of Lieutenant Huse, who took charge of one of the platoons, we moved around it stealthily.

At the critical moment a carbine, in the hands of a recruit, was discharged. We rushed in but found the camp empty. The Indians had taken the alarm and had had time to get away. But they left behind much property, blankets, sheep and horses.

Dawn broke and the sun appeared. Looking down into the plain, I saw numerous bands of sheep, accompanied by their Indian herders. I resolved to seize the sheep as hostages, and demand the surrender of the murderer, Marianna.

Detachments sent out at a gallop had no difficulty in rounding up the sheep and the herders. The herders, however, were armed and hostile in demeanor. I placed them under charge of the soldiers. At a signal, "halt!" (arranged in advance), the soldiers wrested the guns from the Indians.

I then told the herders to go out and find

Marianna; that if they did not bring him back in three hours I would kill their sheep. I reported my action to Colonel Crofton at Fort Wingate and it was approved.

At the end of three hours the herders returned with tears in their eyes, reporting they could not find Marianna, but if I would give them more time they would.

I said, "Very well, I will take the sheep to the post." I then marched there, bringing 936 sheep, 11 horses, and a wagonload of guns, pistols, blankets and so forth. I found some of the infantry officers and ladies greatly excited—they said I was trying to stir up an Indian war. "No," I said, "I am trying to prevent one. I am showing these Indians they cannot afford to fight."

Some hours after I returned Colonel Crofton sent for me. He said he had received a telegram from the District Commander at Sante Fe disapproving my action and ordering that the sheep and property be returned at once to the Indians.

I reflected a bit and said, "Colonel Crofton, you will do me an immense favor if you will postpone carrying out this order until tomorrow morning. I am convinced that by that time the murderer will be given up."

To my great relief he agreed to this proposition. Equally to my relief, Marianna was surrendered and placed in the guardhouse that night.

To me it was a complete demonstration that the way to make Indians peaceable is to make them proprietors, not of beef cattle, as was tried with Comanches and others, but of sheep. Cattle can be driven off in raids, but a tribe possessing sheep will not go to war for fear the sheep will be killed or lost. Cattle on account of their size are to an Indian only an occasional source of food; sheep provide them constantly with meat and with clothing.

The disorder which has reigned for a long time in Mexico, and which bids fair to last indefinitely, is due to the fact that the Mexican Indian possesses nothing, and therefore can lose nothing by war. Would sheep solve his problem?

In May, 1884, we received news that the regiment was to be ordered from New Mexico to Arizona. The information was a great shock to me, for it was accompanied by a proposed schedule by which my troop would march to Fort Apache, Arizona, and there by a devious route over mountain and deserts, to Fort McDowell in the western part of Arizona, a trip of fully 700 miles, in which my wife and babies would be forced to accompany the troop. She was not in the best of health and I was consequently at my wit's end seeking for an alternative. Finally I thought of my friend, General Logan, and telegraphed him, saying I would prefer to go to Fort Apache and giving my reasons.

A curious thing happened. When he received the telegram Logan was on the floor of the Senate arguing against the Fitzjohn Porter bill, which was a demand on the part of General Fitzjohn Porter for a review of the action against him by General Pope in the Civil War. General Pope was in the gallery. Logan took my telegram and scrawled on the back, "General Pope, I would be glad if this could be done." Pope scrawled below, "General Logan, I have instructed my adjutant general to revise the order as Lieutenant Parker desires." Logan put the telegram in an envelope and sent it to me.

I was appalled at what I had done. I never dared tell my friends about it. It did not comply with my ideals or the ethics of the profession. But my wife and children were saved from the ordeal and I was satisfied.

Our troops left for Fort Apache June 11th, cheered by our friends of the 13th Infantry. The distance was 165 miles over a fair road. We had few incidents. At Nutria Hill, fourteen miles out, my private wagon, loaded with an assortment of little pigs, hound pups and chickens, upset, broke the cages in which they were confined and made a merry rout, much enjoyed by the pups. My family traveled in an ambulance and lodged at night in tents which, in the rain, leaked somewhat to the consternation of my wife. But we arrived in good health.

VII

THE GERONIMO OUTBREAK

One June 19, 1884 our command, Troops "A" and "K," 4th Cavalry, arrived at Fort Apache, Arizona. The post, built partly of light frame buildings, partly of log houses, lay in a picturesque situation between a canyon in which flowed the White Mountain River, and some high timbered hills. The garrison after we arrived and had added our force to it consisted of a company of the 1st Infantry under Captain (later General) Wm. B. Dougherty; one troop of the 3rd Cavalry, Captain Morton commanding, and two troops of the 4th Cavalry, one commanded by Captain Allen Smith, the other by myself. There was also a company of Apache Indian Scouts, commanded by Lieutenant C. A. Gatewood, 6th Cavalry. The complete garrison was commanded by Major Collins, 1st Infantry, a Civil War veteran. Near by was Geronimo, in his camp on the Bonito.

The behavior of the Indians there was very far from that of a beaten enemy. Armed to the teeth, they were haughty and surly in demeanor. By order of General Crook everything was done to ingratiate them. They had from the army a special ration of one pound of beef and one pound of flour per day for each man, woman and child, even though the child was at the breast. That they received it I know, for when the great outbreak occurred I had been commissary officer for months and personally issued the food. They received a large amount of money for the wild grass they cut and cured for hay; also for barley which they cultivated in the creek bottoms. They also received supplies from the Government, like other Indians.

At Fort Apache during the first year of our stay conditions were peaceful enough. Having a substantial government ration, together with fruits and berries from the woods, and what they obtained from barter at the traders' stores, the Indian bucks spent their time in loafing, while the women were busy performing their "household" duties. One rarely saw an Indian hunting. In the haying season, however, the Indians, or rather the squaws (for the women performed all the work) at the gathering of the crop presented a picturesque scene. The hay yard was filled with squaws, papooses and donkeys, each donkey loaded down with hay. The bundle of hay was taken off the donkey, weighed, and a penciled receipt given the squaw; this she took direct to the trader's store receiving in exchange goods, credit or money. At the end of the week the post trader turned over the receipts to the quartermaster, who paid the total amount by check, making out at the same time a receipt for the sum, which was signed by the chief of the Indian tribe. This was a very irregular method of accounting, but was the best that could be done under the circumstances. The full amount of hay paid for was secured by it.

Sometimes the squaw would produce two bundles of hay, one very small, and with cries and gestures demand two receipts, one for the small bundle of "Mi papoose!"

Our quartermaster at Fort Apache in 1884 was First Lieutenant George A. Dodd, 3rd Cavalry, my classmate, and always an original and interesting character. He lived next door to Mrs. Parker and me and we were very intimate with his charming family. During the worst part of the winter of 1885 he was suddenly ordered to Fort Thomas, Arizona, a long march over the mountains through a desert country, traversing a road, or rather trail, impassable for vehicles. On the trip Dodd and his wife rode horseback, while his two children, warmly wrapped up, and securely tied in, sat in boxes lashed to the sides of a mule. It was in this primitive fashion that they "changed station." Dodd was a fine soldier, of few words, imperative in his manner, extremely zealous, brave, not afraid of responsibility. In 1895 he had the best trained troop of cavalry in the army and his exhibition attracted great crowds at the yearly horse show in Madison Square Garden, New York City. In 1899 I served with him in General Young's command during the pursuit of Aguinaldo and the subsequent operations on the west coast of the Philippines, where, for gallantry in action, he received three brevets. In 1916 during Pershing's pursuit of Villa in Mexico, Dodd, being then sixty-two years old, won a reputation for extraordinary energy and gallantry, which resulted in his immediate promotion to the grade of brigadier general.

The winter of 1884-85 was extremely cold, with deep snows. In the spring the Chiricahua Apaches encamped in the valley of White Mountain Creek, just above the post, were hard at work under Lieutenant Britton Davis planting and tilling fields of barley and corn, in order to learn self-support, and make their life more comfortable. We heard that Lieutenant Davis had raised a body of Chiricahua Indian Scouts, as such sworn to defend the flag, who received the pay and allowances of regular soldiers. A guardhouse had been established in which drunkards and other offenders were confined. On the whole the Chiricahuas seemed well fed, well clothed and contented.

Geronimo we saw constantly; he was friendly and good natured. I particularly remember one day when we were out hunting how he laughed at Dr. Fisher, the post surgeon, when Fisher, wanting to light a cigarette, picked up two pieces of wood, and asked Geronimo how to produce a light by rubbing the pieces together. Geronimo, when he came to understand what Fisher was driving at, fell into paroxysms of laughter at the thought that a white man could hope to produce fire with two damp twigs.

But early in May news came that Geronimo and a party of Indians had against orders gone out near Turkey Creek and were having a "tiswin" drunk. (Tiswin is made of the root of the maguey plant, baked and then fermented.) On May 17 at sunset came the news that he had gone on the warpath and had started for Mexico.

Geronimo's band consisted of forty-two men with ninety-six women and children. It was said that after getting the men very drunk he had spread the report that there had been a mutiny in the main camp, that Lieutenant Davis had been killed, and that the troops were about to attack and punish them. But many of the bucks went simply because they were tired of an unexciting peace; they went on a murder orgy, as some men deliberately go on a drunken spree.

We started in pursuit. At 7 o'clock that evening we were on the road, Troops A and K, 4th Cavalry, eighty men, and a party of White Mountain Scouts, perhaps thirty, under Lieutenant Gatewood. As transportation we had a pack train laden with fifteen days' rations. We traveled light, without tents and with the merest necessities.

It soon grew dark and over the uncertain trail we moved slowly. At one place we came to, the Indians had cut the telegraph which connected the post with

Department Headquarters. Near by the forest had been set on fire.

It was dark as pitch when we arrived at Bonito Cañon. Descending in the darkness many men and horses lost the trail and some plunged down precipitous slopes with injury to horse and rider. The ascent was nearly as difficult. To reassemble the command on the other side of the canyon took over an hour. Fire were lighted and the men finally got together. One man had his leg broken, and some horses had to be abandoned.

The officers with the column were Captains Allen Smith, commanding; with Troop A, 4th Cavalry: Lieutenant James Lockett; with Troop B, 4th Cavalry: Lieutenants Parker (4th Cavalry) and Finley (10th Cavalry); with the Indian Scouts: Lieutenant C. B. Gatewood, 6th Cavalry. Lieutenant Britton Davis accompanied us during the first twenty-four hours' pursuit.

Some miles beyond Bonito Cañon the command was halted, the scouts having brought word that the Indians were at the crossing of the Black River, a short distance ahead. It was thought by Lieutenants Davis and Gatewood that it would be better to approach this crossing in the early dawn. There was some delay in starting again, however, and when we reached the crossing of the Black River it was broad daylight. The scouts reported the hostiles were fleeing across the Prieto Plateau, a plain some fourteen miles long and that they were six miles ahead. Here we found some of our horses had to be left, being in terrible shape; their shoes had come off during the night and their unprotected feet, worn down by the malpais lava rock, were bleeding badly.

The scouts were in wild excitement. "Come on!" they cried. "Hurry! Hurry!" It was evident that by a supreme effort we would be able to overtake the hostiles before they reached the end of the plateau and disappeared in the rocks. My troop being at the head of the column I took up the trot, when I was ordered by Captain Smith to desist and come down to a walk. At a walk then we continued our march. I was greatly exasperated. When at the end of the fourteen miles, plodding across the plain we came to the end of the plateau where it borders on the deep and broad valley of Eagle Creek, the scouts pointed out, and we could see with our glasses, the hostiles eight or ten miles away leaving Eagle Creek and ascending the slopes of the high mountains on the farther side.

We marched down to Eagle Creek and at 2 p.m. encamped near Straus' ranch. We had gone sixty-five miles. The pack train did not reach camp until 9 o'clock that night.

It was at this camp that, hearing of some killings by the Indians, I exclaimed bitterly to Captain Smith, "The rest of your trip will be a funeral march, burying dead bodies!"

The next day, May 19, the trail led us through the mountains, ascending one peak after another, climbing up a mountain and down the other side, only to pass in the same way over the next mountain. The trail moreover often led through the roughest rocks where only a man on foot could climb. Riding was impossible, our horses could be led over the rocks with the greatest difficulty. It is not remarkable that marching all day on foot we made only twenty-five miles. This trail was made by the bucks; the women and children had scattered to meet farther on. We camped near Blue Creek.

May 20 we marched twenty-five miles. After we had crossed Blue Creek and gone eight miles through the mountains, we came to a dead man lying on the trail. A short distance away was his dead horse. From letters in his pockets we found that the man was a former soldier of the 6th Cavalry named Lutter; he had evidently ridden to Clinton, the nearest town to get his mail; coming home belatedly he lay down to sleep, first tying his horse to a tree. When the Indians shot him his horse broke away, whereupon the Indians shot the horse also.

Four miles farther on we came to the Lutter ranch, a single log house. It presented a picture of devastation, everything being thrown out of doors, the ground being strewn with broken furniture and scattered papers. About the ranch were a number of dead cows and calves; our scouts said they had been stabbed with lances by the Indian women and children. The attention of our soldiers was attracted by the howling of a dog on a hill near by. They went there and found the body of a man, Lutter's brother, shot through the heart. He had evidently in the early dawn gone to this hill and was looking down the trail for his brother; an Indian crept up close behind him, took deadly aim, shouted and, as Lutter turned, struck dumb with terror at the sight of the enemy, his executioner slowly pulled the trigger.

Eight miles farther on, this trail crossed a little creek, and there by a spring, in among the rocks, lay another dead man. He was evidently a miner or prospector, for his tools lay around him; he had been asleep when the Indians shot him through the heart. He was evidently a former friend of the Indians, or they may have had some superstition about the killing, for they carefully folded up his bedding and laid it on top of the body. On top of the blankets, which were new, was a brand-new pair of shoes.

Four miles farther we found the body of a dead man dressed in a red shirt. He had evidently discovered the Indians and was shot while running away; on his face was an expression of horror.

All these men we buried and we became very expert in the business. There was no opportunity to dig graves, but there were plenty of loose rocks and so at the command "dismount," "bury this man," the horses were left with the horse holders and each dismounted man, picking up a heavy stone, placed it on the corpse until it was hidden from sight. Then we mounted and marched on.

May 21 a march of ten miles brought us to the San Francisco River, on which there were numerous settlements, including the Alma Ranch. Many of the people living along this river, being so far from the reservation, had never seen an Indian in their lives. We found them in a state of terror almost amounting to collapse. Husbands, mothers, sons had been killed, but by an invisible enemy who left no sign except an occasional moccasin track under their windows. It seemed as if the spirit of the evil one was abroad. Families huddled together; women feared to close their eyes in sleep for fear that while they slept they would be murdered.

This day we marched twenty-two miles, following the trail of the hostiles as it passed north up the San Francisco River. Some miles north of Alma we found and buried the bodies of two men. They were two of a party of four men with pack mules; two stopped at the base of a hill to adjust a mule's pack, then started on and when they reached the top of the hill they found there the bodies of their companions, just slaughtered.

May 22nd we marched up San Francisco River, then, turning east, ascended a long slope into the Mogollon Mountains, a wooded and broken territory. By this time, disgusted apparently at our slowness, most of our Indian scouts had deserted us, leaving only five who were now with us. Instead of scouting well in advance, they remained close to the head of the column, fearful of ambush.

Having marched about twelve miles we came to the canyon of Devil's River, running in a southern direction, into which we descended by a long, steep and circuitous route. Arrived at the bottom, where we were shut in at the foot of steep slopes 600 feet high, in a little valley not forty feet wide, I was amazed to hear Captain Smith give orders for going into camp. The situation invited attack. Unsaddling, the men led the herds of horses a short distance up the slope, where retaining their foothold with great difficulty the horses attempted to graze. I sent one of my herd guard to the top of the mountain as a lookout or outpost. I found out afterwards he went only half-way up. Captain Smith announced that he and Lieutenant Lockett would go down the creek to bathe. He also said that the five Indian scouts, when they had finished their dinner, which would be in about half an hour, would ascend the mountain to act as videttes beyond the camp.

It was perhaps thirty minutes or more later while Gatewood, Leighton Finley and I were having a quiet talk together, Captain Smith and Lieutenant Lockett being absent bathing, that the hostiles suddenly attacked the camp. I can give no better description than the one given by Leighton Finley in a letter written me September 7, 1885, and afterwards forwarded to the War Department.

"You, Lieutenant Gatewood and myself were seated under a tree on the easterly bank of the creek. All of the enlisted men, except those of the pack train, were in camp on the west bank of the creek. Troop K nearest to us and Troop A lower down. I do not believe the canyon was fifty feet wide. You, Lieutenant Gatewood and I got on our feet at the first shot, and the quick subsequent firing immediately indicated what was up. Sergeant Warren of Troop K called to the men, 'Get to the herd.' (*I think the sergeant's idea was to get the horses and get out of there. J.P.*) I heard you say 'Never mind the herd, get your guns!' I repeated that order, and when I looked around, not three seconds later I saw you with your four or five men starting up the easterly hill. I called to the rest of the men, 'Come on!' and ran after you. The first line which reached the top of the hill consisted of about seventeen men all told, officers and enlisted men; most of the enlisted men being of Troop K, Sergeant Atkinson and Private Meyers being the only men I noticed of Troop A, although perhaps there were others of that troop. (*Note: We were greatly exasperated during the charge by having some men of Troop A, down in the bottom of the canyon, firing through our ranks at the enemy. J. P.*) You took us up by rushes, taking advantage of various ledges of rock to rest us. The hill was particularly steep and I cannot believe it was less than 500 feet high.

"Lieutenant Gatewood came up the hill immediately behind this first line. When we got about half way up, as I remember, we met the herd being driven down; the members of the herd guard doing their duty splendidly. After we passed the herd some little distance, we met the Indian scouts running down. I heard Lieutenant Gatewood shout to them and rally them, and he brought them up to the summit immediately after we arrived there.

"The hostiles continued their fire until we were nearly to the top. On reaching the summit (*Note: At the summit was a high perpendicular wall of rock; we rested a moment under its shelter and then*

I called out to Finley, and ran up a fissure in the rock followed by Leighton. J. P.) we discovered that the hostiles had run from the crest, scattering in every direction. In a few minutes some of the men pushed forward and discovered the hostile camp on the plateau, about 500 yards from the summit. Seventeen fires were still either burning or filled with live or hot coals. The hostiles left behind them in their haste several articles of clothing and equipment and a lot of beef. (*Note: They had butchered a number of cattle and had been engaged in drying or jerking the meat. J. P.*) One of the scouts captured a pony saddle and bridle. Between five and ten minutes, as I remember, after we reached the summit, Lieutenant Lockett got up and about five minutes later Captain Smith arrived. (*Note: Captain Smith's costume was not exactly warlike; he was attired in drawers and top boots! J. P.*) I heard Captain Smith say to you, 'Parker I am very much obliged to you, or words of identical effect, shaking hands with you as he spoke."

My reply was, "That's all very well, Captain Smith, but we should push on and pursue the hostiles at once." To which Captain Smith replied agitatedly, "Certainly, certainly. You hold the heights up here with your troop, and I will have your horses saddled at once, and rejoin you with the command, bringing your horses up here." He then disappeared. Throwing out outposts I remained on the heights, waiting vainly for his coming. At last about 6 P. M. he sent me word that he had postponed the pursuit until the next morning; that I would guard the heights during the night. The next morning I went down to camp when I was informed by Captain Smith that he had concluded not to follow the hostile trail; that he had only six days' rations left, and he was told by Lieutenant Gatewood that the trail led into a wild country where he would be likely to run out of food before he could get back; that he must send to Fort Bayard for rations before proceeding farther. I was indignant. I said, "Captain Smith, at least make a show of pursuing before you go back, otherwise they will say that you got licked here." "All right," he said, "I will." Mounting we followed the trail over a level plateau for about four miles when we took the back track, camping at Alma after a twenty-mile march.

About this fight Lieutenant Finley in the above letter further says: "If you will permit me to say so, I would like to state that in my humble opinion, you saved the command from probable grave disaster. The command was taken utterly by surprise. The canyon, as I have said, was hardly more than fifty feet wide; the surrounding hills were hardly less than 500 feet high. The hostiles were admirably posted. The easterly hill which we charged made a slight turn towards the southwest. The crest of the hill including the slight turn was fortified by stone rifle pits in which hostiles were posted. The eastern boundary of the canyon was continued northerly by another equally high hill which made a decided turn northwesterly. This crest was also fortified and posted with hostiles. (*Note: Thus the hostiles were not only firing into the canyon from the east side but they were firing up the canyon from the south and down the canyon from the north. Add to this the fire from the west side and it is evident there was no possible cover. To attempt to take cover and return the fire would have meant disaster. J. P.*) On the westerly side across the canyon we got the fire of perhaps two or three hostiles. It was a case of being almost 'all surrounded' in a very bad fix. In my judgment if you had not done what you did do, or if you had hesitated a moment, it is

Horace Jones, Indian Interpreter. Fort Sill, I. T.

not pleasant to contemplate what might have happened.

"I trust you will permit me to add that I cannot believe that men could possibly act better than did the enlisted men of our first line, and to commend particularly from my personal observation Private Lawler and Corporal Pearson of K Troop and Sergeant Atkinson of Troop A, 4th U. S. Cavalry.

"Very respectfully your obedient servant,
"Leighton Finley,
"First Lieutenant, 10th U. S. Cavalry."

Attached to the official letter is the following statement from Gatewood:

"Fort Apache, Ariz., Sept. 7, 1885.

"The foregoing statement of Lieutenant Finley is correct as far as my remembrance goes. He has narrated minutely the circumstances and occurrences during the fight with the hostiles. I was present and had command of a few scouts. Lieutenant Parker aided by Lieutenant Finley made the fight. To the best of my recollection Captain Smith appeared after the firing had ceased and the fight was over and had nothing whatever to do with the fight.

"Chas. B. Gatewood, First Lieutenant, 6th Cav."

The following is what Captain Allen Smith, in his official report to General Crook, dated June 15, 1885, has to say about the fight:

"On the 22nd, started on the trail and marched fifteen miles over a very rough trail; the Indians were making through the Mogollon Mountains. As no one with me knew anything about the country we were in, and as this was the first water we had found since leaving camp, I determined to go into camp. The creek was between two mountains about 600 feet high and very steep. About an hour after going into camp I sent some scouts up the mountain on the south side to look up the trail. When they got near the top they were fired on by the Chiricahuas. The scouts came down on the run, but rallied and went up the hill with the men who immediately charged up. The Indians had selected a good point to receive us but we got to the top so well and so rapidly under the circumstances that they broke and ran before we got to the top. About 600 yards farther we found their main camp. I believe this was the first camp they made from the time they left Turkey Creek. In the camp we got a large quantity of meat, drying, a saddle horse and two other horses. There were nineteen fires in this camp. The fight lasted half an hour and the Indians fired very rapidly and a great many shots. Two men, Private Haag, Troop A, shot in right thigh and Private Williams, Troop K, slightly wounded in the arm, and one scout shot quite badly; one horse killed and one wounded belonging to Troop A, were the casualties on our side. From the indications, blood near the rifle pits, etc., I am of the opinion we wounded some of the Indians. The officers (Lieutenants Parker, Gatewood, Lockett and Finley, 10th Cavalry), men and scouts all behaved remarkably well. Lieutenant Parker who was closest to the point of attack was the first officer on top of the mountain."

It is noticeable that in this extract from Captain Smith's report which was furnished me by department headquarters, he says nothing about being absent from the camp at the beginning of the fight, bathing, and leaves it to be inferred that he commanded during the fight and accompanied the men and officers who charged up the hill.

Discussing the dispositions of the Indians in this

fight it is very evident what their intentions were. Since their outbreak at Fort Apache, May 17, they had made in two or perhaps three days a march of 140 miles through a mountainous country; having few pack animals; men, women and often children, during the hurried flight, running along on foot. In no place did they stop to camp or even to make fires or cook. Arrived at their stronghold, on Devil's Creek in the Mogollon Mountains, they established a camp and raided the country for beef which the squaws were busily engaged in drying. In the meantime the men worked at fortifying the ground they had selected for the ambush. This was an ancient stronghold of the Apaches. That they were perfectly certain that they would cause a disastrous repulse to the troops is evident from the fact that the camp with their squaws and children was so near.

In their belief the troops, who they had ascertained were preceded by the five scouts at a distance of only a few feet with no advance guard, would come down the trail into the canyon in single file leading their horses. They did not imagine a commander could be so rash as to camp at the bottom of the hole without posting the heights; they expected that the column, with a view to camping on the plateau beyond would cross the creek and climb up the winding trail leading to the heights, the high ground beyond, in order to camp there.

This was their opportunity. The column of about 100 horses and men in single file, stretching a distance of almost a quarter of a mile, painfully climbing the ascent, would be played on by a frontal cross and rear fire. Cover there was none, the men hampered by their horses and separated from their officers would not be in a position to return the fire, and panic was inevitable.

If, however, the troops camped on the creek and were then fired upon, they expected the men individually to attempt to take cover behind trees and rocks in order to return their fire. This also would have been disastrous to the troops, as the Indians were shooting at them from every direction and no cover was possible.

Our instant advance on the enemy prevented the soldiers from taking cover, from which later it would have been difficult to dislodge them and lead them forward. It is, I believe, when ambushed, always the safest course to attack. The enemy's belief in his secure position fades, he loses morale, he is in turn surprised. This has always been my opinion, and later, during the expedition of my column into Mexico, strict written orders were issued to that effect.

The immediate counter-attack that I made had another beneficial effect. The hostiles were divided into four different parties widely separated. My attack was made on one of these, which was consequently outnumbered. Also this party being in their rifle pits on the crest, while they could see a portion of the valley, could not always command the slopes over which I was ascending. I was fired at by the other parties but at long range and ineffectively. The Indians are not good shots at long distances. The successive outcroppings of rock at times also sheltered me from the party I was attacking. My arrival near the top must have been in the nature of a surprise to them. This is shown by the fact that we captured one of the horses, saddled and bridled, belonging to this party, which they abandoned in their hurry to escape.

Captain Smith's excuse for not continuing the pursuit seemed to me utterly indefensible. We had rations for six days. We could have pursued for three days and then had time to get back to the settlements before the food supplies were exhausted. And it is probable that in that time we could have driven the Indians out of the mountains.

The plans for the ambush of the troops were a credit to the intelligence and warlike instinct of Geronimo and of Natchez, the leading chief under him.

In 1928 I received the War Department silver star citation for "gallantry in action" at Devil's Creek.

On May 24 our command marched back to Alma twenty miles and, marching south on the 26th, encamped on the Gila River, twenty-three miles. Here we came across three troops of the 10th Cavalry, Captain Lee, Lieutenants Beck and Watson. They had received news of Indian depredations on the Gila River and when we met them were proceeding to the place at a gallop, full of ardor, in striking contrast with our leisurely march.

There I received orders from Captain Smith to proceed with the pack train to Fort Bayard for rations. Starting at once I arrived there the next day after a toilsome march of forty miles. Here I met General Bradley, formerly of Fort Wingate, now commanding the district of New Mexico. Also Captain Wm. H. Carter, 6th Cavalry, post quartermaster, later major general. Most of the 6th Cavalry officers stationed at Fort Bayard were absent in the field in pursuit of Geronimo's band.

On May 26 I was at work all the forenoon drawing rations and loading the pack mules. Starting in the afternoon we marched twenty-eight miles, arriving at Mangus Spring late at night.

At 11 P. M. we had scarcely taken the packs off the mules, when two troops of the 6th Cavalry came along. They were commanded by Captain Adam Kramer, an old soldier of German birth who had risen from the ranks. He informed me in a testy manner that he was in pursuit of the hostiles, and preëmptorily ordered me to pack up at once and follow him. I protested that I belonged to another command, that the supplies were for Captain Smith's troops which were greatly in need of them. He would not listen to my expostulations and departed, leaving a detachment of the 6th Cavalry to see that I obeyed his orders. Concluding that it was a matter of life and death and being not averse to seeing some fighting, I obeyed him and at 12 midnight was on the march southward towards the Burro Mountains where the hostiles were said to have been located.

I marched all that day following the 6th Cavalry, which skirmished through the hills in a country bare of trees, with a scrubby growth. There were numerous wild dashes of the cavalry caused by false reports of Indians, and on one occasion the troops had an encounter, fortunately bloodless, with a party of citizens from Lordsburg, out to fight the savages. The whole affair was rather ludicrous. I had had no sleep for over thirty-six hours, and my poor mules had traveled 117 miles in three days. We camped at a place named Malone's Mine.

Finding the next day a telegraph station at Malone's I telegraphed to General Bradley, the district commander, that I was being arbitrarily detained and as a result Captain Kramer on May 29 gave me orders to rejoin my proper command which I reached after a march of sixty-two miles on May 31st.

I found the command still on the Gila River, where it had been retained by General Crook's orders, awaiting the result of the operations of a force of Chiricahua scouts, commanded by Lieutenant Britton Davis, which in the meantime had arrived from Fort Apache. It was said that the hostiles were in the mountains to the north of us, and that Lieutenant Davis with the scouts was endeavoring to "surround" them. Later I heard that the scouts were in communication with the hostiles endeavoring to persuade them to return to the reservation, which I think is more likely. I knew Davis at the time was rather disgusted with the order he had received, and I know that Crook's policy at that time was diplomacy rather than war. It was rumored that Crook had sent secret orders to Chatto, the chief of the scouts, at variance with the orders he had given Britton Davis, whereby Chatto was to treat with the hostiles for their return to Fort Apache.

Whatever may have been the policy it did not succeed, for on the night of June 2 the hostiles escaped from the mountains and fled south towards Mexico, scattering death and destruction in their path. This was not known to Captain Smith's command until June 5, which fact does not say much for the efficiency or the loyalty of Davis' Chiricahua scouts.

Before the news came I had started for Fort Bayard, having been ordered to return to Fort Apache to resume my duties as quartermaster and commissary and having been relieved of the command of Troop K by its proper captain, Captain Joseph H. Dorst, late adjutant 4th Cavalry. Performing these duties I remained at Fort Apache until January, 1886, when I reported at Fort Huachuca, I. T., as regimental adjutant.

VIII

THE GERONIMO CAMPAIGN

At Fort Huachuca the regiment and post were commanded by Colonel William B. Royall, an officer of a rather uncertain disposition on which I will not now dilate. The other officers stationed at the post were Lieutenant Colonel Alexander Forsyth; Captains Wirt Davis, H. W. Lawton, A. E. Wood, C. A. P. Hatfield, Jack Martin; Lieutenants Patch, Wheeler, Walsh, Benson, R. A. Brown, A. L. Smith, J. B. Erwin, Guy Huse; and Post Surgeons Paul R. Brown and Leonard Wood.

Wood was then a contract surgeon awaiting his commission as First Lieutenant Medical Corps. He told me at the time that he had entered the medical corps in hopes of transferring to the line. In this he eventually succeeded, as we all know.

Besides being adjutant of the regiment, I performed the duties of acting adjutant general of the Fort Huachuca district in the campaign then going on. All of the troops belonging to the post, except the band, were in outlying camps.

Captain Lawton with Troop B, a detachment of infantry, and a large body of Indian scouts, generously provided with wagons, pack mules, supplies and funds, with orders to proceed into Mexico, and hunt down Geronimo, had left the post May 10th. He was accompanied by Lieutenants Finley, Benson, R. A. Brown, A. L. Smith, Richards and Clay, and by Dr. Paul A. Brown. Dr. Brown soon fell sick and was replaced by Dr. Leonard Wood.

About the beginning of June General Nelson A. Miles, the new department commander, made a visit to Fort Huachuca. On his arrival he told Colonel Royall, the regimental commander, that he wanted the next morning to climb up the mountains to get a view of the country; I was detailed to guide and escort him.

We started, mounted, at 9 A. M. Leaving the post I pointed to a long incline leading to a high peak in the west and proposed we go up that. "Pshaw! That is not the highest mountain; let us go up this one," said Miles, pointing to El Moro (Nigger Head), which towered above us.

Up El Moro we rode until the mountainside was so steep our horses almost fell backwards. Then dismounting we neared the top. Here we found an outcropping of black rock (the head) over fifty feet high. To scale it I at first thought impossible, but I found a crevice, climbed half way up, with great difficulty, and called to the General to come that way. I laughed to myself for I never thought at his age and with his bulk he could accomplish it. I was amazed when he came puffing up to the top and still more amazed when he looked around the horizon and said, "There's a mountain higher than this; we'll go over there!"

While we rested General Miles began talking about the system of heliograph lines he intended to establish. He would put detachments with heliographs on the highest mountains, thirty or forty miles apart, and thus cover the territory with a network of stations. If hostile Indians appeared on the plain they would be seen from the stations and their position heliographed to the troops in the posts and camps.

I pointed out how difficult or impossible it would be to see parties of Indians on the plains from the lofty heights, but General Miles adhered to his idea. In actual practice, however, when the heliograph stations were established, they were placed on low foothills so as to be easily reached and to be near water. Arranged in this way the system was a success, though it would have fared hard with the isolated detachments quartered in tents and without protection from bullets had they been attacked by the Indians. But Miles' luck stood by him and after the system had been established it happened there were no raids made north of the Mexican line.

I have never been slow at suggestions and I took this opportunity to ask General Miles if I could make one.

"I have recently come from Fort Apache where the Chiricahuas not with Geronimo are located," I said. "Whenever there is news of a raid, the Chiricahuas, in order not to become involved in the fighting, go into the post and are quartered in the quartermaster corral. I would suggest that a false report of a raid be spread. When the Indians are in the corral, surround them with troops, disarm them, take them to the railroad and ship them east as prisoners of war. Geronimo's band in the field will then be isolated, will no longer receive aid and comfort, as heretofore, and will surrender."

"Why, that would be treachery!" exclaimed the General. "I could never do that."

"Treachery or not," I replied, "it will end the war and save the lives of hundreds of innocent citizens."

The General appeared to regard the proposition with disfavor. Nevertheless in a few weeks the Chiricahuas at Fort Apache, being assembled to receive rations, were surrounded by troops, disarmed and sent by railroad to Florida. This was in July or August. In September Miles, in his negotiations with Geronimo, used this fact to bring about the surrender.

Descending from El Moro we climbed another mountain, and at the end of that day we had ascended five peaks. This gives an idea of Miles' physical energy.

In June, 1886, I resigned the adjutancy of the 4th Cavalry and asked to be sent to a troop. Accordingly, I was assigned to "H" troop, 4th Cavalry, at Cloverdale, Arizona, which I reached four days later after a march of over a hundred miles. I had two men with me. At Cloverdale, an abandoned ranch, I found Lieutenant Abiel L. Smith, whom I relieved of the command of "H" troop. Also at the camp was a company of the 8th Infantry, Captain John F. Stretch, First Lieutenant James Pettit and Second Lieutenant R. L. Bullard.

Thirty-six hours after I got there, there arrived at the camp two Americans, Anderson and Jones, fine-looking frontiersmen. It appeared that their profession was smuggling, carrying tobacco and other wares into Mexico. They informed us that they had picked up a trail of hostiles in Guadalupe Cañon.

I hastened to mount my troop and start in pursuit. Anderson and Jones led me to a point in Guadalupe Cañon where the Indians had killed a cow and had camped for several days. It was apparent that they had been there when I passed two days before. Hidden among some rocks they had not seen me, or it would have fared hard with my party.

The trail led north, passing over the crests of the mountains. Being obliged, on account of the roughness of the trail, to dismount often and lead our horses, we made only twenty miles that day.

The day following we made thirty miles.

We made seventy-seven miles in the next three days, through appallingly rough country. Near Cajon Bonito, a remarkable and beautiful canyon descending into Mexico, the trail was finally obliterated by a heavy downpour of rain.

July 2nd we returned to Cloverdale when I forwarded my report of the scout to the district commander, Colonel Beaumont, at Fort Bowie. The substance of this report having been telegraphed to General Miles, at Albuquerque, he at once ordered that I proceed into Mexico with a command "on the trail of the hostiles."

The treaty with Mexico providing for crossing the boundary says, "It is agreed that the regular Federal troops of the two republics may reciprocally cross the boundary line when they are in close pursuit of a band of savage Indians. The pursuing force shall return to its own country as soon as it has fought the Indians or lost the trail." While the conditions in my case were not exactly those mentioned in the treaty it was evident to me that General Miles, a man of resources, thought he could stretch them to justify my expedition. Only a First Lieutenant, I felt flattered at being selected for the command.

After some delay due to the late arrival of pack mules and of scouts, I started for Mexico July 24, 1880. The expedition consisted of thirty cavalrymen, twelve infantrymen, eleven packers, forty pack mules, two wagons with teamsters, Interpreter Montoya, and the scouts: Hank Frost and fifteen Yaqui Indians. The officers with me (and a more congenial, efficient lot I never saw) were First Lieutenant W. B. Banister, surgeon, Second Lieutenant W. T. Richardson, 8th Infantry, in charge of the cavalry, and Second Lieutenant R. L. Bullard, 10th Infantry, quartermaster and commissary. Bullard became in the World War a lieutenant general. Richardson, for long years on duty in Alaska, as commissioner of public roads, later as brigadier general, commanded our forces at Murmansk and Archangel, Russia.

My orders were to "take up the trail of six hostiles you were pursuing, follow it into old Mexico and try to intercept or overtake, destroy or capture them." Of course it was understood that in attempting this I might have to fight the main body of the hostiles. I carried forty days' rations. I was further ordered to communicate, if practicable, with Captain Lawton, whose expedition was still in Mexico, in which case, the order stated, we might "be of mutual assistance."

The only flaw in the program, and it was a serious one, was that my scouts were very inferior. Instead of furnishing me with Indian scouts, I was given a body of Yaquis under Hank Frost. This individual was a tall, lank American from Calabesas, a loud-mouthed, boastful ruffian, who in some way had impressed himself on General Miles. The Yaqui Indians he had with him differed little from the ordinary sedentary Mexican peon, and most of them had worked under Hank Frost, as I afterwards discovered, as adobe makers. Far from knowing the country, they were continually getting lost, and so far as following a hostile trail, not only were they incapable of doing so, but if they found one they were probably not anxious to follow it or even to report it. In the language of the army, "They had not lost any Indians."

The two wagons were to carry rations and forage by the wagon road to Carretas, Mexico, eighty miles distant, and then return to Cloverdale. Sending Lieutenants Bullard and Bannister in charge of the wagons by the main road, I marched south by the direct trail, scouting the country east and west for signs of Indians. On the fifth day I reached Carretas Ranch, where I found Lieutenants Bullard and Bannister, with the wagons, under surveillance by Mexican *Guardias Rurales* or rural guards (revenue officers) who considered their presence suspicious. The country we had traversed was a high plateau, with numerous isolated, volcano-like mountains and deep canyons. On our way we passed "Battle Mountain" where troops of the 4th Cavalry and 6th Cavalry fought the Chiricahuas in 1882.

At Carretas a courier from Cloverdale reached me with orders to halt my column and await the arrival of Lieutenant C. B. Gatewood, 6th Cavalry, with a party consisting of Interpreter Wratten and two "Indians." On July 21st Gatewood arrived. He showed me his papers. One was a letter from General Miles to Colonel Beaumont, district commander. In it Miles said, "Lieutenant Gatewood with two Indians will pass through your post. The Indians have instructions to go to the hostile camp to carry a communication to the hostiles. . . . It is desirable that they be put on the trail of the six Parker was following, as there are indications that they desired to surrender. You may hold that command of Parker's near the line for further service or until the disposition of the hostiles can be ascertained."

The orders from Beaumont stated, "The District Commander directs that you furnish Lieutenant Gatewood with a sufficient escort to enable him to perform the duties he is intrusted with. The escort need only be large enough for the protection of Lieutenant Gatewood and his Indians against Mexicans and hostiles. The District Commander further directs that you keep your command in readiness for further orders, either at Carretas or at Cloverdale as you may judge best."

"But," said I to Gatewood, "this trail is all a myth; I haven't seen any trail of hostile Indians since July

1st, three weeks ago, when it was washed out by the rains!"

Gatewood seemed startled by the statement. "Well," said he, after some reflection, "if that is so I will go back and report there is no trail!"

"Not at all," said I. "If General Miles desires that you be put on a trail I will find one and put you on it. In any case I can take you with me and hunt up Lawton and he surely will be able to find a hostile trail; he is probably on one now."

Gatewood dissented. He pleaded he was sick and was not in fit condition to travel. "Very well," said I, "we will wait here until you are better." Gatewood, with some unwillingness, assented. He said that in any case he would require an escort of at least twenty-five or thirty mounted men.

After reflection I determined to escort Gatewood with my entire command. I accordingly wrote the district commander as follows:

" . . . To furnish an escort of this size, twenty-five or thirty men, will take half of my command . . The small remnant of this column remaining after Lieutenant Gatewood's escort is deducted would possess no efficiency and be of no use. I have therefore determined to take along the entire outfit. While this determination conflicts with the orders I have received, I believe it is the only course open to me consistent with the interests of the service and the ends desired by the department commander."

I have taken pains to go into this matter at length for, as a result of this decision of mine, the way was opened for the negotiations with and the final surrender of Geronimo.

We remained in Carretas for six days after Gatewood's arrival. He then announced that he was sufficiently recovered to proceed.

My orders for the march were that the scouts with six infantrymen should march in advance, followed at two hundred yards' distance by the cavalry, commanded by Lieutenant Richardson; the pack train in rear of the cavalry, never more than a quarter of a mile distant, with a rear guard of infantry following the pack train. In case of an attack the orders were to dismount and charge. "To drive off a concealed enemy he must be attacked; to hide behind rocks and attempt to reply to his fire is useless. No firing will be indulged in unless the command is given. The officers and men of this command are asked to get rid of the notion that the duty they are about to perform is not serious or dangerous and does not require the utmost attention to details."

In our bivouacs we suffered much from ants and various insects that crawled under our bedclothes. Scorpions, tarantulas and centipedes abounded. Several men and animals were badly bitten. Mescal, a fiery stuff, in taste like gin, could be had cheaply, too cheaply, in fact. This and the immorality of the women, who made up for their lack of beauty by their generosity, caused disorders at times among the men. One corporal had to be reduced and a number of men led their horses in rear of the column as a punishment for drunkenness.

South of the valley of Bavispe is a rough and rugged mountainous region where General Crook's column in 1883 caught up with and made a treaty with Geronimo. It was said that somewhere in this region the Apaches had a stronghold that they claimed was impossible for troops to reach; it was situated on a mountain around which the thorny undergrowth was so thick that animals could not pass.

Sixty miles from Bavispe we arrived July 3rd at Bacadehuachi; a curious-looking town situated on a rock at the base of some remarkable mountains, where we heard for the first time of Lawton's whereabouts. They told us he was south of Nacori on the Yaqui or Haros River; that he had been there some days, and was vainly searching for an Indian trail; that the Indians were in hiding and had committed no depredations for some weeks.

The next day we marched almost to Nacori, twenty miles. This place, isolated in the midst of the most rugged part of the Sierra Madre Mountains, was a poor, miserable town, surrounded by a wall and much exposed to depredations by Indians. We found near here Apache Indian lookouts, fortified, and commanding the road for long distances. From these lookouts the Apaches signaled the approach of unwary travelers. The roads were lined with crosses, marking the graves of victims.

Marching south thirty miles down the Nacori River we arrived August 3rd at Lawton's camp on the Haros or Yaqui River.

Before reaching the camp we came upon a party of Lawton's scouts under Assistant Surgeon Leonard Wood working on a raft which they were building with a view to crossing the river in order to scout southward towards Sahuaripa. Wood, who seemed in excellent spirits, was in the river tying together some palm tree trunks which barely floated. The crossing looked to me like a somewhat hazardous proposition.

At the camp I found Captain Lawton, Lieutenants R. A. Brown, Walsh and A. L. Smith (all of these officers have since distinguished themselves, Walsh and Brown as brigadier generals in the World War, Smith as assistant quartermaster general). I found Lawton in a pessimistic mood. He had been in the field since May 5th, three months, trying vainly to overtake Geronimo in the immense area of northern Mexico, wild and rugged in the extreme, difficult to traverse. As a result of his exertions his command was pretty nearly used up; all the officers except Wood were suffering from minor ailments (Wood himself had been sick). The weather was very hot with rains every day or night. Many of the men were sick. For several weeks he had lost touch with the hostiles, who had disappeared; he was sending Wood and the scouts south of the Haros River towards Sahuaripa to see if he could locate them in that direction.

When told about Gatewood, Lawton objected strongly to taking him with his command. "I get my orders from President Cleveland direct," he said. "I am ordered to hunt Geronimo down and kill him. I cannot treat with him." I said, "Lawton, you know as well as I do, that now General Miles has made up his mind to open negotiations for Geronimo's surrender, that that is the way he will be brought in. As for finding him and killing him, it is as difficult to find him in this immense mass of mountains as to find a needle in a haystack!" I said further, "If I keep Gatewood with me, I may in the end effect the surrender of Geronimo. But my scouts are worthless, while yours are good; and furthermore you are liberally supplied with transportation, money, guides and spies; your command is larger and your facilities are much superior; I, myself, am nearly out of rations. And again, if there is any honor to be gained from this surrender you, after all you have done, deserve it."

I stayed three days with Lawton. Before I left him he agreed to take with him Gatewood and his Indians. "But," said he, "if I find Geronimo I will attack him; I refuse to have anything to do with this plan to treat with him. If Gatewood wants to treat with him he can do it on his own hook." "Oh, nonsense, Lawton," I said.

I must admit that my action in turning over Gatewood to Lawton was not approved by my officers Bannister, Bullard and Richardson. They did not share my great admiration for him and they thought I was doing myself an injustice by depriving myself of this opportunity. I think, however, that in doing as I did I was acting in the best interests of the service. My action quickly bore fruit.

At Lawton's suggestion I determined to scout eastward from Nacori across the Sierra Madre towards Casas Grandes where Lawton thought the hostiles might have taken refuge. Accordingly, leaving Gatewood with Lawton, August 6th, we arrived August 7th, at a point east of Nacori, looking down on the enormous canyons and broken country which we were to traverse.

But we were not destined to cross the mysterious country. News came by courier from Lawton that the hostiles had appeared in the west near Ures. So sending word to Lawton that I would march to co-operate with him, we set out the next morning for Bacadehuachi and Huepare which we reached August 11th.

August 16th Lawton's command arrived at our camp at Huepare. Lawton confirmed the news received by courier that the hostiles had been located to the west, and asked me to move north through the valley of the Bavispe keeping on the east of the Terras Mountains while he moved on their west side. He still expressed great reluctance to taking along Gatewood and his Indians. The next day he left for Oputo to pursue the hostiles.

On the 18th I started on my march north.

When near Nacosari, Lawton wrote me saying the hostiles had passed Nacosari going north, killing and plundering, and that some of them came down a hill near Fronteras calling for José Maria (a guide of Lawton's) and saying they wanted to surrender. Lawton asked me to move towards Fronteras, keeping southeast. This letter did not reach me until I had passed the border—too late to comply with it.

Making short marches we moved north on the American border through the difficult country between Bavispe and San Bernardino Ranch. That we were not attacked is probably due to the fact that negotiations were pending for Geronimo's surrender, for he told Lawton afterwards that in a canyon to the east he had seen a command of soldiers led by a tall officer wearing spectacles. I had reason to believe afterwards that my scouts saw a hostile trail on this march and did not report it. August 23rd, the day before Lawton met Geronimo near Fronteras, I was almost directly east of the hostiles at a distance of about fifteen miles.

August 24th we arrived at San Bernardino Ranch on the border. Two couriers passed us carrying dispatches from Wilder who stated that the hostiles had surrendered. This was probably a soldier rumor. August 25th I proceeded to my old camp at Cloverdale.

September 1st, in accordance with instructions from Colonel Beaumont, I moved my troop eight miles to a camp at Cottonwood Springs on the west side of the mountains. From several sources we had heard that Geronimo had *surrendered* and was with Lawton's command, north of San Bernardino. So taking Bannister, Bullard and an orderly with me I started out to find him.

Riding down Cottonwood Cañon toward the plain we saw at a distance a herd of horses, which we believed without doubt to be Lawton's. Presently we neared a place where the stream entered a ravine on the edge of the plain. Here to my great surprise Geronimo, with whom I was well acquainted, passed, riding a white mule, and, apparently ignoring our presence. Going a little farther we entered the ravine or, more properly speaking, canyon. It had been selected by the Indians as their camp and it was with feelings of astonishment and some trepidation that we saw the bucks, seated upon the walls of the canyon, with their rifles in their hands, eyeing us grimly.

Pretending not to notice them we passed through the canyon to the farther end. Looking out over the plain we saw no signs of Lawton's camp, so we retraced our steps through the canyon. It was only when we emerged that we breathed freely.

Several miles to the northward we found Lawton with his men, and I had a long conversation with him in which he described the situation. What it was can best be judged by a typewritten statement sent me recently by Brigadier General Abiel Smith, who at that time was with Lawton's column. The correctness of Smith's account is vouched for by General R. D. Walsh, who also was with Lawton. It also agrees generally with Lawton's and Gatewood's official reports, which I have in my possession. The statement follows:

"The first intimation that Lawton had of a desire on the part of the hostile Indians to surrender came from Wilder, who interviewed two squaws from Geronimo's band that came into the town where Wilder was encamped.

"When Lawton received this information he directed Gatewood with his two friendly Indians, that Miles had sent down from the reservation in Arizona, along with R. A. Brown and his U. S. Indian scouts and a few regular soldiers, to push ahead on the trail, so that the two Indian messengers from Miles could join the hostiles. This was done and after traveling about thirty-five miles Gatewood and Brown went into camp on the Bavispe River. The two Miles Indians had by this time joined the hostiles.

"The next morning one of the Indian messengers returned to where Gatewood and Brown were encamped and asked Gatewood to go out a short distance and meet representatives of Geronimo's band for a talk. This Gatewood did, with an interpreter and one or two others of his party. During the talk Geronimo himself appeared. He told Gatewood that they would not come in as Miles' Indians had requested. Gatewood, after informing Geronimo that he could not add anything to what the Miles messengers had brought them, returned to his camp where Brown and the rest of his party were.

"By this time Lawton with one officer (Smith) and a couple of civilian guides, arrived at the camp. Gatewood reported the result of his visit and interview with hostiles and announced his mission was ended and he would report back to Miles.

"Lawton decided that the party should remain where they were on the Bavispe River with the hope that the hostiles would again seek an interview.

"The main part of Lawton's command with the supplies were back on the trail thirty-five or forty miles at this time. Lawton directed one of the officers with him (Smith) to go back and hurry forward a few mules loaded with food.

"The next morning a request from Geronimo came into the camp for Lawton, himself, to come out and meet him. Lawton went out and was greeted most affectionately and effusively by Geronimo. This time the principal topic of conversation seemed to concern the question of food. Lawton told Geronimo that they had little or nothing with them in the advance camp, but that one of his officers had gone back to hurry forward rations. Geronimo then said when the food came in he would come back and have a talk with Lawton.

"The following day early in the morning, six pack mules with supplies arrived, and almost at the same time Geronimo and Natchez, and a couple of his warriors joined Lawton in camp.

"After eating a hearty meal they all sat around and listened to the terms on which Geronimo was willing to surrender. Lawton told Geronimo that he could not grant him any terms, but would take down his demands and forward them to General Miles; if the general would not accept them he, Lawton, would give Geronimo twenty-four hours' notice to get away.

"It was further agreed that Geronimo's band should be supplied with rations and the two commands should travel back to the U. S. border together.

"After arriving on the border, Lawton communicated by heliograph with Miles. At first Miles declined to come down and listen to any terms. Lawton was informed that he should not bring the Indians back to the United States unless he had hostages; and to take possession of the bodies of Natchez and Geronimo by any means whatever, and to hold them beyond any possibility of escape.

"Later, on the same date, Miles decided to come down to Skeleton Canyon where the Indians were and to listen to what Geronimo had to say.*

"He came on September 3rd and after a conference in the ambulance with only Geronimo, Natchez and an interpreter and himself present, Miles announced that Natchez and Geronimo should return with him in the ambulance that day to Fort Bowie, and that the other hostiles would follow the next day into the post with the troops.

"Immediately after the conference Natchez came directly to my tent from the ambulance and informed me as he stated, that the war was over, and that he and Geronimo would go with Miles."

During my interview with him on September 1st, Lawton told me he had sent word repeatedly to General Miles begging him to come, but that Miles had failed to do so. Miles wished Lawton to bring about the surrender. This Lawton had tried to do but the only effect was to make the Indians intensely suspicious and ready for flight. Miles had sent word to him, Lawton said, to "secure at all hazards the persons of Geronimo and Natchez." Discussing this with his officers, he told me, they had suggested, if the worst came to the worst, that he arrange a conference with Geronimo and Natchez and at an appointed signal shoot them, certain officers being selected as executioners.

"Lawton," I said, "for God's sake, don't think

*Smith says in a footnote: "I was present at this conference."

of such a thing—you will ruin your entire career. What you want to do is to force Miles to come down here; tell him if he does not come you will not be responsible for the outcome; send him the strongest kind of message." Lawton said I was right, but he had his doubts whether Miles would come. "Parker," he said, "this thing has worried me so I have not slept for three nights and days. At any moment those Indians may decamp."

We returned to Cottonwood Springs without further incident.

The next morning, September 2nd, I got the following order from Colonel Beaumont, dated San Bernardino, September 2, 1886.

"Move your command tonight to the camp Lawton left today. Tomorrow, if Lawton moves, move your command so as to be at a convenient distance in his rear, moving from day to day, being advised by Lawton in the matter." I sent this order to Lawton, saying, "the clause which requires me to be advised by you places me, I am glad to say, under your orders and I trust you may give me such directions as you think proper. To conceal from the Indians the fact that a force is moving in their rear, I believe, would be hardly possible; you are the judge of that. I trust that after tonight you will be easier in your mind about the Indians."

To this I got the following answer: "Camp at mouth of Skeleton Canyon, September 3, 1886. My dear Parker, to carry out your instructions from Beaumont would be *fatal* to a surrender. Neither you nor *any* of the troops can move a *step* now. They are fully on the alert and are watching you night and day. I do not think Colonel Beaumont understands the situation. I do not wish a soldier moved for the present. I will try to send you word in time if it is necessary to move at all. If General Miles would only come the Indians will lay down their arms to him. They will *not* lay their arms down while troops are moving on them and they know it and see them. I sent a courier to Fort Bowie last night and this morning Geronimo's brother went in to Bowie with George Wratten, the interpreter, to see General Miles and tell him their wish to surrender. We will be here two or three days; unless the troops scare the Indians away again, as one of the squaws had a child last night and they don't want to move. I have asked the General to meet them here; if he will not, then I can do no more. Do not send any more couriers than you are absolutely obliged to; they keep the Indians constantly excited. Richards has gone back today and will see and explain to you as well as Beaumont. I *hope* we are near the end, but *God knows*.

Yours, Lawton."

It is well I did not obey Beaumont's order to move that night; there is no question but that the Indians, wrought up as they were by their fears of foul play, would have skipped.

On the afternoon of September 3rd, General Miles arrived at Lawton's camp; the hostiles receiving the terms of surrender from his lips, were reassured, laid down their arms and surrendered. What these terms were, no one knew. The Indians taken to Bowie station were placed aboard a train and sent to Florida, there to rejoin the rest of their tribe which had previously been deported. Later the tribe was taken to Alabama, and still later to Fort Sill, Indian Territory.

It was be conceded that Geronimo, who had engendered this causeless outbreak which had cost the country millions of dollars and unnumbered lives of peaceful settlers foully murdered, received but little punishment for his crimes. Geronimo differed from a common murderer only by the fact that he was an Indian and an assassin on a large scale.

It is not improbable that the authorities at Washington were in favor of punishing Geronimo and his men for their crimes. There was a story widely circulated at the time that after the Indians had been put on the train at Fort Bowie, and as the train was about to start, a telegram from Washington was handed to Captain William A. Thompson, 4th Cavalry, then acting as Miles' adjutant general, and that Thompson after reading the telegram put it in his pocket. The train departed, and the telegram was then given to General Miles. Did the Government in this telegram disapprove of General Miles' disposition of the Indians? And did it later reverse their decision?

It was generally supposed at that time that the hostiles had surrendered, unconditionally, to Lawton. It is probable that when the authorities learned the true facts of the case, they must have felt bound to concur in Miles' action. Their hand was forced. After all, the principal thing had been accomplished; the territories of New Mexico and Arizona and the northern part of Mexico had been rid forever of a band of thugs and assassins that had been like a dreadful nightmare for centuries. The question of the punishment of the Indians was a minor one.

It was generally claimed at that time that the hostiles surrendered because they were followed so closely that they had no alternative. "Pursued so that they had no rest," says Gatewood in his report. "They looked with favor upon a chance to lay down their arms with a hope of having their lives spared." This is somewhat overdrawn. The history of the campaign shows that on numerous occasions the Indians were able to hide and obtain considerable periods of rest.

But they knew they were hunted without intermission and that they must always be on guard against a surprise attack. Many of them were probably worn out mentally by the strain of fear and anxiety.

But one of the principal reasons that they surrendered was that they knew by this time that the rest of the tribe had been removed to Florida. Geronimo's small band then was isolated; they no longer had any friends or relatives in that country to give them aid and comfort. The hope of gaining recruits was gone. They could not expect again, as often before, to be restored to their reservation.

Curiously enough, in Captain Lawton's report of the campaign my name was not mentioned. He says in his report: "During this time Lieutenant Gatewood, 6th Cavalry . . . joined me," but when, where, and how is not stated. He indeed said to my wife afterwards, "If it had not been for Jim, I would not have got Geronimo." But I was disappointed not to have my services mentioned officially. I had to be content with a letter from Gatewood in October, then aide to General Miles: "I am directed by the department commander to say he is cognizant of the facts and circumstances attending the services of you and your command in the last campaign and of the orders under which your action was taken, referred to in your communication. Furthermore, what you did meets his full approval and commendation."

September 30th I returned with my troop to Fort Huachuca, having marched, since June 18th, over eleven hundred miles. I felt chagrined that in reports and orders my services had received so little recognition. But I was proud to feel I had been, nevertheless, a factor in the success of the campaign. On May 22, 1885, at Devil's Creek, I had commanded and beaten the enemy in the only serious fight during the campaign. In May, 1886, I had suggested to the department commander the removal of the Chiricahua tribe to the Eastern states, which suggestion, afterwards acted upon, proved the key to the situation. On June 28, 1886, I had intercepted and driven back into Mexico a party of hostiles. On July 27, 1886, being in command of an important expedition, I had taken the responsibility of disregarding my orders, marching two hundred miles away from my post in order to make the mission of General Miles to the hostiles a success. On September 2, 1886, I again failed to obey an order which would, if carried out, have made fruitless the negotiations with Geronimo for his surrender.

In conclusion, what Lawton and Gatewood accomplished was a remarkable achievement, and both of these officers should be awarded, if possible, posthumously, a medal for distinguished service.

Curiously enough, the only actor in this drama who was given a substantial reward was Leonard Wood. He received a Congressional Medal of Honor for "distinguished conduct" in this campaign. The award of this medal has been the subject of considerable discussion.

A photograph of Geronimo and Natchez, now in the pictorial division of the hostorical section of the general staff, bears an inscription written by Britton Davis, substantially as follows: "Gatewood deserves all the credit for capturing Geronimo; Lawton never saw Geronimo until after the surrender." This is a sample of some of the fables told about this campaign. How Britton Davis picked up this astonishing information I do not know; at the time of the surrender he was out of the service, employed at the Corralitos cattle ranch in Mexico, over a hundred miles distant.

It is not necessary for me to say more than that this

statement is confuted by the story of the pursuit and capture as Smith and I have given it and as related in the printed reports not only of Lawton but also of Gatewood. A. L. Smith, commenting on this statement of Britton Davis', told me Lawton had, in fact, many interviews with Geronimo.

The real credit for the success of this campaign was due to General Miles. He supported Lawton in every way. He deported to Florida the remainder of Geronimo's tribe, and thus deprived Geronimo of a base of operations, and a home. He discovered that to run down and capture Geronimo's band within a reasonable time was not practicable, that it would be better and save more lives of citizens to treat with him. He sent Gatewood into Mexico for that purpose. To obtain Geronimo's surrender he promised to protect him from the civil authorities of Arizona and New Mexico, who were keen to arrest and hang him. To carry out this program, in spite of orders from Washington, he shipped Geronimo and his band out of the dangerous territory before the civil authorities had become aware of what was going on. For this he received the censure of the President. But he delivered the southwest and northern Mexico from a century-old thralldom of murder and ravage.

FORT MYER AND SAN FRANCISCO

IX

In July, 1887, Captain Lawton with his troop "B" 4th Cavalry was transferred from Fort Huachuca to Fort Myer, Virginia, opposite Washington. This was then a very desirable station. It was not long before Lawton, who had many influential friends, became a candidate for appointment to the inspector general's corps. On October 2, 1888, he was promoted major and inspector general. Since I was at the top of the list of first lieutenants in the regiments, I took Lawton's place as captain of "B" Troop.

I was greatly pleased. After twelve years' service on the frontier, the change from an Arizona desert to a Washington ballroom, was to Mrs. Parker and myself a delightful one. We were at the right age to enjoy to the utmost the pleasures of society. We knew many of the older residents. From Lawton I purchased a Coupé-Rockaway, a vehicle which had seen hard usage but was still serviceable. I acquired also two carriage horses and a colored driver, and soon we were on the go among the gayest of the gay in that beautiful and gracious city.

Washington at that time was not yet overgrown, as it is at present. Evidences of great wealth there were few. But there were many old Washington families of culture and refinement who, with the high officials of the Government and the best of the diplomatic corps, formed a society which was in quality unequaled ever in this country. There was something extremely gracious about their hospitality, as if they truly felt honored by the presence of the guest. I was but a captain then, but our army was so small, and so widely scattered and had so few superior officers that a captain's rank was appreciated fully as much as that of a colonel is now.

Georgetown, then a city by itself, had a great many Southern families resident there. They prided themselves on having a distinct set, and it was difficult for even a Washington belle to be admitted to their dancing parties. I felt greatly honored, when shortly after my arrival at Fort Myer, my friend, Frank Johns, of Georgetown, invited Mrs. Parker and myself to the Georgetown assembly and without more ado took me down one side of the room and up the other introducing me without exception to every person there. After that, whenever on my way from Fort Myer to Washington, I was kept busy doffing my hat to Georgetown girls.

Fort Myer has been entirely rebuilt since those days. The houses then could not properly be said to be frame houses for they were built of massive timbers, jointed at the ends, like a log house. It was said this unique style of architecture was the product of the brain of General M. M. Meigs, quartermaster general during the war. The garrison consisted of one troop of the 6th Cavalry commanded by Captain (later General) George A. Anderson, and one troop of the 4th Cavalry ("B") which I commanded. Colonel (afterwards General) Louis Carpenter commanded the post. Among the lieutenants were William Baird, A. L. Smith, Barrington West, Chas. P. Elliott, Samuel Reber, and A. G. C. Quay. Lieutenant Pershing was for a few weeks attached to the command. Our duties were not onerous. Our drills ended at midday, and in the afternoon, in fair weather, most of the officers went to town, returning in the evening. Some-

Major General Henry W. Lawton. Killed in Action,
San Mateo, 1899

times the only officer left in the post was the officer of the day. During the two summers I was at Myer the command marched to Mt. Gretna, near Cornwall, Pennsylvania, where, in company with militia troops we spent several weeks in camp.

The two troops were well drilled, and Colonel Carpenter, a fine officer and a lovable character, was very proud of them, and anxious that the Secretary of War, Mr. Proctor, should see them. The Secretary, however, for a long time put off visiting the post. One day when I was officer of the day and all the other officers had gone to town, I was called to the only telephone we had then, the orderly informing me that someone in the War Department wished to speak to me.

A stern voice said, "The Secretary of War wants to know if the troops will turn out this afternoon!" As it seemed to me likely that some civilians intended to visit the post and wanted to know if they would see a drill, I announced calmly, "No, the troops will not turn out this afternoon." "The Secretary of War wants to know if the troops will turn out this afternoon," the voice said, quite ferociously. "No! the troops will not turn out this afternoon!" The voice became ferocious. "The Secretary of War is going to visit Fort Myer and wants to know if the troops will turn out!" I collected my thoughts quickly. "Tell the Secretary the troops will turn out and give him a review and drill!" "Very well, sir; the Secretary has already started!"

Rushing to the barracks I ordered the first sergeants to saddle up the troops and report at the drill field; then at the guardhouse I had the prisoners load and prepare to fire a salute with the old reveille gun. These preparations completed, the sergeant major and I galloped to the field.

And we were just in time! As the Secretary behind some fast trotters came into the post, the gun began to boom; when he reached the drill field, I stood in front of my two troops at the present. I gave the preliminary commands and we defiled before him at a walk, a trot, and a gallop.

The review over I saluted again, and asked the Secretary if he would see a drill. He assented, and for a half hour we maneuvered about, charging, cheering, dismounting to fight on foot, deploying, firing on an imaginary enemy, etc.

I then formed the squadron in line, saluted, and said, "Is there anything else the Secretary would like to see?"

Old Secretary Proctor from Vermont had a down-East accent. He cleared his throat and replied, "I am very well pleased with the evolutions of the troops. But it seems to me there are very few officers present!"

I had rather expected this remark. For while the Secretary, by himself, might not have noticed that I was the only officer there, I feared that the then Quartermaster General Bachelder, and his aide, Major Jesse Lee, who were with him, might out of a spirit of mischief enlighten him.

"It is true, Mr. Secretary," said I, "that the other officers have gone to town, but as you see, these troops are so well drilled they do not require the presence of their officers!"

"Yes, sir, I see they are very well trained," said the Secretary, who then got into his carriage with his two companions and drove off.

An hour or two later the "glass wagon" bringing the officers back from town came into the post. When Colonel Carpenter stepped out, I said, "Colonel, the Secretary of War visited the post this afternoon!"

The good Colonel turned red to the roots of his hair. "What?"

"The Secretary of War was here this afternoon and I gave him a review and a drill!"

"My God! Were there any officers present?"

"No, sir," I said, with a secret malicious joy, "but I told the Secretary it showed how well the troops were trained that they put up such a fine drill when their officers were not present!"

"My God!" said the Colonel and jumping into the glass wagon he drove furiously to the city. Arrived there, he hunted up his boon companions in the War Department. They must have reassured him, for when he returned to the post, after a short absence, he grasped my hand and said, "I am glad the officers were not present; it showed how well the troops were drilled!"

It was early in the year 1891 that the detail of Troop B came to an end, and in command of the troop I was ordered to the Presidio of San Francisco where part of my regiment, the 4th Cavalry, was already stationed. I found that my horses were not to go with us but were to be left at Fort Myer to be turned over to the cavalry command which took our place.

We traveled in Pullman sleepers as far as Chicago where my men turned back to the railroad authorities cars which were, they said, unprecedentedly clean. From there we journeyed on tourist sleepers, not without incident. For at Ogden, Utah, the cars were taken to the yard to be cleaned. On their reappearance my own car was missing, having been taken by a subordinate official with mistaken zeal, anxious to give the Government inferior service for its money. It was replaced by a dirty car, with broken windows. I refused to embark my men, the railway officials stormed and the regular overland train to which we were to be coupled was waiting. In the midst of the hubbub the senior railroad official arrived; enquiring the cause of the delay, he rushed an engine to the yard, brought back my car and we embarked and resumed our journey.

At the terminus at Oakland, California, we found the Government steamboat, on which I met for the first time our new commander, Colonel (Brigadier General) William Montrose Graham, 5th Artillery. General Graham was a nephew of General George S. Meade, a first cousin of my father's, and was therefore in lesser degree my cousin. He received me and my family with much kindness. At the Presidio, when we landed, the wind coming in from the Pacific was cold and blowing fiercely.

The military post of the Presidio was a large one, containing six batteries of artillery (one a light battery) and four troops of the 4th Cavalry. I had never before served with artillery. Due to their good stations and easy service the artillery had at West Point been considered, next to the engineers, the choice branch of the service and the academic board recommended the highest graduates for that branch. It was preferred by a certain element. As one of my classmates said to me, "I had rather be a second lieutenant in the artillery and be able to go to theatres and balls than a captain of cavalry on the frontier." But with such an easy life there were few casualties and little promotion, the latter intensified by the fact that in each battery of artillery there were three lieutenants, while in companies of cavalry and infantry we had only two. The effects of slow advancement were especially evident in the 5th Artillery where in 1891, serving at the

Presidio, there were nine lieutenants of twenty-four years' service each. (After twelve years' service I became a captain.)

San Francisco was in truth at the time a most beguiling and entertaining city. The earthquake and fire had not come to change its whole aspect and make it into a town of lobster palaces and high prices. It was then more like an overgrown mining camp or Deadwood City. It was a town where pleasure reigned. Restaurants like Marchand's, Café Riche, "The Poodle Dog," "The Pup," "The Maison Dorée," and others devoted their upper stories, like Parisian cafés, to private rooms and suites. The best season for the theatres was the summer, when dramatic companies from New York and the East played at prices less by half than those charged in the eastern states. The Tivoli Theatre, admission twenty-five cents, had an excellent opera company, which, during a season, went through the whole gamut of opera bouffe, and comic opera. The hotels were good and excellently conducted. At the Hotel Occidental the proprietor was in the general habit of presenting his guests on departure with baskets of fruit and flowers.

The post occupied an extensive reservation near the "Golden Gate," the strait leading into San Francisco harbor. Several batteries of heavy guns fronted on the ocean and on "Golden Gate." Other posts there were around the harbor similarly armed, as Fort Mason, Alcatraz Island, looking like an immense battleship in the middle of the harbor, Goat Island, Angel Island, etc. These posts secured the harbor and the city from attack from the sea. But our military engineers who seem to ignore land fortifications, had (and still have) left the city open to an attack from an enemy landing on the coast to the south, say at San Pedro Creek, fifteen miles away, and marching up the peninsula. As a few guns on San Bruno Mountain just south of San Francisco would avert this danger and make useless such an attempt it is not easy to see why this opening so tempting to an enemy is left. Such an attack would take all the batteries about San Francisco in reverse. Also San Francisco would be a fine place to loot, containing, as it does, many banks and the Government mint, stored with untold millions of gold and silver.

In command of the four troops of the 4th Cavalry at the Presidio was my old friend of Fort Clark, Lieutenant Colonel (General) S. M. B. Young. My old acquaintance, Dr. Leonard Wood, now married, was stationed at the post.

Under such a strict disciplinarian as General William Montrose Graham, commander of the post, guard duty was necessarily conducted with great precision.

Some amusing incidents occurred. I remember, as an officer of the day, questioning an Irish sentinel on duty at the car station. He said, "My orders is, to allow no kodiaks or cameos to be brought on the reservation." It took a moment's thought to discover that the sentry meant *"kodaks* or *cameras,"* these being prohibited to prevent photographs being taken of the fortifications.

At night, the sentry at Battery Hamilton gave as his orders, "If I see a red light hoisted on the flagstaff on Alcatraz Island I am to call the corporal of the guard." After several tours of duty as officer of the day my curiosity urged me to inquire why this order was given the sentinel, but no one knew. Even General Graham could not explain it.

The thing finally came to light. It appeared that four or five years before, old Captain Josh Fessenden, stationed on Alcatraz Island, was at the point of death. Everybody loved Old Josh, but his demise meant promotion to a popular lieutenant who had waited many weary years for an increase of rank. So they arranged with the commander at Alcatraz, if old Josh died, to half-mast a flag, or a lantern should he die at night.

Unfortunately for the lieutenant but fortunately for Josh, he recovered. But a sentry order once given is hard to rescind! As a result of my investigation this particular order was stopped for a time by General Graham, but two years later I found it again being repeated on that same sentry post. And it would still survive, if Battery Hamilton had not in 1900 been demolished.

Part of the duty of the cavalry troops at the Presidio was, during the summer, to police, under the orders of the Secretary of the Interior, the national parks in the State of California. In 1893 I was with my troop assigned to that duty, and was appointed acting superintendent of the Sequoia and General Grant National Parks, a position I filled for two years—1893 and 1894. Early in June we started on our march there, a distance of 289 miles.

Our main duty was to patrol the park and keep sheep from entering and destroying its shrubs and grass. As is shown in Syria, Palestine and other old countries, sheep and goats will soon convert a smiling country into a desert. This they do by eating the grass down to its roots, killing it, and also by eating and destroying the bushes. This is particularly injurious in a mountain country; the hillsides being left bare, the loose dirt is washed by the rains down into the valleys, covering the floors of the valleys with detritus. What was before a green smiling country becomes a bare and ugly waste.

The flocks of sheep which threatened the damage belonged to a noted wool raising company. They were wintered in the San Joaquin Valley. In summer they were driven into the mountains, moving slowly under their herders over a predetermined route of several hundred miles. These herders were Basque natives, some totally ignorant of the English language.

My days were spent in visiting the different patrols, and exploring the country.

The snows of winter stay late in the Sierras, and come early. Accordingly, it was in September that I usually began my march back to the Presidio.

I remained in California three years.

THE SPANISH-AMERICAN WAR

X

In August, 1894, I received an order to proceed to West Point, New York, for duty as instructor of cavalry tactics.

The position of riding instructor and instructor in cavalry training which I occupied has always been an envied one. The cadets are not fond of foot drills. But the mass of them love to ride. This being so the cavalry instructor finds it easy to enforce discipline. He rarely has to "skin" or "report" a cadet for delinquency. The cadet craves excitement. With me they got plenty of it.

Nevertheless, the cadet does not receive enough mounted instruction to make him a "good" rider. He begins riding in the second year; that year he gets sixty hours of riding the next, forty, the last year, eighty. In all, one hundred and eighty hours. A recruit in a cavalry troop, riding four hours a day, has received at the end of two months some two hundred hours of instruction, or more than the cadet. Neither is a finished rider.

In the cavalry drills on the plain falls were infrequent, but in the riding hall, owing to the disposition of cadets to take chances, they occurred often. But the floor was covered thick with tan bark, and it was rare that anyone was hurt. But that tan bark is not as soft as it looks, I one day had forcible proof.

The platoon of cadets had not yet arrived and the horses were being held in line by the detachment of cavalry. I was riding around the hall practicing my horse, Brer Fox, in changing foot in the gallop. On making one of these turns I became conscious that his forelegs were crossed and that he had not "changed foot" and was falling. The next thing I knew I was drilling the cadets at jumping hurdles.

I called the corporal of the detachment to me. "Corporal, did anything happen to me before drill commenced?" "Yes, your horse fell on you; we pulled him off, you mounted and have been conducting the drill ever since!" "Corporal, have I made any bad breaks?" "No, sir, you have drilled all right." I looked at my watch and discovered that I had been drilling for a half hour without knowing it!

I dismissed the platoon early. I found I had such a splitting headache I could hardly sit on my horse. On my way to my quarters I met a young lady who was a constant gallery attendant at the drills. "Oh, Captain Parker," she exclaimed, "I was so delighted with your drill; it was the finest I have ever seen!" I learned afterwards I had used a form of drill which I had adopted when I first came to West Point and which I had afterwards abandoned.

The doctor called my temporary aphasia "second consciousness." He said football players after a sudden blow or shock often play through a game and waken afterwards with no memory of what they have been doing.

The summer before I left West Point I found myself, due to the illness of Colonel Mills, the acting commandant, and as such in charge of the annual cadet encampment.

The two things which I regard as of greatest value in the course at West Point are the code of honor, and discipline. Mathematics and the sciences, law and history are taught as well or better in civilian colleges. As I have said, as much riding is taught a recruit in two months as during the entire academic course. Apart from riding, the hours of practical military instruction amount to, on an average, less than one hour per day. The graduate has only a smattering of military science.

But nowhere is there such discipline. In the four years that the cadet spends at West Point he is always under discipline. When he goes to meals he marches under the close surveillance of cadet officers, at the table he is under their charge. To go to recitations he falls into ranks and marches to the academic building, there he sits or stands in his section room, at all times silent and under close surveillance. In his sleeping room during study hours he is liable to be inspected and have to stand at attention at any moment. When in ranks, at drill or elsewhere the slightest departure from rigid soldierliness will be punished. In his studies he works "under the lash of failure"; poor marks mean dismissal. The class is divided into numerous sections, the best men in the top section. The men in the lowest section are fighting to get away from the bottom; those in the other sections struggle to keep from "going down." It is the discipline of unremitting work. It is this discipline, this thoroughness, of which West Pointers are so proud and which makes them a class apart. It is this discipline which they bring to the army, the leaven which creates a martial army in a democratic country. The motto of West Point is, "Duty, Honor, Country." It might well be changed to "Discipline, Duty, Honor, Country."

In 1897 I became a contestant for a prize essay on the "Organization, Arming and Training of Volunteers for War." The prize of fifty dollars was offered by the U. S. Military Service Institution. I failed to win the prize, which was awarded to a purely theoretical proposition well thought out by Captain Foote of the artillery; but I received four times the value of the prize shortly after when the Spanish-American War had commenced by selling my essay, which was a study of the methods used during the Civil War, the errors we made and how they should be corrected, to the *North American Review.*

By reading the reports of the adjutants general of the various states, and of the provost marshal general of the army, I discovered the following (to me) curious facts. That with the exception of the comparatively few troops who enlisted in 1861, the "volunteers" were the direct result of the threat to apply the draft. That is, the general government would call for, say, 300,000 volunteers. According to their population each state and county would be required to furnish its quota, or proportion, else the draft would be applied. Recruiting offices were opened, but volunteers did not freely present themselves. The county, in order to escape the draft which might force into the ranks fathers of families, men of wealth or distinction, determined to pay a bounty to each volunteer. These bounties, beginning at $300, rose rapidly to much higher figures, the counties bidding against each other. The money to pay these bounties was obtained by issuing bonds, on many of which we may be still paying interest. Examined closely, it will be seen that these volunteers were in fact substitutes, for which the community, not the individual, paid. We drew many "volunteers" thus paid for, from Canada and foreign countries, and the state of Massachusetts actually raised several regiments of "volunteers" to fill its quota by enlisting the liberated slaves of Louisiana and Mississippi.

During my tour of duty as instructor in equitation and cavalry tactics I had as assistants Lieutenants Butler, Lindsey, and for a short time Pershing. Butler met a tragic death before the World War, Lindsay became a general, and Pershing a general-in-chief. When the Spanish-American War broke out, Pershing was among the officers at West Point whom the War Department refused to allow to go to the front; he appealed to me, and I am pleased to think my application in his favor (with perhaps others), gained him permission to join his regiment. At Santiago he met Roosevelt; the rest is history.

In all I instructed six classes, graduating perhaps seventy-five men each; or in all four hundred and fifty officers. Over three hundred of these are now in the army, some colonels, the others general officers. They all seem to retain pleasant memories of "Captain Jim" and it is a pleasure to meet them. I never had a more agreeable tour of duty than my four years at West Point. Socially it was delightful; we had many charming acquaintances there, and many visitors; my children went to good schools; the two eldest become young ladies, danced and rode with the cadets, with whom they were great favorites, and made among them many lifelong friends. In the professors and instructors and their wives, comprising a list too long to enumerate, we found many congenial and delightful companions. As for the cadet, upright in mind as well as in body, as yet unspoiled by contact with the world, with ideals untouched by failure, spotless in honor as in dress, having the joy of splendid ardent youth as his aureole, I love him, and it ever thrills me to look upon him. Discipline, Honor, Duty, Country; may he ever be worthy of his glorious watchwords!

In 1898 we had so long remained at peace that many of us hardly considered war a possibility. I remember that at West Point a classmate, instructor in ordnance, even after the country's cry of rage at the sinking of the *Maine,* hotly characterized the idea of war as absurd! And this from an army officer! It is sufficient proof of my contention that cadets often enter West Point merely for the education, intending to resign on its completion; but finding it easier and more remunerative to remain in the service, do so, but are never real soldiers.

As for me, I was thrilled at the opportunity, at last, to serve in war. My troop there, the detachment of cavalry, had now reached a degree of discipline and drill that made it in my opinion the equal of any troop in the country. It was much admired, particularly at the annual horse show at Madison Square Garden, where for two seasons it had given exhibitions. In view of its record in war in 1861-65, and thinking that some cavalry might be immediately necessary, I telegraphed to the adjutant general of the army suggesting its use. I met with a polite refusal.

All eyes were centered on Cuba. It was not thought there would be any serious fighting in the Philippines. I still retained my captaincy of Troop B, 4th Cavalry, at San Francisco, but there seemed no intention of sending it across seas.

It can be said of the war with Spain, as of the Civil War, that the country was taken by surprise. Our army numbered only 25,000 men. Our National Guard was in many states unworthy of the name, poorly officered, poorly disciplined, with little or no effective training. In some parts of the country it was still mainly a social organization. Regiments had to be reconstituted, almost from the ground up. The ranks were full of ineffectives, men who through defective physical condition, or for other reasons had to be discharged. In most regiments a mere skeleton of men and officers remained; to mobilize the regiment was like creating a new one. With two-thirds of the men and officers raw recruits, a regiment was not fit for active duty for many months.

But trained officers were at a premium. My somewhat remarkable experience in seeking a command or a billet is indicative of this fact.

I first went to Trenton, capital of New Jersey, my native state. I was accompanied by my father. The governor, Voorhees, said he had given no thought as yet to the raising of troops. However, he was extremely courteous, and promised me the command of one of the first regiments raised.

This sounded very satisfactory, but as I was not at all sure that troops would be called for from New Jersey and as I wanted to get to the front at once I proceeded to Washington where Congress had given authority for the raising of "immune" regiments to be made up of men who had had yellow fever and were therefore immune to that disease. As it turned out I might have had the New Jersey Regiment if I had waited long enough.

I arrived in Washington May 1, 1898. The next day accompanied by my brother, R. Wayne Parker, Representative in Congress, I went to see President McKinley, who received me very kindly and sent me to see Mr. Alger, Secretary of War. May 3rd I visited General Miles and Secretary Alger. On entering the Secretary's office I saw at a desk my old friend, Dr. Leonard Wood. Said I, "What are you doing here, Wood?" "I am busy organizing the 1st Regiment of Cavalry Volunteers of which I am to be colonel and Theodore Roosevelt lieutenant colonel!" In the course of our conversation, which was brief, he intimated he had a *majority* unfilled, and he gave the impression that if I wanted it I could have it! Unfortunately, the idea of serving under "Doctor" Wood did not appeal to me! If it had and I had accepted it

I would have been the senior regular officer with the "Rough Riders," and the only one with long experience in training cavalry. When Roosevelt became colonel I would have been his assistant. And Roosevelt never forgot friends and companions.

My interview with Secretary Alger was brief. He said I had been highly commended to him, and told me to come and see him again before I left Washington.

Leaving the Secretary's office I learned that my old friend General Shafter had been selected to lead the first expedition to Cuba, and I went in search of him. I was anxious to be in the first fighting.

Shafter, when I found him, seemed pleased to see me. He said that unfortunately all the vacancies on his staff had been filled, but he would be glad to take me along as "volunteer aide." As volunteer aide I would have ranked Lieutenant Miley who at the battle of Santiago was Shafter's representative on the line of battle. It was another chance missed.

I was still considering whether to accept, when I was handed an order from the War Department to proceed to Peekskill, New York, as mustering officer of the New York volunteers. As I had been directed by Secretary Alger to report to him before I left Washington, I went to his office where Lieutenant Devore, military secretary, told me the Secretary of War was closeted with some senators. Devore took my name in to the Secretary who sent word by him that he wanted to know "if I had ever had the yellow fever!" I was disgusted. I sent him word by Devore that I had had everything else but yellow fever and took my departure.

I took the night train from Washington and arrived at Peekskill the following day, May 4th. There all was hustle and confusion. Three regiments of the

New York National Guard were assembling there; the 8th, the 9th and the 12th. I was particularly taken with the 12th, commanded by a fine old soldier of the Civil War, Colonel R. W. Leonard, which, it was said, would be the first sent to the front. The men were a rough and tough lot, teamsters, longshoremen, and the like. They were in fact a lot of "Bowery boys," and the regiment later adopted as the regimental march the popular air "The Bowery, the Bowery, the things they say and the things they do, on the Bowery!" The officers on the other hand were of a superior class—most of them were members of the Union Club of New York City, the most select club of that town. Aided by my assistants, Lieutenants Granger Adams of the artillery and W. C. Babcock of the cavalry, the work began of organizing these regiments.

I joined the 12th New York as a major. We were mustered in on Friday, the 13th of May, an unlucky weekday, date and month, according to superstitions. And in some respects the regiment was, during its career, unfortunate. But in other respects we were favored by fortune. For instance, I never served with a finer set of fellows than the officers of the 12th, or with men who worked together better; we were a band of brothers. And every year since, for twenty-six years, we have celebrated the 13th of May by a dinner at the Union Club, when with our dear old colonel at the head of the table we have revived old memories, and drunk to the splendid 12th.

Being ordered to Chickamauga Park, Georgia, and leaving Peekskill Camp amid the cheers of the assembled crowds, the regiment embarked at Jersey City on three trains, each train carrying one battalion with its baggage.

May 19th we arrived at Chattanooga, Tennessee, finding a great blockade of troop trains and the main line to Chickamauga unable to transport us there except after several days' delay. But Colonel Leonard arranged with a branch railroad line which reached Rossville, a place not far from the park, to take us to that town. There we bivouacked for the night.

The next morning, May 20th, the regiment formed and started for our camp. It was an excessively hot day and the men, not used to heavy packs, suffered greatly.

Chickamauga National Park, four miles square, was situated on a plateau, through which the Chickamauga River ran. It was a forest with occasional openings and fields. In the woods the troops were camped to the number of 50,000. The open fields were reserved for drills, reviews and parades.

In September, 1863, this forest was the scene of perhaps the bloodiest battle of the Civil War, over one quarter of those engaged being killed or wounded. The battle was decided on the second day by an irresistible charge of the corps under Longstreet and Hood which broke through the center of the Union Army line, sweeping the right away and driving back the center. A curious feature of the battle and one which has never been stressed by historians was that after Longstreet's charge, the center having been driven back to Snodgrass Hill, there existed for hours and until the end of the battle a gap of three-fourths of a mile in the Union line. This gap was between Snodgrass Hill (the center) and the advanced position of the left. On account of the dense woods it was never discovered by the Confederates.

Chattanooga, ten miles away, a railway and manufacturing center, was a town of 30,000 inhabitants, nearly half of them negroes.

The commander of our brigade was Brigadier General McFee, a National Guard appointee from Texas.

The division commander was Brigadier General Joseph Sanger, lieutenant colonel and inspector in the regular army who had been a noted battery commander during the Civil War. His adjutant general was Major Hugh L. Scott, afterwards chief of staff of the army.

I was promoted to lieutenant colonel, and also had another offer of a job. General Thomas H. Wilson, commanding the corps, had Major W. E. Wilder as his inspector. Wilder was to get the 14th New York, vice Colonel Fred Grant promoted brigadier general; and General Wilson promised me the vacant inspector generalship. But kisses go by favor. The General was asked to appoint J. J. Astor, the millionaire, and he did so. Astor knew nothing about military affairs.

The 12th Regiment was several times ordered to the front in Cuba and several times the orders were revoked.

These repeated disappointments depressed the officers and men greatly, lowered the morale, and added to the epidemic of sickness.

On one of these occasions when we were under orders to proceed to join the expedition to Porto Rico I received a telegram from the governor of New Jersey offering me the lieutenant colonelcy of the 4th New Jersey, then being mustered in.

I wired the governor thanking him and declining, as I was under orders for Porto Rico. He wired back commending my soldierly spirit. He gave the lieutenant colonelcy to Captain Quincy Gilmore of the army. In two weeks the old militia colonel resigned and Gilmore became colonel! But I stayed at Chickamauga.

The dreadful feature of the camp at Chickamauga Park was typhoid fever—called first by the doctors typho-malaria and treated as a form of malaria.

In August, 1898, General Wade who, following

General Brooke, commanded the camp, was relieved by General Breckenridge, then Inspector General of the Army. August 8th General Breckenridge appointed me sanitary inspector of the camp.

It was my business to make the camp more sanitary, to clean up, to correct adverse conditions. I was reminded of the task of Hercules, cleaning up the Augean stables. Unfortunately I could not, like Hercules, turn a river through the camp. But the next best thing was to get the troops out of the camp and that quickly. The camp was rotten. It was full of garbage and dung heaps. Every breath that blew carried foul odors and infection.

The filth which had been deposited in trenches and covered with earth had rotted and the gases engendered escaped to befoul the air. The tent hospitals for divisions of 10,000 men were filled to overflowing with poor devils lying often on the bare ground, their faces black with the flies which covered them. The volunteer divisional surgeons were helpless and hopeless. I will give one instance. At one divisional hospital I called for the chief surgeon. He had, after many attempts, received a few boards and I found him on his knees making a tent floor; he explained he had no other person competent to do this work. While we were talking the hospital steward came up, "Major," said he, "three more cases of measles have just come in, where shall I put them?" "Put them in the measles tent!" "But I have already fifteen men in that tent!" "No matter; put them in the measles tent!" The measles tent, a conical wall tent could have held comfortably six patients!

The average medical practitioner was not fitted by training for administrator in a camp hospital, especially when confronted with the red tape of the army.

Requisition after requisition for supplies remained unfilled because they were found to be made out improperly and were returned for correction. Despairing of satisfying the bureaucrats at headquarters the volunteer surgeon would go without the medicines or supplies. What was needed was an inspector who would force these incompetent administrators of hospitals to take what was needed and receipt for it. The system of requisition did not work and the patients suffered.

I saw that the only thing to do was to recommend the immediate abandonment of the camp. This I did in a report dated August 19, 1898. In my report I commented on the fact that with a strength of 43,000 officers and men, the sick had reached the appalling number, on August 12, of 6,485, and were increasing at a twenty-five per cent rate every ten days. I added that it was only a question of time when the well would not be able to take care of the sick. I detailed the condition as to the camp's water, soil, hospitals. Finally I stated that the camp was "incurably infected" and the only remedy was the immediate evacuation of Chickamauga Park.

It stands to the eternal credit of General Breckenridge that he at once gave the report to the press, although he must have seen that in dispersing the troops he would probably lose his command. The publication of the report made an immediate sensation, and the bitter comments of the newspapers placed the Government in a disagreeable position. The evacuation of the park commenced August 23rd.

A reformer does not often profit. A Chattanoogan immediately directed on me a violent attack, claiming among other things that I had not cleaned up the place! As if in two weeks I could do much toward remedying such conditions!

Portions of my report were read to General Brooke, former commander of the camp, while he was testifying before the Commission on the Conduct of the War, headed by General Horace Porter. He did not hear my name aright. "Give me that young officer's name and I'll see that he is court-martialed!" shouted the irate General Brooke. "No, you won't, General Brooke, no you won't!" replied General Porter.

The training of the troops was good except in rifle practice. Not a shot was fired in the camp until after Santiago had been taken and the fighting had practically ceased. The Ordnance Department pleaded that it could not furnish ammunition for target shooting; it had only enough for the troops actually engaged in hostilities! It took no measures to have cartridges manufactured by civilian firms. In consequence, in July over two-thirds of the men in camp had never fired their pieces! It was the old idea again of the Civil War that the least important thing to teach the riflemen was to shoot! As a battalion commander I protested against this state of things, but in vain.

From Chickamauga the regiment moved by rail to Lexington, Kentucky. Here in the healthful and beautiful bluegrass country we pitched camp three miles from town. The city, founded in 1779, had many handsome residences dating from the first days of the Republic, and contained many old and wealthy families.

Most of the young New York officers brought letters of introduction to the leading families. The regiment became very popular; it was the fashionable thing in Lexington to attend our parades. We were made members of the principal clubs. We gave a military ball in town; it was a grand success. We were looked upon with some envy by officers of other regiments, and I fear with dislike by some of the young civilians of the city who did not relish the decided manner in which their fair companions favored our younger officers.

It was the fashion to dispense mint juleps to callers. "Julia," the hostess would cry to her colored maid, "bring us two juleps; a small one for me!" "Julia, being two more juleps!" It was hard not to be fascinated by such hospitality.

On November 15, 1898, in order to obtain a milder climate, the regiment moved by train to Americus, a town of 6,000 people, two-thirds colored, situated in the southwest portion of Georgia. This town was only about ten miles from Andersonville, site of the Civil War prison pen.

December 26, 1898, we started at last for Cuba. Our long delays, our many disappointments, our sickness and hardships were forgotten in the joyful expectation of more active service. Proceeding by rail to Savannah, thence to Charleston, South Carolina, we embarked there on the transport *Manitoba.* At Charleston I had the pleasure of seeing my parents and my wife and daughter from whom I had been separated for nearly eight months.

On January 1, 1899, we arrived at Matanzas, unloading the transports by means of lighters because of the shallowness of the bay.

The work of unloading being done too slowly to satisfy General Sanger, he detailed me in charge and I worked for nearly twenty-four hours continuously day and night forcing the reluctant men to hurry their task. On one occasion, during the night, I fell overboard and I heard one of the men shout, "I hope the damn —— of —— drowns!" Fortunately, I was able to get back on the dock, but I afterwards suffered a severe malarial attack as a result of the exertion and exposure.

The camp of the division was established on the northern shore of the bay, east of Fort San Severino, an ancient work, still in perfect order, built of stone, with its portcullises, ramps and antiquated bomb proofs and shelters; a beautiful specimen of a Vauban fortress. Its armament, dating from the preceding century, was still in position. The ground selected for the camp was mostly coral rock, in which it was very difficult to drive our tent pegs.

The town of Matanzas of 30,000 population was handsomely built with many fine residences in the Cuban style. It was a beautiful town on a beautiful bay. It contained an opera house, a casino, a large hotel and many restaurants. The finest residence in town was occupied as headquarters by our division commander, General Thomas H. Wilson. Wilson was one of the great cavalry leaders of the Civil War, and still in his prime.

The war with Spain was officially terminated on the first of January, 1899. We found the town full of Spanish soldiers and officers, embarking for Spain on some ships in the harbor. The extent to which these poor soldiers, many of whom were sick or ailing, were crowded on board these ships, owing to Spain's niggardly policy, was incredible. As a result many of them died before reaching home.

The Spanish policy had been to "clean up" the country districts by driving all of the country people into the towns, thus making the interior a desert, in which the rebel forces could obtain no supplies. The country people who thus lost their homes and all of their belongings received in the cities insufficient sustenance and died in shoals. To stop this barbarism had been one of the main reasons for our declaration of war. These *reconcentrados* we found in great numbers in Matanzas, a desperate, unhappy lot of people, many on the point of death from starvation. Energetic measures were taken by our Government to feed this population. Ration tickets were issued and long lines of people, black and white, stood daily before the food depots.

But there was a class of people, still starving, who were too proud to take advantage of this charity. A month after my arrival I found an instance of this in a house of the better class. It was inhabited by a mother and two daughters, all perfect skeletons. Their income, consisting of rents and mortgages, had failed them. They had no servants. They were too proud to stand in line with negroes and common people and await their turn to draw rations, so they starved. They had the aspect of those who have just recovered from a long and wasting fever. They were too weak to be hungry. It appeared from what they said and the way they acted that there comes a point in starvation when one has no longer any energy to remedy his situation. Deprived of food up to a certain point, inanition sets in, and starvation becomes easy.

Through this family I met others in the same fix, personal friends. This coterie was like a club. If any of them received food, the rest were notified and came to partake. Thus all got a very little. Among their friends was a father and mother and fifteen children all looking like wraiths. They lived in a handsome house.

I did what I could for these poor devils. I sent them twenty-five dollars' worth of beans, flour and other food bought in the commissary. I put the old lady and her daughters in touch with people in the United States who bought their needlework. They reported afterwards that conditions were improved. Perhaps the relief officers reached them. Their gratitude was touching.

I had always made a point of keeping up the Spanish I had learned at West Point, and I now found it very useful. However, few of the other officers spoke the language.

Among the Cubans and the *reconcentrados* there was intense hatred of the Spanish soldiers and of the Spanish residents, which threatened an outbreak of rioting and disorder. The local police still acted. To support them and to suppress riotous demonstrations a guard was formed, at the head of which I was placed as provost marshal.

I made my headquarters at the Cristina Cuartel, just outside the city. There the troops were lodged, after we had cleaned it up, for it was in a filthy state. (In fact, the whole town was in a distressingly filthy condition, partly due to the war, but mainly to the unsanitary habits of the Spanish race.) I placed outposts through the town, which is divided into three nearly equal parts by two rivers running through it, each crossed by one bridge. At the entrance of each bridge I placed a large outpost on the flat roof of a building commanding the bridge. Thus, in case of disorder, I could isolate each section of the city.

When the Spanish soldiers had all embarked, we permitted the Cuban forces to enter. This entry the people made the occasion for a grand public demonstration. Young Cuban girls in white dresses, with unbound hair, escorted the conquering heroes. These last mounted on jaded ponies made but a sorry-looking procession. Poor devils, clad in rags and tatters, they had none of the pomp and panoply of war. But they were received with enormous enthusiasm. Escorted to the grand opera house they were hailed with florid eloquence, as the saviours of their country. A large proportion of these troops, as indeed of the population of Cuba, was colored. In fact, the color line has never been closely drawn in Cuba, where intermarriage between the two races is common. Few families have not a "touch of the tar brush." Several of the leading Cuban generals were coal-black negroes.

One of the causes of the revolt against Spain was the discrimination made by Spanish law against the natives of the colonies. These, even when born of Spanish parents, were excluded from office and from many privileges and rights possessed by natives of Spain. It was a foolish policy, and alienated from the mother country many of the wealthiest and high-born families.

But the main cause of the rebellion was economic, the failure of the sugar market, and the consequent distress of the sugar workers. And curiously enough this was caused by the action of an American president. During the Harrison administration, between 1889 and 1893, Mr. Blaine, our Secretary of State, had negotiated reciprocating treaties with many countries, and notably with Spain, admitting with a greatly reduced duty Cuba's principal crop, sugar. To Mr. Cleveland, who succeeded Harrison as President in 1893, these reciprocatory treaties as acts of the Republican administration were anathema and in 1894 they were annulled. This brought widespread commercial distress in Cuba, and the revolt soon began.

In February, 1899, I was relieved from duty as provost marshal and ordered with my battalion to Cardenas, Cuba, by rail. We there relieved a battalion of the 4th Kentucky Regiment, and I took command of the district.

We left Cardenas March 21, 1899, going by rail to Matanzas and there embarking for New York on the transport *Meade* (the old liner *Berlin*).

On March 26, 1898, we arrived at New York. The regiment, in parade formation, marched up 5th Avenue, and being a very popular one, was received with acclamation. Our triumphal march ended at the 12th Regiment Armory on 69th Street. Entering the armory the command for breaking ranks was given. The officers and soldiers dispersed, surrounded by their rejoicing relatives. It was the old National Guard regiment of militia again; I had no place in it! Except for a few formalities connected with the muster out, it was no longer in the U. S. service! I was no longer the chief whom the soldiers of my battalion supported. I was an outsider! I felt almost as if I had lost by death my dearest friend. I had loved the regiment; I felt I had possessed its confidence; it was a living thing to me. It vanished! I could almost have wept.

Although I had the joy of rejoining my family, my depression did not leave me for weeks. As soon as I had been mustered out I applied for and received a leave of absence. During this leave I took occasion to visit Washington, where I tried to impress upon General Corbin the necessity of making a record of the failures, deficiencies and blunders of the war, with a view to escaping them in future. I asked to be allowed to devote a few weeks to this work. General Corbin seemed favorably impressed, but later informed me that he had no desk room!

Hearing my troop (B, 4th Cavalry), still at San Francisco, was about to be ordered to the Philippines I threw up my leave in order to rejoin it. I made a hurried departure. The worst accounts were then being received as to the conditions in those islands; there was much fighting, many casualties and deaths. The Philippines were regarded as extremely unhealthful. On my departure I was accompanied to the railroad station by father, brothers and wife. For her it was a heartrending leave taking. I had been absent nearly a year, and now I was going to the other side of the earth, 10,000 miles distant.

XI

THE PHILIPPINE INSURRECTION

On June 28, 1899, I embarked my troop B, 4th Cavalry, on the transport *Valencia,* for Manila, the force transported being two troops of the 4th Cavalry and two companies of the 24th Infantry, under command of Major Morton. The horses of the two troops of cavalry were sent by another ship.

A large crowd was assembled at the dock to see us off, and there was much cheering and music, weeping of sweethearts and wives, and shouting of farewells. People had little idea of the Philippines in those days; it was a voyage into the unknown, where sickness and death prevailed. The enthusiasm of a national war was absent; even to a soldier there did not seem to be much glory in fighting a weak race whose only crime was a badly timed desire for freedom.

Our voyage was not all a pleasure excursion. In fact, before we reached Manila, the heat, confinement and bad water had a noticeably depressing effect on all of us in spirits and in health.

Manila is on the western side of Luzon, fronting the China Sea. To reach it we passed around the northern end of the island and steamed down the western coast. As the northern part was still in the hands of the insurgents who possessed a number of steam launches, some armed with small cannon, it was remarkable that no naval escort was provided for the defenseless transports coasting the islands for hundreds of miles. It was our first experience of the haphazard way in which the war was conducted by our authorities. We learned afterward there was friction between the army and navy.

It may not be altogether out of place to say that there have been occasions in the history of our country when jealousy between the two services, Army and Navy, has been of great detriment in operations of war. In fact, it has been truly said that a personal friendship between the commanders of the military and naval forces might on certain occasions be worth millions or billions of money to the Nation. But no steps are taken to cultivate a feeling of comradeship between the two services. On the contrary, one of the first things a cadet at West Point learns is to regard the Naval Academy in much the same way as collegians at Yale regard Harvard. Rivalry in athletic games at times assumes much of the appearance of antagonism. Cadets and midshipmen seldom meet except as opponents. After graduation military and naval officers meet more often, but it is notorious that in an Army and Navy Club, the members of each service usually flock by themselves.

It seems inevitable that there should be some latent jealousy between the services. But this should be minimized as much as possible by the authorities. I believe one method of bringing together the boys from the two schools is to have games between the two academies always on the home athletic fields, the middies being quartered with the cadets and vice versa. Only games with other colleges should be made the subject of semi-gladiatorial contests in the immense arenas of our large cities.

We reached the entrance of Manila Bay on the morning of July 30, 1899. Passing the Island of Corrigidor, the armed sentinel at the entrance, we moved into the broad expanse of waters of the bay, mud colored, under a leaden sky. Nearing the town, with its shipping and Spanish-looking houses, we passed the wrecks of the Spanish fleet, sunk by Dewey, May 1, 1898.

Since that date, over fifteen months before, little had been accomplished to bring the islands under American control. The islands were blockaded, it is true, and the insurgents cut off from communication from without. U. S. troops also held Manila and some points near by, Iloilo, on the Island of Panay, and a few other seaports. But all the remaining territory of the islands was in the hands of the insurgents. They had their own government, modeled on ours—President, Judiciary, Houses of Congress; their own newspapers, telegraph lines, mail lines, postage stamps, etc.; their own church, for they had expelled the Spanish priests and installed Filipinos in their stead; they had municipal governments and numerous schools. Everywhere they had besieged and captured the Spanish garrisons. In the towns and provinces order reigned; offenses of the most trivial description were promptly punished by due process of law.

Some of these statements may be contested. However, I am in position to maintain them, having been with the advance of our invasion, from Manila to the north and from Manila to the south, thus having had an opportunity to see things as the insurgent government left them.

It is a curious fact that in their rebellion against the Spaniards the Filipinos were inspired by the

Fort Riley, Kansas, 1880

Fort Bowie, Arizona, 1876

Fort Wingate, N. M.—"the Boardwalk"—1883

Fort Sill, I. T., 1876

example of the American colonists in their revolt against Great Britain! And in the houses of the educated the most popular book was often the lives of the American presidents in Spanish. In the fighting against the Spaniards the people were constantly being called upon by their priests to emulate the example of the American Colonists in the Revolution, and this spirited example was upheld, even after our Philippine War had commenced, as I discovered by reading a captured Philippine newspaper. They admired us even while fighting us, which largely accounts for the humane manner in which they treated American prisoners fallen into their hands.

The city of Manila, where we landed July 30, 1899, lies on both sides of the Pasig River, a considerable stream which connects Manila Bay with the "Laguna de Bay," a large, shallow, muddy lake, ten miles distant. The old town of Manila on the south side of the river was a crowded mass of habitations, monasteries, convents, churches and government buildings, with narrow, winding streets. It was surrounded by a high stone castellated wall and a ditch. New Manila, north of the river, divided into various *barrios,* or wards, was a straggling settlement, though containing the principal business streets.

Our horses not having arrived, we marched out on foot to Deposito, a large granary, the headquarters of General S. M. B. Young, my old friend of Fort Clark and Presidio. Young was in command of the brigade, the division being under another close friend, General H. W. Lawton. My troop was assigned to outpost duty and was quartered on the outskirts of the city at the church and convent of San Juan del Monte. It was a dilapidated place, having been the scene some months before of a fierce fight between the insurgents and the Colorado Volunteer Regiment.

A few days after landing I visited the city and called on General Lawton, whom I found comfortably quartered in a handsome house, the former residence of a high Spanish official. The floors of the house were of dark mahogany kept highly polished. Lawton, with whom I had last served in the Geronimo Campaign of 1886, was the fighting general of the islands, and had distinguished himself by much intrepidity and energy.

We had arrived during a lull. The State Volunteers raised during the Spanish-American War were being sent home, and the newly raised United States Volunteers had not as yet begun to arrive. General Otis, in command of the forces on the island, was evidently waiting until the arrival of the new contingent before taking the offensive. As I was to discover later, an important part of his policy was not to extend his lines beyond their present positions. Meanwhile, the army, continually harassed by the insurgent forces, murmured. This policy of inaction was especially distasteful to General Lawton. The hospitals at Manila were crowded with the sick. The prevailing atmosphere was one of depression. From my interview with Lawton I became convinced that he felt, to raise the morale of the troops, some action was necessary.

On August 10, 1899, I was summoned to General Young's headquarters at Deposito, where I found with him Captain M. D. Cronin, 24th Infantry, and Captain Tyree Rivers, 4th Cavalry. Here we received orders for an advance on San Mateo. This town, fourteen miles from Manila, was on the Mariquina River, and was garrisoned by a force of 700 insurgents, General Geronimo in command. The position of the town was strategic, since lying in a valley between the U. S. forces on the west and a chain of rugged mountains on the east, its capture could close the valley and cut off communication between the insurgents south of and those north of Manila. The troops at San Mateo were said to be some of the best the insurgents possessed. This insurgent position had been attacked previously by a force under General Hall, but without success.

The plan of the advance was as follows: with 280 men I was to march east, cross the Mariquina River, and then move north through the valley. Captain Rivers on the high ground of the west bank, with two dismounted troops of cavalry, was to move north, supporting my left flank; Cronin coming from Novaliches, ten miles northwest of San Mateo, with a battalion of infantry, was to attack the enemy in flank and rear. To anticipate, I took San Mateo; neither Rivers nor Cronin aided me.

On the evening of August 11th I assembled my command at Santolan, on the west bank of the Mariquina River, near the pumping station. It consisted of two companies of fifty men each, of the 21st Infantry, two companies of forty men each, of the 24th Infantry (colored) and my troop B, 4th Cavalry (dismounted), 100 men. The officers were: Captain Wilhelm, Lieutenants Boniface, Spurgin, Weeks, Howland, Dudley. From Lieutenant Spurgin, who had been in the former attack on San Mateo, I had learned that the principal position to be attacked was a line of trenches extending east and west across the valley, and approached by a road running north through a flooded rice field. On this road we were to march. I arranged that the column should march in three sections, each section 300 yards in the rear of the preceding one, in order to lengthen the column and thus to minimize the effect of the fire when the enemy opened on us. All this I illustrated and explained to the officers by a diagram.

The next morning we started early to cross the ferry. We left the ferry at 7 A. M. and marched north along the river. It was eight miles to San Mateo and we moved briskly forward, with an advance guard out in front, Captain Wilhelm commanding.

As we advanced things began to look portentous, white flags on the houses, people running for the mountains, cattle being driven away. At a village five miles from San Mateo the houses were entirely deserted. Finally the road, crossing a wooded stream, entered a plain of flooded rice fields about 1500 yards long and a mile wide. Cattle were disappearing off the plain. In front of a line of trees, which evidently marked the course of a stream, an occasional white figure could be seen. Could this be the position of the trenches? The advance guard was about 1000 yards from this point when suddenly a perfect hail of mauser bullets came roaring down the road. The troops, previously instructed as to their positions on the line, deployed to the right and left like magic, wading through rice ponds a foot deep with mud and water. We were accompanied by Chinese pack bearers carrying the cooking utensils of each company, and these comically tried to dig into the bottom of the rice ponds, some at first actually putting their heads under water. As I was the only mounted officer and perhaps the most pronounced object there, I was the target of numerous bullets, which struck the road and the water around me. Finally I had to leave the horse standing in a pond, gazing around wildly, alarmed at the "pop pop" which the mauser bullet makes when it goes past. The troops having deployed into line, I immediately ordered a forward movement, and sent word to my dismounted cavalry, which was on the right of the line, to make a circuit and attack the enemy's flank. But we were doing what the textbooks declare is well-nigh impossible of success: a direct attack on trenches over a level plain without cover and the plain was covered with water! The injured were falling fast. A wounded negro near me, rolling around in the water, looked like a big seal. The men behaved magnificently. There was as little confusion during the deployment and forward movement as on a drill field; in fact, Lieutenant Munro, 4th Cavalry, who, from the heights on the other side of the river, viewed the fight with a powerful telescope, told me afterward that it looked like an ordinary field exercise.

My line being over 1000 yards long, I used the trumpet to direct its movements and action. It was pretty to see my young lieutenants commanding companies. Sitting upon the rice dykes behind which the men were lying, they gave their commands coolly and distinctly: "Fire three volleys, at 800 yards' distance. Ready! Aim! FIRE! Load. FIRE!"—the volleys sounding like a single shot. The insurgents also fired volleys, the bullets passing over with a devilish roaring, buzzing and popping. In the line in front of me was Captain Wilhelm; he apparently preferred death to getting in the mud, for he stood upright on the road until ordered to take cover. The men, loaded down by the weight of the water which soaked their belongings, threw off their haversacks, canteens, shelter tents and raincoats (we carried no blankets), leaving the field covered with scattered accoutrements. At the trumpet command "Double time, march," given by me to indicate an alternate rush by companies, they would laboriously stagger forward to the next dyke and throw themselves down in the water, which would splash upwards for six feet; a faster gait was out of the question. As we neared the enemy in his trenches, the casualties decreased and it was evident he was firing over our heads. Our fire was to a greater extent taking effect. Soon the enemy's fire, at first continuous, was resumed only when our line was advancing; we kept it down by alternate rushes of companies, while the other companies fired. B Troop, the flanking company, was working farther and farther up toward the enemy and pouring in an enfilading fire. At times I would sound the trumpet call for "Cease firing" and shout instructions. At last, the flanking company having got well up, the enemy's fire ceased and it was apparent they were making a getaway. We were then about 500 yards from the trenches. The trumpeters were ordered to sound a march and the men got up from their muddy beds and marched forward in line, the soldiers cheering and yelling like demons!

I had seen a number of men wounded but we had made no attempt to rescue them. Our continuous advance carried us away from them. Besides, to attempt to carry off a wounded man on that bullet-swept field would have been sure death. I believed the safest course, even for the wounded, was to drive the enemy from his trenches, so that the wounded could be taken care of by the first-aid detachment in rear. So I was considerably startled when Major Cassatt, General Young's aide, hurriedly rode up and announced that we had fourteen casualties. Cassatt said, "General Young wants to know what you will do now."

I replied, "I am going on to take San Mateo. Why do you ask?"

"Well, General Young thought in view of your losses you might decide to forego a further advance!"

"You tell General Young I came out here to take San Mateo, and I'm going to take it!"

We passed over the trenches without stopping to count the enemy's dead. Beyond the trenches was the Canda River, which we forded, waist-deep. Emerging on the other side we found a second rice plain a half-mile in length. At the farther end of this plain was the Ampit River, and in front of the river a second trench from which, as we emerged from cover, we were again greeted by a hail of bullets.

To give an opportunity for Rivers, on the high ground on my left flank, and Cronin, maneuvering in the flank and rear of the enemy, to come forward, we pursued this second attack more slowly. Some cover was found both on the right and left of my line and my flanks were accordingly pushed forward, the line assuming the form of a crescent, the points in advance. I accompanied the left wing. During this advance I was made, on several occasions, the object of especial solicitude on the part of some Filipino sharpshooters firing at close range. The hostile rifle under such conditions has a devilish, hateful sound. On another occasion, lying flat to escape a particularly warm outburst of fire, I found myself being painfully stung by a colony of red ants; it was necessary to run the gauntlet of fire to escape the ants. Another time in crossing a ravine I had the ludicrous experience of finding myself in a well-like hole washed out by the water in the rainy season, and so deep and with such steep sides, I was unable to climb out. I was accompanied by a colored trumpeter only, adjutant and orderlies having all been despatched as messengers. Calling him to me he slid down the hole and I climbed on his shoulders and got out, leaving him there. How he got out I don't know. Working up with the left flank close to the trenches, Van Duyne's company (colored) accompanied by me made a charge and what was left of the enemy retreated in haste to the brushy border of the river and disappeared.

Crossing the Ampit River we came in sight of San Mateo, a handsome town of 3,000 inhabitants. Here again we were saluted with bullets; thinking Cronin near I did not make a quick attack but sent forward Dudley and Spurgin with their companies on the right flank. The fire came at intervals from some hills off to the right; this soon ceased and we entered the town.

The inhabitants, full of trepidation, came forward to meet us, bowing, cringing and fawning. They were ready to give us all that they possessed. My soldiers had thrown away everything except their guns and cartridges; they had no food, and were terribly exhausted. The people brought us some boiled rice—personally I was so fatigued I could not swallow. We took possession of the barracks and public buildings in the town and established our outposts. I learned that the insurgents had fallen back to a strong position at Montalban, about four miles distant. I thought of pursuing, but found my men too much used up to proceed farther. I waited for General Young to appear; in the meantime Cronin with his two hundred men marched in.

When General Young, who had been observing the fight from the rear arrived at San Mateo and told me we had lost two men killed and sixteen wounded (about seven per cent), I was thunderstruck. I had no idea my losses were so great. As for the Filipinos, they packed off and concealed many of their dead and wounded. We saw casually eight dead bodies; it was afterwards said they lost about twenty killed. We had no time in the advance to search the bushes for their dead. Each of my men expended nearly a hundred rounds of ammunition. The insurgents, armed with Mauser rifles, must have made quite as liberal an expenditure. Their good shooting (most of our losses occurred at a range of between 800 and 1,000 yards) was accounted for by the fact that they had with them an Englishman who had carefully instructed them in rifle practice. This man, by name McDonald, was afterward killed in action near Imus.

I quartered my men in the barracks and the convent. During the night the enemy attempted to run a large boat filled with armed men down the Mariquina River past the town; they succeeded, but thirty shots were fired by the outpost at close range into the boat, with deadly effect.

The next morning I was stupefied to receive orders from General Otis to evacuate the town and fall back to our original lines. Was all this loss of life for nothing? And what could be the mentality of a commander who did not recognize the necessity of holding this strategic position, once taken? I never have been able to answer this question.

To deceive the enemy who might attempt to harass us on our return march, I let it be known generally in the town that I was about to move to attack their position at Montalban. Then with a strong rear guard and flanking detachments we retired down the valley. Examining the trenches we had taken, we found them simply riddled with bullets, the upper portion of the embankment in places being raked as by an immense comb. Greatly depressed, we regained our cantonments.

The next day I reported to General Otis and gave him a verbal account of the fight. When I visited General Lawton at the same headquarters building he said quizzically, "Well, you have got me in bad with Otis!"

"How is that?"

"Why, by going ahead and taking San Mateo; Otis will hardly speak to me!"

He did not explain further. But it is likely Otis wanted a small reconnaissance, not a battle. General Young alludes to it in his official report as a "reconnaissance." But as a matter of fact, Young told me to "take" San Mateo, which I accordingly did.*

As showing one of the characteristics of the high-powered rifle, Lieutenant Weeks, one of my officers, during the early part of the fight was shot directly through the liver, the ball making a clean-cut hole about the width of a lead pencil through his body. We all thought he would die, but he recovered so quickly that in two weeks he was attending a dance. The worst wounds with the modern rifle are made at very short range and very long range. At these ranges the bullet, when it strikes, has almost an explosive effect. This is due to the fact that the spinning bullet, like a top, rocks from side to side at the beginning and end of its course. Encountering a semi-solid body, it is upset. Weeks was hit at about 1,000 yards range, where the bullet goes straight.

I should not complete this sketch without mentioning the wonderfully efficient service of Acting Assistant Surgeon Coffin, who followed my column with an ambulance and hospital attendants. I had no sooner

*I may be pardoned for stating that in a private letter of August 14, 1899, Gen. Young spoke of his "great admiration" for my "skill and ability and great gallantry on the battlefield." "He is simply superb," he wrote.

entered San Mateo than he rode up and enthusiastically reported he was ready for further duty. He had dressed the wounds of sixteen men and sent them to the hospital and was now looking for further trouble!

In a letter written home August 13th describing this fight, I said, "Otis could hold this place but prefers not to do so. He will probably lose a lot of men when we go back later."

This prophecy was too true. Four months later, in taking the place, General Lawton, the most brilliant fighter of our army, was killed. Instead of advancing north up the Mariquina Valley as I did, he attacked from the west. While standing on the bank of the river, superintending the crossing of his troops, he was hit by a Filipino sharpshooter and instantly killed. At that moment I was in Fernando de la Union, one hundred miles away, and in conversation with some officers. I suddenly experienced a strange feeling of depression and exclaimed, "I feel as if something has happened!"

We remained on outpost duty at San Juan del Monte until August 21st when the horses of the troop having disembarked, the troop proceeded to Pasay barracks south of Manila to refit. In the meantime I was notified I had been appointed lieutenant colonel of the 42nd Infantry (afterward changed to 45th Infantry.) I was also notified that I would be examined for promotion to the rank of major, regular army, on August 28th and accordingly spent a week studying up my military textbooks. I remember that week especially. It was in the midst of a typhoon that I worked, the rain fell steadily, the ground under my house was six inches deep with water, the tree toads shouted loudly and spitefully, and the wind coming up through the bamboo floor whirled my papers about the room.

My examination, which I greatly dreaded, was after all ridiculous. It took place in the city hall of Manila. In a library filled with old Spanish books, with a lot of officers, I stripped awaiting inspection by the surgeon. Absorbed in the books, after I had been there an hour or so, I finally asked one of the surgeons when I was to be examined. "You have already been examined!" said he. I put on my clothes in much dudgeon.

Next day, primed with military lore, I appeared before the board. My friend, Colonel Rodman, was president. "What does Wagner say is the principal role of cavalry?" asked he. I remembered the paragraph and answered correctly. I waited for the next question; the board looked at me quizzically and smiled. Finally I grew impatient and asked them if they were not going on with the examination.

"No, that is all," said Rodman. "We think you know your business, Captain Parker."

For a week I had wasted the midnight oil!

By this time I had been gaining some idea of the Filipinos, who are an interesting branch of the Malay race. While most other Malays are Mohammedans, the Filipino, having been under the suzerainty of Spain for three hundred years, has become an ardent Catholic. It is true there are Igorots and Negritos in the mountains, mere savages, and Moros, who are Mohammedans, in the southern islands. But these together number only one-tenth of the total population. So pious is the Filipino that in the villages the principal authority often was the priest. In one village I lived in the priest had been in the habit of trumping up charges against peasants who did not attend communion, and having them beaten with a stick by the civil authorities. In another a colporteur having sold the natives some tracts containing the gospels in the

Bicol language, the priest, the following Sunday, threatening with hell fire all those who did not deliver up the tracts, collected them and burned them up in a grand public *auto-da-fe*. A frequent occurrence of our first night's occupation of a town was a continuous buzzing, like that of bees. Investigating we would find that the noise proceeded from rooms where the people were on their knees praying! This gives an idea of their piety. It was not generally published at the time, but one principal reason for the continuance of the insurrection was the opposition of the native priests to the "barbarian," heretic Americans. Their religion was of the most credulous character. I remember on my retreat from San Mateo I entered a native's house adorned with pictures of Hell which gave me the creeps. Most of them represented stark naked men and women being devoured by enormous snakes!

In fact, not only the religion but the government of the small towns of the Filipinos was of the Middle Ages. Not only freedom of thought but freedom of travel was interdicted. Towns, five miles apart, grew up each with a different patois incomprehensible in the other. Unidentified peasants found in a town were regarded as ladrones and locked up. Their other customs reminded me of the Middle Ages. Street lighting was the duty of the householder, who hung out lamps consisting of lighted wicks floating in coconut oil. Night watchmen carried staves and ancient lanterns. Town criers, beating drums at street corners, published ordinances. The people of each town were under a sort of military discipline; the alcalde or mayor would order certain work on a public road or street, specifying the number of laborers from each *barrio* or ward; the order would be published by the town crier, the lieutenants of each *barrio* would select their men and march them at the appointed time to the work. Great religious processions were frequent. The church was the great building of the town and was provided with numerous bells which constantly jangled. In the large cities were many monasteries and nunneries. A large portion of the arable land belonged to the church and was worked by peon labor.

The better class were generally Mestizos (mixed), that is: half-breeds, tracing their white blood to alliances made with the natives by Spanish officers, soldiers or priests. A great scandal among the Filipinos were the unions made by Spanish priests with native or Mestizo women. At Nueva Caceres the bishop had a large family, as had numbers of the minor priesthood. As a rule they took good care of their children, often sending them to the best schools in Manila.

Some of these Mestizos were very handsome, besides having the natural courtesy of the Spaniard. In the matter of good looks, however, the native of pure blood was lacking. The women especially were very ugly—so ugly that our soldiers seldom courted them. The mayor at Iriga was in the habit of boasting what a splendid race would come from a mixture of American and native blood. He announced that he was going to adopt and bring up the first five "American Mestizos" who were born. But after that town had been garrisoned thirteen months by four hundred men, search failed to find more than one "American Mestizo"!

As a matter of fact, it is my experience that the morals of the natives are very good. This is, I imagine, largely due to their religion. Another thing in their favor is their modesty. When the men of my regiment, arriving after a long, hot march at Nueva Caceres, stripped and plunged naked into the Bicol River the native women heard of it and were horrified.

A terrific scandal was the result. The native woman bathes daily, but covers her body to the neck.

On account of the excessive rainfall and dampness during certain seasons, it would be unhealthful in the Philippines to sleep on the ground floor. That part of the house is used for the storage of carts, implements, etc. In the better class buildings, the construction is commenced by first erecting at the four corners a heavy upright. To this at the height of ten feet are fastened strong horizontal sills. On these sills are laid the floors, walls, etc., of the second story. The basement is enclosed by a stone wall. Around the entire second story is often a veranda into which the rooms open. This veranda, an enclosed balcony, is lined with sliding sashes, which may be left open or shut according to the direction of the breeze. These sashes are glazed, not with glass, but with a translucent flat shell common in that country.

With the lower classes it is different. Their houses, resting on piles, are not enclosed on the ground floor. They are made of bamboo (the cost of a house used to be $10), the sides and roof being thatched with the nipa palm leaf. The floor of the second story is of split bamboo, through which crumbs freely fall to the ground beneath, where they are gobbled up by the family scavenger, the pig. On the second floor the family sleeps, using mats, which are rolled up, with the pillows inside during the day. As the daytime costume is as light as a pajama, there is no change of costume at night. There is little furniture. These houses are so clean that we had no hesitation in quartering our men in them when empty, as they often were when we captured a town. For the people were very timid and at our advent usually hid in the woods for two or three days before we could prevail on them to come back. But ordinarily we put our men in the "convent," a large schoolbuilding adjoining the church. Sometimes the people left in such a hurry that valuable personal possessions were abandoned in their houses; to prevent depredation I had to forbid the soldiers leaving the convent until I established security patrols in the streets. I remember yet the look of amazement with which a Filipino received from my hands a small bag of gold he had abandoned in his haste and which our soldiers had preserved for him.

As my promotion to lieutenant colonel made it no longer possible for me to act as captain of Troop B, 4th Cavalary, and as my regiment, the 45th Infantry, had not arrived from the United States, I was assigned to duty with a regular infantry regiment, the 21st Infantry, stationed at Calamba on the Laguna de Bay.

Calamba, thirty miles from Manila, was at the southern end of the Laguna de Bay, a shallow lake sixty miles long and lined on the southern shore with towns and villages. Calamba was the largest of these, and in order to check the enemy's activities in this region a garrison of ten companies of the 21st Infantry was stationed there, the lake being patroled by a stern-wheel gunboat, the *Napindan,* in charge of Lieutenant Larsen of the volunteers. The troops at Calamba were commanded by Colonel Jacob Kline. Kline was in poor health, and I had been confidentially informed by General Lawton that he thought it possible that Kline on my arrival would go to a hospital, leaving me in command. But nothing of the sort happened.

Colonel Kline had disposed his troops strictly on the defensive. Exposed to continual attacks, the men, instead of being quartered comfortably in town, occupied trenches around it. This reacted unfavorably on their health and the conditions when I arrived were such that Kline informed me he did not have one hundred men capable of marching five miles! The prevailing disease was dengue fever, of which I had a touch shortly after my arrival. It affected me like a bad case of grippe, and while I was never on the sick report, I never recovered from certain of its symptoms while I remained in the Philippines. It affected particularly the stomach and digestion.

By an energetic offensive the enemy could easily have been punished and driven away. But due to orders from General Otis, or other reasons, Kline would not allow his troops, when repelling an attack, to advance farther than certain designated points. The regiment was practically besieged. To be continually awaiting and expecting an attack has a curious effect upon the psychology. Kline had a sergeant as chief of his secret service. This sergeant employed a number of Filipinos as spies. Whether or not these spies were also serving the enemy I know not, but they were continually reporting we were about to be attacked at a certain time and place. The sergeant would bring the report to Kline and Kline would assemble his chief officers and notify us to be on guard. As these predicted attacks never materialized, the news would be received on the lines with shouts of laughter.

An important part of the garrison was the artillery detachment of Lieutenant Summerall, afterwards one of our great generals in the World War.

From the rice plain to the east of Calamba rose a solitary wooded hill called Lecheria Hill. It was outside our lines but within easy rifle shot of the town. I had told General Kline that the enemy holding that hill would command the town, when a few days afterwards, on Oct. 2, 1899, he was seen to be busily throwing up intrenchments there. Fortunately, he had but a small force assembled, and we easily drove them away, leaving a platoon to hold the position. But the insurgents had evidently discovered the value of this position, for the next day, October 3rd, they attempted to capture it by assault. Failing in this, they made an attack at the bridge over the San Juan River. Here, besides infantry fire, they were using a revolving cannon. Summerall and I crossed the bridge; climbing a tree I was able to reconnoiter their position. The enemy were concealed by trees and brush, but the cannon was visible, about 600 yards away. Bringing up infantry and artillery a fierce fight ensued, in which we lost two killed and seven wounded. The heat was intense. I obtained permission from Colonel Kline to charge the enemy with a view of capturing his cannon. I gave the preparatory command for the charge, when numbers of soldiers came running back from the lines.

"Stop! What is the matter?" I shouted.

"We are all out of ammunition," was the reply.

Before we could replenish our cartridges the enemy retreated. General Kline reported, "The most conservative estimates from the outside place the number of insurgents killed yesterday at sixty!" I doubt it.

In this connection it was shown during the World War that our count of the enemy's losses is always overestimated. Particularly was this true in the Philippines. The spy or friendly Filipino found it to his advantage to exaggerate the losses of his people. To account for the small number of dead bodies found on a captured field of battle, we invented the fiction that the Filipinos carried off their dead and concealed them. In 1903, in response to the demand of some pacifists, the clerks in the War Department were set to work figuring up the total number of Filipinos killed in battle as shown by the reports of troops. They found the total was over 26,000. I doubt if the number of killed was really much over half of that figure. I was told by a participant of one "battle" in the Philippines that the commanding general generously reported 1,000 Filipinos killed. This officer said he saw the killed—they numbered exactly six!

On October 8th we had an infantry duel between Lieutenant Conley's company on Lecheria Hill and the enemy in trenches, about 1,200 yards distant. In the course of the fight we saw an enemy officer on a white horse riding in rear of their line. Presently he was hit and fell off his horse. A number of men rushed out to bear the wounded man away, whereupon the fire of the whole company was turned upon the body bearers. It was only afterward that we appreciated that the body bearers were protected by the laws of war and should not have been fired upon. But it was the only thing the men saw to shoot at and in their excitement they shot. Similar incidents, considered as barbarities, often occurred during the World War.

The next day, October 9, 1899, we had an artillery duel, the enemy commencing by bombarding us with four field pieces at the "Sugar Mill," on the road to San Tomas, about 3,000 yards away. Their practice was poor and the shells often failed to explode; one 4½-inch shell which made a hole in the mud a few feet from me fortunately proved a "dud." In the meantime Summerall with two 3.2-inch guns came up at a gallop, and went into battery. Having previously determined the distance to all prominent points around the town, he had the exact range. He opened with his guns, firing with the utmost rapidity. A moment elapsed, when, looking towards the sugar mill, the air was seen alive with bursting shells, flames and smoke. This lasted for a minute or so, when a dark mass appeared, pouring out of the mill. Through our glasses we saw it was the gunners abandoning their battery and running for cover. The sugar mill went up in flames.

Our spies reported next day that the enemy's loss had been fifty-six killed and wounded.

The conditions of virtual siege at Calamba continued until January, when the garrison there was reinforced by the 39th U. S. Volunteers under Colonel Robert Lee Bullard, my old lieutenant in the Geronimo campaign, afterwards lieutenant general in the World War. To the astonishment of Kline and the 21st Regular Infantry, Bullard paid little heed to General Otis' orders to remain on the defensive. On January 2, 1900, on pretext of making a "reconnaissance," he advanced on the enemy and in a series of severe engagements drove them entirely away from Calamba, "cleaning up the country" for miles around. This to the great chagrin of my friends of the 21st Infantry. They were mortified that these raw volunteers had accomplished what they had vainly waited to do.

In fact, all that was needed in the Philippines was a certain measure of audacity. One hundred men, we afterwards discovered, if properly handled, could defeat a thousand insurgents. Bullard had pricked the bubble. But Otis, who never left his headquarters to inspect the conditions at the front, who with a steam launch at his disposal lying in the river at his headquarters never made even the short trip to the Laguna Bay, who depended merely on the map and the information gained from Spaniards, thought otherwise. "You did right in attacking the insurgent's line near Calamba, but should not have pursued," Bullard was informed. "Do not move from Calamba without orders from superior authority."

We had heard that a forward movement under Lawton and Young was about to be made. I had become so depressed by the condition of affairs at Calamba, the sickness, the loss of morale of the officers and men, the tragic and disheartening failure to take the initiative, being low in health as well, as the result of the dengue fever, that I felt that if I remained in that accursed spot longer I would surely collapse. I had written and begged Lawton to send me with General Young, who I heard was preparing for a forward movement.

It was, therefore, with infinite joy and a sense of relief that I received the order to join him.

I arrived at Manila coming from Calamba October 19, 1899. In Manila I found that my beloved horse, Brer Fox, had arrived. I had him shipped by railroad to San Fernando de Pampanga, where I found him the next day, tied to the iron grating of a building near the station. It was the first time he had seen me since I had placed him in the hands of the quartermaster on my arrival in New York from Cuba seven months before. As soon as his eyes lighted on me, he recognized me, and then did a thing which for a horse showed uncommon intelligence: he pulled back and almost broke his fastenings attempting to get to me!

There were four troops of the 4th Cavalry and seven troops of the 3rd Cavalry at San Fernando, all waiting to get their horses shod. Aboard ship the shoes had been removed. The troop of Captain George A. Dodd, 3rd Cavalry, however, being shod, I made the march to Arayat with him the next day.

My destination was San Isidro, General Young's headquarters, nineteen miles from Arayat. I found the town of Arayat on the Pampanga River a scene of confusion, being choked with troops. Here strenuous efforts were being made to forward supplies by water to San Isidro or beyond. Temporarily no troops were leaving for San Isidro, so I asked the commanding officer to give me an escort. He was evidently not one of those who looked with pleasure upon "Mex" officers, and flatly refused me. I was not to be denied, however; I discovered that the place contained many enlisted men detached from their commands and anxious to join. Accordingly, without further consulting the combative major, I posted a notice in the barracks that I would start for San Isidro the next morning at 8 o'clock and would take with me any soldiers who wished to make the trip.

The next morning I found myself in charge of a nondescript crowd of twenty or thirty men, consisting of infantrymen, cavalrymen, engineers, signal corps men, hospital corps men, and what not, most of them armed.

Forming them into column, I marched them down to the flat scow which was to ferry us across the Pampanga River. With my detachment I crossed the river and proceeded north along the road on the east bank.

In marching north towards San Isidro we were traveling up the great valley of central Luzon, 120 miles long and 40 miles wide, reaching from Manila to the Gulf of Lingayon. Near us was the extinct volcano Arayat, 1330 feet high, a conelike mountain visible for many miles. I wondered that this mountain, visible from every direction, had not been used as a heliograph and signal station to maintain communication between the American forces operating on both sides of the valley.

Otis had received considerable recent accessions to his strength. A plan of campaign had been determined upon, roughly as follows: Aguinaldo and the seat of the Philippine Government were at Tarlac, on the railroad running north from Manila to Dagupan and about half way up the valley. General MacArthur, with a division of six regiments of infantry, was advancing north along the railway from Manila, pushing the enemy back on Tarlac. On the east side of the valley General Lawton's division, consisting of five regiments of infantry and a brigade of cavalry under Young, was to march north from San Isidro, threatening the flank and rear of the insurgent army near Tarlac. This movement was to be combined with that of a brigade of infantry (three regiments) under General Wheaton, which, moving by transport from Manila to Dagupan was to move southward down the east side of the valley, making a junction with Lawton, and cutting off the escape to the east and north of Aguinaldo and his army.

In the Philippines, due to difficulties of travel and transportation, "combined movements" were rarely a success. My fight at San Mateo was an instance of this. This movement, as we shall see, was not an exception to the general rule.

On reporting to Lawton at San Isidro I was assigned to the staff of General Young, commanding a cavalry brigade, consisting of the 3rd and 4th Cavalry, to which the Macabebe scouts (four companies) were attached. The other officers of the staff were Captain W. E. Wilder, lieutenant colonel of volunteers, Captain Dade, of the cavalry, Lieutenants Smedberg and Howard. They were a fine set of fellows and did not fail to distinguish themselves. We messed with General Young, his colored man, Howell, doing the cooking. We were quartered in the municipal building of San Isidro, a considerable town. Lawton and his staff were working night and day to bring up supplies for the forward movement, some being brought by road, some by river boat. The rainy season was not yet over, and the roads were frightful. Much of the cavalry was delayed in coming up by lack of shoeing facilities.

The Macabebe scouts were native Filipinos recruited in the town of Macabebe on the Pampanga River some fifty miles north of Manila. These people who in the previous insurrection had fought on the side of the Spaniards and thus had incurred the hostility of Aguinaldo's force, readily enlisted as our scouts. They were formed into four companies commanded by First Lieutenant Matthew A. Batson, 4th Cavalry. He had under him Lieutenants Quinlan, Boutelle, Faulkner, Chadwick, McMillan and Blount.

The Macabebes were held in fear and detestation by the native population, who accused them of many atrocities—accusations, I fear, in some cases well founded. They had the utmost contempt for their enemies and under their young American officers strode through the country as if they owned it and feared nothing. They were good marchers and courageous fighters. Their officers were mounted on native ponies. As a rule they had no advance guard; with Batson at their head mounted on a white pony they followed in double rank. When halted they faced outwards, prepared for an attack in any direction. When the attack came from the front they deployed into skirmish line at a run, fan-wise to the right and left front.

It was amusing to see the relations between these old veteran fighters and their young American commanders. They seemed to regard them as a superior sort of being, with the loyalty of dumb beasts toward their protectors. On the other hand the lieutenants could communicate with them only to a limited extent by language; they made up for the lack of it by signs. A few words they had in common, the most useful seeming to be *saca* and *sigue* (pronounced seegay).

"Saca mi Caballo, mi sombrero, mi fusil," meant "get my horse, my hat, my gun." *"Sigue"* meant "go" "come." *"Sigue-sigue"* meant "run." *"Sigue"* accompanied by a waving of the arms in the direction of the enemy meant "deploy in skirmish line." I verily believe during the first few weeks most of the officers had at their command not more than eight or ten words. Thus when they wanted a fire built and food cooked they would say *"saca fuego"* (fire) *"saca tubig"* (water) *"saca manok y arroz* (chicken and rice) *sigue, sigue!"* They lived off the country and fortunately there was plenty of chickens and rice to be found. Chicken stew is good food!

October 29, 1899, we started on our march northward to cut off Aguinaldo from possible retreat to the northern part of the island. Marching on the road to Santa Rosa we were halted at the River Taboatin where our scouts had discovered a force of insurgents intrenching themselves on the northern bank, in the angle between the Taboatin River and the Pampanga River. Crawling forward among the bushes I had a good view of the enemy about seventy-five yards away. The bridge over the river had been destroyed and the insurgents on top of the high bank commanding the passage were busily engaged with pick and shovel, apparently unaware of our presence. It is a curious fact that far from possessing the acute vision of our red Indians, the Filipino, even when lying in ambush for the American, was usually discovered before he himself was aware of the presence of the foe.

General Young decided to send a force of cavalry up the river to seek a ford, and debouch in rear of the trenches. While this advance was being made, the troops in front should open up, assisted by machine guns in a gunboat lying at the mouth of the Taboatin River.

Owing to the mud and the difficulty of finding a ford the flank attack was not a success. Firing opened prematurely, the gatling guns on the gunboat made a fearful uproar but the insurgents got away without serious loss. Two of our men were killed. I accompanied the cavalry through the rice fields in an attempt to cut off the retreating googoos, but the mud was almost up to the horses' bellies, and after incredible exertions our attempt failed.

We stayed at Santa Rosa that night; the inhabitants having fled, the troops occupied their houses. The poorer quarters were assigned to the men, and contained nothing valuable. This was our usual custom in the Philippines, as we carried no tents. The more pretentious houses if not occupied by officers had to be protected from looters, who were often Filipinos or Chinese, the latter especially being keen to rob unprotected treasures. The next morning I accompanied a column of the 4th Cavalry commanded by Lieutenant Colonel Hays in a search for a ford to cross the Pampanga River. After a thirteen-mile march we found one above the town of Cabanatuan.

Along the main road houses were frequent. The people in these, when we appeared, displayed white flags as a sign of their peacefulness. Looking down the road and seeing a white flag hoisted by his neighbor, each peaceful inhabitant hung out the same sign. Thus the line of white flags extended far in advance of our column, and probably apprised the enemy of our approach!

Also to placate the invading force the natives often offered us gifts of eggs and fruit. As my stomach was still deranged from the effect of dengue fever and could digest only with difficulty the hardtack and bacon of the ration, these eggs were a boon to me. The natives I discovered were fond of partly hatched eggs, the contents being like custard. I even found these not unpalatable.

The next day, October 31st, I was directed by General Young to take a command consisting of two troops of the 4th Cavalry, Captains Erwin and Wheeler, and two companies of Macabebe scouts, Lieutenants Batson and Boutelle, proceed to and capture Aliaga, which General Otis considered an important strategic point.

Aliaga, a small town made up mostly of the poorer class of native houses, lay in the midst of an extensive plain noted for its fertility. In former times there had been in the vicinity extensive Spanish sugar plantations, but now all these had disappeared. It was probably due to the representations of the former Spanish owners, refugees at Manila, that General Otis considered it of such importance. One feature it had of military value: it was not far from Tarlac and its possession threatened that important place.

The march to Aliaga, ten miles distant, was only accomplished after surmounting considerable difficulties. After crossing the swollen Pampanga we plunged into a sea of mud. Even the Macabebe scouts were sometimes up to their bellies; our American horses plunged and floundered through it with difficulty. Often we had to halt the cavalry to give the horses, who were gasping for breath and trembling violently, a chance to recover themselves.

The scouts who were less embarrassed by the mud reached the town first. There were 200 insurgents there who hastily retreated when they heard of our approach. Riding forward rapidly, Batson captured a cart at the telegraph office which contained all the latest despatches from Tarlac. These, when deciphered and translated, showed that the insurgent government contemplated an early retirement from Tarlac, information of great value. I at once sent them by courier to General Young. I also asked his permission with my force to move fifteen miles to Victoria, a point on the railroad in rear of Tarlac. I believed I could thus cause the evacuation of that city threatened in front by MacArthur's army. It was our experience that the insurgents were always made panic-stricken by attacks in the rear. To this request General Young made no answer.

In the meantime I established my command in the town. One house, superior to the rest, I thought adapted for my headquarters. Climbing up the steep ladder into the house I was met by a corpulent person who evidently was the butler or major domo. Welcoming me and the officers with great effusiveness, he explained that Lieutenant Colonel Patilla of the Philippine army owned the house but was unavoidably absent (!); that the house and everything there were at my disposal. He further inquired when I would like dinner.

We found the house well furnished, with numerous bedrooms. Assigning these to the members of my staff, we presently sat down to a very good dinner. Five or six female servants, part of the household, did the cooking or waited on the table!

The next day our cavalry horses rested while Batson with his Macabebes scouted in the vicinity of the town. On the following day, November 2nd, this reconnoissance was continued. Near the town of Santiago, one and one half miles from Aliaga, Batson's force was fired upon by insurgents in ambush. (They turned out to be a force under Lieutenant Colonel Patilla). Directing Boutelle with his company to stand fast, Batson made a circuit and struck the enemy in the flank, driving them off the field in confusion and with much loss. He then discovered that

Boutelle had been killed! Boutelle had scorned to take cover, and was shot standing in the road, encouraging his men!

News came to me at once. Leaving one troop of cavalry and some scouts in Aliaga to hold the place, I rode with the remaining troops to join Batson. As I approached Santiago it was burning, a majestic column of smoke and fire ascending to the heavens. It had been set on fire by the Macabebes to avenge the death of their leader. Made of bamboo, with roofs and sides of nipa palm leaves, these Philippine houses burn like tinder, the fire spreading with inconceivable rapidity.

I joined Batson at 10.30 A. M. just as the insurgents, who had apparently reformed after their repulse, attacked again. Being mounted, on the road, within a short distance of the enemy, it was only their poor shooting which saved Brer Fox and me. Batson on the left of the line was engaged. My adjutant, Lieutenant Boniface, had left me to carry orders, when I discovered that Boutelle's company of Macabebes, without a leader, were not engaging in the fight. Leaving my horse with my orderly, Hannum, I took command of the company, and waving my arms, and commanding *"Sigue-sigue!"* as I had seen the lieutenants do, attempted to deploy them in skirmish line. But they looked at me like a lot of dogs ordered to "sic" (is it the same word?) and not seeing what to "sic at"; "Oh, the devil, come on then!" I cried and rushed forward. Instantly they deployed and followed me.

The enemy was on the other side of a canal. Reaching this I jumped in and thereby spoiled a perfectly good watch. I could wade across. But the little Macabebes would have had to swim; they cut bamboo poles and hauled each other across. Emerged on the other side we were soon in a hot fight; my adjutant,

Boniface, appearing, I turned the company over to him.

The skirmish was soon over. Meeting Batson: "Batson," said I, "let's follow these damn insurgents and wipe them off the face of the earth." "All right," said Batson and took the advance.

Then ensued a merry chase. Moving through the flooded country, we crossed in turn five rivers, some of them swimming deep. Bridges there were, but all wrecked; Batson and his men crossed by the stringers and I was astonished to see Batson's little pony walk across on the stringers as on a tight rope. Our big cavalry horses plunged through the streams. The enemy retreated to Zaragosa, where they ambushed us. This force was soon routed and a number of insurgents killed. We then advanced towards Carmen, where we had another fight and drove off the enemy.

It was then getting late. We could have gone farther but the river Chico stopped us, being too large to cross except in boats. We were near Tarlac and must have given Aguinaldo a pretty fright. In fact, it is likely this advance hastened Aguinaldo's flight from Tarlac.

We were fortunate in finding in Carmen a Filipino school teacher who spoke good Spanish and promised to lead us back to Aliaga by an easier route. By heading the rivers we arrived in front of that town without having to ford a single stream!

It was 10 P. M. and dark. As we approached we were fired on by the pickets. I halted and sounded on the trumpet "cease firing." More shots! I sounded "mess call." More shots! We sounded various calls, each time being greeted by shots from the pickets; it was 11 P. M. before we satisfied them we were not insurgents and were allowed to enter the town. We had been marching and fighting twelve hours.

Tired out, covered with mud, I climbed up the ladder into my quarters. I was met by the major domo, who announced calmly "Gentlemen, dinner is ready!" I felt I was campaigning in luxury!

In the morning I slept late. I was awakened by the crowd of servants rushing into the room crying, "Colonel, save us, save us, they are firing cannon at us!"

Sure enough, little shells about an inch in diameter were coming into town, bursting on the tin roofs. We turned out hastily. A force of insurgents about two miles from town, beyond a deep river, in the direction of Licap, had brought up a small gun, and were shelling us.

I deployed the Macabebes toward Licap. One troop of cavalry dismounted extended on their right in a cemetery surrounded by a wall, the other was held in reserve. The horses, which otherwise would have afforded a good target for the enemy (there was no cover in this flat town, the houses being erected on piles), were dispersed, each separate set of fours hiding behind a house. After an engagement of half an hour, in which we fired volleys, the enemy retreated.

Later in the day Dodds' troop of cavalry and Castner's company of scouts arrived. General Young at Cabanatuan had heard the sound of the cannon, and thought we were seriously engaged, and needed reinforcements! On the way Castner had had a fight and killed a number of insurgents.

Two days later I was ordered to return with my command and rejoin General Young at Cabanatuan. Knowing the town was full of spies and not wishing to be ambushed on my way back, I made all my preparations (inquiring the way, etc.) as though I intended to march in the opposite direction toward Tarlac.

The newspapers published this as "Parker's raid." Batson reported we killed forty insurgents.

I had often begged General Young to abandon his usual carabao transportation of ten miles per day and live on the country. "General," I said, "we will never be able to accomplish anything until we *shoot* all our carabaos!" I was accordingly pleased when he gave orders, before leaving Cabanatuan, to leave all property behind except what we could carry in our saddle bags. My rubber tub, extra toilet articles, most of my bedding and so forth were left here. I did not get them again for eighteen months! From that time on we lived on the "emergency ration," with what chickens and rice we could pick up.

We, the members of the staff, had considerable difficulty about messing. General Young's colored man, Powell, got some liquor and as a result went on a strike, declaring he would cook for the General, but not for his staff. So Young told us we must shift for ourselves. This was a serious deprivation. Employed often on separate missions carrying orders to the various commands, we were not in a position to establish a separate mess. Sometimes our orderlies were able to find and cook something for us, but often we were up against it. On several occasions I got food by carrying my meat ration can and tin-cup near a soldier's cook fire. Presently a soldier would politely say, "Would the Colonel like some coffee, some chicken and rice?" And in an absent-minded, careless way I would accept!

November 7th I marched with Young to Talavera, ten miles. November 8th to San José, sixteen miles. Here we had a skirmish and much night firing. We also captured an insurgent deposit of arms containing, among other things, shells for 6-inch and 8-inch cannon. Why the poor devils of insurgents carted these

Leonard Wood as Army Surgeon. Later Major General

enormous projectiles through the country I do not know. They certainly had no cannon which could use them!

November 10th to Lupoa. Had a small action. It rained heavily. Arriving at night in this little place the houses were all occupied when the cavalry came in.

As the soldiers, wet to the bone, marched to and fro in this little town seeking shelter, I heard one poor boy, in the pouring rain, sobbing. It was hard luck.

November 11th we marched to Humingan. Here the Macabebe scouts, in advance, had a considerable fight. With Dodds' troop I charged through the town and beyond for two miles, trying vainly to cut off the insurgents.

At Humingan I was left in command of the town for two days, having under me Batson and the Macabebe scouts, until I was relieved by Captain Ballance with his battalion of infantry. It was a considerable town. One night we thought we were to be attacked and I rode along the outpost line in the moonlight, listening to the bugle calls of the enemy. It was a weird experience.

The town was the headquarters of an insurgent regiment of *Milicia Nacional.* They were armed with wooden guns! They were part of the *levee en masse* of Aguinaldo's government; copying our laws, every ablebodied man belonged to the militia. (It is said that near Manila some of these poor devils with their wooden guns had been shot down by our troops, who of course thought they carried rifles.) While at Humingan I encouraged the officers to "present themselves," issuing a *proclama* that if they did so and should give their parole not to fight against the United States, they would not be disturbed.

One great reason why the insurgents did not fight

more effectively was that they were short of rifles and especially of ammunition. And many of their guns were old-style Remingtons. Important garrisons, like the one I encountered at San Mateo, were armed with the Spanish Mauser. Some of the *Milicia Nacional* were armed only with bolos, others with bows and arrows and spears. Of course these latter were not much used against our troops.

The insurgents were in great straits for bullets and powder, wherewith to reload their cartridge shells. For power some of them used the heads of safety matches; these are made of an explosive nitrate compound. But it took a great many matches to load a cartridge and matches were hard to get!

November 13th from Humingan I rode to Tayug. This was the most considerable city we had encountered, the seat of a bishopric and well-built town. We occupied the bishop's palace. Captain Dodd had just captured at San Nicolas, near Tayug, a train of insurgent carts on its way northward. It contained among other things a complete newspaper printing press and a cart containing many thousands of silver dollars in bags. These we piled up in our quarters.

That night General Young got information that Aguinaldo with a considerable force had passed through Urdaneta going east. I was ordered the next morning to go to Asingan, not far from Tayug, and join there Major Swigert's squadron of two troops of the 3rd Cavalry, and with them, as General Young's representative, start in pursuit.

Accordingly the next morning, November 14th, accompanied by my orderly, Private Hannum (I had no other escort, although it was a risky proceeding), I rode to Asingan, six miles. Thence, with Swigert's command I marched to Urdaneta. Here we found the trail of a considerable force of insurgents going towards Binalonan, the soft mud being patted down by hundreds of bare feet.

At Binalonan, at 2 P. M., we met General Young with Chase's troop of the 3rd Cavalry. The trail we were following turned toward Manaog and we proceeded in that direction, followed at the distance of one mile by General Young with Chase's troop.

The afternoon became very dark and it threatened rain. The troops marched in the following order: platoon of Troop K, 3rd Cavalry, as an advance guard; then the two troops of cavalry, Major Swigert and I riding at their head.

At about 5 P. M. being in a wood, the advance guard halted and began to dismount. I rode up at a trot. "Get on your horses; why are you dismounting?" said I. "The enemy are just in front," replied the non-commissioned officer. Major Swigert then rode up. "Major Swigert, you had better charge them," I said. "Do you think General Young would want me to charge?" asked Swigert. "That is exactly what General Young would want!" I replied.

At this juncture a non-commissioned officer called out, "Get off the road; they are going to fire a volley!" I turned to Swigert, he seemed undecided what to do. Ignoring the proprieties of the occasion, by which Swigert, not I, should have given the order to the troops, and seeing that delay was fatal, I drew my pistol and shouted "Draw pistols. Charge!" and dashed to the front, in order to give the lead.

In a moment I was among the insurgents. They were in column, on the road leading through the forest. They were hampered by the fact that to fire they had to aim over each other's heads. Some discharged their pieces wildly and then jumped aside, some jumped to one side and then fired, others threw down their guns and plunged into the bushes. My horse, Brer Fox, was moving along the road at full run, in a series of tremendous strides, jumping mud holes. When I had fired six shots from my revolver (it was the one with which in 1877 I had killed buffalo) and it was empty, I looked around for the head of the column of our troops. It was not in sight! I was alone, except for the presence of two men!

Just in front of me (I did my best to pass him but his horse was too fast) was Private Lugenbrouch, Troop K, 3rd Cavalry, a member of the advance guard. Behind me came my orderly, Private Hannum. The column of insurgents we were charging through seemed to have no end. I muttered to myself, "What a damn fool I am!" and though my pistol was empty continued snapping it at the googoos and as I passed them, like a flash of lightning, relieved my feelings by giving them a hearty cursing, bestowing upon them a volley of all the opprobrious names in the category. As for them, while they were continually firing and bullets whizzed by me, we were going too fast, and we arrived upon them too suddenly, for accurate aim. As for our fire I doubt if we did any considerable damage to the enemy.

Private Hannum says in the affidavit made July 3, 1900, that we were "about 300 yards in advance of any support whatever. . . . I fired one shot to my left front, then turning in my saddle to the right rear I discovered an insurgent in the art of raising his rifle at us. I shot him through the left breast just above the heart. The ammunition in my revolver then failed to explode."

The column of the enemy extended a half mile or more. At the rear of their column was some open ground where a hundred or more men had climbed a high fence and were running across an open field.

Here I ordered Hannum and Lugenbrouck to dismount and open fire with their carbines.

They were engaged in doing this when the leading troop of the 3rd Cavalry came up, and I requested the captain to dismount and open fire on the enemy, in plain view, about 200 yards away.

And here came in his West Point training. Instead of commanding, "Dismount, as skirmishers, commence firing!" as a volunteer would have done, he first gave the command for "forming fours," berating the men for not getting in their proper squads. He then gave the orders for dismounting and forming line and counting fours, preparatory to deploying!

The insurgents were fast disappearing. "For Christ's sake, open fire!" I yelled. I fear his feelings were hurt.

Leaving him to pursue the enemy I galloped back to where General Young with Chase's troop had halted during the action. I hurriedly explained the situation to him; it was getting dark, and at my suggestion he had Chase's troop dismount and advance in skirmish line through the woods. A lively action was the result, and a number of the enemy were killed or captured. But it was too dark to accomplish much.

Without waiting to see this action begun I asked authority from General Young to push on with Swigert's cavalry towards Posorubio, where we had heard the insurgents were heading and, if possible, capture Aguinaldo. General Young assented. I rejoined Swigert's column, and we assembled for the march.

Rain was coming down in torrents, and the darkness was pitchy black. Perhaps it was because of this that the guide lost his way. At any rate, at about 9 P. M. arriving at a village, we found we were traveling in a direction directly opposite Posorubio. As our horses and men were thoroughly exhausted we halted and got under shelter, remaining there until morning, when we rejoined General Young at Manaog. There we were informed that in the fight twelve insurgents had been killed, and eight captured, also thirty-six rifles with ammunition, and some carabaos, pack animals, loaded with supplies.

Major Swigert, an old and experienced officer of cavalry, resented my being placed over him, and was especially angry that I should have presumed to give the command for the charge. It was perhaps for this reason that in Swigert's report of the fight there is no mention whatever of my being present. However, that did not prevent General Young from recommending that I be given a brevet of lieutenant colonel, regular army, for what I did at Manaog. (I had already been recommended for the brevet of major for my services at San Mateo.)

But neither General Young nor any of our officers present realized, for years, the importance of what was accomplished at Manaog. We had cut off and dispersed a force of over 1,000 well-armed men, nearly the whole of the troops remaining to Aguinaldo.

United States Senate document No. 331, Part 3, gives the diary of Simeon A. Villa, Aguinaldo's secretary, of the flight and wanderings of Aguinaldo.

He details how Aguinaldo and his party left the railroad at Calasiao on November 13th and marched to Santa Barbara, where they were joined by General Pilar's brigade, a total of "more than 1,200 armed men," thence to the "extensive forest of Manaog." Here they were joined by the troops coming from Urdaneta, reaching it at dawn, November 14th. "After everybody had breakfasted the honorable President ordered that our forces be divided into two columns, one to serve as vanguard under General Pilar himself, the other to form the rear guard, commanded by Colonel Montenegro. . . . Some 250 troops composed the vanguard. . . . November 16th daylight came in the midst of rain. At 7 o'clock we were all awake when Lieutenant Colonel Joven, one of the rear guard commanders, presented himself to the honorable President saying he had arrived last night after we were all asleep. He also reported that the rear guard soldiers disbanded and scattered in the town of Manaog on account of being surprised by a large American column while they were passing through that town, and that he had been able to collect only seventeen of his men, whom he brought with him to this place!"

The diary shows that no other detachments of the rear guard force ever joined Aguinaldo.

In 1902, being an adjutant general at Washington, I met Buencamino, Aguinaldo's Secretary of State, in the office of Mr. Root, Secretary of War. Buencamino, who was with the force we attacked in the forest of Manaog, made a written statement to General Young and myself that Aguinaldo's force comprised in all 2,000 men and that the rear guard consisted of 1,300 armed men. "The onslaught of the American cavalry was so terrible," he says, "that the Filipinos were dispersed, that is, separated into smaller bands. At twelve o'clock midnight Leyva, Montenegro and Joven met me and said they had been completely routed by the Americans; that they tried to rally their forces but could only collect about 150 soldiers." It is thought that most of this detachment of 150 went back on the back trail and formed part of the force routed near Mangataren November 27, 1899, by Colonel J. Franklin Bell. Bell, shortly after, was promoted brigadier general of volunteers.

The situation, briefly explained, was this: General Wheaton with his command had landed at San Fabian, some twelve or fifteen miles northwest of Manaog, on November 7th. His orders were to connect with Lawton and cut off retreat to the northeast by Aguinaldo. He pushed forward but slowly. On November 12th one of his regiments, the 33rd Volunteers, had a fight with the insurgents at San Jacinto near Manaog, at which Major Logan, son of my old friend General Logan, was killed. The troops then occupied Manaog but after some hours withdrew, in spite of the fact that they were informed by Lieutenant Thayer, coming from Asingan, that our troops were there.

On November 13th Aguinaldo, hearing of Wheaton's landing and fearing he would be cut off, left the railroad en route to Posorubio. He had probably heard that the route via Manaog was open. Coming from Calasiao the direction of his march was east. At Manaog the road turns north, crosses the river and then continues east. He left his rear guard just south of the river at Manaog, the head near the ford over the river. As we were marching south of the river westward it was the head, not the rear, of the rear guard that we struck. We scattered it, driving the remnants back west. Aguinaldo with some two hundred and fifty troops pursued his march to Posorubio and beyond.

It seems apparent that Aguinaldo's rear guard expected the pursuit to come from the west, that is from MacArthur's command, but not from the east. This is shown by the fact that the baggage was found at the head of the column. But in every way it was a faulty disposition. The Filipino troops were a tried force, however, veterans of many fights with MacArthur's troops in front of Tarlac. Had they reached the northern part of the island (Aguinaldo's destination was Bayambong on the Aparri River) and united there to the troops under Tinio and others, they would have given the Americans a long and hard campaign, difficult through lack of railroads or other communications. But their dispersal put fear into the soul of Aguinaldo and from that moment his only object was to hide. He disappeared from sight completely, and was no longer a factor in the insurrection. Otis, who had sent a telegram, "If a certain personage is captured keep him on a ship, by no means bring him to Manila," was glad, for political reasons, he had not been captured. Aguinaldo could have said too much! "Dead men tell no tales!" No steps to discover his whereabouts were taken until March, 1901, when his hiding place was discovered at Palanan, an isolated mountain town on the northeast coast where Colonel, afterwards General, Frederick Funston, in an ingenious and extremely gallant way, effected his capture.

It was well that at Manaog we did not dismount to attack. The insurgents had the coming of nightfall on their side, and the shelter of the forest; the attack would have progressed slowly and ended with the darkness; the insurgents would have made good their escape. This instance shows the great value of cavalry in certain contingencies.

It is a curious commentary on our prevailing lack of information in this campaign, that this action, a decisive one to the insurgents, should have been regarded by our superiors as little more than a skirmish! As a fact: *I had altered the whole course of the war!*

The next morning I said to General Young, "General, Major Swigert is an old and experienced officer; he ranks me in the Regular Army; he resents my being placed over him; he will probably do well if placed on his own responsibility. Let me join your staff with the other officers!"

Young replied, "Oh, damn it, all right; you come with me!" He then gave orders to Swigert to make a reconnaissance to Posorubio. In the meantime Young, to hurry forward reinforcements (he had with him only three troops of cavalry), went back to Asingan, taking his staff and Captain Chase's troop of the 3rd Cavalry. Up to this time we had heard nothing from Wheaton's command, and did not know whether it had landed.

November 16th, the Macabebe scouts having arrived at Asingan, we marched back to Binalonan, six miles through water. A typhoon with heavy rains had continued since November 14th and the whole country was flooded. At Binalonan we were rejoined by Swigert's cavalry squadron returning from its reconnaissance to Posorubio. Asked if he had heard anything about Aguinaldo, Swigert replied, "Oh, yes, he was there; he left Posorubio as I entered!" "Why did you not pursue him?" "I had no orders to pursue him, sir!"

Young afterwards said to me, bitterly, "If it hadn't been for you, I would have caught Aguinaldo!" "How do you mean, sir?" "Why, you begged off going with Swigert!" I could hardly suppress a laugh.

From Binalonan, November 17th, General Young with Chase's troop, following the Macabebes, marched to Posorubio. I was sent with a detachment of ten soldiers to San Fabian with dispatches for General Wheaton whom we heard was there. I also was to obtain some food supplies for the staff. At Manaog I found a detachment of the 33rd Infantry which had finally occupied that place. At San Jacinto, a few miles beyond the headquarters of the 33rd Volunteers, I found to my great surprise Lieutenant Thayer of the 3rd Cavalry. He had been sent from Asingan November 13th to San Fabian to ascertain if Wheaton were there. Running into ambush, and his detachment being partly scattered, he had arrived safely. But

Wheaton would not let him go back! In the meantime we all thought he had been captured or killed, and we remained in ignorance of Wheaton's arrival.

I cannot help thinking it was General Wheaton's fault that the gap at San Mateo between the two forces was not closed.

Toward the end of the month I was at Vigan and picked up in a toilet room a crumpled telegram. It was from General Tinio at Posorubio to General Allessandro at Vigan. It read: "Had a severe skirmish with the Americans, November 12th, at San Jacinto, in which one company and one platoon of my battalion (150 men) were engaged; my loss eight men killed of whom Lieutenant ——— died fighting like a hero."

In his statement Buencamino says Tinio's force was three hundred and fifty armed men. And in this same encounter Wheaton estimated his (enemy's) loss at three hundred!

Continuing on towards San Fabian I rejoiced in the fact that the typhoon was over and the sun was at last shining. I had been wet through for three days and I was now getting comparatively dry. Just outside of San Fabian I came to a place where some soldiers were mending the road. There was a large pool and they pointed to the safest place for me to cross. Riding at a trot I arrived at the middle of the pool: my horse went down and I fell between his legs. At the same moment Private Hannum's horse, before he could check him, fell alongside of Brer Fox, the legs of Hannum's horse also towards me. After much floundering of man and horse we emerged, I soaked through and covered with mud from head to foot!

Arrived in the town I at once took my despatches to Colonel Bisbee, commanding officer. He was keen to learn the news, and there I sat dripping, for a half hour, telling him of our campaign. I was glad enough when he let me go! I went to the quarters of my old friend, Captain Faison, who to my immense gratitude provided me with a bath and dry clothing.

Poor old Brer Fox, my faithful horse, was now exhausted. By the kindness of Captain Faison I obtained at San Fabian a place where he could rest and recover while I procured a new mount from the Government.

The next day, November 18th, with my detachment, I started to rejoin General Young at Posorubio. Ten miles from San Fabian, with two men ahead as an advance guard, I discovered, coming down the road from Posorubio, two men, a big man in white on a big horse, and a little man in khaki on a small horse. Halting and looking through my binoculars, I recognized in the big man, Lawton! He was accompanied by his young son, Manly Lawton, and was riding through this hostile country *in front* of his advance guard!

I was amazed at his recklessness; it looked as if he wanted to be killed. On joining him I did not fail to expostulate with him on the chances he was taking and especially on his wearing white clothing, a shining mark for a sharpshooter. He answered ironically, "Well, if I am killed, it will be the fault of the Government; this white suit was originally khaki color, and if they don't dye it properly it isn't my fault!"

He was in a pessimistic mood; he had, on crossing the Agno River a few days before, lost by drowning his aide, Lieutenant Luna, 34th Infantry, and two men of his escort. The abundant supplies he had accumulated for his division at San Isidro and Cabanatuan he had been obliged to leave behind, not being able to forward them on account of the bad roads.

He directed me to accompany him back to San Fabian, there to meet Swigert's command and take it north, along the shore road. The men of my detachment, carrying the commissary supplies, continued on towards Posorubio.

As to these commissaries there is a sequel to be told. Among them was a large plug of chewing tobacco that I had bought for my own use. When the detachment reached General Young he opened the bag of commissaries and said, "Here is a plug of tobacco I didn't order. Does anyone here want a piece?" Lieutenant Quinlan of the Macabebe scouts (now colonel and judge advocate) took one-half of the plug. Two days afterwards at Aringey the Macabebes had a severe fight with the insurgents and Quinlan was hit over the heart by a bullet, knocking him down. Finding he was not hurt he arose and discovered that my plug of tobacco which was in his shirt pocket had saved his life! The bullet had hit it squarely, tearing it into shreds, but not penetrating beyond.

When I joined the cavalry at San Fabian, Swigert said in an angry tone, "Before we go any farther I want it settled—who commands this force, you or I?" I said, "Major, you know very well I don't presume to command your force; you are the commander, not I!" "That's all very well," Swigert rejoined, "but you did not seem to think that way when you gave the command to charge, three days ago!" That riled me. "Suppose we visit General Lawton," I said, "and you make your complaint to him!" But Swigert would not go.

Swigert was then fifty-three years old, having graduated from West Point in 1868. He was not the only officer in his squadron who seemed disgruntled and disappointed. Truth is, the 3rd Cavalry, after having gone through the disenchantment of the Santiago campaign with its attendant sickness and hardships, was apparently not in a frame of mind to show much enthusiasm at fighting "googoos."

Next morning, November 19th, we marched northward along a road skirting the ocean. Nearing the town of San Tomas, I noticed the natives seemed much alarmed, chasing their cattle off the fields toward the mountains. Presently we came to a small river running across the road and emptying into the ocean. I was with the advance guard. At the place where the road crossed we plunged into the river and found the bottom was of quicksand. We regained the farther bank with much difficulty and I sent a man back to advise Major Swigert to avoid the river by riding in the ocean around its mouth, which he proceeded to do.

Going on a few paces I suddenly discovered in front of me and not two hundred yards away, on the right side of the road, a body of armed men dressed in a uniform like that worn by the Macabebes, marching in single file from a house and disappearing into a trench. They looked so peaceful that I dismounted and waved my handkerchief to them. I received no response and we perceived that they were getting ready to fire. We had hardly time to jump into a grove of guava trees on the left side of the road, when they fired a volley, not at us, but at the two troops of cavalry on the beach. Several horses and men were hit.

Leaving my horse with my orderly I ran back to the command. They had dismounted, and I led them along the beach, taking care to keep low down near the water, where we were out of sight from the people in the trench.

When we had arrived opposite the trench I led them up towards it. What was my surprise to find raised ground between us and the trench. When we reached this shelter we found we were protected by the earthwork of a redoubt facing the sea; all we had to do, to see the enemy, was to look over the top and there they were, only sixty-five yards distant, a row of hats showing above the edge of a deep "standing" trench! It was as if for this duel they had taken one trench and given us another! There were seventy-five to one hundred men on each side.

Then ensued a scene of indescribable excitement. Both sides fired as fast as they could; the uproar was ear-splitting. Some of our raw recruits were so frantic that they did not aim or even look over the top of the battery but fired up into the air. Oblivious to all else, it was necessary to shake them before they could comprehend that they must aim at the enemy.

Presently I noticed some soldiers aiming off to the right at what seemed to be a dark mass on a hill a thousand yards away. With my glasses I discovered they were a crowd of troops. As General Young and the Macabebes were likely to come from Posorubio in that direction, I checked these men.

We were about to arrange a flank attack when we noticed the enemy's fire was slackening. They had a covered "getaway" leading to a brushy ravine. Leaving our shelter and running across the road to cut them off we were greeted by a shower of bullets from the force on the hill. Against them we went into action. A few volleys made them retire. In the meantime the force in the trench had disappeared.

Our losses were one killed and seven wounded. We also had several horses wounded. In the trench we found seven dead Filipinos, all shot through the head.

We put our dead soldier in the trench, and covered him with earth. I read a short prayer from my prayer book and we marched on.

Nearing the town of Agoo, fourteen miles from San Fabian, we found the outskirts deserted. But looking up the principal street we saw two figures in white, who seemed by their actions to regard our approach with some trepidation but were resolved to stand their ground. Riding forward and waving my handkerchief I found them to be the *Presidente* of the city with a Frenchman. The *Presidente* welcomed us and invited the officers to stay in his house.

It was a large structure with plenty of room for all of us. We were tired and hungry. The *Presidente* said we should soon have dinner. Great preparations for a feast began. Quacking ducks and geese were carried through the house and despatched—chickens, turkeys and even a calf. It was like a Biblical scene. We finally sat down to a big repast. There were few vegetables, but there was plenty of meat, sweets and fruit. We did full justice to this peace offering. The *Presidente* was a nice old fellow, very conciliatory. That evening our outposts heard firing to the north, which soon ceased.

Next day we marched to Booang, fifteen miles. Here we met the Macabebe scouts. They had come with General Young from Posorubio by an inland road following Aguinaldo's trail, reaching the main road the evening before at Aringay. There they had had a fight with the insurgents, the noise of which we had heard at Agoo. One scout was killed and Quinlan was saved by my tobacco. I wanted it back, even in its shattered condition, but Quinlan wouldn't give it up.

Our most serious casualty in the fight was Batson's gunshot wound through the foot. At first he made light of it. But it finally was the cause of his retirement from active service.

Next day we marched to San Fernando de la Union and rejoined General Young. This place, one of the few harbors on the coast, had been strongly fortified by the insurgents. But it was all in vain, for the reason that General Young, with Chase's troop of cavalry, in advance of all other troops, arrived there before the bulk of the Filipino garrison, which was dispersed about, working in the fields, could be collected. The cavalry troop marched so fast that the news of its coming had hardly been received before the defenses were attacked. Dismounting in open ground, Chase had gallantly attacked on foot the apparently formidable defenses. It was a risky thing to do but it was successful. To have waited for reinforcements would have been fatal.

At San Fernando General Young had ascertained that Aguinaldo had left the shore road at Booang and started via Naguilian through the mountains. Accordingly with the cavalry and scouts we made a hurried trip to Naguilian. There apparently orders and information Young received caused him to abandon temporarily the direct pursuit. Leaving the Macabebes under Colonel Wilder to follow Aguinaldo, General Young returned to San Fernando, in order to pursue his march northward by the coast road. It was not certain at this time that Aguinaldo was not making for Candon or Vigan, points on this road near which considerable forces of the enemy had concentrated, and it was General Otis' desire, as shown by his despatches, that these places be occupied by our troops.

General Young, with three troops of the 3rd Cavalry, was now far in advance of the bulk of his command. The remainder of the 3rd Cavalry, delayed by the typhoon, the high rivers and lack of horseshoes, were still south of San Fabian. The troops of the 4th Cavalry had apparently been held back near Cabanatuan for work in that vicinity.

It was a proof of General Young's wonderful fortitude in the face of drawbacks that he did not falter in the least. With him the command was always "Forward! Forward!"

XII

VIGAN

At San Fernando the gunboat *Samar* was lying, commanded by Lieutenant Mustin of the navy; a gallant officer and extraordinarily plucky, who afterwards became a captain and chief of the Navy Air Service, dying prematurely. The sea was high and Mustin, unable to land in the usual manner, in order to bring General Young some dispatches, came ashore by swimming through the breakers from his rowboat, which remained outside the combers.

That evening General Young sent for me and we had the following conversation.

"I want you tomorrow to go on board the gunboat *Samar,* proceed to sea and intercept the gunboat *Callao,* which is coming here with one company of the 34th Infantry. Go with it to Vigan, capture the town, release the Spaniards held as prisoners there, and operate against General Tinio who is at the pass of Narvacan, eight miles from Vigan with 1,500 men, fortifying it. General Tinio has 3,500 Spanish prisoners, which you will, if possible release."

"Very well, General. But how many men did you say you would give me for this job?"

"Oh, you will have a company of infantry!" But apparently seeing some surprise depicted on my face he added, "That will be enough. Anyway I am marching up the coast and will be along in a few days!" I made no reply, but I was proud to think that General Young believed I could do all this with one company.

Vigan was about eighty-five miles north of San Fernando.

The next morning General Young, with the cavalry, pursued his way north, while Mustin and I with Batson, who was to be transferred to a hospital at Manila, boarded the *Samar*. This was a matter of some difficulty. The sea was high. Commandeering a lot of natives at a fishing village near the town and getting into a large native boat on the beach, the natives carried the boat on their shoulders with us in it, out through the breakers. Once beyond the broken water we rowed to the gunboat which was rising and falling in the enormous waves. From a boom that stretched up over the stern hung a rope and belt. Navigating with some difficulty to a point under the boom, and fastening the belt around the body, each of us in turn was hoisted into the air and lowered and dropped on the deck of the ship.

The gunboat *Callao* did not appear and we went up the coast hoping to confer with General Young. The gale increased in intensity, and it became necessary to return.

We went back to San Fernando and anchored. The next day the gale subsided; we ran up the coast to report to General Young, but no communication was possible. We then proceeded south to San Fabian and anchored near the battleship *Oregon*. The *Callao* was there. We learned that the infantry company, on account of the high sea, had not been able to embark and had marched by land, with Major March's battalion, to San Fernando.

Mustin agreed with me that the navy might be of considerable assistance as a landing force in the capture of Vigan. He thought he could arrange it. "Go on board the *Oregon,*" he said, "and do the polite to Commander Wilde but don't be too insistent about

Vigan. I will go on board later and jolly up the old man!"

Accordingly I made an official visit to the *Oregon.* I must say I felt cheap, in my dirty khaki suit and muddy boots, as I climbed aboard the spotlessly neat *Oregon,* with its glistening brasses and holystoned deck and was conducted by a white-clad officer to the commander.

Commander Wilde was very cordial, and much interested in the progress of the troops. After drinking several highballs—they had ice in them, unheard of commodity!—and congratulating him on the very great aid the navy was giving us, I retired.

Later Mustin visited him and returning said Wilde had agreed to go to Vigan and look the ground over and that he thought everything was all right. We set sail that night for San Fernando, but in the darkness missed the port and did not arrive there until ten the next morning.

Landing, I found Major March and asked that he embark all or part of his battalion on the *Samar, Callao* and *Oregon* for transportation to Vigan. I showed him my instructions from General Young. He refused, alleging contrary orders from General Wheaton. "General Young ranks General Wheaton," I said. "I don't know about that!" replied March. We had quite a sharp discussion; finally I made my demand in writing, to which he adjoined his written refusal. I then left, and we steamed to Vigan, anchoring at Carayan, the port of Vigan, three miles from the town, in company with the *Callao* and *Oregon* which had already arrived.

There was a curious sequel to this refusal of March to obey General Young's orders. Scouting north the next day March fell in with General Young who took him along with him. A week later when Young was near Candon he got news of a body of insurgents near Cayan, Lepanto Province, and sent March with his battalion in that direction. So March, on December 7th, met and destroyed a force protecting Aguinaldo's march, killing General Pilar and capturing General Conception, for which he received great applause, and was in high favor with General Young when I next met Young. March afterwards became major general and chief of staff of our army in the World War.

The next morning early, the *Samar* steamed near the beach, where it was fired on from trenches on the shore. This was what Mustin was hoping for and he immediately replied. This was the signal for the beginning of a grand fusillade on the part of all of the ships. In a few minutes they were firing their six-inch guns, their three-inch guns, their gatling guns, their rifles. The noise on the deck of the steel-walled *Samar* was frightful. I believe that the *Oregon* even fired one of her 13-inch guns. One of the shells took off the leg of an old woman five miles away! The effect of the shells hitting the sand dunes on shore was like the explosion of volcanoes.

This was a new kind of fight for me. I reclined in an easy chair on the deck of the *Samar,* looked on and laughed. "How long are they going to keep this up?" I asked Mustin. "The insurgents have left long ago!" "Why, I guess the old man will shoot until he has used up his annual allowance; he hasn't had any target practice this year!"

Suddenly, on the *Oregon,* flags ran up and we ceased firing. Then more flags ran up; boats were lowered and marines and sailors tumbled into the boats. Mustin sent me ashore.

We landed through the breakers with some difficulty. Once ashore I proceeded to a house near by; it was part of the *Camarin* or storehouse of the

Tabacalera company. An old Frenchman who was in charge was at breakfast and as I had not yet eaten anything that morning I sat down with him gladly. I asked him for a horse in order to ride to town; he gave me a horse and also a mounted servant. I set out for the town. After proceeding some distance, I overtook the sailors and marines (about two hundred), Commander McCracken in charge. He was very busy giving some instructions to his men. Presently a horde of people in *quilezes* and *carromatos* (Filipino vehicles) came down the road. They turned out to be mostly escaped Spanish prisoners, among them Albert Sonnigsen, an American photographer whom the insurgents had taken captive near Manila. "Come on!" they cried, "the insurgents have all left the town! There will be no resistance!" I asked McCracken what he was going to do. "I must give these men a little instruction in *advance guard* and *patrol duty* before I go any farther," said he. "All right," said I, "I'm going ahead!"

I was joined by four sailors carrying guns with fixed bayonets. Whether they were sent by McCracken I don't know but they looked to me exceedingly comical. As we neared the town we heard the bells of the church ringing. Entering it we found the sidewalls lined with people shouting, *"Vivan los Americanos, mueren los Tagalos!"* (Hurrah for the Americans, down with the Tagalos.) As I proceeded along the street, in my torn and dirty uniform, on my dejected looking pony, my feet almost touching the ground, amid all these acclamations and ringing of bells it seemed to me much like the celebrated entry into Jerusalem told of in the Good Book. Presently a band of music appeared and bore down on me. In front of it walked a man with an immense bamboo pole, on the end of which was a green wreath, in token, I suppose, of peace. The band was followed by dignitaries: the *Presidente* of the Province, the *Presidente* of the town, the lieutenants of the various *barrios,* the chief of police, some priests, etc. On seeing the band my pony refused to go any farther; I slid to the ground and was at once surrounded by the officials, who were profuse with felicitations and loud expressions of friendship toward the Americans. I was overwhelmed. I expostulated: *"Yo no soy commandante—el Capitan de los marineros es commandante!"* (I am not the commander—the captain of the sailors is the commander.) But they seemed to pay no attention; they conducted me through the streets, lined with huzzaing crowds to the municipal building where they made more speeches. And the bells rang and the band played!

It was half an hour after my arrival that McCracken with his sailors came up, and by that time the enthusiasm had nearly subsided. I was pleased that we had taken the town; McCracken promised me that the navy would at once send a gunboat for troops to relieve the sailors, and in the meantime I felt it was up to me to take a back seat and let the navy manage things their own way. So I hunted up a comfortable room and bed in the municipal building (my baggage consisted of a saddle, bridle and a pair of saddlebags containing one change of underclothing) and established myself there. I did not think it worth while to bring up the subject of relative rank, attempt to take command, or even to give advice. The regulations require that when combined forces of the army and navy serve on shore the senior officer takes command. If my orderly had been present I might have pointed to him as my "troops," but he was unfortunately absent, sick. In the meantime I studied the town, the system of civil government, the military situation, and became acquainted with the civil officials. The navy was busy patrolling and reconnoitering and perfecting its outpost system.

Vigan, one of the largest and handsomest towns in the Philippines, with a population of more than forty thousand, was the capital of the Province of Ilocos Sur and the seat of a bishopric. The inhabitants, *Ilocanos,* spoke a distinctive dialect and were noted for their thrift. The town was well built and contained many public buildings of stone. On the main plaza on the south side were the seminary and the municipal building, where we were quartered. On the north side were a large convent and bishop's palace. On the east were the cathedral and a separate bell tower. On the west were a building we called the "Spanish hospital" (some sick Spaniards were there) and a roofless stone building formerly the casino. Around the park-like plaza extended a stone coping which had supported an iron fence. In front of the Spaish hospital was a stone balustrade with stone pillars supporting a railing. These details are essential to understand the murderous fighting which later took place on the plaza.

The river Abra skirted the town on the south, the road to San Fernando de la Union crossing it by means of a ford, and eight miles south, leading from this road to the province of Bangued, through the mountains, was the pass of Narvacan, where Tinio with fifteen hundred men had thrown up fortifications. Tinio, of course, had his spies in the city, and as we heard later, he personally, in disguise, visited it.

The governor of the province, Senor Acosta, was very friendly, as were also the mayor of the town and the principal officials. Acosta, a large Filipino, was exceedingly timid, besides being a great toper. Whenever I met him he pressed on me his bottle of *vino,* a Philippine decoction made of the distilled sap of the palm. He assured me it was *"bueno por el estomago"* (good for the stomach) and in the absence of other stimulant I found it, in small quantities, to be a satisfactory tonic.

Two days after my arrival the *Callao* brought Company B, 33rd Infantry, Captain Van Way, Lieutenants Lipop and Pickel. Next day the transport *Castellano,* in charge of Captain Hacker, arrived with a hundred and thirteen sick and footsore men of the 33rd Infantry picked up at San Fernando. They were under charge of Major Cronin, 33rd Infantry, sick. The transport also brought 50,000 cartridges and some rations. Commander McCracken and his sailors and marines then went back to their ships and I assumed command. I quartered the officers and soldiers in the bishop's palace on the main plaza. Some of the sick and footsore men later became fit for duty, making my total effective force eventually a hundred and twenty men. Our position was protected by five outposts on the outer edges of the town, by a night and day patrol in the principal streets and by sentinels at the quarters and commissary.

The officers were a fine lot. I had trouble with Major Cronin, who on first arrival refused to obey my orders on the ground that the 33rd Infantry belonged to Wheaton's command, not to Young's, and that I was a staff officer and could not exercise command. On receiving this information I took out my watch and said, "Cronin, agree within five minutes to obey my orders, else either you or I will have to go into irons!" For I was faced with the possibility of having my command taken from me and rather than have that happen I had determined personally to use physical force. Cronin's resistance vanished, and he did good work afterwards.

The men were a rough and tough lot. The wealthy Filipinos were in the habit, on the approach of our troops, of burying their money in the ground, sometimes under their houses. Our men, unknown to their officers, often discovered these treasures by poking in the ground with their bayonets and ramrods. The favorite crap game, played under my windows, was for seventy-five pesos a throw!

One day in the street I saw a big crowd of these soldiers around some object, hee-hawing at the top of their voices. Curious to see the cause of their merriment I made my way through the crowd. In the center stood two Igorrotes, just come down from the mountains. I had never before seen these savages. Totally naked, except for a "necktie" around the loins, they were of a nearly white color. Well built, clean and healthy looking, they were rather pleasing to look at. Each man carried as a weapon, a club. As for the merriment of the soldiers, the Igorrotes seemed to understand there was nothing offensive in it.

General Young, whom I had last seen on November 23rd, failed to arrive, though we had several false alarms of his approach. In the meantime I paid some attention to civil matters, seeing that the streets were cleaned up and so forth. For cheapness, the city government was unique. The mayor got fifty pesos per month (twenty-five dollars), the chief of police twenty-four, policemen twelve, school teachers twelve. But it seemed to be a perfectly good government.

When we first came to the islands the Filipino, when told the advantages of learning English, often said, "Why should I learn English? I want to learn *American!*" So I got to talking about the "American language" before I left the island. Some day, may that be its name!

Finding a printing press in town I published over my name a *proclama* or proclamation to the inhabitants of Vigan. I told them the war was at an end, that Aguinaldo was a fugitive hiding in the mountains, that the Americans brought them peace and prosperity, that it was the duty of every good citizen to swear allegiance to our flag. To this Tinio, the insurgent general, replied by a counter *proclama* (written, not printed) that the war was not over, Aguinaldo was not a fugitive, and that they had a bullet for every Filipino who joined the Americans.

It was early on the morning of December 3, 1899, that Second Lieutenant Pickel brought me word that we were to be attacked the following night. Pickel, a good-looking fellow, was a favorite of the ladies, and this information had been whispered to him by a pretty *mestiza,* the daughter of a Spanish sergeant. Later in the day two Filipinos, in strict confidence, made individually the same statement. However, such reports were so frequent during this insurrection, and so often turned out to be erroneous, that I did not attach undue importance to this one, beyond reinforcing the patrol in town, and determining where, in case we were attacked, I should post my detachments. That night I slept soundly.

It was 3.50 A. M. December 4th when we were awakened by a fusillade in the streets. The patrol had encountered a body of insurgents. We immediately turned out. There was no moon, clouds obscured the sky and the night was pitch black. The company was speedily formed in front of the barracks and I divided off two detachments of sixteen men each; one under Lieutenant Pickel to reinforce the patrol, and one I took and posted behind the stone coping at the west end of the plaza, facing the Spanish hospital, where it was reported insurgents were in position.

In the darkness nothing could be seen. I took two men of this detachment with me and proceeded to reconnoitre the stone casino at the northwest corner of the plaza. I had arrived perhaps thirty feet from this building when a tremendous volley was fired, coming from the windows of the casino, but particularly from the stone fence in front of the hospital. Fortunately it hit none of us. I threw myself on the ground and partly rolled, partly crawled back to the stone coping. Here we were about forty yards from the enemy behind the stone fence. In rolling over I had lost my revolver, but this did not particularly worry me; I had other things to do than to act as sharpshooter. Further, the only mark for the enemy was the flashes of our guns. The enemy was firing from the loopholes between the pillars of the balustrade.

I ordered the men behind the coping to hold out to the last extremity; this they did, some of them eventually being killed there.

I quote here from my report. "I then ran back to the barracks and posted Lieutenant Lipop with sixteen men in the 'seminary,' a stone building looking out on both plazas, and having a wing which flanked the rear of the buildings west of it. I then rejoined the men behind the stone coping, and the fire from the hospital slackening, called for men to charge it. Eight men responded, but on nearing the stone fence a tremendous fire belched forth, and three of the men with me were killed, those remaining resuming their former positions. About this time outpost No. 5 was attacked, and was reinforced by Captain Van Way with sixteen men, who eventually killed nine or twelve insurgents in the sand banks on the river.

"It was reported about this time that outpost No. 3 had been surrounded and one man killed and one wounded. My attention was then called to the fact that there was a body of insurgents in the cathedral.

The doors were tried, and being found locked, a guard was posted in front of each door. It was now getting light and the fire of the insurgents was redoubling in intensity. Running across under a hot fire into the convent, I found the west end of that building, on the second floor, an admirable position from which to fire down on the insurgents posted behind the fence in front of the hospital. It also cut off retreat from the hospital to the river. Going back I took about twenty men to this position, and a tremendous fire was now opened on the hospital and casino. In this fire (as I learned afterwards) joined outpost No. 1 of four men. These men who were in the midst of the enemy, we had supposed were killed; but protected by a large stone sentry box near the jail they had maintained bravely their position.

"About this time Captain Van Way, at outpost No. 5, having a serious skirmish, the guard at the rear end of the cathedral left and joined him, whereupon a company of insurgents escaped from the cathedral.

"In crossing the plaza three of them were killed. Lieutenant Lipop, from the seminary, had an opportunity about this time to pour a destructive fire into insurgents retreating from the hospital, killing three.

"Lieutenant Pickel had joined Captain Van Way. In the church tower six of our sharpshooters dominated the plaza. Major Cronin controlled the fire from the barracks. At about 8 A. M. several insurgents were killed crawling out of a tunnel, hitherto unobserved, leading from the river under the stone wall to the hospital. Shortly after, with six men, I passed up along the bank of the river, joining the outpost, and thence into the rear of the hospital, which was found deserted. Thirteen dead bodies were found and several prisoners were behind the stone fence, which was literally shot to pieces. Eight or more insurgents had been killed in the casino but had been dragged a short distance away.

"Patrols were immediately sent through the town to cut off the retreat of the insurgents. This resulted in a number of skirmishes in which insurgents were killed. Seventeen were found with arms in their hands in a courtyard and forced by a single soldier (Epps) to surrender, and thirteen were captured in the cathedral and other places. Altogether, as a result of the fighting, over forty dead insurgents were counted, thirty were taken prisoners and eighty-six Remingtons and one Mauser were captured. The prisoners included a captain and two lieutenants, all badly wounded.

"It speaks well for the forbearance of our men that so many prisoners were taken, as, owing to the desperate nature of the fighting, there was a strong inclination to give no quarter.

"During the rest of the day and the succeeding night there was almost continual firing from the outposts, a few shots being returned from the surrounding heights. In places the enemy was reported to be constructing trenches. During the evening of the 4th communication was established with the fleet. On the 5th a force of one hundred and fifty sailors and marines was sent to the city. About the same time, at noon, on the 5th, Brigadier-General Young, with three troops of cavalry and trains, arrived from near Narbacan, where his infantry and cavalry had had a severe fight on the 4th, and had captured a formidable series of trenches, forcing the pass to the province of Bangued.

"It is to be presumed that the division at Vigan took away from the defense of this pass many insurgent troops which would otherwise have joined in the resistance there.

"I cannot conclude without paying tribute to the magnificent fighting done by the 33rd, Texans. Many were really sick, but all turned out for the fighting, and nothing could equal the coolness, intrepidity, and determination shown by them. The steadfast defense of the position at the west end of the plaza, almost at the muzzle of the guns of a numerous enemy for four hours, half of the time in darkness, deserves to be commemorated as a striking example of American valor, and to the seven men who died there, on the spot where they perished, it is only just that a monument be erected bearing their names. I desire also to commend the conduct of the officers under me, Major Cronin, Captain Van Way, Lieutenant Lipop, and Lieutenant Pickel, all of the 33rd Infantry. I would have liked to add to this report a report from Captain Van Way of his operations. During nearly the whole of the fight he was separated from me, and with a small detachment he rendered invaluable service in defending the ford at outpost No. 5, where he killed many of the enemy, fighting at close range.

"He afterwards was instrumental in capturing most of our prisoners. I have had occasion for two weeks to observe this officer closely and to know him intimately. He would be an ornament to our regular army. He is anxious for a second lieutenancy, and I recommend that as a reward for his services in this fight he be appointed to a vacancy.

"For extraordinary gallantry, fighting for hours

lying between two dead comrades in the position in the plaza, notwithstanding that his hat was pierced and his clothes ploughed through by bullets, I recommend that a medal of honor be granted Private McConnell, Company B, 33rd Infantry.

"While searching the town for insurgents at the close of the fight, Private Epps, Company B, 33rd Infantry, asked Captain Van Way permission to search a particular house. Looking over a wall he discovered seventeen insurgents armed, and mounting the wall he covered them with his gun, forcing them to stack arms and surrender. When some surprise was expressed at this incident he replied, 'What else could they do? I had the drop on them.' For extraordinary gallantry I recommend that Epps be given a medal of honor.

"During the whole of the fight Corporal C. C. Calloway maintained his outpost, No. 1, directly in rear of enemy's position at the hospital and about seventy-five yards from it. When it became day and his position became known to the enemy it must have had considerable effect in determining the length of their stay. I recommend that for his gallant conduct on this occasion he be given a certificate of merit.

"The killed on December 4th were Sergeant Fry, L; Sergeant Bell, B; Sergeant Spencer, B; Corporal Wachs, B; Private Bennett, E; Private Brandon, E; Private Puckett, D; Private Wright, A; all 33rd Infantry.

"Force of the enemy present 700, 500 on plaza. General Tinio and Lieutenant-Colonel Alessandrino in command, battalions from Abra and Ilocos Norte. Estimated loss of the enemy in

Major General George Crook

1st Lt. Chas. B. Gatewood

killed, wounded, and prisoners, 150. Direction of retreat not known. Arms, Remington; a few Mausers. Ammunition expended by us, 15,000 rounds. Enemy uniformed. A number of officers' horses were captured, some blood-stained; also a large quantity of ammunition. Twenty-eight Spanish prisoners rendered loyal assistance during the fight carrying ammunition and water. One seized a rifle and killed an insurgent. People of town panic-stricken. A piece of artillery should be in every town garrisoned by a small force.

"There is no question but that the severe losses in killed of the insurgents were largely due to the remarkable marksmanship of the 33rd, due to previous training."

Captain Van Way in his report says in part:

"By far the fiercest of the fight occurred on and around the plaza. This plaza is covered with decorative masonry, monuments, and trees, and behind these, by direction of Colonel Parker, sixteen men took position. Many others, the number I am unable to give, stationed themselves in the adjacent buildings that afforded a fire on the hospital and there stayed during the whole of the fight.

"The hospital contained nearly two whole companies of the insurgents, who from the windows and from the balustrade, a most magnificent protection to them, poured a fierce and almost incessant fire upon our men.

"Stacks of over two hundred empty shells marked the places where our most gallant men lay, while that balustrade and the bodies behind it spoke eloquently of their coolness and marksmanship. The distance from this balustrade to the positions of our men was but from twenty-five to sixty yards. At this remarkable range one of the fiercest of fights raged nearly four hours.

"At a lull in the firing just before daybreak, ten men, led by Colonel Parker, charged and attemped to enter the hospital, only to receive a volley, killing Sergeant Spencer and Corporal Wachs of B Company and Private Puckett of D Company and wounding one other man. The rest of the little band, unable to stand such a fire, dropped back some twenty yards to the plaza masonry, where, partially protected, they awaited the return of Sergeant Spencer, the only man missing, who was supposed to be behind some protection in front of them. Calling to him to get away that they might fire, he replied: 'I can't; I'm hurt.' Then this mortally wounded man, realizing the situation, crawled over twenty feet in a direction that would soon have placed him well out of his comrade's fire. Unable to go farther he feebly called: 'I can't make it,' turned around, emptied the five shots from his magazine into the balustrade at a distance of thirty feet, and died.

"In the little ring of masonry where those in charge dropped, four more were killed and three wounded. Here during the hottest of the fire someone expressed the opinion that the little force, so outnumbered and in such an inferior position, would have to retreat. To this, Private McConnell, B Company, who at the time was lying between two dead comrades replied: 'Never will we retreat! We'll die! We are Americans!' This same man, his gun rendered useless by a shot which struck it, his face cut and bruised by flying gravel, his clothing torn, still stayed. Taking a dead comrade's gun he continued to fire until the last of the enemy were driven from the hospital.

"To McConnell's remarks, Sergeant Bell, Company B, added: 'No, we will die or win right here.' Die he did, poor fellow, but a few minutes later, as he was changing his position to get a better shot.

"Colonel Parker, ever exposed, ever exerting every energy toward increasing the action, was first on the plaza, then in the buildings, then on the plaza again, and no doubt had much to do with the remarkable determination and steadiness of the men.

"No pen in my hand can do full justice to the valor displayed by the officers and men on the plaza that morning.

"Lieutenant Lipop with Sergeant Conklin, Sergeant Thomas, and sixteen men of B Company were in a building on the south side of the plaza and did splendid work, Lieutenant Lipop killing four of the enemy, one a captain, as they were retreating down a street commanded from his window. These he killed as fast as he could use the rifle and at a distance of a hundred yards. . . .

"It was impossible to keep all the men under control; it was each man's fight, and he fought it. For hours after the beginning the result was uncertain; but with men like these annihilation was possible but not defeat. Men with feet on which they could not stand the day previous, men sick with fever, fought alike with those of Company B who were well and strong. Outnumbered by an enemy, who on the start had the advantage, these men of the 33rd Volunteers fought in a manner characteristic only of soldiers who knew not the word 'defeat'." . . . .

"The *insurrectos'* loss is variously estimated from forty-two to sixty-seven killed. One *presidente* puts it at over a hundred, with many more wounded. This included one captain and two lieutenants killed. Many were killed at long range along the river several hours after the town was cleared. The firing really did not cease for twenty-four hours, for, during the night following, many of the enemy were in town carrying dead and wounded, secreting them in houses we were unable to search on the day of the fight.

"During all this time the citizens of the town were in hiding behind the masonry of their homes. Those living in houses of bamboo either went to their more fortunate neighbors or dug pits in which they stayed. In spite of these precautions two were killed and three were wounded. . . ."

The fighting lasted four hours, two hours in the dark, two hours after daylight. It should be remembered there is no dawn in the tropics; there is a faint daylight and then the sun rises. The fighting naturally became more murderous in the light of the day, and the fusillade became continuous. Not long after the sun rose I put six sharpshooters in the bell tower of the cathedral from which lofty position they could aim advantageously at the enemy below. Towards the end of the fight the insurgents' fire ceased; deeming the fight won I had the men in the tower ring the bells as a signal of triumph, but instantly a heavy fusillade again broke forth. Early in the fight, outpost No. 4 was approached in the rear by a body of insurgents. When our men challenged, the enemy opened fire, killing Private Wright and a bullet grazed the head of Private Bircher stunning him and knocking him down. The other two men escaped. Bircher, reviving, crawled into the river, getting under a raft from which he was afterwards rescued.

A little after 8 A. M. the attack of the insurgents having apparently ceased I took six men and making a long circuit went around to the rear of the Spanish hospital and into it. Throwing open the folding doors of the front of the hospital and standing there in the sunlight waving my arms, my sudden appearance indicating that the fight was over, I was greeted with great cheers by the men on the square and in the different buildings.

Truly there was enough fighting for everybody. I was told that men, in the upper part of the barracks, sick with dysentery, too weak to stand, would turn over in bed, fire a shot out the window at the insurgents, and sink back exhausted but satisfied. I did not notice a case in which any man seemed to think we would not eventually win. It was beautiful to see the steadiness of the Texans. In one instance, while I was standing beside one man, I saw him raise his rifle slowly as at target practice and take deliberate aim before he slowly pulled the trigger. When the discharge took place he slowly lowered his gun, saying calmly, "Well, I got that fellow!"

After the fight was over we had an exciting time in the cathedral routing out some thirteen insurgents who had hidden behind the organ and in various other places.

Carts came and carried away the enemy's dead. On the plaza we dug a great grave for our eight dead heroes; splendid fellows they were, lying side by side in the trench, and I could not but weep as I looked at them and read from my prayer book their funeral service, while distant shots from the outposts indicated the enemy were still surrounding the town.

About noon I sent word to the provincial governor that I wanted to see him. He was found miserably crouching in the cellar, afraid to come out, and sent me a letter begging to be excused on account of the *sifflando de las boletas* (whistling of the bullets).

That afternoon, trying to take a little rest, I was almost asleep when a burly Texan rushed into the room and fired a shot out of my window at an insurgent crossing the road a long distance off. The range was eleven hundred yards and he hit the man in the leg! That is some shooting!

All that day we were unable to communicate with the naval vessels at the port, three miles away, although we could plainly see their masts.

The strain I had been through was almost too much for my nerves and I tried in vain that night to sleep, my mind rehearsing again and again the tragic incidents of the morning before.

On the morning of this day, December 5th, a force of one hundred and fifty sailors and marines, under Commander McCalla of the navy, coming from the port, marched up into the plaza. Without paying his respects to me, or approaching me in any manner, McCalla took possession of the municipal building, opposite our barracks, and established himself and his men there.

Shortly after the arrival of the sailors and marines General Young came in with three troops of cavalry. Meeting him, we had an amusing conversation. Without any preliminary he began to expatiate on the wonderful success his infantry and cavalry had had at the trenches of Narvacan, the day before. "But, General, I have been doing some fighting here!" I interrupted. "But I want to tell you about our fight at Narvacan!" the General went on, going into some details. "But, General, perhaps you don't know that I have had a tremendous fight here!" I again interrupted. "Oh, damn it!" cried the General, "I know you've had a big fight, haven't I been passing dead bodies for the past five miles? But I want to tell you about my fight!"

The trenches they had taken were very strong, but they were taken while most of the forces of General Tinio were absent at Vigan, trying to annihilate the garrison I commanded. As usual the insurgents had bad luck.

In spite of mistakes and blunders in the Spanish-American War, the Philippine Insurrection and even the World War, how often it has been found that luck was on our side! Is it proof of the old adage, "Fortune favors the brave"?

In forwarding my report General Young made the following comment: ". . . . . Lieutenant Colonel Parker (captain 4th Cavalry) deserves great credit for his heroic, gallant, and successful work, and he and his little command deserve high recognition for this grand defense. S. B. M. Young, Brigadier General."

On reception of the news of the fight General Lawton recommended that I and every member of my command be awarded a medal of honor. The board charged with the distribution of such medals, however, awarded them only to Private McConnell and myself.*

*"For most distinguished gallantry in action. While in command of a small garrison repulsed a savage night attack by overwhelming numbers of the enemy, fighting at close quarters in the dark for several hours."

I had barely time to write my report, and, in fact, insufficient time to acquaint myself with many minor details of the fight, when I was ordered by General Young to proceed to San Fernando. General Otis at Manila had sent a despatch to General Young in which he said it was reported atrocities had been committed by the Macabebes near San Fernando and ordered an immediate investigation. I left Captain Van Way and his officers with regret; we were bound together by the tie of common danger and triumph. Both Captain Van Way (now a colonel of cavalry) and Lieutenant Lipop later joined the regular army; I afterwards served with Van Way, who never failed, when at a distance, to write me a letter on the anniversary of this extraordinary fight, one of the most murderous and thrilling that occurred during the Philippine insurrection. I also was sorry to quit, if but for a time, General Young and his staff. Young's magnificent conduct in this pursuit of Aguinaldo was equaled only by his gallantry in 1898 at Santiago, Cuba, and particularly at Guasimas. But this is a story by itself. With Shafter's army, having landed with his dismounted cavalry division at Siboney, Young found the camping ground too much crowded. Sending an officer to Shafter, who was on board a transport, he obtained permission to move his camp to higher ground. Once on the march his natural impetuosity carried him away and proceeding some ten miles he encountered the Spanish forces in position. This brought about the battle of Guasimas, in which Young's division of less than a thousand men had a bloody conflict with nearly twice their number of Spaniards, driving them in panic back towards Santiago. In this fight the "Rough Riders" participated and Captain Allyn Capron, formerly of my troop, was killed, the first officer to fall on the field of battle in the Spanish-American War.

As I have already shown, Young's conduct during the chase after Aguinaldo and the occupation of the western coast of Luzon was even more bold and venturesome than his conduct in Cuba. General Otis often complains, in his published despatches, that General Young was beyond reach of communication! As a matter of fact, General Young found himself so much hampered by restriction coming via telegraph from headquarters at Manila, so long as he was within reach of the telegraph line being laid in our rear by our efficient signal officer, Lieutenant (afterwards General) Russell, that he was very glad to run away from it, pushing his way up the coast at such a rate that Russell could not keep up. This partly accounts for his action in operating far in advance of his main body, capturing from the enemy position after position, but having with him only two or three troops of cavalry, sometimes only one! I suppose this struck Otis, who wished to pursue the campaign in an orderly manner, with armies, as extremely irregular.

Young, like a good cavalryman, took chances. One instance of this was the time he sent me with one company to Vigan, there to confront fifteen hundred men under Tinio. With my small force I was, unfortunately, obliged to remain on the defensive, a dangerous expedient in this class of warfare. In fighting Filipinos the best defensive was the *offensive*. As soon as they no longer feared being attacked they themselves attacked. This fact I had already discovered at Calamba.

Shortly after I left him, Young's troops, operating northward along the coast, made themselves master of it as far as Laoag, a distance of some forty miles. Aguinaldo had disappeared in the mountains to the east and his pursuit ended. Young, then in his sixtieth year, commanding a district along the west coast, took station at Vigan. In 1901, in recognition of his brilliant services, General Young was made a major general, and in 1903 was retired with the exalted rank of lieutenant general of the regular army.

It was toward the end of December, 1898, that I was ordered to Manila, to join my regiment, the 45th Infantry Volunteers. I parted with regret from General Young and my associates on his staff.

Manila was full of troops arriving almost daily from the United States. Thus I met many old companions and intimate friends, with whom I had served for a time at frontier posts, and then lost sight of. Such reunions could not fail to be joyful. The import duties fixed by the Spanish Government still were in force. And since the Spanish policy was to tax necessities, not luxuries, we bought champagnes and wines at nearly French prices. Although General Otis had prohibited the coming of officers' wives, many of these ladies, denying his authority to exclude them, had drifted in and were ensconced in the Oriente Hotel and elsewhere. I have always noticed that it is the best looking women who are the most ready to risk danger and hardship. Living was cheap, and for a very small sum one could equip oneself with a handsome little victoria, a team of diminutive Filipino ponies, and a native driver. Many such equipages could be seen dashing around the streets, carrying our army belles. To me it was a delightful and cheering sight, however old Otis may have regarded it. These ponies were all stallions and some of them for beauty of build and appearance could not be excelled by our best horses. Near Pasay I attended several races in which the smallness of the race horses in no way lessened our excitement and interest. Betting was high and for Manila it was a very fashionable gathering!

Otis had proposed to increase the forces operating in the Islands to 75,000 men. For this, twenty-five U. S. volunteer regiments had been temporarily added to the army. These regiments were far superior to the National Guard regiments which preceded them and which were now en route to the states. Of the new regiments the colonels, lieutenant colonels and majors were mostly regular officers. The captains and lieutenants were civilian soldiers carefully selected, many of whom had served in the Philippines or in Cuba. The enlisted men were procured by local enlistment in the same manner as recruits for the regular army. The regiments had undergone a careful course of preliminary training and of target practice. Their recruitments being local, each regiment represented a different section of the country. These men had the individual intelligence and independence of citizen soldiers and soon acquired the discipline of regulars.

We were part of "Wheaton's column," consisting of three troops of cavalry, two batteries of artillery and four regiments of infantry. Our mission was to sweep clean of insurgents Cavite and Batangas Provinces south of Manila.

My regiment, the 45th, was commanded by Colonel Joseph H. Dorst (captain 4th Cavalry), one of my oldest and best friends, who for years had been General Mackenzie's adjutant. Handsome in a marked degree, gallant, brave, Joe Dorst was regarded as one of the most brilliant officers of the army.

A lieutenant colonel, when the regiment is together, is usually a "fifth wheel to the coach," and I did not relish that job. Accordingly Dorst, on my insistence, assigned me to the command of one of the battalions, of which the major, Cole, was absent.

The first day, January 7th, we marched along the shore of Manila Bay to Bacor, thence to Imus, twelve miles. At Imus the 4th Infantry in the advance had a serious fight, in which Lieutenant Ward Cheney, 4th Infantry, was killed. Next day we marched eight miles to Das Marinas. Here I met my old friend and colonel, Bob Leonard, now lieutenant colonel of the 28th Infantry Volunteers.

At Das Marinas the 45th Infantry was detached from the column and ordered to proceed to Quintana. Quintana was an insignificant place, but on the map it looked like an important strategic point, since roads were shown diverging from it in all directions. As a matter of fact, most of these "roads" were mere trails.

The regiment had a tough time reaching Quintana, although it was barely seven miles away. At six P. M. we started, our first hazard a deep, stony ravine. The trail was wide enough for only one man, and the regiment, of nearly a thousand, took two hours in crossing, only to find that we were on the wrong trail! Another two hours was consumed in getting back to Das Marinas, where we took the correct trail and again crossed the ravine, using up another two hours in painful marching and waiting.

It was now nearly midnight and the men were pretty well exhausted. We had emerged on a high plateau. Suddenly the advance guard halted: "The enemy in front is signalling!"

With raw troops, enemy "signals" seem more disturbing than enemy shots. Dorst and I went forward to investigate. Sure enough, there were signals; first a red, then a blue, then a white light!

We regarded them for some minutes in silence. Finally someone broke in: "Why, those are the lighthouse lights on Corrigidor Island!"

It was one A. M. when we finally halted and bivouacked, barely six miles from Das Marinas! We camped on the bare plain. In the darkness I lay down in a furrow made by a plough. We had no supper, we were glad enough to rest and sleep!

The next morning, continuing the march, we arrived at a deep canyon separating us from Quintana; at the bottom was a narrow creek nearly waist deep. Into this our men, with their heavy packs, floundered, scrambling up the opposite bank. At last we surmounted the hill and arrived at Quintana, an insignificant looking place. There were few women to be seen, but a large number of suspicious looking men were around. They were surly and obstinate, evidently insurgents, but we could find no arms.

Shortly after we arrived "officers' call" was

sounded and we assembled at the colonel's bivouac. With the officers grouped in front of him, Dorst read an order just received from the headquarters of General Bates, commanding the department of southern Luzon. The order recited that there had been many cases of "looting," a thing forbidden, under heavy penalty, by laws of war. In future, the order said, anyone guilty of looting would be shot! That the taking of chickens belonging to the natives was not excepted! Considering that we often lived on the country, this order seemed a ridiculous one and would ordinarily have been received with the silence its folly merited. But while Dorst was reading it, his Chinese cook, armed with a long bamboo pole, stole up. He was intent on some chickens in a tree, just in rear of Dorst. Adjusting a noose on the end of the pole he dropped it over the head of one of these chickens. A slight squawk and the chicken was borne away to be cooked for the colonel's dinner!

It was some days before Dorst learned of this incident. In the meantime he must have been puzzled by the grins on the faces of his auditors!

The next day we returned to Das Marinas. The following day we were sent back to Quintana. On January 12th with my battalion I made a fruitless scout to Palangui six miles and back. On this scout we crossed a canyon by a lofty stone bridge, evidently of ancient construction, and we also found a place where two creeks were joined by a tunnel a half mile long, excavated through a mountain! We also found roads worn so deep and so overgrown with brush that for miles vehicles traveled in a kind of tunnel. All these were indications of the palmy days of the friars in this country, the land hereabouts being their property and the people living largely in a state of peonage.

January 14th we marched twelve miles to Naig, a large town near the entrance of Manila Bay. The next day Dorst, with an expedition consisting of my battalion and three troops of the 11th (volunteer) Cavalry, set out for Nasugbu, a town and bay to the southwest. We marched to Magallanes the first night. The next day, after a skirmish, in which the cavalry killed four insurgents, we entered Nasugbu, a small town on the sea.

Here we learned the enemy was in force at the large town of Taal, twenty miles away. I begged Dorst to march there, that while we might run short of rations we had found it perfectly easy in northern Luzon to live on the country, there was always plenty of chickens and rice. Dorst finally concluded to go.

An hour later, after I had turned in, he woke me up and said, "I have been talking to Lieutenant Carson, of the 11th Cavalry, and he has told me how Otis abused Batchelor like a pickpocket for exceeding his orders. I am not going to run the chance of being treated like that!" "Oh, pshaw!" said I and turned over.

As it turned out we would have arrived at Taal just in time to co-operate with Major W. N. Johnson, 46th Infantry, in attacking that place and would probably have had a grand success. We remained a day at Nasugbu and then started back, returning over the same route. As might have been expected, on crossing the canyon of the Duyo River we were ambushed.

The fight was pretty hot. The canyon, just

above the crossing, forked, and I proposed to Dorst that I take one of the companies of my battalion down into the fork, and thus get on the flank of the enemy.

In company with Captain Cogswell, leading the company, we had got nearly to the bottom of the canyon when we encountered a thick growth of trees and vines. Penetrating these we finally emerged into the bare creek bottom, only to be fired upon by three insurgents who rose from behind a rock some thirty feet off and fired a volley at us. How they missed us I don't know, but they did. After the first shots we squatted down, seeking some sort of shelter and shouted to our soldiers to return the fire. But they were still entangled in the vines and bushes and could not use their guns, and so the insurgents after firing one or two more shots at us had a chance to get away. I think it was the narrowest escape I ever had.

In this engagement we killed eight and captured seventeen.

We returned to Naig January 19, 1900. On January 24th Colonel Dorst with Berkhauser's battalion of the 45th, and five troops of the 11th Cavalry, left en route to Taal, leaving me in command at Naig. So Dorst had to go to Taal after all!

During the sixteen days I was in charge at Naig nothing much occurred. Precautions had to be taken against the insurgents, who were numerous in the country about the town, but apparently not organized. I issued to the people a series of regulations prohibiting assemblies, and stopping circulation in the streets at night. I posted strong outposts, which occasionally exchanged shots with the enemy. And I made several reconnaissances to towns and villages in the vicinity. But the inhabitants seemed contented, and the shops had a brisk trade with the soldiers. Spies were numerous. There was one very pretty Mestiza girl who kept a shop, who, we knew had relations with the insurgents. One day I said to her, "Maria, your friends, the insurgents, are no good. We came over here to fight, if they can't give us a fight we want to leave your rotten country and go back home!" Maria looked stupefied!

On February 9th Dorst returned from Taal and on February 15th the regiment boarded the transport *Tartar* for an expedition to the Camarines, a province in the southern part of Luzon Island. The force was commanded by General Bates. It consisted of the U. S. Cruiser *Marietta* and the transports *Tartar, Venus* and *Castellano.* The troops consisted of the 40th Infantry and the 45th Infantry with four pieces of mountain artillery, altogether two thousand men.

We were towed in ship's boats to the fleet. As I came on the deck of the *Tartar* one of the officers of the ship asked me, "Are you Lieutenant Colonel Parker?" "Yes." "I have *a barrel of apples* in the refrigerator for you, sent by your wife!"

This was a remarkable coincidence. I had been cut off from news by mail for weeks, but here came a barrel of apples! I then remembered that I had written home some time before that the one thing I would like to get was a big rosy, tart, American apple.

It turned out that my wife on receiving the letter had written to the forwarding quartermaster, Colonel Long, at San Francisco, begging him to forward to me a barrel of apples which she had ordered sent to him. Being a friend and classmate of mine he complied. The apples crossed the ocean on the *Tartar*. But they would never have reached me but for the happy chance that made the *Tartar* part of our expedition to the Camarines.

We had a stormy passage passing around the southern end of the island and sailing up the east side. On February 19th we anchored in San Miguel Bay, an open roadstead, swept by great rollers.

That evening we had a "council of war" aboard the *Marietta*. Boarding the *Marietta* was an exciting job. The little launch which carried us to her rose and fell on mountainous waves. We climbed aboard at the risk of our lives. At last we were gathered in the cabin. There were present General Bates, commanding, and his staff: General James L. Bell, Colonel Godwin, 40th Infantry, and Colonel Dorst, 45th Infantry, and their staffs, and the field officers of the two regiments. Most of them were plainly seasick! Especially so were my companions, Colonel Dorst and Major Merritte W. Ireland, then surgeon, 45th Infantry, now major general and surgeon general of the army.

I sometimes attributed my appointment to what was undoubtedly the post of honor to the fact that I was one of the few whose brain was not disturbed by *mal de mer*. While the other troops were to attack in front, my battallion was to make a three days' march around Nueva Caceres and attack the enemy's right and rear. To accomplish this we were to start a day in advance of the other troops, so that we could reach our appointed position in front of Nueva Caceres in time to co-operate with the main attack.

Accordingly the next morning (it was on the 20th of February, 1900, my forty-sixth birthday) we started for the shore, seven miles away, in a long string of boats towed by a steam launch. Accompanied by my adjutant and Major Ireland, I was in the last boat. The country in front of us was flat. To the south reared the immense mass of Mt. Isarog, an extinct volcano.

As we neared shore, fire was opened on us by insurgents, but with no apparent effect. It was low tide, and our boats grounded well out among the breakers. The men jumping out found under their feet not a sandy beach, but soft and slimy mud! Some struggled ashore in their uniforms, their clothing splashed with mud and water. Others, including Doctor Ireland and myself, divested themselves of their clothing and carried it in bundles.

Newspaper correspondents in the rear stayed in their boat, refusing to land but focusing their cameras on the ridiculous spectacle we afforded them. To add to our troubles we discovered that the muddy bottom lay in hillocks, giving us an insecure foothold as we slipped and slid over them towards shore buffeted by the waves and in places sinking deep in soft slime!

Arrived on the beach our troubles were not at an end. The lower part of our bodies was covered with mud; we would have liked to wash it off, but the only water available was beyond our reach! I was reduced to the expedient of scraping the mud off with chips of bamboo; the Doctor used a bayonet! This gave us a criss-cross appearance but did not remove all of the muck, and we finally put on our clothes with much of the mud as a foundation.

In the meantime outposts had been thrown out, but the insurgents did not cease firing. I was engaged in the process of "demucking" when Captain Peter Murray of General Bell's staff appeared and speaking in the name of the General, as I supposed, suggested that I drive off the insurgents who were attacking my outposts! "Oh, damn the insurgents," I had to reply, "I've got to get rid of this mud first!"

However, it was necessary to start, and the battalion formed and got under way. It was excessively hot, and the midday sun poured down mercilessly. We were bound for Calabanga, a town several miles from the shore. The insurgents in our front disappeared.

It was about five miles to Calabanga. Nearing it we met the enemy and experienced a stout resistance. The troops were deployed and a heavy fire commenced. Early in the struggle one of my men was killed.

Shortly after the action commenced we were startled by the report of a heavy gun fired by the insurgents. But looking about I could not see any signs of the fall of its projectile. Again and again the great cannon roared. But nothing was hit! It was probably a smooth bore cannon loaded with bamboo joints filled with stones. But for some reason the stones did not reach us.

Finally the enemy had enough and decamped. He had lost ten men killed and many wounded. We entered and occupied the town, now deserted by the inhabitants, with the exception of a lone native, who, we soon discovered, was insane. Our men were exhausted by the experiences of the day and I decided to remain overnight. A mountain stream coming from the slopes of Mt. Isarog afforded us a refreshing bath, and enabled us to clean off the mud with which our legs were covered.

There was a good deal of firing during the night between our outposts and the enemy. Some of his shots came through the house in which the Doctor and I were quartered. The Doctor complained in the morning of wakefulness, but I slept deeply.

The next morning we marched toward Carolina, a little place on the slopes of Mt. Isarog where the *insurrectos* were said to have a *maestranza* or arsenal. Our arrival was a surprise to the inhabitants, who decamped, leaving all their possessions. We captured and destroyed a few arms and some cartridges. A few boxes and trunks of personal effects were opened, but left intact. We proceeded on our march.

We had brought with us from the transport a native guide. This individual was now to lead us to the town of Palestine about five miles from Nueva Caceres where we were expected by General Bates to camp for the night. But he lost his way. It turned out that it was well that he did, for Palestine was a leper settlement! Imagine arriving at such a place at night!

Instead, we marched by a devious route through a succession of rice fields; part of the time we traveled through water. Several times we were attacked by bolo-men; and two of them were shot.

Night came on. At nine P. M. we found our further progress barred by a deep lagoon. Efforts to find a way around it or across it were unavailing. The men were tired. We were on a rice plain, wet and muddy. But there was nothing to do but to bivouac where we were.

We formed a square. It was impossible to put out outposts on that flat; there was no cover and in case of alarm the outposts might be killed by our own fire. So sentinels were posted at the corners of the square and we lay down in the mud and slept. Fortunately we were not disturbed during the night. The enemy may have known we were in the vicinity but he would not expect to find us in a place like that.

The next morning daylight disclosed at some distance a light bridge across the lagoon. We crossed and occupied Concepcion, a small village lying on the farther side. We were on a broad macadamized road leading east from Nueva Caceres, and about a mile and a half from that town. Our position was screened from the town by a growth of trees.

The combined attack on the town was not to take place until two P. M. While we waited, hostile natives made their appearance. Instead of rifles they were equipped with bolos, spears, bows and arrows. Some carried shields, others wore complete suits of armor made of carabao hide, including helmets and breastplates! They brandished their weapons, and altogether presented a ridiculous appearance. Again and again my officers begged me for permission to fire on them but I refused.

Through an old native I got several of these would-be warriors to come in and talk. I told them they were very foolish to stand there and threaten us; we did not want to kill them; to go back to their farms and work; we would not interfere with them. I was successful and in a short time they disappeared.

At one P. M. we moved toward Nueva Caceres. Emerging from the trees (on the way we were once or twice attacked by isolated bolo-men) we deployed on a broad plain extending towards the town. One company under Captain Capps extended our line to the south, so as to cut off the retreat of the insurgents in that direction.

We expected to hear the firing of the main body of our troops attacking the north end of the town, but in this we were disappointed. A crowd of natives, apparently riflemen, made their appearance at the entrance to the city as if to defend it, and then disappeared. We hastened our march.

Just before crossing a bridge spanning the Naga River and leading into the city, I saw in a large building by the side of the road a shutter partly opened by someone peering out. Soon it opened still more and disclosed the face of a white man. I beckoned to him, he joined us. He was an English agent for the purchase of hemp, Anstruther by name. He told me the insurgents had intended to oppose my entrance, but at the last moment had changed their minds. But they had said that before they left the city they would burn the nunnery and massacre the occupants. He had heard that the nuns, some of them were Spanish, were greatly alarmed.

"Where is this nunnery?" I demanded. Anstruther led; the Doctor and I followed. As we arrived in front of the large building the folding doors were flung open and we rushed in, to find ourselves surrounded by a crowd of weeping women.

The nuns indeed were greatly alarmed, some of them had hysterics! A pretty girl tried to throw herself on my shoulder, crying, *"Mio Salvator!"* (My Saviour!) The Doctor, not a bad-looking man, had similar experiences. It was a delightful episode! But we had no time to spend with nuns. We assured them as best we could that we would look out for their safety. I rushed off to station my outposts and see that the principal roads leading from the city were guarded.

The next day, dining with Anstruther and a leading Spanish priest, I proposed to visit the nunnery and pay my respects to its occupants. The priest replied unfeelingly, "Gentlemen are not permitted to visit the nuns!"

The combined movement, as usual, didn't "combine"; we were the first troops in the city! Shortly after we arrived a U. S. gunboat came up the Bicol River to the town. But the main body of troops didn't arrive until the next day.

Nueva Caceres (now called Naga) was a rather pretentious place, situated on the Bicol River, a navigable stream emptying into San Miguel Bay. A large and flourishing city, it contained among other buildings, convents, a nunnery, a college, a cathedral and various other stone edifices pertaining to an important bishopric. A company of Franciscan friars had also made their headquarters there—these the insurgents, in their retreat from the town, had carried off into the mountains. The insurgents, too, had taken with them most of the Chinamen in the town, afterwards foully butchering them.

For my headquarters I took possession of the handsome residence of the native governor of the province, Abella, later moving to the house of Arejola, an insurgent leader, which I occupied with several officers of the battalion.

On the 23rd the main body of our forces arrived at Nueva Caceres. Brigadier General James M. Bell (colonel of cavalry) took command. Under the direction of Major General J. C. Bates several expeditions were sent out—one to pursue the insurgents and liberate the friars, one under Colonel Dorst with six companies of the 45th Infantry to the province of Albay, and one to the district of Lagonoy on the eastern side of Mount Isarog. All these expeditions had numerous small engagements.

With my battalion I was to open the road to Pasacao, a port of Nueva Caceres on the western side of the island and sixteen miles distant. It was reported that the enemy had three hundred troops at Pasacao.

I started for Pasacao February 26th. Acting on my theory that the sooner I got there the less time the insurgents would have to collect their men and prepare their defense, I took up a rapid gait. Toward the end of the march the men kept continually shouting, "Pass the word forward, one man has fallen out of Company E!" "Pass the word forward another man has fallen out of Company D!" The men were tired and wanted to rest. Finally the shout, ever repeated, came from the rear, "Pass the word forward, the doctor says to halt the column!" This was too much for me. I had come to the end of my patience. I called out angrily, "Pass the word back for the doctor to go to the devil!" It turned out as I suspected—the doctor, Captain Sparrenberg, had sent no such message.

Thirty small dilapidated bridges spanning ditches and creeks added to the difficulties of our march, but we finally arrived at Pasacao, only to discover that the insurgents had fled!

We found in the harbor of Pasacao the transport *Venus,* sent to meet us and bring us supplies. Two days afterwards, leaving two companies of infantry to garrison Pasacao, I started for Nueva Caceres with the remainder of my battalion.

Our march was delayed; after nightfall, to be prepared for bolo-men, we marched with fixed bayonets.

To arrive at Nueva Caceres we had to cross the River Bicol in two large, cranky native dugouts, hauling ourselves over by a rope stretched across the river. It was night and when we arrived in the middle of the river the rope broke! The stream was in flood and running swiftly and violently. I had in these canoes perhaps one hundred and fifty men. I feared a disaster was imminent. Not far below us was a ruined bridge and when we struck that I feared the canoes would overturn. Ordering the men to take off their belts and packs and to sit low in the bottom of the canoes I waited in the darkness for what would happen. We were now whirling swiftly down the river.

Presently, with a resounding crash, we struck the sloping piles of the bridge. Fortunately we struck square. If we had struck diagonally, God knows what would have happened. Soldiers are helpless in the water. Hundreds had already drowned in the Philippines.

The boats remained upright. With infinite care the soldiers one by one climbed up the sloping abutments of the bridge and in the darkness they crawled along the stringers to land. There I checked them up. Not one man had been lost!

On March 22nd the 40th Infantry under Colonel Godwin departed for the Island of Mindanao. From that time on until June 10th, under General Bell, I commanded the post of Nueva Caceres. It was a thankless job. General Bell had few troops, enough to occupy only the largest towns in the province. Dorst's force of six companies occupied five towns near Nabua. The rest of the towns were under the domination of the insurgents. It was death to a native, unless he was guarded by our troops, to side with the Americans. Even those in towns that we occupied, those who showed friendship for us, were liable afterwards to find out their mistake. For if such a town was abandoned by us, the "Americanistas," as friendly natives were called by the insurgents, were exposed to every form of vile insult and injury. And the native could never be sure that his town would not be deserted by us. The native *had* to be "on the fence." He had little to fear from us, much from the insurgents. Thus the Filipinos got the reputation from some of our people of being "treacherous." After we had left the island news came that our newly arrived troops were continually being exhorted by "hell-roaring Jake Smith" and others never to trust the "little brown brother." I fear it was an unfortunate day for the Filipino when the army of volunteers which had conquered the country and got to know the people was replaced by newly raised regiments of regulars "who knew not Joseph."

While occasional scouts were made in the vicinity, the situation of the small garrison at Nueva Caceres was that of troops on the defensive. Strong outposts had to be maintained. The town was full of spies in constant touch with the insurgents. The more precautions were taken the more false alarms we had. I remember one night the troops in a convent were found firing volley after volley into the dark convent yard. It was only after I had taken a lantern and explored the yard thoroughly that they agreed they were mistaken in thinking the enemy was concealed there. Put troops on the offensive and they are bold; put them on the defensive and they are the prey to panic.

One day the commander of an outpost reported that the night before, in a house looking down the road towards Concepcion, a native had been signaling, using a lantern, which he flashed through the window. I had come to the conclusion that most of the "enemy signals" reported were something different altogether and I did not in any event attach much importance to "signals" when it would be easier and safer for the enemy to send a written message. But I investigated this case and found it was an actual fact that someone was signaling, using the Morse code. I therefore ordered that if the following night the signaling was repeated the outpost should fire a shot through the window.

The outpost commander, however, actuated by motives of humanity, when the signaling recommenced, "rushed" the house. They caught in the act a young man of the upper classes, who had formerly been a telegraph operator. He was locked up in the jail.

In the morning I had a visit from his mother, a very handsome, very fat Spanish lady. Tears rolled down her cheeks and, embracing my knees, she implored me not to punish her son. I had some difficulty in inducing her to take a chair and in persuading her that instant execution would not be the lot of the young man. In fact, after a few weeks I released him.

The Filipinos, in some of their aspects, are like wayward children and should not be taken too seriously. War is hell, but it is not up to us to make it more hellish than it need be. I believe in chivalry in war and I am in favor of carrying on war like a gentleman.

It was part of my duties while at Nueva Caceres

to act as provost judge. As such I was the police court justice of the city.

In the jail I found an astounding state of affairs. There were numbers of prisoners against whom, apparently, no charge had ever been made. They had been locked up as suspicious characters; therefore, they were probably *ladrones* (thieves or robbers). Being too stupid to find means of clearing themselves of this "charge" they had remained in custody, some for years.

It should be explained that the common *tao* (peon or peasant) is, in intelligence, little better than a brute. Again, in the Philippines there was little intercommunication between the towns, especially in the mountain country where *ladrones* infested the roads. Strangers were looked upon with suspicion.

While acting as provost judge I had occasion often to investigate offenses in which *taos* were witnesses. They often reminded me of the phrase "dumb driven cattle," for they were little better. It was another aspect of the Middle Ages so often found in the Philippines, which included the political domination of the church, the participation of the church in agriculture, trade and commerce, the owning and working by it of great estates upon which the laborer was a serf, and the companies of friars directed operations; the dense ignorance of the common people; the feudal and almost military organization of the inhabitants of the towns; their primitive methods of lighting, of spreading information (by a town crier with a drum), of sanitation, of police, jails, and so forth. This likeness to the Middle Ages, as described in the books dealing with that period, met you at every turn.

We lived in the house of Arejola, who afterwards became chief of the insurgents in that part of the islands. When I first went there I met him one day on the street and he accosted me in surly fashion, demanding that I vacate his house. This I refused to do and he left me; it was after this I heard he was with the insurgents. Three other officers lived with me, including Major Cole, who had by that time joined the regiment. By some mischance for him and good fortune for us the Quartermaster Department had forwarded to him all of his household furniture, including his library of books. It is not necessary to say that books in the English language were a boon then in the Philippines. The house was old and was infested with great numbers of enormous rats which ran freely along the rough walls. Cole slept and perspired on a big American mattress, the only one I ever saw in the Philippines. There the beds usually had a rattan bottom, woven like the seats of chairs; on this one spread a sheet and reclined without further covering than pajamas—a method of sleeping necessitated by the hot climate, but one rather hard at first to become accustomed to. In the morning you were likely to be well marked with dots and criss-cross lines made by the rattan.

In addition to rats we were bothered by wild monkeys prowling around in the dark. We had a piano in the house and one of these monkeys was in the habit of playing on the piano at night; at least, he amused himself by striking the keys. These discordant notes would wake us up and cause much profanity.

Having a good regimental band, guard mounting was each day conducted with all the formality of a regular garrison, attracting crowds of spectators. The band also gave nightly concerts on the plaza, much to the contentment of the inhabitants.

Our piano was a source of great joy. Jazz was then coming into fashion and Captain Sparrenberg, the surgeon of the battalion, was an accomplished performer, able to convert anything, even the most solemn hymns, into syncopated music. He could "pound the box" to perfection. Whenever we went into a town we commandeered the best piano there and thus beguiled the monotony of our existence in a foreign and not always inviting land.

Upon the occupation of Nueva Caceres the headquarters of the insurgents had been transferred to the District of Lagonoy, on the eastern side of Mt. Isarog. Lagonoy could only be reached by trail or by sea. There the insurgents were able to collect hemp and by barter, with Japanese vessels which called there, to obtain arms and ammunition. In February, 1900, when we first landed, the District of Lagonoy had been traversed by a battalion of the 40th Infantry. But this was not much more than a raid. The insurgents fled to the hills, but returned as soon as the troops disappeared. I was anxious to be allowed to take a detachment and occupy Lagonoy, but General Bell seemed to think he had not sufficient troops to spare for this expedition. It was reported the insurgents there had a thousand troops.

One of the outposts of the insurgents occupying the Lagonoy district was at Mabattobatto, on the road to that district. On June 11th Colonel Lockett, commanding the 11th Cavalry Volunteers, set out with two troops of cavalry, some artillery, and four companies of infantry to attack the enemy there. On his occupying the village of Mabattobatto the enemy was seen almost a mile off, throwing up a considerable trench on the slopes of Mt. Isarog. In battle array Lockett formed his command to make an armed reconnaissance according to the best methods of warfare. The cavalry, supported by infantry, moved out in advance, rode up to near the trench, drew the enemy's fire and then returned. "The reconnaissance was successful"—the enemy's force and disposition had been ascertained. But none the less, as the cavalry retired the insurgents mounted the trench and hurled defiance, insults and jeers at our troops. Our volunteers, who had wished to push home the attack, were enraged.

The next morning the little army formed for assault. After a prolonged "preliminary bombardment" by the artillery the infantry in two lines advanced, the cavalry on the flanks and the artillery in the center. At 1,000 yards from the enemy the infantry opened fire, the companies and platoons advancing by alternate rushes. At 200 yards from the trench bayonets were fixed and the infantry charged the position. What was their surprise on arriving at the trench to find *no one* there! In fact, there were no signs that anyone had been there during the whole battle! The insurgents the night before had decamped.

The volunteers returned to Nueva Caceres loudly cursing and expressing great contempt for the formal, classic method of attack!

There were no casualties!

Apaches at Home

Apache Scouts Stripped for Action

En Route to Bowie after Geronimo's Surrender

Geronimo and Natchez, Prisoners of War at Fort Bowie

XIII

THE CAPTURE AND DEFENSE OF LAGONOY

Some days after, General Bell decided to occupy Lagonoy and entrusted me with the job.

The District of Lagonoy, lying between Mt. Isarog and the sea, is a flat plain sloping down from the mountain, a plain about fifteen miles long and six to eight miles wide. At the north and south it was shut in by rugged hills. The only means of approach were a rough road (not much better than a trail) around the southern side of Isarog and a second trail, devious and difficult, around the northern side. The Bay of Lagonoy afforded a good anchorage. The district was almost entirely devoted to the culture of hemp which, like cotton in the Confederate States during the Civil War, was commandeered by the insurgent government, and traded for arms and ammunition brought by the Japanese.

The insurgent forces in Lagonoy numbered over one thousand men under Lukban and Bellarmino. As the sequel will show, our occupation of the district and continuous aggressiveness forced Lukban to emigrate to Samar where he became famous as a partisan chieftain. Bellarmino also found Lagonoy too hot for him and went over to the other side of the mountain to annoy Joe Dorst and his six companies in the District of Iriga.

The insurgents under Bellarmino had thrown

up trenches to obstruct each of these two roads of approach. They also had built a deep trench, seven miles long, facing the ocean. They also had numerous trenches and insurgent barracks on the slopes of Mt. Isarog and the hills to the north.

It was my experience that the insurgents would never stand if their rear or flanks were threatened. Instead, then, of moving my entire force by the road, I proposed to threaten them by detachments coming from three different directions while I arrived with the main force from the fourth.

For this operation General Bell gave me three companies of infantry, three troops of cavalry, two guns of the Astor Battery, and the steamboat *Montanes,* containing some soldier prisoners and their guard. The latter was to arrive in the bay. Some Sibley stovepipes protruding from the sides were to give the boat a formidable appearance, as if armed with cannon.

Major Dennis E. Nolan, now major general, with a troop of the 11th Cavalry, was to threaten the insurgents from the northwest by traversing the rugged trail around the north side of Mt. Isarog. Captain Cogswell's company of infantry, eighty men, was to come in from Iriga, threatening the insurgents from the south and southwest. My main command, consisting of two troops of cavalry, two companies of infantry and two pieces of artillery, in all 188 men, was to go around the south end of Mt. Isarog and come in to Lagonoy from the southwest.

To anticipate, the effect of this operation was as I expected. The insurgents, greatly disturbed by the appearance of the heavily armed (?) ship *Montanes,* were about to man the trenches facing the bay when they were informed of the approach of bodies of troops on their right, their rear and their left rear. It was too much for them; they fled and separated into small bands! The engagements which attended our entry were few and inconsequential.

Starting from Nueva Caceres on June 24, 1900, with my force of 188 men, I reached on June 25 the small town of Mabattobatto, a sad-looking place, with a poverty-stricken population, some of them lepers. On the mountainside were the trenches that Lockett's command "captured," now deserted.

Next day, June 26th, about noon, our column, after a march through a forest full of huge rocks, approached the village of Mabalukbaluk. This place was in a pass in the mountains where the insurgents, we were told, had thrown up trenches and expected to make a stand. It was indeed a formidable position if well defended. At the top of a high, steep ridge was the trench. In front of the trench were numbers of man-traps. Some were pits, cunningly concealed, and having at the bottom a sharp stake on which the unwary soldier would be impaled. Others were trees bearing a huge arrow or bolt, released by a combination of cord and trigger set in action by the foot of the unsuspecting soldier who, it was expected, would be pierced by the arrow.

But my guide, Victor Sanz, formerly a lieutenant colonel of insurgents, knew about these tricks. Finding a herd of carabaos near the trenches he suggested that we drive them over the insurgents' position. This we did. There was but a small skirmish, and the soldiers, following the trail made by the carabaos, avoided the pitfalls and traps. We had some difficulty hauling our artillery over the pass. At one o'clock after a rather light skirmish we arrived at the town of Tigaon. It was entirely deserted by its inhabitants but contained much hemp. There we were met by Captain Cogswell's company, 45th Infantry, coming from Iriga. I left here as a garrison twenty men under Lieutenant Odell, 45th Infantry, and started by a good road for the large town of Goa, five miles distant. It was a beautiful country through which we were passing, the road lined with hemp plantations, looking like banana groves. Above loomed the immense mass of Mt. Isarog, a black and picturesque height.

At Goa, a good-sized town, which also was deserted, we found tracks of a considerable force, including artillery, leading northwest. We also heard that a force of three hundred had just left the town. We pursued them four miles, when night coming on we returned to Goa. Total distance marched, twenty-one miles. My infantrymen were very tired.

Next morning, leaving Captain Cogswell's company quartered in the church convent at Goa, we started for San José, the chief town of the district, two miles from Goa. When we arrived at San José we found it deserted. The town boasted a large church and convent and many good buildings, including a large edifice belonging to a Spanish company, the latter admirably suited for my headquarters, containing as it did a large hall, with several bedrooms on the second floor, and good accommodations for a guard on the first floor.

Leaving a company of infantry in the convent at San José we at once started for Lagonoy, a small town two and a half miles from San José, and at the northern end of the district. We now had traversed the entire district, from south to north, without experiencing up to the present time any appreciable resistance. Just beyond Lagonoy was a fair-sized river. We marched down to that and found that beyond the river the district ended in a range of high hills. As the river was deep, I concluded to go no farther. About a mile distant, near the summit of some high hills, was a small trench, but I concluded to leave that for later exploration.

I had with me Captain Agnew's troop of cavalry, Captain David Hand's company of the 45th Infantry, and the two small pieces of mountain artillery. We went back to the convent in the town to rest and eat our midday meal. At the request of Lieutenant Lyle, commanding the artillery, I left him on the bank of the river; he wanted to throw a few shells at the trenches.

We had not been long in the convent when there was a terrific uproar. It appeared that when Lyle fired the first shot, a large force of insurgents concealed in the bushes on the opposite bank of the river opened up on him at short range. We hastily reformed the companies and rushed down to the river to aid him. I, with one detachment, ran down the main street; the insurgents were firing directly up the street, and the way we had to dodge from house to house reminded me of some of the methods of street fighting.

By good luck, although bullets had struck Lyle's pieces three times, none of his detachment had been hit. He stood his ground and, cutting his shell fuses at zero, fired in among the enemy only 100 yards distant. Soon Agnew's troop and

Hand's company got into action. The engagement lasted about two hours, when the insurgents retreated. It was said their losses were heavy.

During the fight I had an amusing experience. Mounted, I was visiting different portions of my line (the two companies were about a quarter of a mile apart) and was riding unattended through a hemp plantation, when a bolo-man, knife in hand, suddenly came at me. Putting spurs to my horse I rushed at him, shouting a loud "Boo!" He hesitated, turned and ran! I had not time to pull my pistol before he disappeared.

Cheatham's troop of cavalry in the meantime had been scouting the country southeast to Sangay, twelve miles distant. Thus, during two days, the district had been pretty well covered.

Hearing that General Bell had arrived in a gunboat, I rode to Baybay, the port four miles distant. There I met the general, who came ashore and with me visited the town of San José, returning that evening. He informed me that to hold the District of Lagonoy he could spare me only one company of infantry and one troop of cavalry! That the rest of the troops would have to be sent back. Furthermore, as I would not have enough men to hold all the towns, the town of Lagonoy would have to go ungarrisoned. This decision later turned out to be disastrous.

My problem was this: with a troop of cavalry and a company of infantry I had to garrison four large towns and the port, and keep the rest of the country free of the enemy. I solved the problem in the following manner.

The best defense is the offensive. Only by continuous aggressiveness could I keep my garrisons from being beleaguered. For the duty of keeping the enemy always on the defensive I assigned the cavalry troop. It was to march every day, scouting for the enemy, attacking him wherever found.

The port, Sabang, would be held by a corporal and six men, established in an ancient Moorish fort at that place.

All the towns and also the port should be linked up by telephone lines; each town garrisoned by a small detachment, established in a secure position. Infantry detachments on native ponies, commandeered from the people, scouted, during the day, the country immediately adjacent to the town. At night, sheltered behind the stone foundations of the house in which they were quartered, using but a single sentinel, they stood on the defensive. I established night outposts around the town, using the native police. These were always ready to give the alarm, to protect their families, for in street fighting the inhabitants had no shelter and would suffer from the bullets which traversed the light bamboo houses unchecked. Fortunately, the insurgents seldom cut the telephone lines, and when at night a post was attacked, the alarm would be given and the cavalry was ready to fly to its assistance.

The infantry was disposed as follows: at Tigaon, a lieutenant and twenty men; at Goa, a lieutenant and twenty men; at Baybay, the port, a corporal and six men. At Sangay I put a sergeant and ten men of artillery, armed with rifles and having a field-piece. At San José, my headquarters, I had the remainder of the infantry company, the artillery detachment, and the troop of cavalry; making with the pack train and hospital attendants, a total of perhaps ninety-two men.

The telephone line running from Sangay to Tigaon, then to Goa, then to San José, then to Baybay, was about seventeen miles long and was very expeditiously constructed by my efficient signal officer, First Lieutenant Frank J. Lyman.

Lagonoy, two miles distant from San José, was visited daily by the patrols. At first it was deserted. When the inhabitants returned to it, a force of native police was organized and armed with rifles; they did good service.

June 28th Major Nolan with his troop arrived, having marched around the north side of Mt. Isarog and participated in two fights. Part of the infantry troops were used to land and haul supplies from the *Montanes* and haul them to San José The cavalry scouted.

June 29th and 30th Major Nolan's troop and Captain Agnew's troop returned to Nueva Caceres. Hand's company and Cogswell's company also departed. The cavalry scouted. Many inhabitants returned to the towns, including the former mayors of San José and Goa, Forregrosa and Padilla, who took the oath of allegiance and were continued in their duties. The chief priest of San José, a native of much influence in the community, who had hitherto been with the insurgent forces, also came and presented himself.

My troops now consisted of only one company of infantry, one troop of cavalry, and one section of artillery.

July 1st, after consultation with Forregrosa, the mayor, we decided it would be well to have a service in the church at which the priest should preach a sermon of peace and conciliation. The mayor assured me that the ringing of the church bells would bring in many of the common people hiding in the woods. Accordingly the church bells were rung and about ten o'clock the mayor and I got into a native coach drawn by two ponies. Preceded by a native brass band we proceeded to the church. Alighting from the carriage and mutually sprinkling holy water on each other we took seats in the pew of honor, directly underneath the pulpit. The church filled rapidly. The priest, a powerful, hard-looking native, spoke his piece, in the Bicol language. Then we went back in state, again in the coach, with the brass band!

The priest, who had a granary filled with rice, promised to distribute it among the poor, many of whom were starving.

This day the cavalry had a fight, killing two bolo-men. Insurgents made a futile night attack on Tigaon.

July 2nd, with the cavalry, I marched to Tigaon, thence to Licod, around the south side of the mountain. I had a small fight, killed one rifleman, wounded and captured another, captured five saddled horses and much grain. We also burned the barracks. Left San José at eight P. M., returned at six P. M.; distance, twenty-six miles.

July 3rd Captain Cheatham with his troop had a fight near Lagonoy; killed one and wounded two. Lieutenant Schuman at Tigaon reported he was about to be attacked by Colonel Perfecto and forty rifles. I answered by messenger that that was what he should want!

July 4th we observed "Independence Day." Seeing a Filipino flag waving over a house we hauled down the flag and took the owner in custody. When asked for an explanation the owner answered that it was "Independence Day" and because of that he hoisted the Philippine flag. I told him that later when the insurrection was over he could use his flag all he wanted, but so long as his people were fighting us he would have to defer its use! I then released him.

July 5th—Cheatham with his troop was resting near Lagonoy when he was attacked by fifty rifles. Killed four, including a lieutenant and a trumpeter.

July 6—Cheatham with cavalry had fierce fight with the enemy in trenches near Estacahan, had two men dangerously wounded. Took trenches and killed six. I sent out reinforcements.

A number of insurgent officers came in, and on taking the oath of allegiance were paroled, but told they would be watched. We hear that Segovia, an insurgent chief, is tired of Lagonoy and has left the district, taking seventy rifles.

Seized six thousand pesos, presumably belonging to the insurgent government; also many thousand bales of hemp.

July 10th—The insurgents were said to be leaving the district. Many insurgent officers had surrendered and been paroled. The telephone line was completed. One of Cheatham's men wounded near Estacahan died; he was buried in the churchyard. As I was reading the service over the poor fellow I heard the natives saying, *"El Coronel dice amen!"* (The Colonel says *amen.*) It was a great surprise to them that I should say amen! It appears the priest had been telling them the Americans had no religion; that they were barbarians and that we were in the habit of "eating little children!" This was told me by Juan, my servant, who is a constant attendant at church.

This Juan was a simple-minded Bicol who on

one occasion reminded me of George Washington. I was in the careless habit of keeping my silver money in a cigar box on the table in my bedroom. One day I found that some of it had disappeared. I questioned Juan, who replied without hesitation, "I took it, Colonel, I wanted to buy a shirt." "But, Juan, in future when you are going to take my money, please let me know."

It must have been about the middle of July when I made up my mind it was time to have a *baile*. My proposition was, that the way to pacify was to dance. For while our officers would not readily associate with the Filipino men of the upper classes, they would be glad to dance with their pretty wives and daughters. And the chivalry of the American is such in their behavior towards women that it wins the hearts of not only the fair sex but of their male companions. And so a dance is a great help toward bringing about more cordial relations.

The hall of the headquarters building made a good ballroom. For a band we collected the musicians from five different towns; these were equipped mainly with horns and drums; stringed instruments were lacking on account of the dearth of catgut, hemp was not a good substitute. Consequently the five bands when assembled in one company—a forest of forty horns and drums—produced music that was brassy and thunderous. But we were not in a position to be critical.

Hostilities had somewhat abated, although the cavalry still scouted daily for the enemy, and I believed I would have a satisfactory response to my invitation.

Dances, or *bailes,* as they are called in the

Philippines, usually commence at about five P. M. At that hour the brass band had assembled, and many guests were making their appearance, including the native officials of the various towns, the priests and a number of the *principales,* or more wealthy citizens. But not a woman had appeared!

We opened up our stock of beer, whiskey, et cetera, and engaged in animated conversation. The band discoursed and we were having a pleasant time. But it was time for the ladies to arrive, and at six o'clock I mentioned that fact to the native chief of police.

"I do not think any ladies will come to this party!" said he. I strove to conceal my astonishment and asked him why he thought so. "Because the insurgents have issued an order that any ladies coming to this dance will be killed!"

I told him I thought the ladies would come all the same. But I must confess I was a little doubtful.

At six-thirty a message came from Goa, two miles away, "Lieutenant Odell has just passed through Goa on his way from Tigaon, with four wagonloads of *bailarinas!*" (dancers).

It appeared that Lieutenant Odell, who had become very influential and popular at Tigaon and Sangay, had gathered up, nilly-willy, the belles of those towns and was transporting them in army wagons.

Presently they arrived. Seeing their rivals on the way to the dance the ladies of Goa and San José hastened to imitate their example, and we soon had the ballroom crowded.

The ball costume of the Filipino women of the upper class is rather antique and very picturesque.

Their skirts and waists are of stiff, heavy, silken brocade. Their necks and busts are covered with a fichu or neckerchief of pina cloth or of finely woven hemp. They wear on their feet dancing slippers, sometimes without stockings. After each dance the lady and gentleman are supposed to separate and sit at opposite sides of the room. The dances indulged in are the waltz, two-step, and an ancient square dance called the *rigadon*.

My officers present were: Captain Cheatham, Captain Rogers, Captain Sparrenberger, Lieutenants Lyman, Odell, Tyner, Luthi, Lyle, Schuman and Ryan; also two officers of the 47th Infantry, from the town of Tobaco. We opened the ball as was the custom with the *rigadon*. In my set were Dr. Sparrenberger, who is 6 feet, 4 inches in height, Lieutenant Lyman, 6 feet 3, and myself, 6 feet 2. We were all excessively thin and in our white dress uniforms we looked, as someone remarked, like long white snakes! In the *rigadon*, which is a somewhat complicated dance, we made various and ludicrous mistakes. The Filipinos, who at first had been looking rather sour and solemn, burst out laughing, the ice was broken and the ball became a merry one. The rather timid ladies were enchanted by the gallant manners of the American officers, and the Filipino men, who preferred to look on rather than dance, beamed their approval.

Señorita Luisa —— was in beauty and accomplishments the belle of the ball. The daughter of a Spanish priest at Sangay, a man who was, nevertheless, a most devoted father, she had been educated in a convent at Manila. She was rather frail, but was a beautiful dancer. I was therefore surprised when at two A. M. she told me she feared she must go home.

"My dear Señorita," I said, "are you trying to break up my ball?" "What do you say, Colonel?" "Don't you understand you are the belle of the ball and if you leave us, the others will follow?" "Oh, no, Colonel," she cried with much emotion, "I am not trying to injure your ball; believe me—but my home is twelve miles away and I ought to go; besides, I am ill!" "My dear, we will see you home safely; you must stay to the end of the ball; and in the meantime Dr. Sparrenberger will give you something to make you feel better!" So Sparrenberger fixed her up a mixture of coffee and brandy and soon she was dancing again.

At four A. M. some more people tried to leave. I detained them in a similar manner, with many excuses for my insistency.

It was seven o'clock and broad daylight when the ball broke up. An officer who served at San José ten years afterwards told me that the people there were still talking of our "grand military ball." This officer also told me that two of the principal streets in San José had been renamed "Aguinaldo" and "Parker." I am not sure, however, that I like the association of names!

It was at about this period that I re-established the schools in the district. I detailed a soldier to give the children lessons in English; they seemed glad to learn, and soon in my daily rides to the different towns my ears would be pleasantly saluted by voices of little children calling out, "Good morning! Good-bye!" The teacher at Sangay was Señorita Luisa Algarrate. She remarked in her plaintive voice, "I did not want to be teacher but *El Coronel me mando!"* (The Colonel ordered me.)

On these rides I was careful, as always in the Philippines, to take along an escort of several men, and whenever possible, to return by a different route, thus avoiding ambush. But there was one officer, the efficient Dr. Frederick Sparrenberger, who being often hurriedly summoned to the scenes of trouble and an escort not being immediately available, was sometimes obliged to ride alone, at night, by unfrequented roads. His behavior on many of these occasions was extremely gallant and should have received from the War Department official recognition. As soft-hearted as he was brave, Sparrenberger ministered alike to natives and Americans, and his work was an important element in the pacification of the district.

I should not neglect here in speaking of gallant conduct, to mention Captain Cheatham, commander of the cavalry troop who day after day scouted for the enemy, almost certain of ambush. Or his lieutenant, Luthi, who was as gallant in his way as Cheatham in his. I was also ably assisted by Captain Rogers, Lieutenants Odell, Lewis, Ryan, G. P. Tyner and John Schuman. Ryan, Tyner and Schuman afterwards joined the Regular Army. Cheatham went into the Philippine Scouts. Luthi, when I last heard of him, was chief of police of Manila. Lieutenant Frank P. Lyman, of the signal corps, was another officer who should have received official recognition. He braved many perils in the arduous work of establishing and maintaining our telephone line.

We had many privations at Lagonoy. The first letters from home did not arrive until we had been there nearly two months. There was no fresh beef, no fresh vegetables, no ice. When we first arrived we found we had no means of making yeast, no potatoes with which to ferment yeast; no yeast powders. Thus we had no bread. Our hardtack came to an end. In this predicament we finally discovered that some Chinese shop-keepers made bread of rice flour, using a yeast produced from a *beer* made of the sap of the palm. Some of this yeast we obtained and found it answered our purpose; after that we made good bread.

On August 21st the Spanish ship *Salvadora* arrived with commissaries. But many of the supplies of food on the manifest were missing; the Spaniards had evidently sold them. Particularly we mourned the absence of the potatoes invoiced to us. I looked up the "Laws of the King of Spain," which General Otis had adopted *ad interim* for the military government of the Islands. For a failure of a ship captain to comply with the manifest the fine was one thousand dollars. This I imposed on the Spanish captain; he readily complied, and brought me two sacks containing each one thousand pesos. But later Otis, always favorable to the Spaniards, remitted the fine. Two years afterwards when serving as adjutant general at Washington the proceedings of a board of survey on the loss of these commissaries passed through my hands, covered with endorsements! The Spaniards had been whitewashed. The government sustained the loss.

To add to our difficulties the rinderpest attacked the carabaos in the district and nearly all died. It was a baneful sight to see the fields covered with their rotting bodies. Later we had a rice famine, the poorer people especially suffering. I appealed to the authorities at Manila and they brought our merchants in the transport *Tartar,* 10,000 *picals* of rice or about one million three hundred thousand pounds. I saw that it was sold to the people at a reasonable price.

Speaking of the "Laws of the King of Spain," this was a large book, published at Manila, largely dealing with fines and taxes. The taxes were extraordinary; they may be said to have dated from the Middle Ages. Their object seemed to be to discourage civilization and progress. Thus a bale of hemp pressed by hand power was taxed, say, one dollar; if baled by horse power, two dollars; if baled by steam power, three dollars! A house with one window was taxed so much, with two windows still more, etc. Under orders from Manila I was obliged to detach an officer as tax-gatherer; he even had to visit the market place each day and collect pennies from the poor peasants who came to sell their little stocks of fruits and vegetables.

We officers despised the "Laws of the King of Spain." The people, on their part, could not understand why we, representing a country of progress and liberty, adhered to the laws of tyranny and superstition. As for me I never could comprehend why Otis, instead, did not adopt the "Laws of the State of Ohio," or of some other enlightened community.

Insurgent officers still continued to come in and surrender, giving up their swords or bolos. I let them know that if they told a straight tale I would let them go, but that if they attempted to deceive me I would punish them. Some of the most ornate liars I locked up for a time in a granary under the convent. I called this *"El refugio de los Mentirosos,"* or "Liars' Retreat." It was my only prison.

The town of Lagonoy, as I have said, I was ordered to leave without a garrison. Under these circumstances the inhabitants were slow in coming back, exposed as they were to raids by the insurgents. Later, however, we organized a native police and reinstated the former mayor. I issued to the police four rifles, with ammunition. A patrol visited the town each day; schools were begun and the place began to revive.

August 30th I organized an expedition to make a raid on the town of Caramoan on a peninsula thirty miles from San José. There was said to be a force of insurgents there. We were to go there in the gunboat *Quiros,* Lieutenant Worlick, U. S. Navy, commanding, which had recently made its appearance on the coast. I was about to start when the chief of police of Lagonoy made his appearance. I asked him what he wanted.

"No hay nadie in Lagonoy," he said calmly. "What?" said I. *"No hay nadie in Lagonoy."* (There's no one left in Lagonoy.)

It was too true! During the night the insurgents had attacked the town. The mayor had locked up the rifles for safekeeping and they were not available. They killed the mayor, also his aged father, and carried off their wives. They captured the rifles. They took the eight policemen prisoners, carried them to a high cliff hanging over the sea, tied stones around their necks and threw them over the precipice. They also killed two Chinamen. The entire population fled, leaving alive in Lagonoy only stray cats and dogs!

I did not know all these details until later. Sending a detachment to pursue the insurgents I embarked with thirty men for Caramoan. The expedition was not a success. Caramoan, two miles from the sea, was deserted. There was no opposition. We stayed overnight (experiencing quite a severe earthquake) and returned the next day.

To prevent further depredations in Lagonoy, and ignoring General Bell's orders, I established a garrison there, Lieutenant Luthi and twenty men. But it was some time before the people returned.

September 1st, at the invitation of Lieutenant Worlick, I embarked with a party of officers on the *Quiros* and steamed to the town of Tobaco. This place, at the foot of the volcano of Mayon, was a considerable city, garrisoned by some companies of the 47th Infantry. The mountain behind the town is one of the grandest sights in the Philippines. Immensely high, it is a perfect cone, its sides covered with lava and ashes, a column of smoke perpetually issuing from its summit. In perfection of form it rivals Mount Aetna or the Japanese Fujiyama.

We were hospitably welcomed by our brother officers of the 47th Infantry. Calling on the mayor of the town, he proceeded to organize a *baile* for our benefit. It took place that evening. The mayor, in the kindness of his heart, insisted that I should dance with the belle of the ball, his *chere amic,* a pretty young lady, having a decidedly Chinese cast of countenance. In fact she was a Chinese Mestiza, the daughter of a wealthy merchant from the "Flowery Kingdom."

It is quite proper in the East to ask one's age

and it is also a compliment to a middle-aged man to add to his years. Sitting with the young lady at supper I said, by way of conversation, "My dear, how old are you?" *"Tengo doce anos, Señor,"* (I am twelve years old, sir), was her reply, deprecatingly and in a timid voice. I had to laugh and so did Lieutenant Lyle, seated on her left. "And how old do you think I am?" I incautiously asked. "Oh, about sixty-five!" she replied. I was not so well pleased, particularly as Lieutenant Lyle burst into a roar of laughter. The sweet young thing, wishing to be polite, had added twenty years to my age!

It is a fact that in the tropics a woman at twelve years is mature!

The *baile* was a great success. We returned to San José the next day, well pleased with our visit.

On the night of September 5th Lieutenant Odell at Tigaon telephoned me a fight was going on at Sangay; that he could hear the rattle of musketry and the roar of cannon! I saddled up and with a detachment made a rapid night ride to Sangay, a distance of twelve miles. Arrived there all was quiet; the sergeant in charge of the artillery detachment reported he had been attacked but had driven the enemy off. He also said surlily that they wanted to be relieved. They objected to being used as an infantry garrison.

There was something fishy about his story. I investigated and found that they had been drinking and had staged a sham fight. The people of the town were greatly alarmed by this and the previous conduct of the artillerymen, and I had no recourse but to take them away. I locked them up for a while in the *"Refugio de los Mentirosos."* They had always been an undisciplined lot—great looters. One favorite trick of theirs when on the march was for each man to provide himself with a number of stones. When the detachment arrived opposite a fat goose, the sergeant would command, "Battery, fire!" when each man would let fly at the goose which had but a poor chance of escaping the volley of stones.

During the latter part of September and the early part of October, we had eight or ten small engagements. On September 24th the insurgents even made a night attack on San Jose, firing a few shots into the town. While I sent forces to drive them away, I rode through the streets of the town carrying a lantern and reassuring the alarmed people.

October 6th, with a force of eighty men, I marched against an insurgent force on the higher slopes of Mt. Isarog. After an engagement in which they suffered a number of casualties, they scattered; we burned six barracks and captured a quantity of ammunition. It was a picturesque affair. The mountain on which we were attacked by some naked savages, similar to Igorrotes, was heavily wooded. The savages, one of whom was killed, were armed with spears and bows and arrows, and seemed to have no connection with the insurgents. For several days after this expedition I suffered from a very painful sore throat. In the chase after the insurgents I had become exhausted and overheated. In this condition I incautiously took a drink of raw whiskey; it scarified and blistered the skin of my throat, so that for days I suffered intensely. It was the first time whiskey ever affected me in that way!

During my stay in Lagonoy District I was able to seize for the United States much hemp, the property of the "Compania Co-operativa," a company organized by the insurgent government for collecting and disposing of the hemp crop. Also a large amount of money accumulated by the same company. In this I was greatly aided by my interpreter, Victor Sanz. Sanz, who spoke no English, and with whom I had to communicate in Spanish, was a fluent conversationalist in the Bicol language. Son of a Spanish officer, he had attached himself to our cause, and he served us with the greatest zeal and loyalty. Personally, I was greatly indebted to him for many acts of devotion.

It was not an easy job that we accomplished in the District of Lagonoy with our two small companies. Our only communication with the outside world was by sea, and that rarely. We were in the midst of a large population, much of which was at first hostile or semi-hostile. We had to hold a large territory and drive out the insurgents. We had difficulties in supplying the troops, in sanitation, and in making our small force suffice for our needs.

Personally, I had to order the marches and combats of the troops in which often I took part. I had constantly to inspect my outlying detachments. I supervised the schools, the construction and repair of the roads, the civil government of the towns, the civil police, the supervision of spies and former insurgent officers, the confiscation from the insurgent government of hemp and funds, for which I accounted to the civil government at Manila. When famine came I saw that food was bought and the population was fed. And I had to gain the people's confidence.

All this required ceaseless activity, ceaseless

vigilance. But I felt that I had been successful.

On the morning of October 11, 1900, I heard a noise of horsemen under my window. What was my surprise, on looking out, to behold Colonel Lockett at the head of a troop of cavalry!

He announced that by order of General Bell he had come from Nueva Caceres to relieve me of command. In command at Nueva Caceres, he had been "ranked out" by the arrival of Colonel McGregor with his regiment, the 9th (colored) Cavalry. And being himself ranked out, he had been sent to rank me out!

I hastened to make my preparations for departure. Saying good-bye is often an unnecessary and painful task; it was especially so in this case. I let none of the natives know that I was going. But as I was about to start for the port, the *Presidente* of Goa, Padilla, happened to come in, on a matter of business. He saw my baggage and asked me where I was going. I had to tell him.

The poor fellow, burying his face in his hands, burst into loud sobs. I had been his friend; I had supported him against his enemies who hated him for being an Americanista, and for enforcing the laws and who would be glad to see him with his throat cut! And now he was going to be turned over to a strange commander who, maybe, might not support him!

He did not tell me this; he was too overcome by grief and terror. I left him weeping and proceeded on my way.

Sure enough, shortly afterwards he was deposed. And I have no doubt his enemies wreaked their vengeance upon him.

But it was for me to obey orders. Lagonoy

was a thing of the past. That chapter was closed. I was going to new scenes, new problems.

It was true that I had received, so far as I knew, no credit for what I had accomplished, but how was anyone to know my difficulties? It was no longer the policy to publish official reports and I never saw the accounts I forwarded even referred to. But that is a common occurrence in war. To be appreciated you must be under the eyes of your superior.

I sailed from Sabang on the Spanish freighter *Serrantes* and arrived at Nueva Caceres October 16th. Being not in the best of health and needing a rest, I would have liked a leave but heard that it was not the policy to grant leaves. Instead, they occasionally ordered officers, who needed relaxation, to Manila on court-martial duty. For such a detail I applied by telegraph, and received an affirmative answer. Under orders to report for court-martial duty at Manila, I left Nueva Caceres November 1st. Arrived at the mouth of the river I boarded the transport *Francisco Reyes,* arriving after a voyage of two hundred miles at Legaspi. Legaspi, south of Nueva Caceres, was the principal port of the province of Albay. On November 4th we took aboard Company F, 47th Infantry, Captain Garwood, which by orders of the governor general was to be landed on the Island of Bataan. On this island, at a place called Calanan, there was a coal mine, owned by Spaniards, which this force was sent to protect. At Legaspi, however, the natives informed us that no coal had been mined at Calanan for years and that the only inhabitants were wild savages, who went about stark naked!

We arrived at the beautiful, landlocked little

bay of Calanan at three that afternoon. Manning boats, we started on a tour of exploration. The place was deserted. A family of savages, alarmed at our approach, rushed from their rude shelter and disappeared in the woods. There were some sunken hulks here and there and some vestiges of coal sheds, burned to the ground.

Next day we continued the exploration. The place was savage and wild beyond description. There was nothing to protect. There was not even a place to camp, the mountains sloping steeply down to the water's edge. The company, having no boat, would have no way of communicating with the mainland fifty miles distant. It was a regular "Robinson Crusoe" isle.

Under these circumstances should the company take station there? Captain Garwood asked me this question. I replied that I would suggest that he take his company back to Legaspi, report the circumstances and request further orders. In my belief the authorities had been misinformed.

This he did, and received telegraphic notice that the orders for garrisoning the island had been revoked. To me it was a commentary on the government of the island, that on the sole testimony of a lying Spaniard (the commercial class of Spaniards we had in the Philippines seemed to be natural and inevitable liars), a company of infantry should be sent to an unknown, uninhabited island, to be left there without means of transportation, or means of communication with the mainland. And this, notwithstanding the crying need of important districts like Lagonoy for larger garrisons.

Before we could take the company off the ship, however, the barometer commenced to fall rapidly. The captain was alarmed, a typhoon was approaching! And we were in an open roadstead. We pulled up our anchor and started to Sulat Bay. There, for forty-eight hours, during a tremendous tempest we rode safely at anchor.

November 7th we returned to Legaspi and landed Captain Garwood and his company. November 9th we arrived at Manila.

I think during the month I stayed at Manila I had almost the most joyous time of my life. The pleasure of the transition to the gayety of the metropolis was enhanced by escape from care and responsibility. The trials of the past months were to be put out of sight.

This was the feeling of hundreds of officers who had for a short period "come in from the lines" and who were determined to enjoy themselves to the limit. Their reckless feeling affected all classes of Americans. It was what we called afterwards "the days of the empire." Manila was truly a "city of pleasure." Champagne cost little more than in Paris, so did excitement. Accommodations were poor, food was mediocre, but what did that matter to men who had lived as we had?

To our jaded eyes the sight of white women was refreshing. I remember as I drove up from the steamer I took off my hat to the first woman I met, as a salute to the whole company of my fair compatriots. And I discovered before long that the city had many of them and that they were not the least beautiful of their sex. The husbands of some were in the city; of others out on the lines; and still others had no husbands. Was it any fault of ours that we sought in their society comfort and pleasure; or of theirs that they took pity on us?

Captain Ryan, of the commissary department, had journeyed with me from Nueva Caceres. He had come to obtain commissary stores for the troops in the province of Camarines. He took a vow that until his ship was loaded *he* would not be, and I consented to join him in the resolution. So, for a time, we mutually promised we would drink nothing stronger than beer. Fortunately the ship was not long in loading.

One of the most unique characters in Manila at this time was Mayor Brown; of Jewish extraction, he was "hail fellow well met" and liked by everyone. Why he was called "Mayor" no one knew, except that for every stranger or newcomer, particularly of the army or navy and not too low in the social scale, Mayor Brown did the honors of the city. Everyone knew him and he went everywhere. Those in pursuit of pleasure hunted up Mayor Brown; those who needed funds got them readily from him. I am inclined to think that some of his loans were never repaid, but Mayor Brown did not complain. He kept open house. It was said that he arrived May 1, 1898, on Admiral Dewey's flagship, a guest of the Admiral; that when the Spanish fleet had been sunk and the troops entered the city he came with them and, finding a house deserted, took possession and had been there ever since. As an importer of wines and liquors and later in supplying our post exchanges, he was said to have made quite a bit of money. On one occasion when I asked him what he intended to do when the insurrection was over he told me that when peace came he was going back to the United States and spend his time making visits to army posts, where he was sure of a welcome from his old friends. I believe his ambition was never realized and that later he lost much money. But as a man who befriended hundreds of officers he deserves to be celebrated. I am particularly indebted to him.

In Manila I met many classmates and old friends. One does not realize all that friendship means until he tests it far from home and in a strange and foreign land. There the word "old friend" acquires a new and almost sacred significance. I experienced many times while in Manila the joy of seeing reborn the affection of early days.

I think one of the reasons why that period was called "the days of the empire" was on account of the lavish way in which things were done. Otis had gone home and General MacArthur was in command. Money was dispensed freely for storehouses, offices, docks, ships, roads, barracks, quarters, residences for the higher command, ice plants, et cetera. Each officer stationed in Manila was provided with horses, a carriage and a driver; also each of the higher clerks and civil employees. It was amusing to see in the neighborhood of the headquarters' offices the long line of native equipages waiting for the clerks. These civilian employees also brought their wives to Manila, swelling the female contingent.

My duties on the court-martial were light and generally confined to the earlier part of the day. I was getting the rest and relaxation I so long had needed. But all good things come to an end, and on December 7th I again sailed for Nueva Caceres, this time via Pasacao, where I arrived the next day.

At Pasacao, garrisoned by a company of the 45th Infantry, I was detained by a violent typhoon for three days. At the end of that time I started for Nueva Caceres with a small escort of mounted men in charge of a pack train laden with sacks of mail. Most of the country we passed through was a vast lake of water caused by the storms and floods. Through this the mules and horses waded with the water often up to their hocks or bellies. Near Nueva Caceres the flood made it impossible to march any farther and I commandeered some boats, into which we loaded the sacks of mail and paddled down the river to Nueva Caceres.

December 14th I started for Iriga, the headquarters of my regiment, twenty-four miles distant. I had already corresponded with Colonel Dorst, who welcomed me to his headquarters. I had with me four wagons and twenty men. When I arrived at Baao, four miles from Iriga, I telephoned Colonel Dorst to tell him that I would arrive shortly. Joe happened to be in one of his contrary moods. He replied, "Jim, I wish you wouldn't come with that big detachment to this place; take them to Nabua" (a place two miles from Iriga and four miles from Baao). I was perplexed. I wanted at least to see Dorst and I knew I could go to Nabua via Iriga just as well. So I said, "Joe, all the same I'm coming to Iriga!" and hung up the telephone. And at Iriga, Joe, in front of his quarters, welcomed me with great hospitality and there was no more talk of going to stay at Nabua!

The district of Iriga, of which the town of Iriga was used as our headquarters, consisted of an area fifteen miles square, containing five towns: Iriga, Baao, Buhi, Nabua, and Bato. It lay at the head of the Bicol River and thus several of these towns could be reached by small boats. The towns, only a few miles apart, were connected by telephone. When I arrived the district seemed thoroughly pacified and the inhabitants on good terms with the military. Occasionally, on the outskirts of the district, skirmishes with the insurgents would occur. Also, at times, the wagon trains, conveying supplies from one post to another, would be fired upon by snipers, and this in spite of the fact that such trains were always guarded by at least two companies of infantry.

On January 2nd Colonel Dorst, who was not in good health, departed for Manila for a stay of nearly three months, leaving me in command of the district. There were in all six companies of infantry.

I determined to remedy a serious deficiency in supplies, brought hitherto by land. I persuaded the chief quartermaster at Nueva Caceres to send us a large invoice of goods by water. To protect the fleet of forty native boats we picketed the course of the river. The distance by river was forty miles, but with the river guarded the insurgents did not dare to attack and the convoy arrived safely at Iriga. It carried an enormous quantity of supplies, of some items enough for six months. Thereafter the troops received the full ration, including freshly baked bread. As a result of the muster out of several companies of the 11th Cavalry there were left a number of surplus cavalry horses, of which one hundred had been assigned to the district. No use, however, had been made of them and they had been turned out on pasture. The arrival of plenty of forage made them available and they were distributed among the posts. Funds were obtained and stables were built. The best riders were picked out, cavalry drills were begun, and in a short time each company had a detachment of mounted scouts. The next time that snipers fired on the wagons the mounted scouts charged and the enemy had difficulty in escaping. This put an end to that annoyance. The fatiguing march of large infantry convoys escorting the wagons was no longer necessary. Ten scouts sufficed to guard a train, where formerly two companies of infantry were necessary. Also, mounted patrols were used to clear the country adjacent to the towns instead of infantry—to the great satisfaction of the soldiers.

To increase the efficiency of the troops we instituted target practice, using the Parker swinging target which I had invented at Fort Wingate, New Mexico, in 1882.

In the snapshooting of skirmishes and ambushes men had acquired the habit of jerking the trigger, a tendency corrected by target practice.

About this time we were supplied with a number of Filipino scouts. They also were given a course of target practice. From the way they handled a gun I saw why in our combats with the insurgents we had so few casualties. Even in firing at a target the Filipinos were so excited that they "couldn't hit a flock of barns." They were "wild-eyed." It was ludicrous. It takes a certain amount of coolness and steadiness to make a good shot. This is one reason why the Anglo-Saxon and particularly the American is so much better with a rifle than the more excitable races.

I found that there were schools in the district, but that the schoolbooks they used, apparently supplied by the church, were largely devoted to lives of the saints and prayers and kindred religious subjects. The arithmetic and geography taught were of the most meager description. I succeeded in getting the authorities in Manila interested in the subject and obtained from them some schoolbooks more up to date.

It was a curious fact that our troops carried with them no flags, and as a consequence many Filipinos had never seen an American flag. My old chum and classmate at Rutgers College, New Jersey, Rev. Joseph R. Duryee, then living in New York, sent me a thousand small American flags, which I distributed to the school children and which they used on festive occasions and anniversaries.

We also detailed soldiers to teach English in the schools, with promising results.

Turning my attention to sanitation I employed the surgeons of the command in the work of inspecting the various premises, fining those inhabitants who did not clean up their homes and using the fines for prizes to clean up their homes and using the fines for prizes to be given those whose houses and yards were neatest. The surgeons also persuaded many of the inhabitants to adopt the use of dry earth closets. While in command I made a practice of inspecting the conditions in the various towns, riding through the country with a small escort. I noticed that while the lower class of workmen invariably took off their hats to a Spaniard (they were afraid of the Spaniards) no recognition or salute was given me or any of the Americans. I determined to change this. Meeting a party of laborers by the roadside who merely glared at me as I came up, I ordered them to join my escort. Marching several miles to the nearest town with the laborers following in my train I called for the mayor. I said to him, "Kindly tell these gentlemen that when I salute them I would be glad to have them return my salute. Say that I am sorry to have been obliged to detain them and that now they can go back to their homes!"

After I had done this several times I was received always with salutes and broad smiles and grins. In fact, the people were glad to be obliged to do the courteous thing, for if they had saluted without coercion, they would have been denounced as "Americanistas!"

Finding ninety natives in prison for unknown causes, I had them released. No charges had been preferred against them and they had been locked up many months before our arrival by the native authorities merely on the pretext that they were not known and, therefore, were "suspicious persons."

In February, 1901, news came that the "Philippine Commission," of which Mr. William Howard Taft was the head, was making a tour of the provinces and would shortly visit the Camarines and probably pass

Major General S. B. M. Young

through Iriga. Summoning the mayors of the five towns and opening a bottle or two of champagne in honor of the occasion, I placed before them the desirability of making a good showing in the district. Their roads and streets, I pointed out, were often grown up with weeds, the gutters obstructed, the bridges broken, the fences in need of repairs.

They entered gladly into the spirit of the occasion. Soon town criers summoned the workers, gangs were put to work on the streets and roads and in a remarkably short time the towns assumed quite another aspect. The bridges and culverts were also all put in order.

This accomplished I called another meeting of the alcaldes (mayors). After congratulating them on the improvement they had effected I said, "Many of your better class of houses, I mean those made of wood, need paint and look very shabby. Is there not some way of painting them?"

One of the alcaldes spoke up, "Near my town there is a creek and in the bottom of the creek there is a lot of fine white paint."

I had never before heard of getting paint out of a creek, but I asked him to bring me some. He did so, and I found it was a deposit of a kind of white gypsum, which would make an excellent whitewash. I expressed my satisfaction with the paint and the alcaldes went to work.

In their zeal the inhabitants painted, not only the wooden houses, but all the *bamboo* houses, so that soon there was not a house or a hut in the whole district, not even in the woods or in the mountains, that was not covered with a coat of virgin white. Not only that, but most of the people, with indigo and other dyes, painted picturesque scrolls of fruits and flowers on the white background. The houses were transformed! With vines and flowers about them they were, many of them, very pretty and quite different from the dirty drab shacks which had preceded them.

We were, however, disappointed in our expectations of seeing the commission; they went by another route. But in their place General Bell, at my request, inspected the district, arriving on February 27, 1901. The general was truly surprised. Every house was painted a pure white and decorated; all the streets, roads, bridges and fences had been repaired. When he approached a town (he came on horseback) the church bells would commence to ring. A short distance from the town he was met by a band, the *principales* mounted on ponies, the school children on foot. A procession would be formed, the band in front, then the little schoolgirls trooping along waving their American flags; next in order, the general, the schoolboys marching on each side and the *principales,* including the mayor and officials, on their little Filipino ponies. At the entrance to the town the procession passed under an arch of triumph made of bamboo. In the streets the inhabitants, when they were able, hung out the American flag or a banner to represent it. (I saw many made of bath towels crudely colored.) On the plaza young women stood on the balconies and threw flowers on the street in front of the general. Alighting in front of the Municipal Building the general was escorted within, where toasts were drunk in his honor and in honor of the American people. Then the general was invited to take a seat on the balcony, where he witnessed, in the plaza below, dramatic performances by natives armed with bows and arrows, spears, shields, and so forth, and dressed in ancient costumes. This over, the general went to the military headquarters. And in the evening a ball was given in his honor.

All this was done, not at my instigation; I was

ignorant of many of the details. It was a tribute to the Americans and it was to me a complete proof of the docility, kind-heartedness and friendliness of the Filipinos.

About this time the Government had distributed to the military posts copies, in Spanish, of the Constitution of the United States and had ordered the military commanders to read and explain it to the people. Accordingly each Sunday, after church services were over, the *principales* used to gather in my quarters and I would "expound the Constitution." I pointed out to them what great advantages they would gain as American citizen; how, with free entry of their products—hemp, sugar, tobacco, and so forth—into the United States their lands would greatly increase in value and even the poor people would be greatly benefited. I was listened to with great attention. I have no doubt this promise that they were to have all the rights of American citizens had much to do with the cessation shortly afterwards of hostilities in the Camarines.

Some months later, after I had left the islands, the Supreme Court announced that Filipinos could not be admitted to the rights of citizens under the Constitution! When my friends at Iriga were told of that decision, could they help thinking that the "expounding of the Constitution" was merely a plot to deceive them —to bring about more quickly their submission? And did they, perhaps, believe that I was a party to the swindle?

The people having complained that travelers on the road to Nueva Caceres were liable to be held up by armed *ladrones* who robbed them, and that in consequence few dared to make the trip, I determined to bring about again free communication between the cities. I therefore had a notice published that at seven A. M. Mondays of each week a mounted patrol would start from Nueva Caceres and protect all wishing to make the trip, returning on Thursdays.

On the first travel day perhaps a dozen people went to Caceres. On the second, thirty or forty. On the third and ever afterwards there was a great procession. It was amusing to see the large throng, laden with all kinds of commodities, reaching for half a mile, trudging along the road, with two mounted soldiers at the head and two bringing up the rear! With such a guard, if composed of *Americans,* they felt entirely secure.

The trail from Bato to the Province of Albay still was dangerous, the towns of Libon and Polangui in Albay not yet being garrisoned and being infested with insurrectos. Finding that the commanding officer of the Albay district would not occupy these towns I placed there small detachments of the 45th Infantry. But the communicating trail, twelve miles long, which followed the course of an old highway abandoned twenty-four years before by the Spaniards, was a difficult one, leading as it did through a forest, over a deep river and through a plain covered with cogon grass ten feet high.

In the interests of pacification and commerce I concluded to rebuild the road. Summoning my friends, the alcaldes of the district of Iriga, as well as the alcaldes of Polangui and Libon, I explained to them how it would add to the prosperity of all the towns should they have free exchange of commodities. I asked them if they could not help me build it.

After considerable discussion and consultation they announced that they could turn out fifteen hundred men to build it, provided I would furnish rice for food. It would take some days to finish the job; the men would have to be absent from their homes and would have to be fed.

There was present at Iriga at this time, inspecting the roads, Lieutenant William Kelly, an officer of the Engineer Department. After explaining the matter to him he telegraphed to his chief at Manila and the rice was furnished. On March 20th the work began.

It was extremely interesting to watch the way they went about it. The force was divided into three companies of five hundred men each. Each company worked on a different portion of the road and was divided up into numerous gangs. One gang with bolos cleared away the brush and dug out the roots. Another, with sharpened sticks for picks, pried up the clods. A third, with ridiculous little wooden spades, distributed the loose earth in the roadway. Still another, with pestles, tramped the earth down hard or, with rudely constructed hand barrows, carried, from the nearest creek, sand, which they spread on the rounded surface of the highway. Some gangs were cutting down trees near the creeks, making timbers and erecting bridges. And finally there was a gang of music makers. These men, using rough instruments made in the forest, producing weird and barbaric strains, played fiercely. The faster they played the faster the bolo men, the men with picks, the spade men, the pestle men, the barrow men and the timber and bridge men worked and toiled. It was a revival of feudal times, of the forced labor of the Middle Ages. In such a way perhaps were the cathedrals built and the castles of the barons. And I have no doubt that the ancients, too, animated and cheered their laborers with rude music.

In a little more than a week a good road, twelve miles long and twenty-four feet wide, was completed. The river, broad and deep, was crossed by a ferry, at which a ferryboat was duly established. Patrols traversed the road. For the first time in twenty-four years the two large and populous provinces of Caceres and Albay were connected by a highway.

During the month of February our efficient quartermaster, Captain Simpson, having completed a set of officers' quarters and headquarters' offices, we moved in, vacating the municipal building. In these quarters we also lodged in the dining-room where, at night roosted on a perch an immense turkey gobbler, presented for a New Year's feast by the *presidente* of Buhi, but which turned out to be such a pet that we had not the heart to kill him. This turkey habitually accompanied the sentinel, who paced up and down in front of the building. Directly opposite was a store kept by a Spaniard and frequented by the Filipino women who went there to buy rice and other food. The turkey, who, by the way, was always in a state of exaltation, trailing his stiffened wings on the ground, objected to the presence of these women and it was a common sight to see him pursuing the poor creatures who, with shrieks and cries, attempted to evade him, as with gobbles he flew across the street. The Spaniard probably consigned (mentally) the Americans and their national bird to the infernal regions!

During my stay there the district of Iriga, in a way, was very gay. We had many *bailes*. At Nabua the alcalde, Señor Perfecto, maintained as part of his establishment a band of perhaps twenty-five pieces. Whether he gave the poor devils who played his horns, flutes and drums anything besides food I never inquired, but it was the common talk that he did not. Accordingly, Señor Perfecto would have a *baile* on the slightest excuse, and there were a number of very pretty Mestiza young ladies at Nabua.

I remember particularly the first ball I attended at Iriga, given by the alcalde of that place on New Year's

Eve. A large addition was erected to his house to accommodate the dining-room, leaving the rest of the house available for dancing. (In the Philippines a temporary addition like this can be roughly constructed of bamboo and banana leaves for a few dollars.) When midnight struck and the New Year was ushered in amid the ringing of church bells, we ran with our partners in the dance across the street to the church, and there knelt during the mass. That finished, arm in arm we returned to the ballroom and resumed the interrupted waltz! Sometimes a mixture of folly and religion is very pleasing!

It was about March 1, 1901, that Congress, under the lash of the prohibitionists, passed a law that beer, wines or liquors should no longer be sold in any establishment under government control. The news was immediately telegraphed from Manila and I was required to publish an order to that effect. We had in our commissary a goodly quantity of champagne, which the authorities, in the kindness of their hearts, had sent us out in the wilderness "for the sick," it being understood that others might partake. I immediately notified my officers that such an order was coming and so each of them bought a case or two of the delightful beverage. I then published the order.

Having the champagne on hand in large quantity, the next problem was how to get rid of it. We had a merry time. Among other things we gave a series of *bailes*. The Filipino belles do not, as a rule, drink wine; the custom is, when it is offered them, to put the glass to their lips, say *Salud* (your good health) and put it down again. But we changed all that. We would cry "no heel taps" and require the lady to drink. "*El Coronel dice* (the colonel says) no heel taps!" the lady would cry apologetically, and take a good drink. Then her eyes would shine and she would become quite natural.

But our attempts to reform the Filipinos came to a sudden end. March 31st the 27th Infantry, a regular regiment, newly organized and almost entirely composed of untrained recruits, came to relieve us. Colonel Dorst had already rejoined us, and on April 4th we left for Nueva Caceres. As we were forbidden to transport animals from the Philippine Islands to the United States I had to say good-bye to my beloved horse, Brer Fox, my companion in so many marches and combats. I left him with Colonel Quinton, the commander of the 27th Infantry, but he soon after died of the *surra,* an epidemic disease fatal to many of our horses in the Philippines.

Brer Fox was a horse of many travels and adventures. He had gone from West Point to Peekskill, to Chickamagua, to Lexington, to Americus, to Matanzas, Cuba; to Cardenas, Cuba; to New York, to San Francisco, to Hawaii, to Manila, to Vigan, to Naig, to Lagonoy, to Iriga. Peace be to his ashes!

At Nueva Caceres, boarding the steamer *Montanes,* we transferred in the Bay of San Miguel to the transport *Sheridan* and proceeded to Manila.

On the way we landed a company of infantry at Pasacao. It fell to my lot to escort Mrs. Crimmins, the wife of one of the officers, ashore. She was a bride and full of romance, a beautiful girl, and the task of carrying her in my arms through the breakers was not an unpleasant one. As her Cicerone, and one who knew Pasacao, I escorted her about the dirty little village. She was an ardent Catholic and wanted to see the church. When she entered and beheld the sordid place, filthy in the extreme, with monstrous misshapen effigies on the walls, she burst into a passion of tears. I felt sorry for her as I made my way back to the boat.

At Manila we occupied a camp near the Luneta. Near us was a regiment, part of which had been raised in Kentucky. There was so much drunkenness in the regiment that finally the colonel was ordered on no pretext to allow any soldier to leave camp. Although tightly locked in, the men still stayed drunk. An investigation finally solved the problem—the regiment was manufacturing its own whiskey! We had all been supplied with sterilizers for boiling water. The Kentuckians had turned these into stills. Making a mash of the grain intended for their horses they distilled the liquid and made their own tipple!

We sailed from Manila March 22, 1901, touching at Nagasaki.

* * * * *

Before leaving the subject I should like to say a few words about the "Philippine question" in general. Our policy on May 1, 1898, when Dewey destroyed the Spanish fleet in Manila Bay, and for many months after was uncertain. Some of our wisest statesmen, particularly John Hay, Secretary of State, were opposed to our taking possession. Even Dewey himself telegraphed home that he considered the Filipinos more capable of self-government than the Cubans, a statement which, under pressure, he afterwards modified. Without our help the Filipinos alone had reduced nearly all the Spanish garrisons in the islands. Outside of the city of Manila, although everywhere blockaded by our fleet, they were supreme. As I have said before, their rule comprised an orderly, progressive system of general and municipal government, including post offices, telegraph lines, schools, a national church, newspapers, and a fairly efficient army.

There is no question but that in the early days we

treated them as allies. Dewey turned over to them large quantities of arms. The Spanish prisoners taken by our naval force, officers as well as men, were delivered to Aguinaldo's forces for safekeeping. With Aguinaldo Dewey had close relations, as with an ally. The Philippine troops aided materially in the capture of Manila.

Suddenly all was changed. McKinley decided the islands should be held by the United States. Prominent politicians, such as Beveridge, described in glowing terms the great advantages which would accrue to us by their retention. We were told that the islands were rich in mineral, in mines of gold and silver, coal and copper, pearls and fisheries and covered with forests of invaluable timber; that enormous profits would come from the production and transportation of rice, hemp, copra and other commodities. These statements dazzled the eyes of the American public, appealed to its covetous instincts. We were further told that it was essential that we should have "a foothold on the Asiatic coast," and that the islands afforded this foothold; that we would receive the gratitude of the Filipinos for teaching them self-government.

Time has shown us the futility of these promises. There are no good mines of gold or silver, of copper or coal, no great fisheries or pearl production. Most of the timber is so far from roads or from water and is so scattered that it is but a small resource. The islands, freed from the harsh and tyrannical rule of the Spaniards and the domination of the priestly castes who made peons of the people, no longer export rice; instead it is imported from other countries. The hemp production has declined. The "foothold in Asia" could have been accomplished by a naval station in the islands, readily granted by the Filipinos.

What has been gained has been, largely, an extension of public roads and improvements in the island and an increase of trade, but not to a greater extent than in Cuba, to which we granted autonomy. We claim we are teaching the inhabitants "self-government"; we forget that such teaching should commence at the bottom and that in no respect have we interfered with the municipal governments which remain almost as medieval as in 1898. Our missionaries clamor for retention in order that they may convert the people. The people perhaps are more pious and devoted to religious practices than our own. The American office-holders and merchants in Manila try to make us believe it is for patriotic reasons they want annexation or retention, as did the Americans in Cuba during the intervention, but it is for their own, not the natives' interests, they are struggling.

In 1901 the military commanders were ordered to instruct the people in the provisions of the United States Constitution and the Administration evidently intended that they should become United States citizens. But our Supreme Court wisely decided that Filipinos could not come in under the Constitution. They are, therefore, *subjects* held by force. (Ninety-nine per cent of them desire autonomy.) Did our forefathers dream that our government could be put to such uses?

It was well for the republic that it was prevented from admitting to the full rights of citizens these Malays, as alien to us as are the Chinese, in an over-populated little island on the other side of the world! Can we allow such a country to elect one-fifteenth of our representatives in Congress to make laws for citizens of Illinois or New York? What an outrageous proposition! Is it not strange that it was entertained?

The advocates of retention think to strengthen their argument by abusing the natives as a race. This is hardly consistent. But they go too far—the natives are not as bad as they make them. They are volatile, but not as volatile as the Cubans. Anyone who has lived among them as I have, knows that they are as good laborers as are usually found in tropical countries. They are docile, orderly to the highest degree. They are clean in habits. They are moral. They are pious. With proper leaders they are good soldiers, as witness the Macabebes and others, who fought on our side in 1899. They ruled the entire islands (except Manila) during eighteen months in 1898 and 1899, and there was nothing during that time to show that they could not "self-govern" themselves. The laws were enforced.

We have spent many hundreds of millions of dollars and many American lives in carrying out McKinley's policy in regard to the Philippines. It may be that the interregnum has been good for the people. But it should not last too long; it may end in revolt more or less general. A fine spectacle would this democratic country then present in the eyes of the world! And it would not, this time, be an unarmed mob opposing us.

Another thing: the Philippine Islands are not an *entreport,* or place through which commerce is maintained with other Asiatic countries. It is not a "foothold" in that sense. Nor is it a "foothold" in a military sense, where we would assemble ships or troops in case of war with an Asiatic nation. It is rather a strategic weakness—a place which would easily be captured from us. And its capture would be a severe humiliation.

If we should give the Philippines autonomy, would some other nation gobble it up? Hardly. For whether we exercise a protectorate or not the Philippine people will always be a ward of our nation, in whose future our country will be always interested. The seizure of the Philippines by a foreign nation would be regarded as an act of war.

It is said the Filipino politician is shifty, uncertain, unreliable. Are our politicians above criticism? But the character of some politicians of Manila is not a proper measure of the Filipino character. The people I found in the provinces were docile, honest, almost humble. They were anxious to be taught, anxious to improve. There was practically no drunkenness, no immorality. Their women were extremely modest. Unlike the Cubans, political passions did not create undue excitement, affrays.

The population of the Philippine Islands in 1903 was about seven millions and a half, one-half million being savages and Moros. The remainder were Christians and civilized. The Mohammedan Moros numbered about 300,000. It is not to the credit of the government that these savage Moros were in 1904 made the principal Philippine exhibit at the World's Fair at St. Louis, convincing thousands of people that these were a fair specimen of the Philippine people!

It speaks well for the morality of the Filipinos that of the total population only a few over 15,000 were of a mixed race, or what is called *Mestizos*. How different in this respect are the Spanish-American countries! The female *Mestizas* in the islands are, some of them, very handsome.

One cannot help being struck with the similarity of face, form and figure between the Filipinos and the Japanese. In truth, both have Malay blood, and many Filipinos, especially the tribe of Tagalos, have, like the Japs, also Mongol blood. Many of their characteristics are similar, too. It is true the Philippines are in the tropics, but in time may we not expect from the Filipinos a regenerative era similar to Japan's?

One of the objections to autonomy is due to our sentimental interest in the savage Moros. Their friends do not wish to turn them over to the Filipinos. If that is so important, let us keep them; they inhabit separate islands where they live in wretched misery. The Filipinos may well spare them to us. Personally I don't think these half-million robbers and pirates deserve much consideration. If they rebel against the rule of those of their own race, let them suffer.

To those who say, "We paid twenty millions for the Philippines and we ought not to give them up," I ask, "Do you consider twenty million dollars for seven million people, or three dollars per subject, the islands thrown in, a fair price?"

It is said that ninety-nine per cent of the Filipinos demand independence. Under such conditions is there not a danger that some overt act might bring about an insurrection? Looking at such a contingency from a military point of view, it seems certain that to suppress a new insurrection would be more difficult than it was to put down the last. Then only a few of the natives were armed with rifles, and ammunition was scarce. Their resistance would have been infinitely greater had they been armed. Yet to put down the revolt required the use of 75,000 troops for several years. But it may be assumed that in the case of a new insurrection arms and ammunitions will not be lacking.

But enough. Let us get rid of this stain upon our escutcheon! We have held the islands over a quarter of a century. A new generation has grown up under our tutelage. And even this generation is not friendly to us. Things have arrived at a point where no further benefit will accrue by their retention, either to us or to the Filipinos. We have a promise to fulfill. Let us fulfill it!

Some day our schoolbooks will say proudly that we held the Philippines long enough to "teach them self-government" and that we then, after having spent billions of dollars on them, with unexampled self-denial and benevolence made them free!

XIV

SERVICE AS ADJUTANT GENERAL:

The voyage in the transport *Sheridan* from the Philippine Islands to San Francisco was tedious in the extreme. And it was with rapture that on the final day of our voyage we came in sight of the beaches, the playgrounds and the amusement resorts of San Francisco, which face the ocean. Soon we entered the Golden Gate and steamed past the Presidio, my old home. We were stopped by the quarantine boat. When it came alongside and we could look down on its decks, there stood, waving kisses to me, my wife, come three thousand miles to meet me! What joy! The mast of the quarantine boat coming near as it rocked on the waves, I seized the cordage and slipped down the rope into her arms!

The soldiers audibly approved my acrobatic transfer, but it was against all rules; I must go back and submit to the quarantine examination. So I shinned up the rope again, got on board, and fortunately was not called to account by the strict quarantine officer, who, perhaps, did not see me.

Landed at San Francisco, we marched through the city to our camp at the Presidio. That the regiment did not receive a triumphal greeting from the citizens on their return from their long and arduous service was entirely due to the ill-judged action of the military authorities, who in our country are too apt to forget what an important part sentiment plays in military affairs. The rifles and equipment of the regiment had been left in Manila; accordingly the regiment marched by byways to its camp. This was the case with all the regiments returning from the islands. Thus the soldier who had looked forward to a triumphal march, applauded by the populace for his heroic conduct, for his many sacrifices, found himself robbed of this satisfaction. Thus mothers, daughters, relatives and friends, who would have looked with pride and rejoicing on the serried ranks of those who had risked their lives for their country, found their heroes had been sneaked through a great city like convicts.

I think there is no government of a nation, great or small, except the United States, that is so regardless of the instinctive feeling of a good soldier, that part of his reward is the greeting and applause of his countrymen, publicly acknowledging and thanking him for his services.

The mustering out of troops is a tedious process, but after staying over a month in camp, we were finally, on June 3, 1901, mustered out, and with my wife I departed for my new post of duty, Washington, D. C. I had been promoted to the grade of major of the 4th Cavalry on February 1, 1901, and later was appointed assistant adjutant general at Washington, D. C.

In concluding the description of my services with the 45th U. S. Volunteer Infantry it is right that I should say something about the twenty or more regiments of volunteer infantry raised for service in the Philippines, of which the 45th Infantry was one.

The raising and organization of these regiments was one of the wisest and most successful acts of the Government. They were enlisted for the duration of the war, and each raised in a different section, so that some were made up in Texas, some in the Dakotas, some in the Pacific Coast states, some in the East, etc. The colonels and field officers were as a rule regular officers, selected for efficiency; the company officers generally had commended themselves by good work in state volunteer regiments during the Spanish War, or had belonged to the National Guard. There was a considerable contingent of old soldiers of the Regular Army in the ranks. Before being sent to the Philippines the regiments were given a course of four months' intensive training, including target practice.

On their first arrival in the Philippine Islands these volunteers were somewhat raw, but that even then they could do good fighting was shown by my experience with the 33rd Volunteers at Vigan, a regiment which had arrived only a month or so before. These regiments, in my opinion, were in 1900 more efficient than the regular regiments. This was partly due to the fact that they were homogeneous, the officers and men having been through the same course of training under competent instructors, while in the regular regiments a large number of old soldiers had taken their discharges at the end of the Spanish War, the vacancies being filled with untrained raw recruits, little training being possible after they landed in the Philippine Islands. The regular regiments also contained a large number of new officers, also uninstructed. Thus when two regiments of infantry were called for, to take part in the Boxer campaign in China, it would have been better, in my opinion, to have sent two volunteer regiments. The two regular regiments that were there did fairly well, but they were not a fair sample of our Regular Army, having many undisciplined recruits and inexperienced officers. Two good volunteer regiments would have done better work because they were better disciplined. And moreover they would have demonstrated to the foreign troops in China how valuable is our principal dependence in a great war; namely, the American volunteers.

In July, 1901, after a short leave, spent at Perth Amboy, New Jersey, where my family was temporarily living in my father's summer cottage, I joined my post of duty at Washington, D. C., renting as quarters a small house at 2212 Q Street.

The President at that time was McKinley, Elihu Root being Secretary of War. The General Staff had not then come into being, their functions being performed by the adjutant general's department. At the head of the army, instead of a chief of staff directly responsible to the Secretary of War and holding office at his pleasure, was the "Commanding General of the Army," at that time Lieutenant General Miles. While the present chief of staff, if he differs from the Secretary of War on a question of policy, is expected to resign, or can be displaced, the general of the army could, and often did, oppose, on questions of policy, not only the Secretary of War, but the President himself. Secure in his position, he was not afraid to appeal to Congress and to the country, whenever he believed the interests of the service were in danger, and in some instances such appeals were effective. Such opposition, however, was naturally extremely irritating to the Executive, and instances where it created bad blood occurred when General Sherman was at the head of the army—on one occasion he left Washington and removed his headquarters to St. Louis. And during the Roosevelt administration General Miles and the President were often at swords' points.

Nevertheless, this system had its good side. We have in the army been singularly fortunate, in recent years, in our Secretaries of War. But numerous instances both in the navy and army show that a secretary unfitted for his office can impair materially the efficiency or the morale of the service. It sometimes happens that a Secretary of War, when appointed, is entirely ignorant and careless of the history or the traditions of the army of which, under the President, he is the head. Under the tutelage of self-seeking staff officers, or under the influence of hasty, half-baked ideas, he may take up a policy of lasting injury to the military arm or its efficiency in peace or war. In the old days the courageous opposition of the general of the army, always a soldier of experience, imbued with the military mentality only gained by long service, was often of infinite value.

In the person of the Secretary of War, during my term as adjutant general, we were extremely fortunate. It is probable that Elihu Root is the greatest man and patriot of the present time. The impression he produced on me, was that of an *intense* nature. I was fortunate in coming often in contact with him while I was in charge of the militia division of the War Department, and I shall never forget the impression conveyed of force, intensity, wisdom, his attitude in considering and deciding a subject. As he held a written paper before him, and read it, he seemed to be *consuming,* devouring, almost masticating the words and ideas it contained. At the end of the perusal, no matter how abstruse the subject, it was rare that he was not ready with a clear-cut, pertinent decision.

In 1901 in consequence of the then recent enlargement of the army the amount of work which required the decision of the Secretary of War was unusually great; nevertheless, as he remarked himself, four-fifths of his time was taken up with non-military subjects. For in the War Department are decided not only matters pertaining to the army but also affairs of the rivers and harbors division, in addition to those of the insular division, a bureau that regulates matters pertaining to our outlying possessions. To decide the multifarious questions which thus arise requires the services of a skilled lawyer and a most competent administrator.

The adjutant general, Major General H. C. Corbin, under whom I served, tall and powerful of physique, was a man of force and great intelligence. Somewhat drastic in his methods, he had many enemies and critics, but on the whole he acted and decided with wisdom. Having upon his hands all the multifarious functions now confided to the general staff as well as those now exercised in the adjutant general's department, he had not an easy task. In addition, his time during the day was largely occupied by conferences with senators, representatives, and other officers of the government. So that his hours of work were not limited to the usual office hours; often he would be found in the War Department toiling until near midnight. He was a most satisfactory man to serve under. He had confidence in his subordinates, gave them, freely, discretionary powers. Words of praise or commendation were from him infrequent, but although unexpressed we knew when we had his approval.

He was a "driver," and got through a mass of business that was extraordinary. Things that would ordinarily be referred to a tedious board, or now would take months in being considered by the General Staff, with him were accomplished in a few days or hours. For instance, one day I invited his attention to the fact that the edition of the Cavalry Drill Regulations had been exhausted and that before a new edition was printed it would be necessary to make a revision embodying later decisions and developments. I urged that a board of officers be convened to make a revision. "Hell!" said Corbin, "I won't have a board; revise them yourself!" It was a pretty considerable work, but I accomplished in less than a month what a board of officers would have probably taken a year in doing. And thus the Cavalry Regulations, 1902, bears the following announcement: "This revision of the Cavalry Drill Regulations . . . . made by a board of officers . . . . is approved and will be complied with. (Signed)

Elihu Root, Sec. War."

The board of officers was myself!

On another occasion shortly after ten A. M. I was called into General Corbin's office to find him in consultation with several prominent officers of the National Guard. "Parker," said Corbin, after introducing me, "these gentlemen want the War Department to publish a course of target practice for the National Guard. Have it ready and bring it in here by noon!"

It so happened I had been acting as president

of the board of officers which drew up the firing regulations of 1902 and so was familiar with the subject of rifle practice. I was also in charge of the division of the militia and fairly well acquainted with their needs. I set to work and at one o'clock, an hour late, was able to produce a scheme which was adopted for the militia substantially without revision.

Nowadays the General Staff would play over such a task for months!

My comrades, Assistant Adjutants General under Corbin, were W. H. Carter, H. P. McCain, George Andrews, W. P. Hall, William Ennis and John Johnston.

The first four of these afterwards attained the head of the department with the rank of major general and adjutant general, U. S. Army. The others attained the rank of brigadier general in the line. They were all fine fellows and earnest workers, bound together by a common interest and zeal.

The range of subjects covered by my duties as assistant to the adjutant general were very extended and included almost everything dealt with in that department except the business of the personnel branch. As I have never been backward in presenting my views I did not hesitate to submit memorandums on matters which, in my opinion, could be improved. Thus I brought about, among other things, action enlarging the scope of discharge of enlisted men by purchase, making it possible for young soldiers who had imperative reasons for rejoining their families to buy their way out of the service. Prior to the passage of that regulation, such discharges could be obtained only "by favor," that is, through the influence of Congressmen or persons of prominence, in which case the Government was not reimbursed. In many cases the soldier, not having friends at court, and having cogent reasons for separation from the service, deserted. Thus this new regulation lessened desertion.

Desertion had always been rife in the army. In the earlier days on the frontier, when the soldier's life was one of hardship, and he compared his pittance of thirteen dollars a month with the high wages gained by miners and other citizens, he often ended his contract with the Government by absconding. Fortunately, conditions changed. In 1910 when I commanded the 11th Cavalry I remarked that compared with conditions thirty years before, military rule was like a Sunday school!

I find from my record of letters sent that I apparently initiated action in the matter of bestowing medals of honor for gallantry in action on dead officers, making as a test case that of my friend, John A. Logan, Jr., killed at San Jacinto, P. I., November 12, 1899. Among other things I suggested that the soldier's financial account with the Government be always kept up to date, as is done at present; that an officer's foreign service registry be kept, also that a reduction of the number of white soldiers sent to the Philippines be made, their places to be taken by native Philippine soldiers.

At that time the offices of the State Department, the War Department and the Navy Department were all in the same building at the corner of G and 17th Streets. It is a curious fact that though the navy and army had offices practically side by side and while they had, in many instances, the same problems (as for instance that of discharge by purchase or favor) we knew nothing of their methods nor apparently they of ours. I doubt if a copy of the Navy Regulations could have been found in any of our offices. Since the World War, however, an effort has been made to bring about some "co-ordination."

In the spring of 1903 I was placed in charge of the Division of Militia Affairs. Up to that time the militia, which by the Constitution included the entire male population of the country, had never been organized or properly provided for. Without the necessary provision of Congress for its upkeep, the militia system proper had languished and had finally become absolutely a dead letter.

In the meantime there had grown up in the states themselves bodies of state troops, used principally for the purpose of maintaining order within the states and these troops, although called the "National Guard," constituted in each state what was practically a state army, maintained in disregard of the provision of the Constitution that "no state shall maintain troops in time of peace." These state troops, however, in a time of civil disorder or war could be mustered as "militia" into the service of the United States and for this reason the United States, through Congress, had passed laws providing for their partial equipment and maintenance.

This was the condition of affairs when in the winter of 1902-03 Congress passed the "Dick Bill." This did reorganize the National Guard as the "*Organized* Militia"; it made one uniform force where we had had so many independent armies. It provided a large sum for its annual upkeep and another larger sum for uniform arms and equipment. It provided for annual service in the field, at the cost of the United States.

Previous to the passage of the Dick Bill, the sum allotted by Congress for the militia was apportioned among the different states according to their representation in Congress, without any reference to whether they had a large or small National Guard. Thus some states, with organizations which existed solely on paper, drew their full allotment. Under the Dick Bill, while the total allotment was increased, it was apportioned to the state according to the number of organized militia therein found by the U. S. Inspectors, to be efficiently trained and equipped.

A minimum of drills required for each soldier by the new law was twenty-four per year. This requirement seems very low, but nevertheless it brought about a revolution in many organizations, in which the social feature had become more important to the members than military efficiency. As a result of these requirements, shortly after the Dick Bill went into effect, some organizations ceased to exist! This was the case particularly in the Southern states where there were many companies of cavalry and infantry more distinguished for their handsome uniforms and for their social status than for their discipline or efficiency.

The inauguration of the new regulations resulted in many curious developments. Thus, one of the inspectors I sent out, my friend Colonel C. G. Starr, reported that a troop of cavalry in the new state, Oklahoma, had for their sole evidence of military uniform the yellow cavalry hat cords! Other parts of the uniform were lacking. The Governor of Virginia, to whom I wrote, repeatedly asking when it would be convenient for him to have his troops inspected by the War Department, refused to make any reply, considering it perhaps beneath the dignity of the chief magistrate of a sovereign state to correspond with an underling of the War Department. It became necessary finally to send to Richmond our Assistant Secretary of War, Colonel Sanger, a very handsome and suave gentleman, who, on paying his respects in due form to the governor, was received with true Southern politeness and completed his mission successfully. The militia of the state of New York, the largest and most efficient body of National Guardsmen in the United States, under the command of General Chas. Roe, formerly an army officer, refused for a long time to equip themselves with the U. S. magazine rifle cal. 30, holding that the Remington rifle cal. 45, an old-style weapon, was better for their use. These are only a few of the obstacles which came up in the application of the Dick Bill.

There was some basis for the contention, made at that time, that the long-range, flat-trajecting weapon was not altogether satisfactory for militia. The putting down of riots had been the most important duty of the National Guard, and the service rifle with its 3-mile range and the new breech-loading cannon with its 5-mile range were not exactly the things to use against mobs in crowded cities, since wild shots were liable to kill innocent persons miles away.

After all the state militia had been equipped, there still remained, of the two-million-dollar equipment fund that Cogress had so generously provided, a sum of three-quarters of a million dollars. Being called upon by Secretary Root to advise what should be done with this money, I recommended that it be used to equip the militia with rifle ranges, of which they were greatly in need. In this I was opposed by my friend and classmate, General William Crozier, chief of ordnance, who desired that the money be used for light batteries wherewith to equip the militia. I pointed out that the suppression of riots was one of the most important duties of militia; that long-range cannon were not fitted for that duty; that the equipment of a light battery cost some $50,000 or as much as the equipment of a regiment of infantry; depleting greatly the allotment of the state, and for these reasons few states would ask for light batteries. My arguments, however, did not convince Secretary Root and the entire sum was allotted to the Ordnance Department for the construction of "light batteries for the militia."

The year after, I was surprised to find that Crozier had asked for a million dollars, "for the construction of light batteries for the militia." Congress was inclined to be much more liberal in its appropriations for the militia, the citizen soldiers, than for the regular army, and the appropriation went through. I saw then what Crozier was up to. He did not expect to issue the batteries to the militia. He was very patriotically establishing a *reserve* of field batteries for use by the militia in the emergency of war. The next year, and during the succeeding years, large appropriations were made by Congress for batteries for the "use of the militia" though few of these batteries were issued to them. It thus came about that in 1917 when we entered the World War, and prominent officers like General Wood, former chief of staff, were deploring our lack of field artillery equipment, it was found that we really had altogether some 850 guns.

In those days my brother, R. Wayne Parker, was a member of the House of Representatives, and a prominent member of the military committee. Wayne had been for a number of years lieutenant and captain of the Essex Troop, a militia cavalry organization of Newark, New Jersey, and was imbued with a true military spirit. Agreeing with me, Wayne was a great believer in the importance of the rifle, of rifle instruction, and of accumulating a reserve of rifles for war. Accordingly each year when the estimates from the Ordnance Department came in for the action of Congress, Wayne saw that a liberal appropriation for the manufacture of rifles was included. In case no appropriation was asked for, Wayne inserted one in the bill; in case the amount asked for seemed insufficient, Wayne insisted that it be increased. That was one thing which he made his hobby and particular care. And I believe it was largely due to his efforts that in 1917 we had nearly 900,000 rifles, enough fully to arm our first contingents in the World War.

The duties of the officer in charge of militia affairs were at that time fully as important as they became a few years later, when Congress gave the head of the division the rank of brigadier general and major general. I was several times urged to allow my friends in the militia to push me for promotion to that grade. But I refused for what appeared to me good and sufficient reasons. For one thing I feared I might be separated permanently from the line and from command of troops.

Of late years, especially since the war, a considerable improvement in the militia has been brought about. While its strength has not been increased as much as one might expect, it has gained the confidence of the people through the good record made by militia officers and men in the World War. As a result Congress has very largely increased appropriations and officers and men are now paid a small amount for attendance at drills, making it possible to exact more drills and better training. During the time I was in charge of the militia bureau the appropriations by Congress amounted to less than ten dollars per annum per man; now they have been increased to fifty dollars. This is not too much to pay, when we consider that the regular army costs the United States annually $1,000 per man. Not that I regard the militia as comparable in value to the regular army; its faults and drawbacks are too obvious. It is fairly efficient in a short tour of riot duty. But we have found that in an emergency of war its ranks have to be so filled with new men that it becomes at once a recruit organization, requiring almost as long a period of pre-war training as an entirely new unit.

Nevertheless, it is a nucleus of patriotic citizens animated by the soldierly spirit, who make considerable sacrifices of time and money in its behalf. It is a school for officers and soldiers who, graduating from its ranks, add to the defensive power of the country. And among those who witness its undoubtedly fine parades and close order drills it serves to keep the military spirit alive.

In 1903 a movement was started in favor of combined maneuvers of regulars and militia and Congress appropriated $100,000 for a preliminary survey of sites suitable for maneuver grounds and camp sites. I was placed in charge of certain features of this work, among other things completing a book of nearly a thousand pages containing descriptions and maps of all available "camp sites." Various officers and boards of officers were dispatched to certain points to examine and report upon the different places recommended to the War Department. What we wanted were tracts of twelve to twenty thousand acres, suitable for camps and maneuvers, near centers of population, with good water supply, drainage, with sites for rifle ranges and artillery ranges, and easy of access by rail or water transportation.

Such tracts were not difficult to find, and while they were invariably covered with farms and dotted with farmhouses, the farmers, curiously enough, were as a rule ready to sell out, *for a consideration.* This was generally arranged by an agent who got the refusal of the land from the farmers for a certain price, and then offered the tract *en bloc* to the Government. Prices widely differed. A tract of desert land near Albuquerque, New Mexico, was offered for almost nothing, while sites in Pennsylvania were priced at two hundred dollars or more per acre.

In carrying out the plans adopted for combined maneuvers of the army and National Guard we had several maneuvers in the summer of 1903. In two of these, namely, at West Point, Kentucky, and Fort Riley, Kansas, I took part as an umpire, our chief umpire being Colonel Wagner, a writer of various books on the art of war and at that time the chief exponent of the service schools. We made decisions which in battle would be made by the enemy's bullets. As a result, in the mimic war, there were commanders who seemed to fear the decisions of umpires, just as in real battle there are commanders who magnify the importance of bullets. And this resulted in similar hesitation and lack of decision. On the whole I am not sure that these early maneuvers, beyond the advantage of bringing the National Guard and the regular army together, accomplished much good. The picture of battle which they presented was incomplete and misleading. It was claimed during the Boer War that many of the disasters suffered by the English troops during the early battles of that war, were largely due to false lessons inculcated at Aldershot.

It was during my tour as adjutant general at Washington that President McKinley was assassinated. On the occasion of the arrival of his body at the capital, I had charge of the troops and police placed to maintain order at the railroad station. It was after dark that the coffin, accompanied by Mr. Roosevelt, arrived—photographers had been rigidly excluded—but just as the troops presented arms there was a terrific explosion. At first many thought someone had thrown a bomb, but presently we discovered it was only a photographer in a house across the street who, to make sure that his picture would be a success, had used with his apparatus an overcharge of magnesium.

Roosevelt I had known for a number of years, and of late date had exchanged several letters with him on the subject of an article I had written in the *Military Service Magazine* about the conditions of the fighting in the Philippines. Roosevelt had dissented from an opinion ex-

Officers of 12th N. Y. Volunteers at Matanzas, Cuba, 1899

Col. R. W. Leonard, Commanding

pressed by me that under certain circumstances it was well to regulate the expenditure of ammunition in battle by using volley fire instead of allowing uncontrolled fire. The last time I ever saw him was in 1916 while journeying westwards on the Pennsylvania Railroad. We were near Indianapolis when the porter told me Roosevelt was on the train; as I passed his stateroom he recognized me and gave me an enthusiastic greeting, inviting me to take breakfast with him. Presently the dining-room conductor appeared; I was surprised to see Roosevelt jump up and give the conductor a greeting even more enthusiastic than the one he bestowed on me, shaking his hand with great fervor! Later in the day I went to Mr. Roosevelt's stateroom to pay my respects. We got talking about the Mexican question, and Mr. Roosevelt startled me by saying that if we had war he would like to serve "under my command"!

It was during my tour of duty as adjutant general that Pershing came home from the Philippines after a campaign among the Moros which had been widely advertised in the newspapers. While the fighting during my time in the Philippine Islands was vastly more important than that which occurred there later, the American public in 1899 and 1900 had their eyes fixed upon England's tragic struggle in South Africa; in consequence the newspaper reporters in the Islands were ordered to cut short their accounts of the engagements of our army. Thus the most serious fighting got only a few lines in the American papers. It was different with Pershing. He conducted a short, comparatively bloodless, but skillful and successful campaign, every move of which was chronicled at length in despatches by the Associated Press. The picturesque halo which surrounded the Moros, a savage Mahometan tribe, added to the interest this campaign excited in America.

Thus when in 1903 Pershing returned to the United States he was a noted man. As he was a particular friend of President Roosevelt it was evident it would not be long before he became a general officer. However, I did not object to adding my name to the long list of officers who had recommended him for promotion, even though in so doing I asked that he be promoted over my head—an action for which Pershing did not fail to thank me.

Speaking of Roosevelt's attitude toward the army, it became very evident before he had been long President, that he took great pride in and proposed to make full use of his prerogatives under the Constitution as "Commander in Chief of the Army and Navy." He had had a taste of military command with the "Rough Riders" and he proposed to be commander in fact as well as theory. During his short experience with the army in Cuba he had formed the opinions usually shared by volunteers concerning the regulars, that they were ruled by red tape; that there was a large proportion of dead wood among the officers, et cetera.

At the same time he had, during the Santiago campaign, met a few young officers who seemed to him to be an exception to this rule; to him they were the few exceptions, apparently, almost the only ones. Thus an officer who had known Roosevelt in Cuba was pretty sure of advancement. When a brigadier generalcy became vacant it was these young officers he wanted to advance to the coveted position; the fact that there were many colonels who by a long life of meritorious service had earned it, did not appeal to him.

Roosevelt, while he was yet a young man, was the great exponent of the theory that in war youth counts far more than experience. It is a creed held by many in our service. But it is a false creed. His sixty-six years did not make Foch cautious. Many of the greatest commanders of history were old men. With experience, a general can be enterprising, take chances; without experience, he may be afraid to attempt uncommon methods. In war the rashness of ignorance has no value. And to imagine that in a few short years an officer may fully learn to command is folly; in my forty-two years of service there was scarcely a day I did not learn some new thing, and it seemed to me that it was towards the end of my career that my eyes were opened most. The art of war is an intricate study. I believe that an officer who fully applies himself to his position has fewer hours of idleness than the average professional man in civil life.

Among other duties that fell to me was the revision of the firing regulations for rifle and pistol. Due to the confusion that ensued after the Spanish-American War, caused by the reorganization of the army and the constant employment of our troops on field duty where facilities for target practice were not to be found, the marksmanship of the army had fallen off. This was also partly due to the fact that a revision of firing regulations issued just before the war with Spain abolished the feature of competition which had been formerly enforced by a "figure of merit." That is, companies formerly had competed for the figure of merit, that company receiving the highest figure of merit which had the greatest number of sharpshooters and marksmen.

As president of the board charged with the revision of the firing regulations, my colleagues were Majors Sibley and Guilfoyle, of the cavalry, and Captain Hale, of the infantry, who acted as recorder.

In the course of our labors on the new book of target practice we restored the figure of merit; we adopted the round bull's-eye instead of the elliptical; we increased the importance of the aiming and position drill and of estimation of distance, and we made a new class of riflemen, namely, "experts."

I had always been of the opinion that the slow drawing of the bead on the bull's-eye of the target shooter was not as useful to the soldier in battle as the deer hunter's ability to shoot quickly. I therefore proposed to the board that we make "rapid fire" a part of the course, the contestant to fire five shots in thirty seconds. It was a new idea to all of us and Guilfoyle and I proceeded to try it out on a rifle range near Washington. It was found successful, was adopted and has remained to this day a valuable part of the course of target practice.

We also incorporated in our Manual of target practice, special Course "B," which I invented, as a means of hasty rifle training of volunteers in time of war when target ranges are not to be had. It is a course of one hundred and seventy shots at miniature targets at fifty feet distance. Assuming that it is just as difficult for the marksman to hit a one-inch bull's-eye at ten yards as an eight-inch bull's-eye at eighty yards, these miniature targets at a distance of fifty feet subtended the same visual angle as the real targets at two hundred yards. As a matter of fact, the problem of hitting is exactly the same. The fact that the shot holes can be seen by the marksman—and therefore the delays of "marking" which cause so much loss of time on the rifle range are absent—expedite the shooting. This fact makes it possible, by erecting a row of, say, fifty targets, to have each man of a regiment of 1,000 men fire twenty or more shots per day. In this course I provided for firing, standing, lying and kneeling, at simulated ranges of two hundred and three hundred yards.

To furnish proof of the value of this scheme, we had a body of recruits at Plattsburg divided in two. One-half the recruits were instructed on the regular rifle range, the other half at simulated targets and distances. It was found that the proficiency of each, when tested competitively, was practically equal.

On the conclusion of our work on the firing regulations I took the manuscript to Elihu Root, the Secretary of War, for his approval. I was pleased to have him remark as he signed his name, "I am glad to have had under me an officer who does his duty with such energy and force!"

In connection with the book of firing regulations and in order to supplement it I afterwards prepared for Hudson and Kimberly, publishers, a small *Soldiers' Handbook of Target Practice,* which was sold at the low price of twenty-five cents. This handbook was not published under my name, nor did I share in any profits that may have accrued to the publishers.

The question of including in the Army a "General Staff," which, under the chief of staff, would be directly responsible to the Secretary of War, had been agitated for some time and in the winter of 1902-3 Congress passed a law to that effect. A board of general officers was convened to make the selections and there was much speculation as to what officers would be honored by appointments. My friend and classmate, General Crozier, chief of ordnance, a member of the board that made the selection, unsolicited was so kind as to assure me I would be one of the fortunate ones.

At last the names of the general staff officers were published and I was disappointed, though not surprised, to find my name left out. As constituted, a large proportion of the general staff were captains, leaving but few places for older officers. Then service in war or fighting characteristics did not seem to count in the selection; some officers who had notoriously "fallen down" in the Philippine campaign were included. Then, as General Crozier naively remarked, "Every man selected had the unanimous vote of the board." That is, while a number of officers were chosen who, while highly extolled by some of the board members, were unknown to others (there was a surprisingly large proportion of officers who had served as the personal aides of the general officer members of the board), no officer could be selected that any member of the board objected to. It was like the black ball of a club.

It so happened that I had incurred the personal hostility of General Wallace Randolph, acting as chief of artillery, by a memorandum which I had written. I had suggested that in the reconstitution of the field artillery the artillery have their share of colored soldiers, then confined to the infantry and cavalry. While this was a perfectly fair proposition, Randolph, as chief of the artillery, violently resented it.

It was a mistake to have included in the general staff such a large proportion of young officers. In foreign armies the general staff is more largely composed of men of experience. It is to these that decisions on matters of policy are left; the younger officers serve in the general staff as in a sort of school. We made no such distinction.

In the War Department the advent of the general staff brought about a certain amount of friction. Not content with their other duties they reached out for the functions of administration; thus the militia bureau was at first turned over to them. They also wished to regulate the functions of the supply departments, to the great indignation of the quartermaster general, the commissary general, and others, who violently resisted their "encroachments." To the outsider was evident a marked change in the bearing and disposition of certain officers appointed to the general staff. Men who were once carefree, almost happy-go-lucky in their ways—boon companions, friendly and free with all the world—after a short period in the general staff became solemn in countenance, judicial in language and exclusive in their choice of companions. Some were pitiably weighed down by the responsibilities that devolved upon them, and I have known one or two who seemed actually to lose their minds under the strain!

With the coming of the general staff we lost our adjutant general, Corbin, who was succeeded by General Ainsworth, former chief of the Record and Pension Office. By the Army Appropriation Bill the adjutant general became "the military secretary"; thus my title became "Major and Military Secretary." This change, however, did not last more than a year, when we went back to the old designations.

In April, 1903, I received my promotion as lieutenant colonel, being still retained in the A.G.O. In this connection it is amusing to see how often I became, in the course of my career, a lieutenant colonel. I had already been lieutenant colonel 12th Infantry, lieutenant colonel 42nd U.S. Infantry, lieutenant colonel 45th U.S. Infantry. I now became lieutenant colonel "military secretary." Later I was lieutenant colonel adjutant general. And later lieutenant colonel 13th Cavalry.

To us line officers it was a bitter pill to find in 1904 the two highest offices in the army filled by the medical profession—Doctor Wood, major general and chief of staff; Doctor Ainsworth, major general and military secretary! Both, however, were men of the highest efficiency.

My three years' stay at Washington will always be a pleasant memory. My family was growing up; my two daughters had just made their debut in society and, with hosts of young friends, took a joyous part in the social pleasure of the capital; my two eldest sons were at good schools, and in 1902 Cortland entered West Point. James also was anxious to join the army, but a rule was then in force that no two brothers could be at West Point at the same time, so with a great deal of reluctance he competed, in 1903, for a midshipman's warrant. Even after he won in the competitive examination he expressed such a strong preference for the army that I was obliged to promise him that if, after spending six months at the Naval Academy he did not change his mind, I would allow him to resign, with a view to entering the army later as a civilian appointee. But in six months he had become so imbued with the spirit of the navy that he scorned the idea of entering the rival service. We were amused to see the meeting of the two boys at the

Army-Navy football game of 1903. The score was 40 to 5 in favor of the army. They did not meet until after the game, when we got them together under one of the goalposts. They shook hands, Jim looking rather fierce. Presently I heard the following remarks on the game. Jim: "You fellows are nothing but a lot of muckers anyhow." Cort: "Forty to five, Jim, forty to five!" Even brothers cannot forego the traditional jealous rivalry of the two institutions!

Jim, though a year behind Cort, became his senior, reaching the rank of commander of the navy several years before Cort was promoted to the corresponding grade of lieutenant colonel in the army. Promotion is much faster in the navy than in the army.

I have already told of the patriotism always shown by my wife. During our stay in Washington, 1901-1904, she spent much time in labors as the chairman of the relief committee of the Army Relief Society, of which she can be said to be the founder. It happened this way. In the winter of 1898-99, during the Spanish-American War, a fair for the relief of destitute Cubans was established in New York City, under the care of General Leonard Wood and General Francis N. Greene. Mrs. Parker wrote to Generals Wood and Greene, asking that one day's receipts per week be devoted to the relief of widows and orphans of soldiers and officers of the regular army who had died in the Spanish-American War. This diversion of the receipts of the fair, Generals Wood and Greene did not see their way to accomplish. Mrs. Parker then consulted her friends, among them Reverend Joseph R. Duryee, D.D., and Mrs. Duryee, Colonel and Mrs. Burbank, Colonel and Mrs. Reber, Mrs. Lamont, the wife of the Secretary of War, and others and, with their approval, wrote out a circular "for our own," asking that all who were interested should join a society to be called the "Army Relief Society." Sections were to be formed, each section to contribute at least twenty-five dollars a year. This circular was mailed to the ladies of the different army posts and to coteries of friends in civil life. It met with instant response. The distribution and handling of the money thus raised, it was understood, should be entirely confidential, the names of the recipients to be kept secret. In some cases the money was to be given, in others loaned, and in others used to educate children. Money thus collected was to be deposited with the Wall Street firm of Morgan, Bliss & Lamont, who promised to audit the accounts. Mrs. Parker became first chairman of the relief committee, and as such for several years conducted the secret correspondence with the recipients of the bounty. When she entered upon her duties the first deposit of funds was only fifteen dollars; but more money came quickly. Under her leadership many cases of hardship needing relief were discovered, the policy of the society was developed, and a successful start was made. Now the organization has a considerable income, a fairly large reserve fund and can pride itself on having accomplished an important and highly useful and beneficent work.

In January, 1904, I was ordered to St. Louis, Missouri, to organize and act as adjutant general of a new territorial division of the army, to be called the "Northern Division." In a letter from Secretary Root in regard to this transfer he says, under date of December 24, 1903:

"My dear Colonel Parker: I am much gratified that the chief of staff should have selected you for the important position of adjutant general of the Northern Division, which is in several respects the most important of the four great military divisions of the United States and which will require in its adjutant general the ability and force of character you possess. That you do possess these qualities in a high degree your service in the militia division of the adjutant general's office in Washington has shown. Your work in that position has been faithful, devoted and effective. Far more has been accomplished during this past year than I supposed would be possible. Now that the position has become less important and responsible, because of the reorganization of the general staff, it is fitting that you are transferred to a broader field.

"With best wishes, I am

"Very sincerely yours,

"ELIHU ROOT,
"Secretary of War"

The World's Fair at St. Louis was then going on, and here we spent an amusing year. I joined the St. Louis Club, where many receptions and balls were held, as well as other clubs. In the Exposition, at the various state buildings and foreign buildings, there were almost daily receptions, attended by the youth and fashion of the city.

A feature of the fair was a number of military parades in which the National Guard and the regular army joined. I particularly remember the parade of November 26, 1904, "President's Day," at which President Roosevelt was the guest of honor. It was advertised by the officials of the fair as "the greatest military parade of the age" and attracted a large number of spectators from the city and surrounding country. General Bates acted as grand marshal and I was his principal aide. In the procession the foot troops first marched past the reviewing stand, which was within the exposition grounds, followed by a large body of cavalry.

The rear troops of the cavalry force were late in

getting the order to start—they lost distance. To make it up and to overtake the colonel they were obliged to take a very fast gallop, almost a charging pace, in which order they arrived opposite the reviewing stand. These rear troops happened to be negro recruits; they passed in the most inextricable confusion, many of the horses running away or entirely out of control; some had lost their helmets, others half out of the saddle, even clinging to their horses' necks. To an outsider it was a comical sight; to me it was a shameful scene of disorder. But President Roosevelt was delighted! He evidently mistook it for a cavalry charge and, waving his hat, he shrieked, "That's the way I like to see the cavalry move; that's the way I like them!"

In the spring of 1905, my four-year detail as adjutant general having arrived at its termination, I was ordered to Fort Riley, Kansas, as director of the cavalry school.

Fort Riley at that time constituted the mounted service school, including a cavalry school and a field artillery school, the whole under the command of Colonel E. S. Godfrey. The artillery school comprised six batteries of field artillery under Lieutenant Colonel M. M. Macomb as director. The cavalry school comprised a squadron each from the 2nd, 9th (colored) and 13th regiments of cavalry. Thus, as director of the cavalry school, I had command of a full regiment of cavalry. Fort Riley had been entirely rebuilt since I served there in 1881, twenty-four years before, only a few of the old buildings being left. The cavalry and artillery occupied different subposts. A large riding-hall gave opportunity for winter training.

The most important feature of the mounted service school, in my opinion, was the school of equitation for officers, under the expert direction of Captain Walter C. Short, 13th Cavalry. Short was a marvel in his knowledge of the horse and his ability to train him and reduce him to thorough obedience to the pressure of the bit and of the leg. As I realized before my stay at Fort Riley, the great defect in our cavalry was the fact that our horses were not properly trained or under control and our officers and enlisted men were without the knowledge of how to train them.

I saw at once the great value of Captain Short's methods and instituted a similar course for the troops of cavalry at Fort Riley, as well as in the regiment and brigade I afterwards commanded.

The work that Captain Short inaugurated in the training of the horse was in the end a great factor in the improvement of the cavalry arm of the service.

While at Fort Riley I conducted a number of experiments. One of these was designed to discover the best and safest manner of advancing over open ground against an enemy in position. We simulated the hostile skirmishers with targets and found in each of these instances the direct run forward of thirty yards required by regulations was safer in the end, due to the fact that in the short runs and oblique runs the soldier would be longer in making the total advance toward the enemy and thus would be longer under fire.

In an experiment to determine the relative efficiency of the rifle and pistol the trooper, mounted and in motion, firing at targets, it was found the rifle was more effective and made more hits than the pistol.

By another experiment I demonstrated that at very close quarters the saber is more efficient than the pistol. In the test the troopers rode down a track with target silhouette on the right and left, close to the track. In every case more hits would be made by the saber than by the pistol.

In the late summer and early autumn of 1906 news

came of a revolt in Cuba, accompanied by great disorder. By the Platt Amendment the duty of the United States was to restore order. Accordingly marines were landed, and in October troops of the Regular Army were ordered there.

My stay at Fort Riley had been highly instructive and socially very pleasant. My command was devoted to me and I was particularly pleased with my officers. But there were some aspects of the place I was not sorry to leave, and as there was a prospect of active service against an enemy in Cuba I made application to be employed there. As a result, early in October, 1906, I received orders to proceed to Havana, Cuba, there to report to the commanding general of the U.S. forces, Brigadier General Funston. I was to be provost marshal of Havana.

At the same time my old friend and classmate, Major Herbert J. Slocum, received orders for Cuba, so we journeyed together, going by rail to Miami, Florida, thence by boat to Havana.

It was a beautiful day when we arrived in the picturesque harbor of Havana. The revolution, thanks to the presence of marines, and to the peace efforts of Roosevelt, Taft and Funston, had subsided. General Funston, as a Cuban officer in the revolution which preceded our intervention of 1898, was well known to the Cubans and was very useful in settling the trouble. But a decision he had made, leaving "captured" horses in the possession of the insurgents, displeased our Government. So when, on the afternoon of my arrival, I reported to General Funston, he told me, with a laugh, that he had been relieved and had been ordered back to the United States; further, conditions did not require the services of a provost marshal.

There was nothing for me to do but to wait for new orders. General Bell had taken command and in a few days settled the question by appointing me president of a general court-martial which was to try all the military cases which arose on the island of Cuba.

On April 18, 1907, the President appointed Earl D. Thomas, then colonel of the 11th Cavalry, a brigadier general, and I being at the top of the list succeeded to his vacancy.

Immediately General Barry, who commanded the troops in Cuba, ordered me to proceed to Pinar del Rio and take command of the regiment.

Pinar del Rio, a town of 30,000 population, was the center of the tobacco district—the "*Vuelta Abajo*" district, so called because, looking at Cuba on the map, there is a "turn downwards," or *vuelta abajo,* of the configuration of the island at this point. The soil of the *Vuelta Abajo* produces the most fragrant tobacco in the world. Pinar del Rio, 125 miles west of Havana, on the Western Cuba Railroad, lies near the south coast of the island in a rolling, fertile country.

The garrison at Pinar del Rio consisted of troops I, K, L, and M; the machine-gun platoon; and the band of the 11th Cavalry. We also possessed a considerable pack train and wagon train. The officers were Captains Rowell, Jones, Lieutenants McKinley, White, Amos, Gardner, Kimball, Grunert, Tompkins, Laursen, Cocke, Shelley, Robinson, Rogers and Miles. Our surgeon was Dr. Shook and our veterinary Dr. McDonald. The soldiers were quartered in an old Spanish barracks, "the Cuartel," a veritable fortress, on a height overlooking the town. In the Cuartel we also had the headquarter offices, the storehouses for supplies and the officers' club. The officers were quartered in buildings near the Cuartel, hired by our Government.

Mrs. Parker and I, with our son, George, lived in a small, rather ornate house, built in Cuban style, the building having but one story, a spacious veranda in front, and a *patio* in rear, containing the cook house, offices, etc. Inside the house the floors were tiled. Our *ménage* was presided over by our colored servant, Gaines, who, as a soldier, had served under me at Fort Riley and who now performed the various duties of cook, housemaid and laundryman. He cooked by the Cuban method; that is, with charcoal, the stove being a mass of masonry containing pot holes, in each of which a separate charcoal fire was built. It is a method much cleaner, neater and handier, as well as much cooler, than our coal stove, the heat from which is a nuisance in hot weather.

When I arrived at Pinar del Rio the finishing strokes had just been accomplished on a wonderful work inaugurated and pushed through by General Franklin Bell, in command of the troops. It was a military map of the whole island on the scale of two or three miles to the inch, the complete map being twenty-four feet long! This remarkable piece of work had been accomplished by military reconnoissances made by the younger officers of the army, each officer provided with a prismatic compass and a sketch book, and accompanied by one or two soldiers, spending months in the field.

As for the preservation of order on the island the attitude of the troops was purely passive. We took, of course, measures to acquaint ourselves with conditions and were at all times ready to turn out for active service.

In addition to the usual drills, target practice, et cetera, of the command, one of our most important activities was field and combat exercises and manœuvres, for which the eastern part of the island was ideally fitted. The field and combat exercises were, in fact, small maneuvers in which the force was usually split up into two parties: a raiding party and a pursuing party. The raiders, given a start of several hours, disguised, so far as possible, the direction in which they traveled; they made long marches, and reaching a defensible position with a good "getaway," halted, hid and ambushed the pursuing party. After a combat had lasted some time the umpire (I usually filled that position) intervened, making his criticism and his decision. The raiders were then given a start, and after a certain interval the pursuit again was taken up. The pursuing party kept out in advance scouts to prevent being ambushed; they also used the best trailers in the command to follow the tracks of the raiders. The maneuver continued day and night; there was danger of attacks at night, which necessitated strong outposts around the camp.

In these field exercises the raiders usually moved towards the Magote country, where there was little cultivation and which afforded many suitable positions for defense and ambush.

In the early part of April, 1908, we had an extensive maneuver, participated in by the third squadron 11th Cavalry from Pinar del Rio, the second squadron of the 11th Cavalry from Camp Columbia, three batteries of field artillery and a signal detachment from Camp Columbia, and a Cuban battery of field artillery, all under my command. General Barry, with his staff, acted as observer. I arranged the maneuvers and acted as chief umpire.

During this, our second intervention in Cuba, it was widely believed by foreigners that the United States had returned to Cuba for good and that we would never again leave the island. Among our officers I was one of a minority who believed that we would be true to our promises and again leave Cuba to the Cubans. As time went on this became increasingly evident. In the fall of 1908 the election for the new president of Cuba took place; on January 28th he was inaugurated, my command, on this occasion, parading and saluting the Cuban flag as it was hoisted on the government building, thus indicating the beginning of autonomous Cuban rule. Soon after this Governor Magoon left the island in a United States battleship, being escorted out of the Bay of Havana by numerous Cuban vessels.

In the meantime I was informed that my regiment, the 11th Cavalry, would proceed to Fort Oglethorpe, Georgia, for station, going by way of Washington, D. C., where, on March 4, 1909, we would take part in the inauguration of President Taft.

In expectation of our departure I was the recipient, with my officers, of numerous courtesies on the part of the people of Pinar, including a dinner and several dances. They seemed unfeignedly sorry to see us go and on February 17th, the day of our departure, the mayor of the town ordered a public holiday and a large portion of the population accompanied us to the railroad depot, cheering us and waving their hats as we rolled away. I was touched by and very proud of this manifestation. I think there were very few of our garrisons in Cuba who were given a similar send-off.

On March 4, 1909, we marched in the inauguration parade at Washington. The regiment of nearly a thousand mounted men made a fine showing and were greatly applauded. We then entrained for Fort Oglethorpe.

Fort Oglethorpe, constructed for the accommodation

of a cavalry regiment, was situated on the outskirts of Chickamauga Park, where in 1898, in the Spanish-American War, I had spent four weary months as a major and lieutenant colonel of the 12th New York Volunteer Infantry. All traces of the sickly camps we had then occupied had vanished.

It was largely due to the superior and unusual facilities for training afforded at Chickamauga Park that I was able, in the next three years, to make the 11th Regiment incontestably the crack regiment of the cavalry arm of the service. In accomplishing this result I was aided by a splendid body of regimental officers, to whom I am under the deepest obligations.*

Chattanooga, a town of many conventions, regarded the troops at Fort Oglethorpe as one of their assets.

In 1910 among the conventions we entertained was the American Bar Association. Besides seeing a parade and drill the members were invited to meet the officers and ladies of the regiment at the Officers' Club, where many toasts were drunk to the 11th Cavalry by the lawyers. In return the Bar Association invited me to their closing banquet. I found myself sitting on the left of the presiding officer; Woodrow Wilson, then governor of New Jersey, was on his right. At the close of the banquet Mr. Wilson made one of his unique and remarkably eloquent addresses. On the lawyers, many of whom had never seen Mr. Wilson before, the effect was electrical. Numbers jumped up and, waving their napkins wildly over their heads, shouted, amid the applause, "He's our man for President!" As I never before heard Wilson's name

*I was particularly indebted to Lieut. Colonels Beach and Morgan; to Captains Langhorne, Haines, Jones, Rowell, Clayton, Leary, Frank Parker, Vidmer, White, McKinley, Gillem, Amos, Tompkins, and to Lieutenants Shelley, E. R. Tompkins, Swift, C. Cox, Grunert, Reynolds and Kimball.

used in that connection I was correspondingly impressed. I think perhaps this was the first time Wilson was publicly saluted as the coming presidential candidate.

Being at Fort Oglethorpe five years, from 1907 until shortly before my promotion to major general in 1913, I had a wonderful opportunity for training, such as is rarely afforded to a regimental commander. Many regiments are split up and the parts assigned to different posts—the colonel commands only a part. Many posts have unfit training grounds. At Fort Oglethorpe I had the entire regiment together.

A civilian has difficulty in realizing that in the service we have not much unoccupied time. To demonstrate this I append a brief table of roll calls, taken from an order of April 1, 1910.

> Reveille, 5.40 A. M. Assembly and drill call, 6.00. Mess call, 6.30. Fatigue call, 7.00. Drill call, 7.25. Recall from drill, 9.30, followed by grooming. Sick call, 10.30. Officers' call (at which I always made a point of addressing the officers for ten minutes, explaining orders, etc.), 11.45. Mess call, 12.00 noon. Drill call, 12.55. Fatigue call, 1.00. Recall from drill, 1.30. Stables, 3.30. Guard mounting, 4.35. Recall from fatigue, 5.00. Mess call, 5.15. Retreat, 6.00. Tattoo, 9.00. Taps, 11.00.
>
> At 3.45 P. M. on Tuesday, squadron parade, mounted; on Thursdays, regimental parade mounted. On Saturdays mounted inspection and inspection of barracks took up all the morning.

The above program does not mention a day's practice march once per month; a field day once per month; daily rides (six miles in an hour) for all officers not attending mounted drill; cross-country work; jumping obstacles, for all officers once a week; endurance rides of three days, for officers once a year, thirty miles per day; a practice march of twenty-one days once a year for entire command; officers' riding schools; officers' garrison schools with recitations in drill regulations, army regulations, field regulations, et cetera; non-commissioned-officer schools; privates' primary schools; night marches; firm-alarm drills, etc.

At our monthly field days we had competitive contests in grooming, pistol shooting, rifle shooting, trumpet calls, saddling and bridling, running at heads with saber, fencing mounted, wrestling mounted, wall scaling, high jumping, one-half-mile race, polo, mounted rescue, machine-gun packing, reaching, tent pitching, fire fighting.

It will be seen that the above table of occasions does not leave much leisure to the enlisted men. But it is a well-known fact that the more time to idle the soldier has the more likely he is to grumble; if you want to make him contented, give him plenty to do, always providing that he can see that the work you provide is good for training, for the command or for the post.

In 1910 the War Department began to introduce "inoculation" for typhoid. We were informed that it was not permissible to *oblige* the men to take the inoculation. But we were ordered to use every means —advice, lectures, et cetera—to encourage and induce the officers and men to be inoculated. I had lectures every week, which all who had not been inoculated were required to attend. As a result, about one-third of the men were inoculated, but that was all.

In the meantime we had a small epidemic of typhoid, nearly a dozen men being in the hospital suffering from the disease. Finally I called up the post surgeon, Dr. William Lyster, and told him that I had determined to *force* the men to take the serum. "But," said the doctor, "you are expressly prohibited by the War Department from requiring men, against their will, to take the inoculation." "It doesn't matter," said I. "I am going to compel them whether they want to or not." In the doctor's presence I wrote out the following order:

Fort Oglethorpe, Ga.
September 7, 1910

General Orders No. 100:

There being danger of an epidemic of typhoid fever at this post and it having been demonstrated that typhoid fever inoculation prevents the disease, all officers and soldiers under fifty years old, except those who have previously had typhoid fever or are already inoculated, are hereby directed to present themselves for the typhoid inoculation. Exceptions will be made in certain special cases, upon written application, *but such men will not be permitted to go outside the post where they run danger of infection.*

By order of Colonel Parker:
HERBERT A. WHITE
Captain and Adjutant, 11th Cavalry
Adjutant

As may be seen, this left a loophole. But the men who resisted inoculation would not be given passes. Fortunately, no one objected. They all took it.

It was near the period of the year when we were required to make a twenty-one days' practice march. I wrote the War Department asking permission to test the inoculation. The doctors had claimed we would be immune. Why not have the courage of their convictions? It was a typhoid fever country. I wanted authority to march without boiling water and to let the men drink any water they desired. I got permission. We made our twenty-one days' march to Knoxville and back. I encouraged the men to drink anything in the shape of water they could find. We returned. The doctors waited a week; no case of typhoid. They waited two weeks, a month, two months; no typhoid.

Then they were full of joy. They wrote full accounts of the experiment. And the medical department at Washington got the Secretary of War to order that the whole army be inoculated.

Dr. Jefferson Kean, colonel medical corps, was then on duty in Washington. He tells me that he became very much interested in my demonstration. That some months afterward he was sent to France to attend, at Paris, a meeting of military surgeons; the account he gave of my experiment, its success, and of the action of our Secretary of War greatly impressed the French surgeons. Kean said that later a bill for compulsory inoculation of the French Army was introduced in their parliament and passed. The English surgeons did not see their way to adopting compulsory inoculation. But during the World War they enforced the rule of limiting passes to those soldiers who were immune, which had the same effect.

Typhoid, or enteric fever, has always been the scourge of armies. As a result of inoculation the world was spared the terrible additional mortality which would have resulted from typhoid epidemics in the filth of the trenches during the great war.

Speaking about training in general, the drill in which I took most pleasure was when I had under my command the entire regiment of nearly a thousand mounted men. Our drill was a fast one, generally in compact formation. With a well-drilled regiment it was a thrilling experience to be able to throw to the front, like a huge thundering projectile, this mass of men and horses; then to transform it from a line into a column; then at a fast gallop to form a new line, without stopping; then, the new line moving forward to wheel it in regimental front, to the right, the troops on the flank moving almost at the run; then moving forward at a fast gait to abruptly halt, dismount and open fire; then mounting, to rush forward in line again, drawing sabers and preparing for the charge; then with the colonel in front of the center setting the pace, to increase the gallop to the run, the earth trembling under the impact of the hoofs, the horses crazy and blind with excitement; and then to give the command "charge!" the trumpets sounding, the men cheering; and then at the command "halt!" to stop short, without disorder, the line intact.

It takes hard work to accomplish such things. We taught our troops to move to the charge from a halt or a walk so that in an emergency no time would be lost, and when in full career to halt within a few yards, so that in mimic combats opposing forces charging each other would not collide. We taught them to dismount from any formation—line, column or mass—and open fire in thirty seconds from the moment of command, the horses being trained to rush to the rear in order to get under cover quickly. We taught the regiment, while moving, to change, at fast gaits, from any formation to any other, a thing not provided for in the drill regulations, and we introduced new trumpet calls, so that there was a different call for each formation. We taught the mounted attack of trenches in successive lines of skirmishes, the men dismounting at the trenches and attacking with the rifle, as was later done in Palestine in the World War. We taught our officers and men the ability to decide quickly, when suddenly attacked or surprised, whether to charge the enemy mounted or, dismounting, to attack him with the rifle, or, if on open ground, to rush to the rear and obtain cover for the horses before dismounting to attack. We learned how to move at high speed through the woods.

In 1909, the War Department having issued a circular letter enjoining on cavalry commanders the instruction of their commands in cross-country riding and passage of obstacles, we began to make a daily practice of hurdle jumping. The hurdles at first, due to the inexperience of the horses and riders, were limited in height. A number of the officers becoming interested in the formation of a hunt club, I facilitated, so far as possible, their desires. I had not previously looked upon drag hunts and fox hunts with much favor, this kind of amusement, as I supposed, being open only to the more favored and wealthy class. But we were fortunate in being presented with some fine hounds; others we bought at a low price, and I found we could make the remaining expenses inconsiderable.

Many of the officers of the regiment, however, were slow in joining. I wanted to make it a *regimental* hunt club. It was my duty according to the War Department instructions to lead the officers each week in an "obstacle ride." At "officers' call" one day I informed the officers that the obstacle ride would take place each Friday. (On Friday the hunt took place.) That if I saw fit to follow the hounds in the ride, they would nevertheless accompany me. Such officers who, for good reasons, were excused from the ride would take charge of the "general fatigue" squads which on Friday cleaned up the post.

The result was that after taking part in several obstacle rides conducted under these conditions the whole body of my officers became wildly enthusiastic about the hunt and joined the club.

Conditions indeed were ideal. Dues were small. The park and the country adjoining made a splendid hunting ground. The courses were chiefly drag hunts ten or twelve miles long. Hurdles, rail fences, ditches, fallen trees, etc., provided the jumps, which were numerous.

Ours was the only regiment in the United States that had an organized hunt club. It added greatly to the perfection of equitation of the regiment, as well as to its fame. Visitors were greatly impressed.

In March, 1911, the Mexican question was again at a critical stage and the regiment received rush orders to proceed to a mobilization camp to be formed at San Antonio. A dispute had arisen between the two nations as to the right of Mexico to cede a tract of land on Magdalena Bay to Japanese citizens. It was charged that the Japanese Government intended to esablish a naval base. Affairs had arrived at such a point that President Taft had decided to send troops into Mexico. Realizing that this would probably result in war, Taft ordered all Americans to quit Mexico. This they did with difficulty, abandoning their houses and property at great loss. About this time the President changed his mind. It was said afterwards that General Witherspoon had informed the President that intervention would require 400,000 troops and four years' fighting. At any rate the orders to cross the Rio Grande were revoked. A division of 15,000 troops was assembled at San Antonio to impress the Mexicans and remained there eight months, but our poor citizens, who in some cases had lost all their property and were afraid to go back to Mexico to reclaim it, were left without recompense.

In anticipation of trouble with Mexico, my regiment had for a long time been exercised at drill in hasty preparation for service in the field, and was quickly on the way.

Arrived at San Antonio, we were met by officers of the general staff, who informed us that conditions were such that we would be probably on the other side of the Mexican border within a week. Troops began to pour into camp, cavalry, infantry, artillery, and special troops. The entire force was under the command of Major General W. H. Carter. The day after our arrival in camp I was informed that 429 recruits and over 400 horses were en route to the regiment. I had hardly got our camp in order before they began to arrive.

I determined that if it could be done, these recruits should be ready for service and fit for fighting when we crossed the Rio Grande. Accordingly we turned over the new horses to the old men for training. The quietest of the old horses were assigned to the recruits, between thirty and forty recruits joining each troop. The recruits would ride, under expert instruction, five hours per day, including Saturday, with a practice ride on the road on Sundays. In addition they had two hours a day of aiming and position drill.

It will be seen that under this system that in two weeks the recruits rode over sixty hours, or as much as a cadet in his first year of riding. The recruit did no grooming; he had no time for it; that and fatigue work and guard duty were left to be learned later, and in the meantime were performed by the old soldiers.

The new men responded nobly. At the end

of two weeks they rode fairly well, had perfect confidence, and were fit to commence target practice. The target range was at Leon Springs, twenty-five miles away. This distance they rode, at a walk and a trot, like old soldiers, and went into camp.

At Leon Springs they had six days of target practice, each recruit firing 170 shots in "Special Course B," the course in firing at miniature targets with service ammunition, which I had devised.

On the sixth day, as a test of comparative efficiency, a regular skirmish run was made, first by experts, then by recruits, firing at the regular skirmish silhouettes. The score of the experts was forty-five per cent and of the recruits twenty-two per cent. Considering their inexperience at skirmish firing this, to me, was an indication that in action they would give a good account of themselves.

During the week of firing the riding was kept up; so that at the end of the third week after the arrival of the recruits I was ready to march into Mexico; my recruits could ride and they could shoot! It was made very evident to me at that time, that in case of a forward movement my regiment would constitute the vanguard. We would probably march on Mexico City via Vera Cruz and Jalapa as did General Scott in 1845. It was with this in view that later I was furnished with detailed maps of that country near Vera Cruz marked "secret" by the War College. It is a long march to the capital, and to attempt to keep open our line of communications with the sea would require many small detachments isolated, exposed to attack by greatly superior forces. A force of 20,000 or 25,000 men well provided with transportation could cut loose, overthrow any Mexican Army in its path, and by not stopping to besiege fortified places, arrive at Mexico City in two weeks. Once near the city there is plenty of food, as the French found out in 1864.

Arrived in the city, form a government of the best citizens, proclaim a protectorate, and raise a Mexican army to be under American officers to do the dirty job of re-establishing order in the provinces. Announce, as we did in Cuba, that when order is restored the Americans will leave Mexico; it being understood that in case of riot or revolution we will return. Reform the constitution and the laws, with special advantages for foreigners. The resulting flood of immigration would soon make Mexico tranquil. Such an act on the part of the United States would end wars, revolutions, banditry, and be a work of humanity.

We worked hard at drills all summer. Later on, for the benefit of the enlisted men, a baseball league was formed to which the fourteen regiments present contributed nines. A polo tournament for the officers was also formed. In the autumn a football contest between regiments took place. We came out victors in all these events.

It is difficult to estimate the value to a regiment of a reputation for excellence, and this applies to excellence in athletics quite as much as in other respects. It creates among the men a pride of regiment, an *esprit de corps,* and reaches far. Men of other regiments want to join, discharged men want to re-enlist. It brings about contentment and contentment means discipline, loyalty.

But these things are not achieved without devoted attention and labor on the part of the officers.

In the fall of 1912 I was ordered to Washington, and from there to Bridgeport, Connecticut, to command the Blue Cavalry in a combined maneuver of National Guard and regular troops. In this maneuver the invading Red Army coming from New Bedford, Massachusetts, and marching on New York, was composed largely of the National Guard regiments of New England. The Blue Army, composed of militia troops from New York and New Jersey, opposed the advance of the Reds. The maneuver began near Bridgeport, Conn.

My brigade of "Independent Blue Cavalry" consisted of twelve troops of New York cavalry and one of regular cavalry. The two regiments of which it was composed were commanded by Colonels DeBevoise and Bridgeman. The officers and men of these regiments were fine fellows, full of enthusiasm and pep. We had good weather, good luck and the whole affair was most delightful.

On several days my brigade acting alone held up the march of the Red Army. On the last day, by a mounted charge we captured "Overlook Hill" dominating their camp in Newtown and making it untenable.

That charge of New York cavalry was celebrated by them in song and story for a number of years.

We learned a number of things on that trip. One thing that particularly impressed me was the facility for defense against an enemy advancing from the east, which the terrain in Connecticut affords. The streams as a rule run southeast across an enemy's path. Between them are ridges, also running southeast, and often covered with almost impenetrable undergrowth. Through these ridges there are few passes so that there are few east and west roads and those very winding and circuitous. The roads and fields are lined with stone walls four feet high and three or four feet thick. Thus the roads are practically defiles and the fence corners entrenchments. These conditions facilitate ambush, concealment of men and horses, and occupation in retreat of successive positions. The strength of these positions behind stone walls makes it possible for small detachments to hold their ground till the last moment, inflicting severe losses on the enemy advancing over open ground.

In the latter part of September, 1912, I was detailed, as a member of a board, on the reorganization of our cavalry. The board was ordered to proceed to Europe and there examine the cavalries of Germany, Russia, Austria, Italy, France and England. The members of the board were Brigadier General E. J. McClernand, Colonel James Parker, Lieutenant Colonel Joseph E. Dickman, and Major Jesse Carter.

Of our visit to Europe, I would say that it seemed to us that the English had to a certain extent gone back on the tactics of their cavalry, adopted just after the Boer War. These tactics declared the rifle "the principal weapon of cavalry." On the other hand, we got the impression that the Germans and the Russians, both of whom had armed their cavalry with rifles, attached great importance to dismounted fighting.

The Austrians, Italians and French were still crazy about the charge, saber and the lance.

Two years later, in the World War, these policies had their effect. The Russian cavalry showed itself good at dismounted work. They would have accomplished much if they had been well led. The English cavalry quickly adapted themselves to the changed conditions and finally in the latter part of the war in Palestine they practically adopted Boer tactics by charging entrenchments, then dismounting and using the rifle. The tremendous successes that the English had in Palestine were entirely due to the cavalry. At first French, Italian and Austrian cavalry in the World War were of little account. They could not fight on foot, not being properly armed and trained. Later they learned.

On this trip we inspected cavalry at Petrograd, Moscow, Vienna, Rome, Turin, Milan, Vincennes, Senlis, Saumur, Aldershot and Tidworth. We were received everywhere, except in Germany, with the greatest courtesy.

The board started on its return journey to America in the middle of December, spending Christmas Day on the seas.

After several discussions on the ship, General Dickman and I came to the conclusion that there was no question but that our cavalry organization was the best. McClernand and Carter did not make known their opinions. Consequently I was surprised in our first meeting at Washington to find that they unreservedly declared for the European system. Thus the board was divided two and two.

It took us over a month at Washington to write up our report, which was then duly pigeonholed and never again was heard of. Incidentally, I did most of the writing.

General Pershing and General Parker, Brownsville, Texas 1916

Capt. Jas. Parker
4th Cav., 1892

Capt. Parker, Cav.
Instructor, West
Point, 1894-1898

Major Allen, of the general staff, who was responsible for our trip to Europe, took occasion immediately after my departure for Texas to reconstitute the board by adding several members, all of whom were for the European formation. Thus Colonel Dickman remained the only true American cavalryman.

Two regiments of cavalry were ordered to Winchester, Virginia, and were used to carry out extensive experiments in the European tactics. This drill finished, the board drew up a drill book modeled on the European practice. This drill book was issued to all our regiments and was tested for a period of one year.

At the end of that time a vote was taken and the large majority of our officers declared in favor of the American organization. Thus the movement to make our cavalry like the European was decidedly killed.

I was appointed brigadier general by President Taft about the middle of February, 1913. When the appointment went to the Senate for confirmation, together with that of Colonel Liggett (afterwards lieutenant general in the World War), who was also appointed brigadier general, both appointments were held up by a Senator from Alabama who was fighting for another candidate. It looked as if the appointment might fail of confirmation. That would have been disastrous, as on the 4th of March President Taft went out, and President Wilson came in. He was known to favor other candidates, and was especially committed to my classmate, Colonel Hugh L. Scott. It was, then, with considerable relief that at 10.20 P. M., March 3rd, with only a few hours to spare, waiting at the door of the Senate room, I was greeted by Senator Bankhead emerging from the Senate Chamber. He clapped me on the back and shouted, "We have made you a brigadier!"

The next day, in the full uniform of a brigadier general, put on for the first time, I rode at the head of the inauguration parade, mounted on my beautiful black stallion, Chattanooga. I commanded a brigade made up of the corps of cadets from West Point and the corps of midshipmen from Annapolis, a splendid command of élite troops. The weather was magnificent. Many of my friends thought that I had been turned down by the Senate and were surprised and delighted to find they were mistaken.

Ordered to the command of the First Cavalry Brigade, I proceeded to San Antonio, Texas, making my headquarters at Fort Sam Houston. This was a large post of infantry, cavalry and artillery. Here also lived the commander of the Southern Department, Major General Bliss. Some troops of cavalry of my command were stationed at Fort Sam Houston. But the remainder of my brigade lay stretched for over nine hundred miles along the Rio Grande River, from the mouth of the river to El Paso, in small detachments, guarding the Mexican border. Their duty was to protect the inhabitants from the Mexican raiders. These banditti excursions were quite frequent on account of the disturbed condition of Mexico, which was then undergoing a revolution. Our troops were forbidden, however, to cross the Rio Grande in pursuit of these raiders. Later, as a result of our occupation of Vera Cruz and of the invasion of Mexico in pursuit of Villa by General Pershing, our patrols along the Rio Grande were fired upon by Mexicans on the other side of the river, and orders were issued from Washington forbidding our patrols from even showing themselves on the banks of the river!

In view of the nine hundred miles front, I jocularly claimed I had the biggest brigade of cavalry in the world!

It was composed of three regiments—the 2nd Cavalry, the 3rd Cavalry and the 14th Cavalry.

Each regiment was composed of twelve troops and a machine-gun platoon, numbering about 1,000 men; thus I had in all about 3,000 men and horses. The detachments along the Rio Grande numbered sixteen. There were also thirty small camps of patrol detachments or outposts. As there is much heat, dust and alkali water in the desert country along the Rio Grande great hardship was experienced in these camps by both men and horses.

The main camps were some distance from the river. Each maintained two or three outposts of ten men each near the river, these outposts, by means of small patrols, maintaining communication with each other and with the main camp.

Notwithstanding the arduous sentry duty this demanded, it was difficult to prevent the Mexican bandits from breaking through the line of outposts.

My brigade headquarters were at Fort Sam Houston, San Antonio. San Antonio was 140 miles from the Rio Grande by railroad, but it was a central point with railroad communication with most of the camps. I had a small office and several clerks. My chief of staff was Lieutenant Colonel W. S. Scott; my aide, First Lieutenant John H. Read. My duties were to conduct the training of my brigade, to inspect it frequently and to make report to higher authority on its clothing equipment, camp economy, physical condition of command, food, care of horses, etc.

The training year, by orders from the War Department, was divided into two periods: the period of garrison training and the period of field training. At the end of each of these periods I inspected every unit of the command. This was not an easy task; to visit the forty or fifty stations of troops or outpost detachments required over a month. In the upper course of the Rio Grande River the detachments were usually near the railroad; on the lower course they were often only to be reached by vehicle or on horseback. I assumed command of the brigade March 25, 1913. After a preliminary inspection of part of the brigade I saw that my task of training would be unusually difficult. As a result of field service the troops had neglected drills. Some of the officers claimed that such training was not possible, that their time was too much taken up by field work. As a matter of fact, the troops which were in camp, having nothing interesting to do and disgusted with their long term of duty, having poor food, poor water, and poor accommodations, living in a desert, had lost courage, energy, morale. The horses, standing at the picket lines, without shelter from the almost tropical sun and rain in summer, uncovered in the cold of winter, were in bad physical shape.

I changed all this, but it took time. I first set the troops at work on my competitive test of garrison training, which I had found so useful in the 11th Cavalry. It gave the men and officers something to work for. They were no longer isolated; they were engaged in a trial of skill with others, a contest. Those of the officers who had ambition found a vent for it. In this competitive test the troops were to be marked by me personally, with marks ranging from

0 to 10, on twenty different subjects, including degree of excellence in uniform, equipment, grooming and care of horse, saddling and bitting, trooper's position in saddle at all gaits, training of horse, jumping hurdles, use of saber, and troop drill, including evolutions, the charge, and dismounting to fight on foot. Every troop and machine-gun platoon was inspected and marked in his annual inspection of garrison training by the brigade commander. The results were published soon after to the command.

I also devised tests for the officers, connected with the use of the pistol and saber, equitation, estimating of distances, et cetera. This was a new idea to many of the officers, many of whom were inferior to their men in these exercises.

I marked the troops on the number of men excused from daily drill. At the tests all had to be present.

There was considerable improvement the first year, 1913. Some commanding officers, however, did not quite understand what was wanted or whether the orders could be enforced. But the response the second year, 1914, was remarkable. For instance, the mark for general excellence in garrison training in the 14th Cavalry went from 57.2 in 1913 to 85.2 in 1914. In 1915 the standing of all three regiments was much above 90. In rifle practice the figure of merit had more than doubled and the total number of men qualified as expert sharpshooters and marksmen had increased from 961 to 1,448. I had troops which lived in an alkali desert, amid the cactus, rocks and mesquite, which, when turned out for my inspection, would have made a profound impression at a horse show in Madison Garden, so well kept and well trained were their horses, so beautifully dressed and well drilled were their men. I was told that the individual soldiers were so enthusiastic about this test that they spent their spare time for a week before I came grooming their horses and polishing their equipment.

Service on the Rio Grande was not without excitement. On June 3, 1913, while inspecting a detachment at Brownsville I was under fire for some hours from bullets coming from Matamoras, where fighting was going on.

It should be understood that in addition to the 1st Cavalry Brigade numerous detachments of infantry guarded the Rio Grande.

A number of serious raids were made by the Mexicans during the three years I was there. Soldiers especially seemed to be objects of the most supreme hatred of the raiders. On a number of occasions the small patrol detachments quartered in tents were fired on at night at close range. The soldiers, totally surprised, would lose several of their number before they replied to the fire, when the Mexicans would flee. To prevent this I placed sandbag walls around the tents occupied by my detachments.

Several long-distance raids were made by Mexican bandits. On one occasion a railroad train was captured near Brownsville and a number of passengers and soldiers killed.

We all supposed, when President Wilson ordered Vera Cruz occupied by General Funston's force, that the Mexicans would fight back and that the long-awaited intervention was at hand. But the Mexicans, with all their bragging, are afraid to fight with the United States and nothing happened except that we cleaned up the dirty city of Vera Cruz and enriched the citizens by spending our cash freely.

Later on the troops were brought back to the United States, Huerta, the murderer of Madero and the object of President Wilson's hatred, having resigned.

In November, 1915, Villa, the powerful bandit of

the northern states of Mexico, marched to attack the Carranza troops holding Agua Prieta, a Mexican town on the boundary and adjoining the large American town of Douglas, Ariz., a railroad center. Our Government, at Carranza's request, transported a large body of his troops as reinforcements for the troops at Agua Prieta through American territory by our railroads. They arrived in time to defeat Villa.

General Funston had told me that if there was any more firing into American towns he would have our troops fire back. I knew that Villa could not very well attack Agua Prieta without firing into Douglas. Being on my way to the World's Fair at San Francisco, I stopped off at Douglas to see what would happen.

Sure enough, a great many bullets came into Douglas. Incidentally several hit the ground very near me. But Funston did nothing. Later he had an interview with Villa, each general with his officers on different sides of the wire fence which marked the boundary. Villa, red with passion, complained bitterly of the action of our Government in transporting Carranza's troops to fight him.

He had his revenge. On January 10, 1916, at Santa Isabel, he took eighteen Americans—engineers, mining men and lumbermen—from a train and foully murdered them. Our government did nothing. Villa then, on March 9th, executed a raid on Columbus, New Mexico, a town on the border held by our troops. The post was commanded by my friend and classmate, Colonel Herbert J. Slocum. The attack took place at night and was unexpected. It was a failure, however, as night attacks generally are, and the Mexicans were beaten back with heavy loss. I think about twenty Americans were killed.

This stirred our Government to action. General Pershing was ordered to organize a large command—

cavalry, infantry, artillery, engineers and aeroplanes, in all 12,000 men—and start in pursuits. I saw at once this would take much time; that Villa's trail, like an Indian trail, required immediate pursuit if anything was to be accomplished. I telegraphed at once to the War Department, asking to be allowed to pursue with one of my regiments, the 8th Cavalry, and a battery of mounted artillery, that I could get on the trail in twenty-four hours. This cavalry regiment was at El Paso near Columbus.

My request was unanswered and Pershing took ten days in getting under way. Once started the cavalry made tremendous marches, but Villa, like an Indian, had long since disappeared. Later on, in June, Carranza practically demanded that the expedition be withdrawn and on June 20th his troops attacked an isolated scouting party of two troops of the 10th Negro Cavalry, killed some and captured others. Mr. Wilson swallowed this insult and ordered Pershing back to the United States.

Early in May, 1916, I was ordered to Brownsville, to make my headquarters there and take command of that district. The district in a straight line was about a hundred miles long. I had under me four regiments of regular infantry, one regiment of cavalry, a battalion of coast artillery, two battalions of field artillery, two companies of engineers, and signal and hospital men.

On May 31, 1916, there came to the district two regiments of Texas National Guard and one Texas battery. General Funston gave me secret orders that in case raids were made from Mexico I was to pursue the raiders. I immediately went to work to organize the district for defense. In the numerous little towns I raised small bodies of volunteers, young men well armed, who at night stood guard and were ready to report any disorders to the troops. Every person in the district who owned an auto was engaged to use it to transport troops when needed and, when necessary, to carry the infantry down to the Rio Grande. I let the Mexicans know that if raids occurred I would take the responsibility of following them.

For some weeks there was quiet, but on June 18, 1916, some Mexican raiders who had crossed were, by my orders, pursued into Mexico by a squadron of cavalry.

The next morning I sent word to my troops to withdraw in case they were not able to overtake the raiders. They mounted and were on the point of marching back when they were attacked by a small force of Mexican soldiers. They immediately dismounted and went into action, killed several Mexicans and wounded others. Then they mounted and charged the Mexicans and pursued them several miles. They then carried out my orders to withdraw across the Rio Grande.

It was on this very day, June 19, 1916, that the President issued orders for the entire National Guard of the United States, about 100,000 men, to be concentrated on the Rio Grande. To my command there came troops from Colorado, Illinois, Indiana, Iowa, Kansas, Louisiana, Minnesota, Nebraska, New Hampshire, North Dakota, Oklahoma, South Dakota, Virginia, and later from New York. In November, including the regular troops there were present nineteen regiments of infantry in addition to units of cavalry, artillery, engineers, signal corps, and hospital corps, in all 31,400 men. The troops were organized into one division and three provisional infantry brigades. I thus had under my command the equivalent of two divisions or one army corps.

The principal camps were at Brownsville, San Benito and Llano Grande.

Instruction of the National Guard troops began at once, six hours a day, four under arms.

In all, sixty-six instruction bulletins, seventeen general orders, thirty-six memoranda, and six letters of instructions were issued dealing with the instruction of the National Guard.

Preparatory to the maneuvers held November 16-24, 1916, tests were carried out for infantry, cavalry, field artillery, and machine-gun organizations.

The maneuvers of November 16-24, 1916, embraced all territory between Llano Grande and the Gulf of Mexico, an area of about six hundred and seventy-five square miles. The troops were engaged in marches, reconnaissance, combat, advance, retreat, construction of and attack and defense of entrenched positions, day and night operations. Each side arranged its own supply, selected its own camps in accordance with the conditions confronting it each day, and the maneuver was conducted under war conditions in every way, except that at a few places wood and water were furnished by prearrangement.

On the whole these maneuvers, lasting ten days, showed the troops of this command to be fit to take the field in active campaign.

In the review of November 25th, in which all the troops, numbering 23,000 men, participated, a splendid showing was made. The cavalry and artillery passed at a trot and exhibited excellent control.

The following officers were commended for remarkably earnest and intelligent effort in the training:

Major Lincoln F. Kilbourne, infantry, D.O.L., officer in charge of militia affairs.

Brigadier General Edward M. Lewis, Indiana National Guard.

Brigadier General John A. Hulen, Texas National Guard.

Colonel Robert L. Bullard, 26th Infantry.

Captain George Grunert, cavalry, inspector-instructor.

Captain John H. Read, 3rd Cavalry, inspector-instructor.

Captain Frank R. McCoy, 3rd Cavalry, chief of staff.

Captain Cortlandt Parker, F.A., D.O.L., aide-de-camp, acting chief of artillery.

In acknowledging a photograph of the review of November 25, 1916, Secretary of War Baker wrote me: "I am grateful for the good picture, but even more grateful for the splendid service you have rendered the country in the present activity."

In the training of the National Guard troops ninety regular officers were detailed as instructors and one hundred and sixty-two non-commissioned officers. These troops had an average of six months' training. The eighteen regiments of National Guard, in addition to other training, completed the course of rifle firing; also twenty-eight batteries of the National Guard light artillery completed a course of firing of 290 rounds per gun. The total number of National Guardsmen who were instructed by me was 29,777 men and 1,630 officers. At the conclusion of their training I estimated that they could be marked as compared to well-trained regular troops, in marching, 98 per cent; manual of arms, 97 per cent; garrison training, 80 per cent; discipline, 90 per cent; field training, 80 per cent; musketry training and battery firing, 60 per cent.

* * * *

It was with great astonishment shortly after the

training commenced that we heard that President Wilson had stated that on no account were the troops to cross the Rio Grande or make an act of aggression on Mexico. At once the soldiers began to murmur. The favorite cry of the men as I rode through the camps was, 'What are we here for? We want to go home." I had some difficulty in contending against this spirit. I used to call the regiments together and talk to them and tell them how necessary and important it was that this intensive training—nearly six hours a day in this hot climate—should be kept up. "We must be *prepared.*"

In that year, 1916, the great World War was attaining dimensions it never had before and it began to look more and more evident that we might be drawn into it. It was apparent to every officer and man, and so this argument of preparedness had a great effect.

But I myself could not understand what Mr. Wilson was up to, especially as we all knew that he did not intend to be drawn into the World War.

The explanation of this appears in the memoirs of General Hugh L. Scott, who at that time was chief of staff.

From his explanation it appeared that Carranza at that time was very hostile against the United States. Pershing's expedition was in the northern part of Mexico and was venturing farther and farther into the Mexican territory. Carranza practically had demanded that the United States take out Pershing's column. It was understood that Obregon, who was Minister of War for Carranza, had threatened to take a large force across the Rio Grande and loot our towns, including San Antonio. Scott said he went to President Wilson and told him that it was quite possible this might occur and that the troops along the Rio

Grande should be reinforced. Mr. Wilson yielded and ordered the National Guard to the border.

This then accounts for the position in which we found ourselves. I am obliged to confess that I am not at all of General Scott's opinion. I believe Obregon, in case of an invasion, would have been beaten back with great loss by the small force at our command. This one great opportunity to settle affairs in Mexico was lost to us. If Carranza's troops had come across and attacked us the Mexican question would have been settled for good and all.

In March, 1917, I had a visit from General Pershing, who then was in command of the Southern Department. He and I inspected all the troops in the district and he seemed to be very well pleased with what he saw. Everyone who served in that command at Brownsville agrees in saying that what we accomplished there was a great work in the way of preparedness for the World War. It was unfortunate that Mr. Wilson, when we sent the troops home, allowed some of the regiments to be disbanded, but in a great many cases they went intact to the World War. Their training at Brownsville was one of the causes of the marvelous results we accomplished in the preparation of our men for fighting in France. It also had the great effect of improving the regular troops, which in some cases sorely needed it.

Without my knowledge, about this time I came very near being ordered to Russia as military attaché, the Russian Government desiring there an American representative of high rank. Fortunately for me, Secretary of War Garrison decided I could not be spared from the Rio Grande. I say fortunately, for I probably would have been kept in Russia after we entered the war and not allowed to do my share in our wonderful accomplishment of preparation.

Speaking about my system of training, as published in my compendium of training in the Brownsville district, I am reliably informed it was of great value to the committee of the general staff which prepared the system of training adopted for our troops when they entered the World War.

On March 20, 1916, I relinquished command of the Brownsville district and proceeded to San Antonio to take command of the First Provisional Infantry Division.

XV

THE WORLD WAR

It was on March 23rd that I organized the first of three divisions in the Southern Department, ostensibly to relieve the department commander of the details of training, discipline, court-martial supervision, etc., of the great number of troops which the department contained. It was really, I think, the result of the feeling, in the minds of the military authorities at Washington that war was not far off; it could no longer be postponed—and so it proved.

I retained command of the division for about two months. The forces which the division comprised were the 4th, 8th, 9th, 19th, 26th, 28th, 30th, 36th and 38th Infantry. I was also in command of the 3rd, 14th and 16th Regiments of Cavalry, and later of the 1st, 2nd and 3rd Regiments of Texas Infantry, mustered at the beginning of the war into the United States service.

I was placed in charge of the administration, general courts, equipment, training and preparation for war of the personnel. I immediately instituted a course of strenuous training, adapting for that purpose the project of training which I had established in the Brownsville district. On April 6, 1917, we were thrilled by the news that war had been declared.

About this time began a series of *miracles* in this country. I call our preparations for war miracles, because in former wars we had never shown similar foresight. That we should ever adopt such wise, far-seeing measures had always seemed to me, under our system of government, impossible. When these measures were actually adopted, it therefore seemed to me miraculous.

In former wars politicians had always large control; they not only decided our policies, interfered with administration, et cetera, but were actually, even without previous military training, placed in command of divisions, army corps and armies. But in the World War the politicians were told "hands off." It seemed as though the President had said to the General Staff, "Adopt your most ideal plan, carry it out without regard to cost. I will see that you are not interfered with!"

I, with many others, had always believed that the adoption of conscription by the people would be possible only in a case of urgent necessity, where the life of the nation was at stake. Conscription during the Civil War, as I have related earlier in my memoirs, was little better than a farce. My friend, General Crowder, in 1917 invented a system of conscription whereby the leading men of communities were induced to lend valuable aid in making it a success; it was by their activities that the draft was enforced, and not, as in the Civil War, by the military officers of the Government.* And, to my surprise, President Wilson made popular the cry, "It is an honor to be drafted!" In the 85th Division, later under my command, a soldier was heard to exclaim, "That

*Crowder tells me that it was on *February* 6, 1927, that President Wilson ordered the preparation of a plan for conscription.

fellow is nothing but a damn slacker—he enlisted to keep from being drafted!"

Indeed if we had relied wholly upon volunteers we could not have done much in the World War; for at the time when conscription was adopted we had enlisted less than 800,000 volunteers and business at the recruiting offices had come almost to a standstill. And it can be said further that the volunteers were mostly boys, whereas the "selective" conscription furnished us with men.

The business of selecting and training officers to lead our army of over three millions was well done, miraculously done. Under the leadership of General Leonard Wood, some time before we entered the war, officers' schools were established at Plattsburg and elsewhere in which selected young men, of patriotism and intelligence, quickly learned the rudiments of the officer's profession.

While we were strenuously making preparation for the war, the pacifists still had their say, and as yet no movement had been made towards sending troops to France. Wilson's idea was, I believe, that our rôle, if possible, should first be one of mediation. But the Allies clamored for our participation; they begged, if only to hearten their troops, we send over at least a division as an earnest of our active assistance. With this in view Marshal Joffre was sent to the United States. He was wildly acclaimed by our people, but when at Washington he pleaded with President Wilson, he met with a cold refusal. At a meeting of the Union Club in New York, early in 1918, Franklin Roosevelt told us Joffre almost wept as he came from that interview. "I have failed, I have failed!" he cried. Roosevelt said: "Marshal, let me take you again to the President, I think this time we will succeed." When the Marshal came back from a visit to St. Louis, the President granted him another interview, and this time Joffre was successful. On June 1, 1917, General Pershing was summoned from San Antonio to make arrangements for the embarkation for France of the American Army, and for the establishment of his headquarters there.

Being next in rank I took command of the Southern Department, being afterwards confirmed as Department Commander by orders from Washington. The Southern Department included the States of Texas, Oklahoma, New Mexico, Arizona and the southern part of California. I very soon received orders from Washington to organize, from the troops in the department, the First Division. I selected for that purpose the 16th, 18th, 26th and 28th Infantry Regiments, the 6th and 7th Artillery Regiments, the 1st Engineers, and the necessary quartermaster, signal service and hospital units. Most of the division had served under me in the Brownsville district, including the 26th and 28th Infantry Regiments, the 7th Field Artillery, the 1st Engineers and other units. The regiments were raised to full strength. The organization and entraining for the East were completed in record time.

Long after the war I learned that I had been designated as the commander of the division, but that the President preferred another man, a personal friend, General Sibert, of the Engineers. As we know now, Sibert did not remain long in command; he was succeeded by my friend, General Bullard.

In the Southern Department I remained in command for nearly three months. Shortly after

I took charge the department underwent a tremendous transformation. Recruits poured in to fill the regiments and other units to full strength, until soon the number of troops in the department numbered over 60,000 men. New regiments and other units were formed. Intensive training was had.

Early in June I was ordered by the War Department to establish six encampments, each for a division of 35,000 to 40,000 men, each site containing room for drills and maneuvers, and to contain the necessary buildings for the care of the troops. The sites selected were San Antonio, Houston, Waco, Fort Worth, Fort Sill, and Deming.

In addition it became necessary for me to establish a number of aviation camps. The chief of these was Camp Kelly near San Antonio, which is still maintained. I named it after my friend, Lieutenant Kelly, who was killed at our concentration camp at San Antonio in 1911. Kelly, on landing, to avoid striking a tent in which there were soldiers, turned sharply, upset, and was killed.

August 5, 1917, I was promoted to the rank of Major General, National Army. On August 26th I was assigned to the command of the 32nd Division to be organized and trained at Waco, Texas.

The 32nd Division was made up of the National Guard regiments of Wisconsin and Michigan. These regiments had received four months' training in the field during the 1916 mobilization on the Rio Grande; thus it was only a few months since they had been serving there. But curiously enough at the end of that mobilization, in spite of the fact that it was evident a crisis with Germany was approaching, the trained soldiers of which the National Guard was composed were not retained, as they could have been; they were mustered out of the U. S. service and in most cases where they applied for it given their discharge by the states. Whether it was because the use of the National Guard in war was not contemplated, no effort apparently was made by the General Staff to bring about their retention. In Iowa, Texas, and some other states, this wholesale discharge of the trained soldiers did not take place. But in the Wisconsin and Michigan regiments only thirty-three per cent of the men who served on the Rio Grande came to Waco.

The 33rd Division had the 66th and 67th Brigades, and the 132nd, 133rd, 134th and 135th Infantry Regiments. The four companies of each battalion had 250 men each, the regiment of three battalions having therefore 3,000 men; the brigades of two regiments, 6,000 men. The division thus had 12,000 infantry. The divisions eventually had three regiments of field artillery and one regiment of engineers. They should have had one cavalry regiment apiece, but General Pershing and the General Staff, notwithstanding their constant boast that the Americans would break the German line and "convert stabilized warfare into maneuver," never asked for cavalry, although it would have been indispensable in mobile warfare.

In his book of reminiscences General Bullard says, in speaking of the American break through at the battle of Soissons, July 18, 1918:

"I would have risked all upon a dash by every cavalryman in my command. I longed for one single American cavalry division, led by an American cavalryman that I knew; he would have gone through or lost all. If on the first day we could have broken through to the great highway and railroad leading south through Soissons into the Chateau-Thierry salient, I see no reason why the capture of Germans in the Battle of Soissons should not have turned out two hundred thousand instead of the actual twenty thousand."*

I am proud to say that General Bullard afterwards announced publicly that the American cavalryman he referred to was myself.

Similarly, General Liggett, who commanded the 1st Army, fighting in the Argonne, wrote to me in a letter of September 23, 1921:

"I remember very well, how, on November second, 1918, I said to members of my staff at Souilly, 'If I had Jim Parker here now, and a division of American cavalry, not one of the enemy's organizations and none of his material would ever get across the Meuse River.'

"And it was so. We did think of you over there, you see."

But enough of regrets. I wrote to General Pershing in the spring of 1918: "If you break

*The value of cavalry was obscured during the years of trench warfare. But in the final break-throughs, in Palestine, at Salonica, and on the Piave, in Italy, the surrender of the enormous masses of enemy troops was due to the cavalry, which dashed through and blocked the enemy's retreat.

On the other hand, in March, 1918, it was Ludendorf's lack of cavalry that saved the Allies from complete defeat.

through the enemies' line you will need cavalry and lots of it. Have you no use for an old cavalry drillmaster to train the horsemen you need?" I received no answer. The two regiments of cavalry he had in France were insufficient to accomplish anything of moment.

I recall a grand banquet given to me and my staff at the Rotary Club, a very important institution in that city. At the close of the dinner the chairman presented to me with due ceremony a handsome silk American flag. I am not good at speeches, but stammered out a fairly acceptable acknowledgment, ending by saying that "when we go across the ocean we intend to put that flag *where it belongs.*" Only the Armistice kept the 32nd Division out of Berlin! As expressed by a French writer, one reason why the Armistice was acceded to was because the English were exhausted, the French nearly so, and in a march to Berlin the American commander "would have had to be given a free hand!"

The system of training developed during my experience in the Brownsville district, and which I had already applied in the 1st Provisional Infantry Division, and afterwards when in command of the Southern Department, was carried out in the 32nd Division.

I want to say a word here about the young officers we sent to France. They were as a rule college men, and besides, were picked, selected for character and attainments, and obliged to pass a competitive examination before entering the Plattsburg and other officers' schools. *They, in my opinion, were the principal cause of the magnificent fighting our divisions did in France.* Take the 1st Division, for instance. In the battle of

Soissons, July 18, 1918, the infantry lost in men killed and wounded (not counting stragglers) *fifty-five per cent.* The young officers who led them, commanding as a rule platoons and companies, lost *sixty-five per cent!* And the division, urged on by Summerall and Mangin, fought for *five* days, most of the time with terribly depleted strength!

There is not another instance in history where a body of that strength took such losses and still kept on fighting. It was not the quality of the men that caused this; they were a lot of new men gathered from cities, many of them foreigners. It is true they had loyal, devoted non-commissioned officers. But it was the splendid example of their young "emergency" officers, afraid of nothing, appalled by no horror, striding on at the head of their platoons, climbing down into the valleys of death and up on the hills of torture, leading on, that made heroic, men who ordinarily were but common mortals.

On September 17, 1917, I received telegraphic orders from Washington to proceed by way of Hoboken, New Jersey, the port of embarkation, to France, taking with me my chief of staff and one aide. I prepared for extended field service.

I left Waco the next day, arrived in New York September 20th, staying there for two days before I embarked. I was met there by all of my family, who were under the belief that I was picked out for high command in France. They did not then know that a number of other general officers had received similar orders. They were full of enthusiasm as well as regret.

On September 22nd, having gone on board my ship, the *Finland,* I found that instead of going to France to fight, it was merely on observation duty and that I would return at the end of two months.

The ship was delayed and started at 12 o'clock, September 23rd. We had on board besides myself and staff, General Morton, General Liggett and General Strong.

The crossing was very stormy. During the night before we reached St. Nazaire we ran through a nest of submarines, a ship being torpedoed on either side of us. Incidentally, both the *Finland* and the *Antilles,* of the same convoy, were torpedoed when they went back.

The next morning we went ashore and took the train for Paris. Here everything was in a hubbub. The "battle of Paris" was being fought by men and women alike. It was a rendezvous where men, coming from the hell of the trenches, had joyous moments with girls from every country, come there to help the poor soldier. Not only the streets, but the lobbies of the hotels and even the rooms, were filled with happy parties. Food seemed plentiful, sugar more so than in the United States. There was no dancing and little music and the streets were dark at night but there were many things to compensate. Hotels were crowded.

The next day, October 9th, I left to join the 8th Division, 8th Corps of the British Army. At Cassel we found on the Flanders plain what out West we would call a "butte" and on the top, the headquarters of the British Army in that section. Reporting to the adjutant general, he directed us to the headquarters of our division, which was at Steenwerck, not far from Ypres and directly in front of Messines ridge. General Henneker commanded.

Here the headquarters occupied the château, the owners of the château, that is, the female part of the family, still living in the house in a detached portion. The young lady of the house gave up her room to me. The ladies were very polite to us Americans. They apparently had no love for the British officers.

We were received with the greatest politeness and hospitality by the English officers, who were so anxious to instruct us that we had difficulty in absorbing all the information we received. This château was on the border of Belgium. The front line trenches were in Belgium. The division was then in a quiet state so far as fighting was concerned, but had received terrible losses at Ypres, of which they spoke in the most casual manner. As a matter of fact, things were not very quiet, a constant cannonading going on. We saw many German prisoners on the road, repairing it.

We spent much time in this division, visiting front line trenches. There was a constant firing day and night. The losses of the division were five to twenty men a day.

On October 12th we left the 8th Division and reported at the headquarters of the 24th Division to General Daly. This divisional headquarters was housed in cylindrical "elephant" iron huts. They afforded protection from shrapnel. A number of them put together formed quite a long building, as was the case with the officers' mess, and in this connection I was very much impressed by the style in which these British officers' messes were conducted. They lived on the finest of foods and wine. Breakfast in the morning was served in the English style. One did not sit down at a table. At lunch a very substantial meal was served, with whiskey and cordials. Dinner at eight o'clock was in full dress. We drank champagne and other wine. We were waited on by English butlers of long experience, men who had been drafted into the service. Of course, there were a number of officers with titles, lords, etc.

On October 17th we went back to Amiens. While we were there we visited the cathedral. Coming out we heard an alarm sounded by trumpets and a noise of firing. Way up in the sky we saw a number of rings of smoke, enormously high, and in among them, darting about, a little speck lit up by the sun, looking not larger than a speck of dust in the sun's rays. It looked as if the German aviator was trying to bombard the cathedral, but he soon gave up and flew away.

On October 18th we went to an English infantry school at some distance from Amiens and the next day and the day after we spent in Paris.

On October 21st we started in our automobiles for Soissons. We stopped on the way at Compiegne, where we were presented to General Petain. We took lunch with him. We reported to the town mayor at Soissons for billets and were housed in a beautiful château, deserted, and much scarred by shellfire. October 22nd we reported at headquarters of the 28th Division, French Army, in a tunnel under a hill; very complete, halls, offices, messrooms, living quarters, etc., electric lighting system, electric ventilating system. The day was spent in receiving an explanation of the part the division was to play in the attack, which was to take place the next morning at 5:15. We found out, however, afterwards that the French had discovered that the Germans knew the hour of the attack and, therefore, set it for four o'clock instead of 5:15. In consequence, the Germans were taken by surprise.

The next morning, October 23rd, we got up at four o'clock and went to division headquarters, four miles. On our arrival the attack had already commenced. In this fight, called the battle of Malmaison, the French took 20,000 prisoners and drove the Germans back four miles.

Extracts from a letter I wrote home: "Arrived here, found a tremendous cannonade going on, 2,000 guns pounding away, preparatory to a battle. Day and night. During our conference with the corps commander, General Margoulet, about five high explosive shells, 6-inch, fell about the hut where the operations were being explained. Pieces rattled on the roof. The boche were shelling corps headquarters. It was all taken as a matter of course, and did not interrupt the narrative.

"Arrived back in town, we found that a gun which shells the town from a distance of fourteen miles away (not known exactly) had landed a shell on a bridge, killed twenty, wounded fifty. This gun is destroying the town. The cathedral is a magnificent building, and has been badly damaged. An old, picturesque tower, of the Middle Ages, has had the top knocked off. Every house in the town is more or less damaged. All night long the guns thunder. Not a light is allowed. The streets of the town are dark and deserted when we go to supper.

"Day of the battle. Got up at 4 A. M. Went to division headquarters four miles. On arrival attack had just begun. We sat in the dugout while the reports came in. Just like election night. Progressing favorably. Only one wire had been broken by return bombardment. Enemy's fire weak, shows his batteries have been knocked out. Reports as they come in are more and more favorable. Towards noon long lines of prisoners come in. Almost all are mere boys; only six out of a squad of twenty were twenty-one. Some pretty boys, others with mean expressions. All dirty. They were taken, many of them, in the tunnels and caves of quarries—540 in one cave."

We witnessed this battle for a week, sometimes under fire. This fight was one of the most successful operations conducted by the French during the war and would have been the cause of great rejoicing had it not been that on the very day that the attack was made on the Chemin des Dames, the Germans obtained a tremendous victory over the Italians at Caporetto, in which they captured 200,000 Italian soldiers and enormous quantities of plunder.

On October 28th we left Soissons and went to Chalons to see a French school. From Chalons we went to Chaumont, the headquarters of the American Army, where I met a great many of my old friends. I lodged in a building called the "House of the Three Kings." It was a house occupied by the Emperor of Russia, the Emperor of Austria and the King of Prussia during the fighting with Napoleon in 1814 and in which was decided the fate of that campaign. From Chaumont we went about and visited the various American camps and schools. I was accompanied part of the time by General Bullard. On November 3rd we returned to Paris; there I had a long talk with Marshal Joffre. At Bordeaux, on November 15th, we sailed on the *Rochambeau* for New York. Very few precautions against submarines were observed on the *Rochambeau,* which they claimed usually carried German spies! Therefore, they said, this line was never attacked by the German submarines! The ship was crowded by a heterogeneous assortment of American officers, correspondents, actresses and American families returning to the United States. There were seven American major generals and one admiral of the U. S. Navy. There were numerous dances and concerts and altogether we had a very good time. We landed at New York City on November 26, 1917.

I was greatly impressed with the French officers with whom I came in contact, high and low. I talked with Joffre, Foch, Petain, Neville, Maistre, Gouraud, Marjoulet, and others. I did not see among them the traditional Frenchman, excitable, nervous, vociferous. They seemed uniformly rather grave, quiet, studious-looking, brainy men.

In the latter part of November I was ordered to Washington, "for duty," and found that my duty, like that of a large number of major generals commanding divisions, was to undergo a physical examination, the general staff thus hoping to weed out the older officers so as to make vacancies for their juniors. This test was conducted by some eminent physicians, including the Mayo brothers. Unfortunately, it had the effect of weeding out some of the best officers we had, including Tom Barry and Franklin Bell, major generals, noted for efficiency. These two died shortly after, deeply disappointed men.

It is not difficult to find something organically

wrong with an old man, and a lot of the oldsters were retired or "canned." One of the medical officers who assisted in the examination afterwards said to my friend, General "Dick" Richardson, "It is remarkable, but the man who was the oldest stood the best examination." "That must have been Jim Parker," said Dick. "It was," said the Doctor, "and his mark was almost one hundred per cent."

I was told that a high medical authority in the French Army remarked, on hearing of this examination, "Apply that test to our army and we would lose nearly all of our best general officers."

Curiously enough, most of the great commanders in that war were old men, many of them over sixty-four years, our age of retirement. There were Joffre, French, Castelnau, Foch, Hindenberg and many others. The modern commander needs most of all *brains and experience.* Physique is comparatively unimportant. The modern commander of a division fights from a point miles in the rear; he does not lead it, as in the old days.

Speaking about "experience," I was perhaps the only officer in the army who at the outbreak of the war had commanded in the field a regiment, a brigade, and the equivalent of an army corps.

From Washington I proceeded to rejoin my division, the 32nd, at Waco, Texas. I found the division in fine shape as the result of the intensive scheme of training which I had inaugurated and General Haan had loyally carried out. Inspectors had been visiting the different divisions under training and the 32nd had received high compliments on its efficiency. A few days after my arrival we received the welcome news that the 32nd Division, on account of its proficiency, had been selected to go to France and would get ready for the trip.

My joy was great. The next day, February 7th, I got the following telegram from Washington:

"Order made relieving you of command 32nd Division and directing you proceed Camp Custer, Battle Creek, Michigan, and assume command 85th Division."

One may judge of my feelings on receiving this message. My retirement for age, February 20, 1918, was but two months off. But I had hoped that in view of my record I would be retained in charge of the 32nd Division and would command it in France. However, I obeyed the order loyally, hoping against hope. One of the last things I did was to address the body of officers detailing my experiences in France. I also telegraphed the War Department asking that General Haan be made my successor in command of the division, a request to which they acceded. Haan was a natural fighter and in France covered himself with glory.

It was hard to say good-bye to my friends at Waco. I hurried off, grief in my heart.

On December 13, 1917, I took command of the 85th Division at Camp Custer, Battle Creek, Michigan. Battle Creek was the most northerly camp in the United States during the World War. The 85th Division, like the 32nd, was made up of troops from Wisconsin and Michigan. But it differed from the 32nd Division, a National Guard division, in that the troops were drafted. In a great many respects this was an advantage, for the men were all of a superior class, coming from the first draft. Instead of being, many of them, boys, as were the volunteers of the 32nd Division, they were grown men, all over twenty-one years of age and a large proportion of them men who had made good in their professions.

Take men of mature age and put them in ranks and whether they come willingly or not, they want to make good, and will work like devils to learn their job. This was the case with the 85th Division and this division had the further advantage in having for its higher officers men who were all officers of the Regular Army.

It was very cold at Camp Custer. The thermometer for weeks would stand below zero. Successive storms had covered the ground with deep snow. A great deal of labor was necessary to dig away the snow and construct regimental drill grounds and to clear the snow from the roads. Much of this latter work was done by the engineers who, as usual, were wonderfully efficient.

But I found the men listless and somewhat castdown because their drilling had been interfered with. I should have to change all this and as one of the best means to that end, instituted a competitive test of each command. I gave them three weeks in order to get ready for this test, which was to determine the best squad in each platoon, in each company, in each battalion, in each regiment, each brigade, and in the whole division. As a preliminary I had one of my English instructors train a squad in what I called a "pep" drill. Having witnessed this drill by a special squad in the assembly hall, the officers went to work and at the end of three weeks I had the pleasure of viewing the competitions for this test, which were all simple movements, but executed with great zest.

To my pleasure, it seemed to transform the men. They lost their listless air. At the same time they were put at other drills, such as bayonet exercise, target practice, etc. These men were so anxious to learn that it was thrilling to look at them. There were a large number of magnificient-looking soldiers, a number of whom came out of the forests, lumber men, boat men, et cetera. I had several companies of North American Indians. To see these great fellows, armed with a bayonet, go at the dummies arranged for bayonet exercise was really a wonderful sight, for they certainly were in earnest.

At the same time I had their instructors spend half an hour each day in reading them stories of the most strenuous work in the trenches on the other side, such as, "The First 100,000," "Over the Top," and "Kitchener's Mob." These stories were drunk in avidly and I have no doubt when these young men first went into action on the other side and saw their comrades struck down beside them they said to themselves, "Why, this is nothing; this is nothing to what we read in 'Over the Top.'" In fact, they were made ready to look upon most dreadful scenes of bloodshed without a qualm. They were guarded against panic by this training.

I inaugurated competitive tests in other things, such as target practice, barrack inspection, etc., publishing in orders the best company for neatness of barracks, for excellence in drill, for accuracy in target practice.

Taking the division all in all, I believe it was a finer division than the 32nd and that if it had gone to the front it would have made a record second to none; but such good fortune was not its share. Part of the division in France was used for replacements and the trained men and officers of the division were sent to the 1st Division, the 2nd Division and other divisions to fill the vacancies occurring as a result of the killed and wounded in the various battles. They were always highly spoken of, but I notice they were lost sight of. However, the 328th Artillery went to the 92nd Divi sion, the 329th Artillery to the 4th Corps, the 330th Artillery to the 2nd Corps, and the 310th Engineers to the 5th Corps.

Part of the division served in Russia.

The 32nd Division, in the course of its operations, was the first division of our army to enter France, which it did in Alsace. The 85th Division has the record of being the last division in the World War to cease fighting. It happened as follows:

In August, 1918, the 339th Infantry, the first battalion 310th Engineers, the 337th Field Hospital and the 337th company, numbering 4,447 men and officers, were detached to join the North Russian Expedition. This expedition was sent to Archangel and Murmansk, Russia, to hold those places and the country in that vicinity in order to prevent the Germans from establishing submarine bases there; also to protect the allied stores at these ports, and for other purposes. Through these ports the Allies had been sending vast quantities of supplies to the Russian government, but when the Russian government became Bolshevik, the Allies did not propose that this property should be surrendered to a government hostile to them. Accordingly, we, the English, French and Italians sent units there, the largest force being composed of Americans. The American troops were promptly divided between the two main commands. With a small reserve at Archangel they occupied a front of about two hundred miles on the Onega River, on the Dwina River and the Tinega River, this front being over 100 miles distant from Archangel. All three of these rivers were navigable by small steamers and the Dwina River was important as being the means of transportation by which these stores had been formerly carried to near St. Petersburg. In holding these positions the Americans had many combats with Bolsheviks, which did not cease during the winters. Some of these fights were quite severe; so much so that of eight officers and two hundred and seventeen men who died in Russia, most of them were killed or died of wounds. For gallantry in battle these troops received 188 decorations. But still the fighting did not cease when the Armistice came. On January 19, 1919, in a fight at Nijni Gora, one of our platoons lost forty men killed or wounded out of forty-seven. On March 31 to April 2, 1919, the Americans fought in the Battle of Bolsheozerki, on the Onega River, the Reds attacking the railroad positions with 7,000 infantry. In spite of being greatly outnumbered, the allied troops repulsed the attack, the Americans taking the most prominent part in it.

In May, 1919, President Wilson withdrew the Americans from Russia.

The condition of the 85th division improved daily, so that when, shortly before my retirement, the division was the object of a close inspection by General Helmick, inspector general, it received from him high praise. The inspector expressed himself as astonished that so much had been accomplished when he considered the disadvantages of climate encountered. He found a division full of pep and enthusiasm and in an advanced state of instruction.

In spite of the deep snow and the zero weather I made a point of riding each day, accompanied by my aides, about the camp, visiting each regiment and separate battalion. Drills and sports continued as though no snow existed. Cannon and small arms resounded, as the men on the target ranges fired all day in the bitter cold.

As the date for my retirement approached I also tried vainly to be continued in service. What I wanted was to command troops in France, in what grade little mattered. I felt that I still had a right to serve my country.

The day arrived. I received from the War Department the customary cold-blooded order severing me forever from the service and from those whom I loved and who looked up to me. I had served my country as an officer for forty-two years and these orders were my farewell:

War Department
Washington, February 29, 1918

Special Orders, No. 43.

Extract

* * * * * *

113. By direction of the President the retirement of Brigadier General James Parker, United States Army (major general, National Army) from active service on February 20, 1918, under the requirements of the act of Congress approved June 30, 1882, is announced. General Parker will proceed to his home. The travel directed is necessary in the military service.

* * * * * *

By order of the Secretary of War:

John Biddle
Major General, Acting Chief of Staff

Official:
H. P. McCain
The Adjutant General

It was a sad parting; twelve hundred officers individually came down to the station to bid me goodbye. I left them standing there; I never saw them again.

My friends were indignant at my fate. At Washington it was proposed to make a strong political effort to reverse the ruling of the War Department. I said, "No, wait for 1919. The war will continue until then and by that time the government will have discovered how few officers of experience it has and how much it needs such officers. With whole divisions in charge of men who have never before even commanded a company it will realize the value of solid acquaintance with the art of war."

I went to my home. Then, from month to month, as the war progressed, I asked for active service. My applications were duly disapproved.

I had the satisfaction, however, of receiving, after my retirement, three silver star citations for gallantry in action: namely, at Devil's Creek, Ariz.; San Mateo, and Manaog. Also I received the Distinguished Service Medal, with a citation which shows that my efforts to prepare my troops for this great exigency were not forgotten.

"Award of Distinguished Service Medal.—By direction of the President, under the provisions of the act of Congress, approved July 9, 1918 (Bul. No. 43, W.D., 1918), as amended by the act of Congress, approved April 7, 1922 (Bul. No. 6, W.D., 1922), a Distinguished Service Medal was awarded by the War Department to the following named officer:

"James Parker, brigadier general, United States Army, retired, then major general, United States Army. For exceptionally meritorious and distinguished services. He served with great distinction as commander of the Southern Department, Fort Sam

Houston, Texas, March 31, 1917, to August 25, 1917; and as division commander, 32nd Division, from August 25 to December 11, 1917; division commander, 85th Division, December 11, 1917, to February 20, 1918, when, having reached the statutory age, he was retired from active service. In these positions of great responsibility he displayed rare and outstanding leadership, the organizations under command at all times showing the results of sound training, a high state of morale and discipline. His unusual professional attainments, sound judgment and devotion to duty were material and important factors in the development of organizations of the American Army and contributed in a signal way to their successful operations in action against the enemy. Address: Care of the Adjutant General of the Army, Washington, D. C. Entered Military Academy from New Jersey."

THE END